R00049 08234

D1789599

A HISTORY

OF

EIGHTEENTH CENTURY LITERATURE

A HISTORY OF EIGHTEENTH CENTURY LITERATURE

(1660–1780)

BY

EDMUND GOSSE

BOOKS FOR LIBRARIES PRESS
FREEPORT, NEW YORK

LIBRARY
EISENHOWER COLLEGE

First Published 1889
Reprinted 1972

Library of Congress Cataloging in Publication Data

Gosse, Sir Edmund William, 1849-1928.
　A history of eighteenth century literature (1660-1780).

　(BCL/select bibliographies index reprint series)
　Reprint of the 1889 ed.
　Bibliography: p.
　1. English literature--18th century--History and criticism.　I. Title.
PR441.G7　1972　　　　820.9　　　　74-39396
ISBN 0-8369-9909-6

PRINTED IN THE UNITED STATES OF AMERICA
BY
NEW WORLD BOOK MANUFACTURING CO., INC.
HALLANDALE, FLORIDA 33009

PREFACE

To call a sketch of English authorship between 1660 and 1780 a history of Eighteenth Century Literature is, on the face of it, to be guilty of a misnomer. Eighteenth Century Literature should include everything between the death of Dryden and the birth of Sir Henry Taylor, and nothing else. At the same time, no other name has occurred to us by which, without confusion or affectation, those literary developments might be concisely described which came to their climax in the early part of the eighteenth century, and seem to be related to what we are in the habit of considering the characteristic features of that age in social, intellectual, and artistic matters. To call this the Augustan period would be to narrow it most unduly; to call it the classical period would be to introduce a series of ideas incongruous as well as inexact. No newly discovered nickname would please all readers at this time of day, and we must be content with a title so patently imperfect as that which we have chosen. The dates on the title-page may at least guard the writer against any misconception of the purpose which he set before himself to fulfil.

In dealing with a section of literary history which has been mapped out so minutely as the greater part of Eighteenth Century Literature, the first problem which presents itself to a critic in attempting to form a general survey of the whole, is that of proportion. The vast landmarks of the preceding century, the colossal Shakespeares and Bacons and Miltons, are absent here; the general level of merit is much higher, while the solitary altitudes are more numerous but considerably less commanding. The first and by far the most arduous duty of the writer was to make a rough plan of his work, selecting and excluding names, determining the relative value of each, and deciding what proportion of the space at his command could be spared for the individual figures. This was done with very great care, and it was when this skeleton was being filled up that the necessity of such a plan became obvious. It was then that the attraction of those fascinating minor figures in which the eighteenth century was so singularly rich made itself felt. It was difficult indeed to pass such names as those of Temple and Arbuthnot and Anstey without loitering longer in their company than the proportions of the plan permitted. But to keep to the plan the writer conceived to be the central feature of his work, and he forced himself to resist the temptation. For the relative prominence given to the various names, therefore, he must take the responsibility, and the critical taste of the reader will decide whether, in the main, the proportions are correctly designed. But those who have made special fragments of the century, or special figures in it, their main study, will recollect, if they glance into these pages, that the first duty of a general critic of literature is to resist the attraction of personal favourites.

In every case I have attempted to set forward my own view of the literary character of each figure, founded on personal study. Hence, in a few cases, it may be discovered that the verdicts in this volume differ in some degree from those commonly held. A few names which are habitually found chronicled are here omitted, and still fewer, which are new to a general sketch, are included. I am conscious that certain writers receive here more prominence than has hitherto been given to them, while others receive less. But, on the whole, I have striven to be conservative in taste. Where my judgment has differed on important questions from that of preceding critics, I have been slow to suppose that I could be right and they wrong. But it was absolutely essential that such an outline of literary history, if it was to have any stimulating quality at all, should be pervaded by the results of a personal impression; and if any reader is offended at an opinion which appears to him heretical, let him acquit me, while he rejects it, of any intention to startle him with a paradox.

The pages have been somewhat copiously starred with dates, for which interruptions of comfort in reading I must offer an apology, I have the impression that dates, if reasonably treated, present a great assistance to the comparative student, and really should prevent, instead of causing, interruption. Moreover, almost the only contribution to actual fact which I could hope to offer in such a critical volume as this was a running bibliography, the accurate chronicling of the original dates and forms of publication being one of the few departments of eighteenth century literature which have, except in certain provinces, been neglected. It is not very important, perhaps, but I may add that in almost every case of a well-known book I have made a point of referring to the actual first issue. Among my thousands of dates, though I have carefully revised them, some must be wrong. Any corrections of fact will be very gratefully received by myself or the publishers.

In the final chapter I have stated my theory with regard to the mode in which the philosophical, theological, and political writing of the period should be examined. But I may explain here that it has been my object, while giving a rough sketch of the tenets of each didactic specialist, to leave the discussion of those tenets to critics of the specialist's own profession, and to treat his publications mainly from the point of view of style.

TRINITY COLLEGE, CAMBRIDGE,
November 1888.

CONTENTS

CHAP.		PAGE
I.	Poetry after the Restoration	1
II.	Drama after the Restoration	38
III.	Prose after the Restoration	73
IV.	Pope	105
V.	Swift and the Deists	140
VI.	Defoe and the Essayists	176
VII.	The Dawn of Naturalism in Poetry	207
VIII.	The Novelists	242
IX.	Johnson and the Philosophers	273
X.	The Poets of the Decadence	310
XI.	The Prose of the Decadence	344
XII.	Conclusion	375
	Bibliography	401
	Index	405

CHAPTER I

POETRY AFTER THE RESTORATION

WHEN the romantic fervour of the age of Elizabeth had completely exhausted itself, towards the middle of the seventeenth century, the poetical field in England was again left fallow, as it had been left in the early part of the sixteenth century, at the decline of the mediæval period. The great poets had spoken in rapturous accents, with a noble and irregular music, and their followers, unable to repeat their sublimity, had exaggerated their irregularity into licence. This rapid decline from the Elizabethan elevation of style was hastened by the general subsidence, throughout Europe, of the fervour of the Renaissance. The form of English poetry was degraded, not merely by its own impetus, but by the nature of the literary changes then being made in France, in Spain, and in Italy. Imaginative literature was undergoing a complete transformation in all parts of Europe. At the moment of deepest decadence it had reached very much the same position which it had reached, at various moments, in the complete decline of mediævalism. In England, for instance, the relation of a writer like Phineas Fletcher to Spenser was almost exactly analogous to that of Hawes to Chaucer. But when it came to the question of revival, it was plain that renovation could not lie any longer on the side of what was fervid, spontaneous, and fantastic. In this direction there was nothing new to be attained, and the tendency had to be rather in the mediæval than in the Renaissance direction, more towards the classic regularity of the great fourteenth century writers than towards the exquisite audacities of the end of the sixteenth century.

The change, then, was one in the direction of repression and revision. It was made in the pursuit of regular form, reasonable thought, and a subdued and chastened ornament. Although the results of the change appear anything but attractive to ourselves, and although the direct and positive gain to English poetry seems very small to us now, the relief from irregularity and licence was eagerly welcomed. The most obvious phenomenon connected with the change in poetry was the gradual substitution, in non-dramatic verse, for the thousand-and-one odd metrical forms of the lyrists, of a single normal instrument in versification, namely, the neatly-balanced and unbroken heroic couplet, containing five beats in each line. It was true that this form, as well as almost all others to be found in English poetry, had been known to the Elizabethans, but it had possessed no special attraction for them, and not one of them had made habitual use of it. But throughout the period with which we deal in this volume, this heroic couplet was the normal and habitual form in which poetry, except on the stage, moved in its serious moments. There were, of course, many exceptions, and about 1725 a very vigorous effort was made, but with only partial success, to substitute blank verse for it. These exceptions will be noted as we proceed, but it is proper here to insist that the employment of the heroic couplet, and the polishing of that couplet, are the most prominent facts connected with the art of poetry during the classic period in this country.

This alteration of form was introduced by one writer, who lived to see it universally adopted. The life of this poet, Edmund Waller (1605-1687), covers the entire period of transformation. When he was a youth the romantic manner was the only one in practice; long before he died the classic manner was unchallenged. The precise and regular taste made fashionable by Waller found a special propriety in resuming a vehicle of expression which had been, it would seem, invented by Chaucer for use in *The Canterbury Tales*, about 1385. The heroic couplet had been employed by its author with extraordinary art, and almost without irregularity. But it was an instrument upon which none but Chaucer seemed to know how to play, and within a quarter of a century after his death it was completely laid aside. When the couplet came into use again, in the Elizabethan age, the form was greatly modified, and the polished distich, as Chaucer had devised it, was lost in a flowing easy measure, kept in hand merely by the recurrent tinkle of the rhyme. Chaucer's artful *cæsura* was exaggerated into what the French call an *enjambement*, and what is called in English an "overflow"; "the sense," as Milton says in describing this peculiarity, "being variously drawn out from one verse into another." In the hands of the best romantic poets of Elizabeth and James, this loose and elastic treatment of the couplet had led to very charming effects; but when inspiration passed away, this laxity of form gave the poetasters occasion for every species of weakness and flaccidity. Waller, without apparently any ambition to restore the couplet as Chaucer had left it, nor on the other hand any suggestion from France, where the Alexandrine was not yet subjected to a like reform, revised and strengthened this form of verse, and gave it the character which it retained for no less than one hundred and fifty years. For that space of time the couplet took the same almost universal position as the vehicle for expression in verse that the rhyme royal had taken in the fifteenth and sixteenth centuries. In this case, as in that, the popularity of the form survived the power of the poets to extract new effects out of so conventional an instrument.

Waller, to whom is due the singular distinction of being the coryphæus of this long procession of the commonplace, was a very wealthy landlord of Buckinghamshire. He entered Parliament at an early age, held completely aloof from the active literary life of his contemporaries, and seemed interested in anything rather than in poetry. His earliest verses, dated apparently in 1623, possess the formal character, the precise prosody without

irregularity or overflow, which we find in the ordinary verse of
Dryden, Pope, and Darwin. To so great an extent is this true,
that a passage of Waller's earliest heroics, if compared at the same
time with a typical passage from one of his coevals, such as Carew
or Crashaw, and with one from Darwin's *Botanic Garden* of 1789,
would be recognised at once as bearing a closer relation to the
latter than to the former. In other words, we hold in Waller's
earliest occasional pieces the key to the prosody of the eighteenth
century, to what Mr. Ruskin has very happily called "the sym-
metrical clauses of Pope's logical metre." For many years Waller
was entirely unsupported in this innovation, and his persistence
in setting his face against the fashion of his own age is very
curious. About 1632 he began to court Lady Dorothy Sidney
in a cycle of poems, under the name of Sacharissa, and some of
these lyrics were, and still remain, justly popular. They are
remarkable for grace, and for a curious felicity in diction; in them
he escapes from his self-imposed chain of the couplet. Waller
plotted to reinstate the king, and in 1644 was heavily fined and
banished to France.

Before this, however, he had obtained his first disciple. The
critics of the succeeding age saw a direct relation between Waller
and Sir John Denham (1615-1668), which has, until lately, been
again obscured. Dryden said, in 1664, "The excellence and
dignity of rhyme were never fully known till Mr. Waller taught it;
but this sweetness of his lyric poesy was afterwards followed in the
epic by Sir John Denham in his *Cooper's Hill.*" This last-mentioned work, Denham's sole important contribution to literature,
is not what we now call an epic; it is a topographical poem, and
the earliest of its class to possess a distinctly national interest. It
was published in 1642, before Waller had printed anything, but
it contains a direct allusion to him as "the first of poets," showing,
as the adoption of the unbroken distich also did, that the author
had perceived and had accepted the reform suggested by Waller.
It is not lengthy, nor very animated, and there is little in its form
or matter to account for the extraordinary reputation which it has

enjoyed. It is a soliloquy of the author's, who, resting on the brow of Cooper's Hill, addresses the Thames rolling at his feet, and enumerates the stately attractions of the great city through which the river is about to flow. Four lines of this address, added in the third edition, are among the most famous of English quotations:

"O could I flow like thee, and make thy stream
My great example, as it is my theme!
Though deep yet clear, though gentle yet not dull,
Strong without rage, without o'erflowing full."

Denham was an architect by profession, and succeeded Inigo Jones as the king's surveyor-general, to be succeeded in his turn by Sir Christopher Wren. The latter part of his life was clouded by insanity. Denham is not a poet of importance, but he supplies a link between Waller and Dryden. Sidney Godolphin (1610-1643), another very early disciple of Waller's, died too young to exert much influence.

A much more versatile and more attractive writer than Denham was Abraham Cowley (1618-1667), but he was not nearly so consistent an adherent of the new school. On one side of his poetical character, indeed, Cowley represents nothing more than the extreme decline of the earlier romantic poetry. He attributed his own start in life to the fact that before he was twelve he had read the works of Spenser through, and his early writings, the precocity of which is extraordinary, are imitations of the great Elizabethans. Before he was twenty he had published two volumes of poetry and a play, all three of which had enjoyed great success. During the early years of the civil war he was engaged in writing the collection of cold and elaborate love-enigmas, which he called *The Mistress*—pieces in which feeling and thought, expression and metrical form, are all tortured in concert. After the battle of Naseby, Cowley, who, like most of the men of letters, was a royalist, followed the queen to Paris, and there came under the influence of Waller. *The Mistress* appeared in 1647, and was immediately accepted and approved by the members of the new school, although it hardly belonged to their camp.

It was his want of colour, his intellectual ingenuity, and his temperate prosaic spirit, which recommended Cowley to the new classic poets. He wrote but little in the heroic measure—his sacred epic, *The Davideis*, and one very noble elegy on Crashaw, being his principal essays in that form. Cowley rarely speaks so simply and sincerely as in these stanzas from the poem on the death of Mr. William Hervey :

> "He was my friend, the truest friend on earth :
> A strong and mighty influence join'd our birth.
> Nor did we envy the most sounding name
> By friendship given of old to fame.
> None but his brethren he, and sisters knew,
> Whom the kind youth preferr'd to me ;
> And even in that we did agree,
> For much above myself I lov'd them too.
>
> "Say, for you saw us, ye immortal lights,
> How oft unwearied have we spent the nights?
> 'Till the Ledæan stars so famed for love,
> Wonder'd at us from above.
> We spent them not in toys, in lusts, in wine ;
> But search of deep philosophy,
> Wit, eloquence, and poetry ;
> Arts which I loved, for they, my friend, were thine.
>
> "Ye fields of Cambridge, our dear Cambridge, say,
> Have ye not seen us walking every day ?
> Was there a tree about which did not know
> The love betwixt us two ?
> Henceforth, ye gentle trees, for ever fade ;
> Or your sad branches thicker join,
> And into darksome shades combine ;
> Dark as the grave wherein my friend is laid.
>
> "Henceforth no learned youths beneath you sing,
> 'Till all the tuneful birds to your boughs they bring ;
> No tuneful birds play with their wonted cheer,
> And call the learned youths to hear ;
> No whistling winds through the glad branches fly,
> But all with sad solemnity
> Mute and unmoved be,
> Mute as the grave wherein my friend does lie."

In 1656 Cowley presented the public with a collection of *Pindarique Odes*—pompous lyrics in what the French call *vers libres*—that is to say, lines of irregular length disposed on a whimsical system, which had lately received the approval of Corneille, and was, long after Cowley's death, to be raised by Racine into momentary dignity in the choral portions of *Esther* and *Athalie*. At that day the elaborate plan on which the odes of Pindar were built up was not understood, and Cowley's idea was that they were formed irregularly and spontaneously, more on a musical than a metrical system. As an example of the vicious Pindaric manner invented by Cowley, of his strange passion for conceit, and of his occasional felicity, the opening strophes of "The Muse" may here be given. It contains what is perhaps the most beautiful line Cowley has left behind him:

> "Go, the rich chariot instantly prepare;
>   The Queen, my Muse, will take the air;
> Unruly Fancy with strong Judgment trace,
>   Put in nimble-footed Wit,
>   Smooth-pac'd Eloquence join with it,
> Sound Memory with young Invention place,
>   Harness all the winged race.
> Let the postilion Nature, mount, and let
>   The coachman Art be set.
> And let the airy footmen running all beside,
>   Make a long row of goodly Pride.
> Figures, Conceits, Raptures, and Sentences,
>   In a well-worded Dress.
> And innocent Loves, and pleasant Truths, and useful Lies,
>   In all their gaudy liveries.
>   Mount, glorious Queen, thy travelling throne,
>   And bid it to put on;
>   For long, though cheerful, is the way,
> And life, alas, allows but one ill winter's day.
> Where never foot of man, or hoof of beast
>   The passage prest.
>   Where never fish did fly,
> And with short silver wings cut the low liquid sky.
>   Where bird with painted oars did ne'er
> Row through the trackless ocean of the air.

> Where never yet did pry
> The busy morning's curious eye,
> The wheels of thy bold coach pass quick and free;
> And all's an open road to thee.
> Whatever God did say,
> Is all thy plain and smooth, uninterrupted way.
> Nay, ev'n beyond His works thy voyages are known,
> Thou hast thousand worlds too of thine own.
> Thou speak'st, great Queen, in the same style as He,
> And a new world leaps forth when Thou say'st, Let it be."

This uncouth and mistaken form of ode was unchallenged for some fifty years, when Congreve attempted a diversion in favour of regularity; no successful stand, however, was made against it until Gray began to write. This so-called "Pindarique ode" was for fifty or sixty years not only the universal medium for congratulatory lyrics and tumid occasional pieces, but it was for a long time almost the only variety allowed to the cultivators of the heroic couplet. Dryden succeeded in putting a noble organ music into it, but there can scarcely be mentioned one other ode than his second *On Saint Cecilia's Day*, which is a perfectly successful poem. The forgotten lyrists of the Restoration found it a particularly convenient instrument in their bound and inflexible fingers, and even the tuneless Shadwell could turn off Pindarique odes. But almost without exception those "majestic strains" are miserably flat. Concerning the value of Cowley's own verse criticism strangely differs. He had a very high ideal of the poetic vocation. He is wonderfully felicitous sometimes in the structure of single lines, and those who are able to appreciate poetry of the class of which France has produced so much, the purely rhetorical and intellectual, will extend their approval to entire stanzas, and sometimes to entire poems. But it must be confessed that to the modern reader most of his "Song" is what, in another sense, he said that Pindar's was—"unnavigable."

Another precursor of the classic school in poetry was Sir William Davenant (1606-1668), an uninspired but exceedingly active professional writer. He was mainly a writer of plays, which will be mentioned in the next chapter, but he also produced an epic which attracted a great deal of notice. Davenant, whose parents were intimate friends of Shakespeare, was that poet's godson. His youth was spent in the house of Fulke Greville—Lord Brooke—the old Elizabethan worthy, until Brooke was murdered in 1628. Davenant succeeded Ben Jonson as poet laureate in 1637, and in 1638 collected his scattered verses into a volume called *Madagascar*. Up to this time he had been entirely identified with the old romantic school, but in 1650 we find him in Paris with Waller and Cowley, and converted to the new prosody of the former. He published in that year the first (and only) volume of an epic poem, called *Gondibert*, on a Lombard story. This poem is mainly interesting because of the extraordinary influence which it exercised over the early style of Dryden, who was slow in quite escaping from the fascination of it. *Gondibert* is Davenant's best production, but it is very obscure and ill-constructed. Its merit consists in the grace of some of the episodes, and in the sententious vigour of single lines. It is written in the four-line heroic stanza, with alternate rhymes, which Gray made so popular in the following century. Davenant's essays in the heroic distich show that late in life he learned Waller's lesson with remarkable adroitness. He was a clever man of letters, but scarcely a poet.

The great writer of the period, the greatest poet in English literature between Milton and Wordsworth, was John Dryden (1631-1700). In comparison with this stately figure, those precursors of the classical school whom we have just mentioned pass into insignificance. Even Waller, though nothing can shake his importance as the founder of the school, is intellectually a dwarf by the side of Dryden. It should, however, be clearly perceived that the change from the romantic to the classical manner in English poetry, the rejection of the overflow in favour of the distich, had been carried out to the full before Dryden came to the front and stamped his own powerful character on the movement. Waller was writing excellent couplets before Dryden was born, but it was part of Dryden's greatness not so much to introduce phases of thought as to adopt and illuminate them when they had once become national. For this reason, perhaps, he was not happy until all question of transition was over. He did not take up poetry in earnest till all intelligent Englishmen had decided what kind of poetry it was they wanted. And then Dryden, confident of his audience, made the distich of Waller an instrument on which to play his boldest music.

Dryden, the nephew of a local baronet, was born near Oundle, in Northamptonshire, and educated at Trinity College, Cambridge, where his famous portrait still adorns the hall. His early life is exceedingly obscure, and we possess very few contributions from it, either in prose or verse. In 1659, at the age of twenty-eight, he took part in the publication of a thin volume of three elegies on Oliver Cromwell. There are two simultaneous editions of this, one by itself, which is excessively rare, and the other in combination with Waller, with whom it is very interesting to find Dryden thus early identified, and Thomas Sprat (1636-1713), an imitator of Cowley, and afterwards Bishop of Rochester. At this time *Gondibert* was in fashion, and Dryden's stanzas are closely modelled on those of Davenant. The next year brought the Restoration, when every bush was vocal, and Dryden presented his share of tribute in his *Astræa Redux*. Here Waller was his model more than Davenant, but still there was little promise of high attainment. Dryden, as was afterwards remarked, was but "faintly distinguished in his thirtieth year." In 1661, in his *Coronation Panegyric*, his heroics are, for the first time, on a level with those of Waller and Davenant ; and the writer has removed from his style a turbid affectation of wit which stuck to it from the bad models of his childhood. This and other short exercises bring us down to the year 1666, when Dryden published his first long piece, the historical poem of *Annus Mirabilis*, closely modelled upon *Gondibert*. It will easily be seen, however, from such a stanza as the following, that Dryden already was a far greater master of metre than Davenant had ever been :

"The ghosts of traitors from the bridge descend,
   With bold fanatic spectres to rejoice;
 About the fire into a dance they bend,
   And sing their sabbath notes with feeble voice."

There can be no sense, however, in which *Annus Mirabilis* can be called a good poem. It is confused, violent, and affected, full of crudities of style and thought, and its fine passages, brilliant as they are, are mere purple patches. The theme was twofold—the progress of our naval war with Holland, and that of the great fire of London.

The character of Dryden's work now changed completely, and the change was coincident with the close of the first period of the classic epoch in England. Within a few months Cowley, Denham, and Davenant died, Waller was silent, Dryden turned his attention exclusively to the drama, and the only non-dramatic poetry produced was that of Milton, a magnificent survival from the romantic age. Late in 1663 Dryden had married the eldest daughter of the Earl of Berkshire, a woman who proved to be silly and peevish; they were not destined to enjoy much happiness together. The personal life of Dryden, however, is very vague to us, and the trustworthy anecdotes preserved about him are singularly few. We know, however, that he stepped at once into the honours and into the consideration enjoyed by his lately deceased forerunners, that he was now in general parlance "Mr. Dryden the poet," and that in 1670 he was made laureate and historiographer-royal. He was gradually absorbed by the writing of plays, of which an account will be given in the next chapter, and about 1667 he entered into an agreement to supply the players of the king's theatre with three plays a year, on exceedingly favourable terms. Dryden was not able to keep his part of the contract, but he wrote enough to bring him in a large theatrical income, and this was a period of high prosperity with him. He was also intimate with the great literary nobles of the court, and sunned himself in their favour almost without an interval, until, in 1675, he had the misfortune to quarrel with the malignant Earl of Rochester. For fourteen years, however, after the publication of *Annus Mirabilis*, Dryden has to be treated exclusively as a dramatist. The peculiar character of his plays, however, was not without influence on his style as a poet. In the heroic plays, which were written in rhyme, he had an opportunity of increasing the volume and polishing the structure of his couplets, and in this way of preparing for his future and purely poetical triumphs. His plays, moreover, contained songs, which are valuable guides to the critic in estimating Dryden's progress as a metrist. "I feed a flame within," in the *Maiden Queen* of 1668, and "After the pangs of a desperate lover," and "Celimena, of my heart," both in *An Evening's Love* (1671), are the best instances of Dryden's early songs:

> "I feed a flame within, which so torments me,
> That it both pains my heart, and yet contents me:
> 'Tis such a pleasing smart, and I so love it,
> That I had rather die, than once remove it.
>
> "Yet he, for whom I grieve, shall never know it;
> My tongue does not betray, nor my eyes show it.
> Not a sigh, nor a tear, my pain discloses,
> But they fall silently, like dew on roses.
>
> "Thus, to prevent my love from being cruel,
> My heart's the sacrifice, as 'tis the fuel:
> And while I suffer this to give him quiet,
> My faith rewards my love, though he deny it."

In these, and still more in later and better examples, he shows that he possessed a genuine lyric grace, the existence of which we should otherwise scarcely have suspected. His songs are entirely unlike those of the earlier English dramatists, and remind us rather, in their grace and courtly turns of thought, of the kind of poetry introduced into France by Voiture and his friends.

These fourteen years of Dryden's exclusive attachment to drama mark a very low spot indeed in English poetical literature. Dryden himself had reached his fiftieth year without writing anything which was really admirable in any very supreme sense, or which, if he had died before 1680, could have secured his name a high place in human memory. What is of greatest importance to poetical students is to observe what progress Dryden made in the new prosody, and how by means of it he drew out those qualities which had been too much neglected in the verse of the previous age— ease, intelligibility, and flexibility. The heroic plays were not wholly useless, if they merely trained the English ear, so long accustomed to discord, to enjoy such harmonious periods as these, in which we see Dryden at his best in 1670 :

> " Ethereal music did her death prepare,
> Like joyful sounds of spousals in the air ;
> A radiant light did her crowned temples gild,
> And all the place with fragrant scents was filled ;
> The balmy mist came thickening to the ground,
> And sacred silence covered all around.
> But when (its work performed) the cloud withdrew,
> And day restored us to each other's view,
> I sought her head, to bring it on my spear,—
> In vain I sought it, for it was not there ;
> No part remained, but, from afar, our sight
> Discovered in the air long tracts of light ;
> Of charming notes we heard the last resounds,
> And music dying in remoter sounds."

Dryden's command over versification, moreover, is shown in the prologues and epilogues which he produced not merely for his own plays, but for those of others. His study of the drama of the Elizabethans presently led him to a certain change of opinion. While continuing to hold the couplet to be the proper vehicle for pure poetry, he began to be dissatisfied with rhyme on the stage. Mr. Saintsbury thinks that a tendency to overflow in the verse of the rhymed tragedy of *Aureng-Zebe* (1676), shows that Dryden was recurring to the form of Shakespeare. Whether this be so or not, in *All for Love* (1678) we find him returning to blank verse, in direct rivalry with the exquisite cadences of *Antony and Cleopatra*. From this time forth Dryden drew a careful distinction between the couplet, which was to be used for serious poetry of all non-dramatic kinds, and blank verse, which, in spite of what Milton had said, was to be restricted to the theatre. His own dramatic blank verse, from this time onward, was more severe than any which had been used, except by Milton, since Ben Jonson.

It was not characteristic of Dryden to invent forms of writing or to introduce fresh material to public consideration. He was never an innovator, since an innovator stands outside contemporary feeling, that he may direct it. This Dryden had no inclination to attempt; he always represented the public and was led by it, his function being, when the town had accepted a certain form or a certain taste, to bring his superlative gifts to the task of making that taste or form as classical and splendid as possible. Hence, when, at the age of fifty, he suddenly achieved the highest distinction in a field new to him, the field of satire, it came very naturally from the fact that the public had within two or three years past become strongly interested anew in that species of poetic work. We shall speak later on of those satires of Marvell and Oldham which led the way for Dryden. He so far surpassed those his forerunners, and made the style so completely his own, that we need not delay here for their consideration. It is valuable, however, to note that these less brilliant writers selected the form of political satire for Dryden, that the Scriptural tissue thrown as a light veil over the story was suggested by an anonymous tract, called *Naboth's Vineyard*, in 1679, and that the very name of Achitophel had been nailed upon Shaftesbury before the great poet stirred a hand. It is highly characteristic of Dryden that he should remain in watchful inaction until all the tools were forged which he needed, and that when he moved it was to produce a work of finished magnificence. When he did speak, it was as a master, and his wonderful fourfold group of satires forms the most faultless section of his work.

The four famous Tory satires were published in quick succession, within the course of twelve months. The first part of *Absalom and Achitophel* appeared in November 1681, when Shaftesbury (Achitophel) was in the Tower; *The Medal* appeared in March 1682, after the bill of high treason against him, a bill which Dryden's poem was intended to support, had been thrown out by the grand jury ; *MacFlecknoe*, which was specially directed against the Whig bard, Shadwell, is dated October 1682 ; and the ensuing month saw the publication of the second part of *Absalom and Achitophel*, written after the arrest of Monmouth (Absalom) at Stafford. The first of these four poems is the most important, and the longest too, and of the last only two hundred lines are certainly from Dryden's pen, the remainder being written under the poet's supervision by Nahum Tate. In the original *Absalom and Achitophel* there is but a thin strain of narrative or allegory, the story of the critical state of English affairs at the moment being told under a Hebrew disguise. The poem really consists of a series of satirical portraits, cut and polished like jewels, and flashing malignant light from all their facets. The sketch of Absalom is indulgent enough, for the secret love of the king to Monmouth was well known, but none of the other Whig leaders were spared,—Shaftesbury himself,

"A fiery soul, which, working out its way,
Fretted the pigmy body to decay,
And o'er-informed the tenement of clay" ;

Zimri (Buckingham), whose death-piece was to be so magnificently added by Pope ; Shimei (Slingsby Bethel), whose

"business was, by writing, to persuade
That kings were useless, and a clog to trade" ;

and Corah (Titus Oates), who proved his "saint-like" grace by

"A church vermilion and a Moses' face,"—

all these were drawn at full length, with a precision never approached by any of the popular "character"-makers of the preceding half-century, and in verse the like of which had never been heard in England for vigorous alternation of thrust and parry. The heroic couplet had become by this time, in Dryden's hands, a rapier of polished and tempered steel.

The success of *Absalom and Achitophel* surpassed anything of the kind which had been witnessed since the Restoration. It was a comparatively short work, containing little over a thousand lines, and the air was darkened by pamphlets of a like size, imitations, parodies, replies, encouragements. None of these possessed any real merit, or gave more than momentary satisfaction or annoyance to Dryden. His next satire, *The Medal*, is less often read at present, although it is much shorter, and shows no less ability. Dr. Johnson's criticism of it still holds good. "It is now [1780] not much read, nor perhaps generally understood; yet, a slight acquaintance with the history of the period removes all obscurity; and though we cannot sympathise with the fervour of politics which it contains, the poetry has claims to popularity widely independent of the temporary nature of the subject." There were, however, none of Dryden's brilliant portraits in this diatribe against the political career of Shaftesbury, and this gave the poem a certain monotony. The most stirring passage in the *Medal* is that in which the poet satirises the instability of public opinion:

> "Almighty crowd! thou shortenest all dispute;
> Power is thy essence, wit thy attribute!
> Nor faith nor reason make thee at a stay;
> Thou leap'st o'er all eternal truths in thy pindaric way!
> Athens, no doubt, did righteously decide,
> When Phocion and when Socrates were tried;
> As righteously they did those dooms repent;
> Still they were wise, whatever way they went:
> Crowds err not, though to both extremes they run;
> To kill the father and recall the son.
> Some think the fools were most as times went then,
> But now the world's o'erstocked with prudent men.
> The common cry is even religion's test,—
> The Turk's is at Constantinople best,
> Idols in India, Popery at Rome,
> And our own worship only true at home;
> And true but for the time, 'tis hard to know
> How long we please it shall continue so;
> This side to-day, and that to-morrow burns;
> So all are God-Almighties in their turns."

MacFlecknoe, on the other hand, a masterpiece in only 217 verses, has remained one of the best known and most read of all Dryden's works. Flecknoe, a scribbling priest whose name had become synonymous with poetaster, had lately died, and Dryden represents him as nominating Shadwell to succeed him on the throne of dulness. The paternal address closes with some lines which, in addition to their irresistible comic force, are valuable as supplying us with early criticism of those exercises of conceited wit in verse on which the *Spectator* was afterwards so severe:

> " 'This is thy province, this thy wondrous way,
> New humours to invent for each new play :
> This is that boasted bias of thy mind,
> By which one way to dullness 'tis inclined ;
> Which makes thy writings lean on one side still,
> And, in all changes, that way bends thy will.
> Nor let thy mountain-belly make pretence
> Of likeness ; thine's a tympany of sense.
> A tun of man in thy large bulk is writ,
> But sure thou'rt but a kilderkin of wit.
> Like mine, thy gentle numbers feebly creep ;
> Thy tragic muse gives smiles, thy comic sleep.
> With whate'er gall thou set'st thyself to write,
> Thy inoffensive satires never bite ;
> In thy felonious heart though venom lies,
> It does but touch thy Irish pen, and dies.
> Thy genius call thee not to purchase fame
> In keen iambics, but mild anagram.
> Leave writing plays, and choose for thy command,
> Some peaceful province in Acrostic land.
> There thou may'st wings display, and altars raise,
> And torture one poor word ten thousand ways ;
> Or, if thou would'st thy different talents suit,
> Set thy own songs, and sing them to thy lute.'
>   He said :—but his last words were scarcely heard ;
> For Bruce and Longvil had a trap prepared,
> And down they sent the yet declaiming bard.
> Sinking he left his drugget robe behind,
> Borne upwards by a subterranean wind.
> The mantle fell to the young prophet's part,
> With double portion of his father's art."

There is no doubt that Dryden's terrible couplets punished his antagonist like the scientific blows of a prize-fighter's fists. In spite of his activity, his energy, his veritable talent, Shadwell never recovered his position, and never will recover it. After two hundred years we need not trouble to pity the victim, but may allow ourselves to taste the exquisite intellectual pleasure which is offered us by Dryden's wit and sparkling malignity. He returned to the attack a month later in that section of the second *Absalom and Achitophel* which is certainly his, and which presents us with the *ne plus ultra* of his satirical vigour. He must have felt that he could not exceed these portraits of Pheleg, Ben-Jochanan, Doeg (Elkanah Settle), and Shadwell once more in Og, and he withdrew with his customary tact from the field of satire.

He was, indeed, occupied with totally different interests. This new study of all public matters seems to have led to his giving an attention to the question of religion such as he had never given before. As far as Dryden had attached himself to any religious section of English feeling hitherto, it rather bears in the direction of Hobbism, or a mild, indifferent scepticism. The fierce conflict now raging between three acrimonious parties—the Catholics, the Anglicans, and the Dissenters—drove him to make a choice among the three; and though his ultimate, and, I believe, conscientious, bias was toward the positivism of Rome, he got no further at first than satisfaction with the balance preserved by the Church of England. This passing mood is revealed in the didactic and argumentative poem, *Religio Laici*, published in November 1682. He did not rest there, but soon after the accession of James II. went openly to mass. Macaulay and others have greatly exaggerated the worldly advantages which ensued to Dryden from this change of belief. We may perhaps admit, with W. D. Christie, that his conversion "was in great measure a movement of calculated expediency," without holding that Dryden acted against any religious conviction. His theological principles were at no time very exacting, but there seems no reason to suppose that they were not genuinely under Roman direction, although a personal reason may have been needed to stir the poet's inertia. He certainly never recanted when recantation might have restored him to wealth and influence. In April 1687 he published his very brilliant and extraordinary poem, *The Hind and the Panther*, in which allegory the hind stood for the Church of Rome and the panther for the Church of England. The opening lines of this poem may be taken as exhibiting Dryden's epic manner at its best, the melody of the verse being beyond all praise :

> "A milk-white Hind, immortal and unchanged ;
> Fed on the lawns and in the forest ranged ;
> Without unspotted, innocent within,
> She found no danger, for she knew no sin.
> Yet had she oft been chased with horns and hounds,
> And Scythian shafts ; and many-winged wounds
> Aimed at her heart ; was often forced to fly,
> And doomed to death, though fated not to die."

The Dissenters are treated with great severity, especially in the opening canto of the poem. The Independents are "the bloody Bear," the Quakers "the quaking Hare," the Hobbists "the buffoon Ape," and the Anabaptists "the baptist Boar." Worst of all, the Presbyterian Wolf appears "with belly gaunt and famished face." The argument proceeds with greater amenity in the later parts, and the final canto is adorned with the story of the Swallows, told by the Panther, and that of the Doves, told by the Hind, which unite to form a very beautiful episode in a poem which is otherwise full of cleverness, but not particularly well constructed or interesting to a modern reader.

It was during the brief reign of James II. that Dryden first began to cultivate the Pindaric ode of Cowley, in which he achieved some successes, and notably the beautiful *Elegy* on Anne Killigrew in 1686. In 1684 he began his interesting *Miscellany* of occasional poems by himself and others; and in connection with this volume and that of 1685 he turned his attention to verse-translation. Thus Dryden was in several ways preparing himself for the noble enforced activity of his old age, and for the troubles which were soon to oblige him to drive hard a professional quill. In 1687 he produced his first *Song for St. Cecilia's Day*, which, though less celebrated than the second one, contains some of Dryden's best-known lines, especially the

> "From harmony, from heavenly harmony,
> This universal frame began :
> From harmony to harmony,
> Through all the compass of the notes it ran,
> The diapason closing full in Man."

The Revolution of 1688 surprised Dryden as much as it did his royal master. The poet had quaintly deplored the difficulty which those birds of paradise, the British Muses, had experienced in extracting their hire and gain from James; "yet something to their share he threw." Under the new Protestant monarch the Muse's fleece became absolutely dry. The Revolution made it needful that all who held office should take oaths in the reformed religion, and thus Dryden found himself no longer historiographer and poet laureate, besides losing his place in the Customs. Neither his honour nor his conviction would permit him to recant, and if it had not been for the generous fidelity of Lord Dorset he might have sunk into penury. Dorset, however, came forward with prompt pecuniary help, until the poet, now approaching the age of sixty, could buckle himself to unaccustomed feats of professional energy. With the year 1688 began the most active period of Dryden's career. His work in the drama and in prose will occupy us in the two following chapters. His contributions to pure poetry for some time took the form almost exclusively of translations—hack-work, indeed, but accomplished with superb energy and skill.

Dryden, who felt the pulse of the age with surprising exactitude, saw that great successes were open to any one who should gracefully and vigorously paraphrase the ancient classics. The study of Latin and Greek had rapidly declined as the century descended, and real scholarship was now a very rare thing. Comparatively few men and scarcely any women could any longer read

Virgil and Homer with pleasure in the original, and yet, at the same time, with the new ambition for correctness, for classic grace, there had arisen a general desire to know in what manner the famous poets of antiquity had expressed themselves. Dryden determined to educate and indulge this taste. A new epoch in translating had been inaugurated in 1682 by an elegant version of *Lucretius* in heroic verse, from the hand of an Oxford poet, Thomas Creech (1659-1700). As the reader may be inclined to compare the manner of Creech with that of Dryden, the version made by the former of the famous address to Epicurus with which the Third Book begins is here given:

> " Thee, who hast light from midst thick darkness brought,
> And life's advantages and pleasures taught,
> Thee, chiefest glory of the Grecian state,
> I strictly trace ; willing to imitate,
> Not contradict ; for how can larks oppose
> The vigorous swans? they are unequal foes ;
> Or how can tender kids with feeble force
> Contend in racing with the noble horse?
> Thou, Parent of Philosophy, hast shown
> The way to truth with precepts of thine own.
> For as from sweetest flowers the labouring bee
> Extracts her precious juice ; Great Soul, from thee
> We all our golden sentences derive,
> Golden, and fit eternally to live.
> For when I hear thy mighty reasons prove
> This world was made without the Powers above,
> All fears and terrors waste, and fly apace.
> Thro' parted heavens I see the mighty space,
> The rise of things, the gods, the happy seats,
> Which storm or violent tempest never beats,
> Nor snow invades, but with the purest air,
> And gaudy light diffus'd, look gay and fair :
> There bounteous Nature makes supplies for ease,
> There Minds enjoy an undisturbed peace."

Dryden, who always required a precedent, determined to surpass Creech, and he pushed on with indomitable spirit, although in failing health. In 1685 he tried his hand at certain fragments of Theocritus, Lucretius, Horace, and Homer. In 1693 he gave a first instalment of his labours and those of some younger friends to the world in the shape of a folio volume of the works of Juvenal and Persius. Of these, five satires of Juvenal and the whole of Persius were his own. The third volume of his *Miscellanies* contained something from Ovid and less from Homer. He then immediately set to work on a vast undertaking—a version of all Virgil, printing the Third Georgic first as a specimen. In January 1694 Evelyn met Dryden, and reported that the poet "now intended to write no more plays, being intent on his translation of Virgil." This huge enterprise occupied him almost exclusively for three years, and was published in July 1697. In order to secure quiet, Dryden retired into Northamptonshire, Huntingdonshire, and Buckinghamshire, several country-seats contesting for the honour of being the birthplace of this celebrated work. Dryden's touch was not delicate enough to reproduce Virgil's best effects, but on the whole it may be securely said that no more satisfactory translation, as English poetry, has ever been produced.

Dryden's next act was the composition, late in 1697, of the famous second song for St. Cecilia's Day, known as *Alexander's Feast*. The final years of his active and arduous life were occupied in writing paraphrases or adaptations to the English style of his day of various stories by Chaucer, Boccaccio, and Ovid. In 1699 he wrote to his beautiful cousin, Mrs. Stewart of Cotterstock, "I am still drudging on; always a poet and never a good one. I pass my time sometimes with Ovid, and sometimes with our old English poet, Chaucer; translating such stories as best please my fancy; and intend, besides them, to add somewhat of my own; so that it is not impossible but ere the summer be passed, I may come down to you with a volume in my hand, like a dog out of the water with a duck in his mouth." When this volume appeared in 1700 (November 1699), it was a great folio of 12,000 verses, entitled *Fables, Ancient and Modern*. This, the last of Dryden's books, has been the favourite with all generations of his admirers. At the extremity of a premature old age, for his body was worn out at the approach of seventy, his genius burned more brightly, and with a younger glow, than it had ever done before. This incomparable volume contains among many other jewels, "Theodore and Honoria," "Palamon and Arcite," and "Cymon and Iphigenia," the best known of all Dryden's narrative poems. In the noble dedication of the second of these tales to the Duchess of Ormond we have an example of Dryden's most polished and magnificent style in elaborate personal compliment. This fine poem closes thus musically:

> "Blest be the power, which has at once restored
> The hopes of lost succession to your lord;
> Joy to the first and last of each degree,
> Virtue to courts, and what I longed to see,
> To you the Graces, and the Muse to me.
> O daughter of the rose, whose cheeks unite
> The differing titles of the red and white;
> Who heaven's alternate beauty well display,
> The blush of morning, and the milky way;
> Whose face is paradise, but fenced from sin;
> For God in either eye has placed a cherubin.
>   All is your lord's alone; even absent, he
> Employs the care of chaste Penelope.
> For him you waste in tears your widowed hours;
> For him your curious needle paints the flowers:
> Such works of old imperial dames were taught;
> Such, for Ascanius, fair Elissa wrought.
> The soft recesses of your hours improve
> The three fair pledges of your happy love:
> All other parts of pious duty done,
> You owe your Ormond nothing but a son;
> To fill in future times his father's place,
> And wear the garter of his mother's race."

Dryden scarcely survived this his last success. On the 1st of May 1700 he died in his house in London, and received a splendid public funeral in Westminster Abbey.

Dryden is the most stalwart poetical figure which will be dealt with in the course of the present volume. In other words, he is the strongest poet of the age of prose, the most vigorous verse-man between Milton and Wordsworth. It is needful, however, that we should comprehend his limitations of style, and not demand from him what his age and temper of mind declined to allow him to produce. The exquisite freshness and variety of the best romantic poetry, with its spontaneous and evanescent beauties, are not to be sought for from Dryden. He never forgets that, as Matthew Arnold has said, he is the puissant and glorious founder of our excellent and indispensable eighteenth century—that is to say, of an age of prose and reason. His native genius constantly clashed in criticism with his acquired taste, and hence his wavering adherence to unfashionable masters of verse, to Chaucer, to Chapman, to Milton. He attempted to extract what he thought was best from these and other romantic poets, and to adapt it to an Anglo-classic taste. His genius was so energetic and his skill so amazing that he partly contrived to do this, but the odour of romance had evaporated. Hence it cannot be denied that the most mysterious and indescribable charm of poetic writing, that charm which is exhaled from the best poetry like a perfume, is wanting, or singularly rare, in Dryden in spite of his acknowledged supremacy as a poet. When this is admitted the reader is placed in a position to do justice to Dryden's genius.

The right way to measure Dryden is to compare him with the other great poet of the period of prose and reason, Pope. We notice, in the first place, that the former has at his command a distinctly richer and deeper music than the latter. We may say that the muse of Dryden has a contralto and that of Pope a soprano voice. This greater depth of tone, or inferior lightness, whichever we choose to call it, was no doubt a survival from the poetry of the first half of the seventeenth century. We have but to study the blank-verse plays of Dryden to see how much he preserved, in his chastened way, of the melody of Fletcher's line. But there was more than this. Dryden was greatly Pope's superior as a craftsman in verse. It is true that though he performed wonders in polishing the heroic couplet, he left something in this direction to be performed by his successor. But

Pope excelled only in the couplet, whereas Dryden was master of blank-verse also, and of a greater variety of lyrical measures than is generally supposed. The least successful of his operas contains such bursts of natural song as—

> " Old father Ocean calls my tide ;
> Come away ! come away !
> The barks upon the billows ride,
> The master will not stay ;
> The merry boatswain from his side
> His whistle takes, to check and chide
> The lingering lads' delay ;
> And all the crew aloud has cried,
> Come away !"

such delicate dactylic melodies as—

> " From the low palace of old father Ocean,
> Come we in pity your cares to deplore ;
> Sea-racing dolphins are trained for our motion,
> Moony tides swelling to roll us ashore,"—

each as dissimilar as possible from the ordinary conception of Dryden's manner as a metrist. This variety of instrument must not be left out of consideration, especially as, until the time of Gray, it was scarcely shared, to any appreciable extent, by another English poet. Nor must it be forgotten that he attained what Waller had seen was needful for the restoration of the structure of English verse, but what no one until Dryden had succeeded in obtaining, full mastery over the balance of iambic verse, so that the poet could rule the line, and not the line carry him whither it would. This energetic harmony in the couplet is admirably described by Gray, in his introduction of the car of Dryden, drawn by "two coursers of etherial race, with necks in thunder crowned, and long-resounding pace."

At the extremity of his life, Dryden wrote of himself as one "who has done my best to improve the language, and especially the poetry," of his native country. It was the opinion of Dr. Johnson and the critics of the eighteenth century that he had done this to such an extent that he found English brick and left it marble. This is, of course, an exaggeration; but he purified the national style to a very marked extent, freed it of uncouth and superfluous ornament, and drew the parts of language into harmonious relation with one another. His fluency, his sustained power, the cogency and lucidity of his logic, polished the surface of narrative and didactic poetry, which, until he came, had been rocky and irregular. He taught the poets to be explicit, where they had been vexatiously allusive; to be perspicuous and vivacious, where they had been dull and crabbed; to pursue the theme which was under their examination, instead of flying off to the consideration of a dozen foreign beauties. More than this it is difficult to say, partly because the great transformation in English prosody, upon which these lessons were founded, was adopted but not invented by Dryden, and partly because it is not correct to consider his purely poetical career without criticising at the same time his contributions to drama and to prose. There is no great gulf fixed between these sections of his work, as there usually is between the verse and prose of a poet. Dryden's social and satirical poems—that is to say, the most characteristic part of his purely poetical work—do not differ in kind but only in form from his prose treatises of similar nature. We may therefore wait for two succeeding chapters before finally summing up Dryden's position as a man of letters.

The period of forty years, during which the supremacy of Dryden lasted, is poorer than any other in our literature in poetry of the second or third order. If Dryden could be removed, the non-dramatic poetry of the age would be seen to be almost non-existent, and when it was not insignificant, it owed its success in almost every case to qualities which were not, properly speaking, poetical. This was peculiarly true of a writer who achieved unbounded popularity in the early years of the Restoration, Samuel Butler (1612-1680). This royalist had served various Presbyterian gentlemen during the Commonwealth, and had secreted in silence an obdurate hatred of the Puritan creed and manners. In the course of an obscure and penurious existence he had read much and had observed intently, goaded into wit by the gadfly of a wounded and rancorous vanity. When the king came back, Butler was at liberty to pour out the vials of his spleen, and in 1663 he published *Hudibras*, a long and voluble lampoon, in which the typical Puritan is described as a hunch-back monster, a pedantic, stubborn, and frowsy country-justice. This absurd and extraordinary portrait was drawn in some thousands of rattling octosyllabic verses, full of wit, and bright with bewildering audacities of rhyme. This elaborate squib pleased Charles II. and his court to an almost indecent extent, and Butler was encouraged to produce continuations of the poem in 1664 and in 1678. He expected to be the recipient of the royal bounty, but was disappointed. Butler left a great mass of MSS. in prose and verse behind him. These, or a portion of them, were published as his *Genuine Remains*, in two volumes, in 1759. From this collection we take a characteristic fragment, probably a chip from the block of *Hudibras*:

> " This reverend brother, like a goat,
> Did wear a tail upon his throat,
> The fringe and tassel of a face,
> That gives it a becoming grace,
> But let in such a curious frame,
> As if 'twere wrought in filograin ;
> And cut so ev'n, as if 't had been
> Drawn with a pen upon his chin.
> No topiary hedge of quickset
> Was e'er so neatly cut, or thick set ;
> That made beholders more admire
> Than china-plate that's made of wire ;
> But being wrought so regular
> In ev'ry part, and ev'ry hair,
> Who would believe, it should be portal
> To unconforming-inward mortal ?
> And yet it was, and did dissent
> No less from its own government,
> Than from the Church's, and detest
> That, which it held forth, and profest ;

> Did equally abominate
> Conformity in Church and State;
> And, like an hypocritic brother,
> Profest one thing, and did another;
> As all things, where th' are most profest,
> Are found to be regarded least."

The temper and extremely limited talent of Butler made it hard to help him. In society he was as surly as his own mock-knight, and the solitary accomplishment which he possessed was that of weaving brilliant rhymes together in the privacy of his own chambers. His poverty, however, was much exaggerated, and it is now believed that Oldham was ill-informed when he said of Butler that "of all his gains in verse he could not save enough to purchase flannel and a grave."

Another writer, far loftier than Butler in genius and character, belongs to the Restoration by only one side of his production. Andrew Marvell (1621-1678), the last of the great lyrical poets of the romantic age, became distinguished as a satirist after the Restoration. His exquisite garden-poems, distinguished for their rich imagery and their loyal study of nature, were composed, it is believed, between 1650 and 1652, at Nunappleton, where Marvell was tutor to Mary Fairfax. These lovely verses do not belong in time or in character to the period we are now considering; but on the return of the Stuarts, Marvell appeared in a totally different light. He had been recommended to Bradshaw as assistant-secretary by Milton, and afterwards Cromwell had made him joint-secretary with that illustrious poet. He was therefore a staunch Puritan, and after the Restoration he stoutly attacked tyranny and crime in Church and State. The literary form which he adopted for these attacks was the satire in heroic couplets. Satire had scarcely been cultivated in English since the extremely rough and shapeless diatribes of Donne, Hall, and Marston had appeared in the beginning of the century. Cleveland, in the preceding generation, and Wild, had suggested its resuscitation, but Marvell was the first to write regular satires in the Latin way. His pieces in this kind, the most important of which are *Last Instructions to a Painter* (1669), and *The Character of Holland* (1672), have considerable vigour of versification, and prove that Marvell had learned the secret of the distich. The second of these pieces opens with this humorous and extravagant strain of hatred and contempt for the Dutch. Marvell never could forgive or forget the burning of the ships in the Medway:

> " Holland, that scarce deserves the name of land,
> As but th' off-scouring of the British sand,
> And so much earth as was contributed
> By English pilots when they heav'd the lead,
> Or what by the Ocean's slow alluvion fell
> Of shipwreck'd cockle and the muscle-shell:
> This indigested vomit of the sea
> Fell to the Dutch by just propriety.
>   Glad then, as miners who have found the ore,
> They, with mad labour, fish'd the land to shore;
> And div'd as desperately for each piece
> Of earth, as if 't had been of ambergreece;
> Collecting anxiously small loads of clay,
> Less than what building swallows bear away;
> Or than those pills which sordid beetles roll,
> Transfusing into them their dunghill soul.
>   How did they rivet, with gigantic piles,
> Thorough the centre their new-catchèd miles;
> And to the stake a struggling country bound
> Where barking waves still bait the forcèd ground;
> Building their wat'ry Babel far more high
> To reach the sea, than those to scale the sky!
>   Yet still his claim the injur'd ocean laid,
> And oft at leap-frog o'er their steeples played:
> As if on purpose it on land had come
> To show them what's their *mare liberum*.
> A daily deluge over them does boil;
> The earth and water play at level-coyl.
> The fish ofttimes the burgher dispossest,
> And sat, not as a meat, but as a guest,
> Or, as they over the new level rang'd
> For pickled herring, pickled *heeren* chang'd.
> Nature, it seem'd, asham'd of her mistake,
> Would throw their land away at duck and drake.'

Unfortunately, the indignation of the writer, which equals that of Juvenal, knows no bound of discretion, and the coarseness of these pieces is beyond credence. Dryden's satires show that the greater poet had studied with interest the angry manifestoes of the Puritan member for Hull.

A further advance in the direction of Dryden's masterpieces is marked by the satires of John Oldham (1653-1683). He was an usher in a country school, where he was sought out when he was about five-and-twenty by a party of noble wits, who had been struck by some of his unprinted verses. These noblemen, however, did little to encourage his fortunes, and he sank into great poverty. Oldham seems to have been of a sincerely independent spirit, and to have boasted with truth that in a venal age he was

> "Lord of myself, accountable to none,
> But to my conscience and my God alone."

The Earl of Kingston, who took a genuine interest in him, endeavoured to induce him to accept a post in his service, but Oldham refused. He was, however, staying at the earl's seat as a guest when he died of smallpox in the thirty-first year of his age. He had published a very successful *Satire upon the Jesuits* in 1680, and in 1684 his *Remains* appeared, with an exquisite elegy on this "Marcellus of our Tongue," by Dryden. The satires of Oldham are distressing to read; the author has no belief in the better part of human nature; he is cynical and bitter to the extreme, and he strikes, not for a party, like Marvell, but wildly, against the world. Oldham is the Ajax among our satirists, and his own contemporaries, not easily moved by personal characteristics, were touched by his strange cold frenzy, his honourable isolation, and his early death. Dryden seems to have been genuinely distressed at the fate of a young man whose personal acquaintance he had but lately formed, and whose work had a character particularly attractive to him. Oldham's versification is better than that of Marvell, in his satires, but still rugged; as Dryden observed, his prosody needed mellowing. Neither Marvell nor Oldham understood that coolness of irony, that polished banter, which gave to Dryden his extraordinary influence as a satirist.

A few years before the Revolution, two peers distinguished themselves above their meaner contemporaries by producing certain critical pamphlets in verse, which were of a kind new in English, and which have preserved a niche for their authors in the history of literature. Of these two writers the one who most nearly deserves the title of poet is John Sheffield, Earl of Mulgrave, and afterwards Duke of Buckinghamshire (1649-1721), celebrated in *Absalom and Achitophel* as "sharp-judging Adriel, the muses' friend, Himself a muse." Mulgrave circulated in 1679 an *Essay on Satire*, and published in 1682 an *Essay on Poetry*, both in heroic verse. These pieces were anonymous, and they were so cleverly versified that the town insisted on thinking that Dryden was their author. In consequence of the following passage in the *Essay on Satire*, the Earl of Rochester had Dryden cruelly beaten by a troop of hired bravos, in a narrow street off Covent Garden, on a winter's night in 1679:

> "Last enter Rochester, of sprightly wit,
> Yet not for converse safe, or business fit;
> Mean in each action, lewd in every limb,
> Manners themselves are mischievous in him;
> A gloss he gives to ev'ry foul design,
> And we must own his very vices shine;
> But of this odd ill-nature to mankind
> Himself alone the ill effects will find:
> So envious hags in vain their witchcraft try,
> Yet for intended mischief justly die."

Mulgrave's *Essay on Poetry* contains some terse and effective lines, one or two of which have passed into current use. He lays down sensible rules for practitioners in the various departments of poetic art, but he was not very successful himself in the composition of odes, tragedies, and epistles. Wentworth Dillon, Earl of Roscommon (1634-1685) was a man who spent the greater part of his life in France, and was steeped in the erudition of the French Jesuits. About 1670 he wrote a short critical poem, called an *Essay on Translated Verse*, which he was persuaded to print in 1680. It is in heroic couplets, but towards the close Roscommon expresses himself strongly in favour of the "Roman majesty" of blank verse, and gives a sort of *précis* of the sixth book of *Paradise Lost* in that measure. In 1684 he published a paraphrase of Horace's *Art of Poetry* in blank verse, and Roscommon is remarkable as the only writer between Milton and the end of the century who discarded rhyme in serious non-dramatic verse.

A word must be said here about the songs which continued to be written almost to the very end of the century, and sometimes with extraordinary charm. Dryden's contributions to this class of poetry have already been mentioned. The Cavalier lyrists of the age of Charles I. bequeathed not a little of their skill to the best of their successors, at least until the Revolution. The finest songs of the Restoration are those of a very infamous person, John Wilmot, Earl of Rochester (1647-1680), but Aphra Behn, Sedley, Lord Dorset (1637-1706), and Etheredge all wrote well-turned verses of this class with considerable charm and grace. These are examples from Mrs. Behn and Rochester respectively:

> "Love in fantastic triumph sat,
>   Whilst bleeding hearts around him flowed,
> For whom fresh pains he did create,
>   And strange tyrannic power he showed;
> From thy bright eyes he took his fires,
>   Which round about in sport he hurled;
> But 'twas from mine he took desires
>   Enough to undo the amorous world.

> "From me he took his sighs and tears,
>   From thee his pride and cruelty,
> From me his languishment and fears,
>   And every killing dart from thee;
> Thus thou, and I, the god have armed,
>   And set him up a deity,
> But my poor heart alone is harmed,
>   While thine the victor is, and free."

"My dear Mistress has a heart
   Soft as those kind looks she gave me;
When, with love's resistless art,
   And her eyes, she did enslave me;
But her constancy's so weak,
   She's so wild and apt to wander,
That my jealous heart would break
   Should we live one day asunder.

"Melting joys about her move,
   Killing pleasures, wounding blisses,
She can dress her eyes in love,
   And her lips can arm with kisses;
Angels listen when she speaks,
   She's my delight, all mankind's wonder,
But my jealous heart would break
   Should we live one day asunder."

All through the seventeenth century the lamp of Doric song was kept alight in Scotland by one interesting family, the Sempills of Beltrees, who passed it on from father to son. Francis Sempill, who died about 1683, was the author of the original version of *Auld Langsyne*, which he opens thus:

"Should auld acquaintance be forgot,
   And never thought upon?
The flames of love extinguished,
   And freely past and gone?
Is thy kind heart now grown sae cauld,
   In that loving breast o' thine,
That thou can'st never ance reflect
   On auld langsyne?"

It is instructive to compare this with Burns's celebrated adaptation of the same theme.

Towards the close of the century there came forward two interesting writers with a notice of whom we may close this branch of our inquiry. Sir Samuel Garth (1660-1719) was a resident fellow of a Cambridge college, until, in mature life, he became a physician, and was called up to London to administer that newly-founded dispensary in the College of Physicians in which gratuitous advice was given to the poor. The apothecaries viciously attacked the pious work of charity, and Garth held their meanness up to ridicule in a mock-heroic poem, *The Dispensary* (1699), which passed through a great number of editions. It was through the zeal of Garth that Dryden received due honour in burial; and he was prominent in founding the Kit-Kat Club. In 1715 his topographical poem of *Claremont* appeared, in direct emulation of Denham's *Cooper's Hill*. The fun has all faded out of *The Dispensary*, and Garth is no longer in the least degree attractive. But his didactic verse is the best between Dryden and Pope, though we see beginning in it the degradation of the overmannered style of the eighteenth century. In the fourth canto of the *Dispensary* Garth sums up, with all his characteristic good nature, and more vivacity than usual, the condition of English poetry at the close of the seventeenth century:

> "Mortal, how dar'st thou with such lies address
> My awful seat, and trouble my recess?
> In Essex marshy hundreds is a cell,
> Where lazy fogs, and drizzling vapours dwell:
> Thither raw damps on drooping wings repair,
> And shiv'ring quartans shake the sickly air.
> There, when fatigu'd, some silent hours I pass,
> And substitute physicians in my place;
> Then dare not, for the future, once rehearse
> The dissonance of such unequal verse;
> But in your lines let energy be found,
> And learn to rise in sense, and sink in sound.
> Harsh words, tho' pertinent, uncouth appear,
> None please the fancy, who offend the ear;
> In sense and numbers if you wou'd excel,
> Read Wycherley, consider Dryden well;
> In one, what vigorous turns of fancy shine,
> In th' other, syrens warble in each line;
> If Dorset's sprightly muse but touch the lyre,
> The smiles and Graces melt in soft desire,
> And little Loves confess their amorous fire.
> The Tiber now no courtly Gallus sees,
> But smiling Thames enjoys his Normanbys;

> And gentle Isis claims the ivy crown,
> To bind th' immortal brows of Addison ;
> As tuneful Congreve tries his rural strains,
> Pan quits the woods, the list'ning fauns the plains ;
> And Philomel, in notes like his, complains ;
> And Britain, since Pausanias was writ,
> Knows Spartan virtue, and Athenian wit,
> When Stepney paints the godlike acts of kings,
> Or, what Apollo dictates, Prior sings :
> The banks of Rhine a pleased attention show,
> And silver Sequana forgets to flow."

Of Anne Finch, Countess of Winchelsea (1660-1720), it is impossible to say whether she was the last of the old or the first of the new romantic school. At a period when the study of external nature was completely excluded from poetry, Lady Winchelsea introduced into her verses novel images taken directly from rustic life as she saw it round about her. Her *Nocturnal Reverie* has been highly praised by Wordsworth, and is a singularly beautiful description of the sights and sounds that attend a summer night in the country :

> " In such a night, when passing clouds give place,
> Or thinly veil the heavens' mysterious face,
> When in some river, overhung with green,
> The waving moon and trembling leaves are seen,
> When freshened grass now bears itself upright,
> And makes cool banks to pleasing rest invite,
> Whence spring the woodbine, and the bramble-rose,
> And where the sleepy cowslip sheltered grows,
> Whilst now a paler hue the foxglove takes,
> Yet chequers still with red the dusky brakes,
> Where scattered glow-worms,—but in twilight fine,—
> Shew trivial beauties, watch their hour to shine,
> While Salisbury stands the test of every light,
> In perfect charms and perfect beauty bright ;
> When odours, which declined repelling day,
> Through temperate air uninterrupted stray ;
> When darkened groves their softest shadows wear,
> And falling waters we distinctly hear ;
> When through the gloom more venerable shows
> Some ancient fabric awful in repose ;

> While sunburned hills their swarthy looks conceal,
> And swelling haycocks thicken up the vale ;
> When the loosed horse now, as his pasture leads,
> Comes slowly grazing thro' the adjoining meads,
> Whose stealing pace and lengthened shade we fear,
> Till torn-up forage in his teeth we hear ;
> When nibbling sheep at large pursue their food,
> And unmolested kine rechew the cud ;
> When curlews cry beneath the village walls,
> And to her straggling brood the partridge calls ;
> Their short-lived jubilee the creatures keep,
> Which but endures, whilst tyrant Man doth sleep."

Lady Winchelsea's temper was so foreign to the taste of her own age that she achieved no success among her contemporaries, although Swift admired her, and from a line of hers, "We faint beneath the aromatic pain," Pope borrowed one of his most celebrated phrases. Her poems, not all of which have seen the light, consist of odes and miscellaneous lyrics, besides several dramatic pieces; the original MSS. are in the possession of the present writer.

As the seventeenth century approached its close, the poetry of England was invaded more and more completely by a Latinism which repulsed and finally silenced all that was not in sympathy with it, and gave an exaggerated importance to all that was. To attribute this tendency to the popularity of those translations of the Latin poets published by Dryden, or to the precepts of the Aristotelian critics of France, is to evade the difficulty. These writings were welcomed, and therefore exercised influence, because the public ear was ready to receive them. The rules of Rapin and Le Bossu did not create a taste—they only justified and fortified it. Every section of poetry responded to the change of manner. The very study of nature was contracted into channels as close as had sufficed to give Horace and Juvenal their satiric picturesqueness of detail. The desire of finding such channels is perhaps the most definite symptom we can point to as leading to such a condition of things. The extreme facility of Renaissance invention had wearied the mind of Europe, and an appetite for individual inspiration gave way to a passion for regularity and intellectual discipline, until only such terrestrial forms of poetical fancy gave satisfaction as Rome rather than Greece or Italy had nourished. The taste for poetry, in the abstract, as a species of literature, retained its hold on the public even when the art had been despoiled of all its lyric and idyllic charms, of half its colour and its music, and of much of its variety. In order to adapt it to these new conditions, there was a curious relapse to the most primitive instincts of men; and as though the age of Hesiod had returned, readers looked to verse for instruction in those common things of life that had been resigned to prose, in the practice of medicine, in the cultivation of an orchard, in the theories of metaphysics, in the conduct of the politics of Europe. Dryden alone had retained to the last some reverberations of the great romantic music of Elizabeth. When he died the Latinists were absolutely paramount, and the poets of the next quarter of a century knew no Apollo but Horace.

CHAPTER II

DRAMA AFTER THE RESTORATION

THE drama took a place in English literature during the last third of the seventeenth century relatively more prominent than it has ever taken since. Certain sections of society were passionately addicted to theatrical amusement, and their appetites had been whetted by eighteen years of enforced privation. All theatres had been closed by ordinance of the Lords and Commons on the 2d September 1642, and in 1647, for fear of a relapse, this order had been stringently repeated. On the 21st of May 1656 Davenant obtained permission to rig up a semi-private stage in Rutland House, but it was not until August 1660 that Killigrew and he secured each a patent to open a public theatre in London. This vacuum of eighteen years sufficed to mark a condition which it did not cause, namely, the complete decline and fall of the exhausted Jacobean drama. In 1642 only one dramatist of the old school, Shirley, was still alive, and of his plays all the most important had already been acted. It was no serious attack on literature to exclude from the boards the plays of such men as Brome and Jasper Mayne. The poets of the old school soon grew tired of writing for an imaginary stage, and their successors were found unprejudiced when the time came for resuming the real drama.

In response to the universal demand for theatrical amusements at the Restoration, various playwrights instantly came forward. But these men had seen no stage plays in England for nearly twenty years, and they did not know what to supply. The names of the earliest purveyors of Restoration drama are remembered only by students, with one exception; without exception their efforts are beneath critical attention. Sir William Davenant alone requires notice, not on account of his merit, but from the fact that he was first in the field. He had been a writer of bad dramas more than thirty years before, and his *Siege of Rhodes* (1656), a clumsy piece which he called an opera, was the first of a series of plays which he brought out at his own theatre in Lincoln's Inn Fields. In writing his Restoration comedies he had the wit to steal from the French, and his last and best play, *The Man's the Master*, performed just before his death in 1668, is taken almost bodily from Scarron.

While the new Cavalier society, released from the intolerable oppression of Puritanism, was looking around it for a stage on which it could see its own face grimacing in the concave mirror of convention, a solitary effort was made to revive the old romantic comedy, as Ben Jonson had instituted it. The first dramatist of talent after the Restoration was John Wilson (1622?-1696?). Of this writer's career very little is known. He was a lawyer of independent means, most of whose life was spent in Ireland. In 1662 he produced, and in the next year published, a comedy of *The Cheats*, which surpassed in talent anything in dramatic form which had been brought forward in England for twenty years. It was in prose, ably but somewhat pedantically written, with the fantastic humours of a magician detailed in the elaborate manner of Ben Jonson. A passage from the third act may be quoted as an example of Wilson's curious belated Euphuism:

"*Mopus.* This is that which we call our Magistrium Elixir, or Rosycrucian Pantarva. The father of it is the sun, the mother of it the moon, its brothers and sisters the rest of the planets; the wind carries it in its belly, and the nurse thereof is the earth.

Jolly. Pray, sir, proceed; and disclose this son of gold.

Mopus. Hermetically, I shall. It is situated in the centre of the earth, and yet falls neither within centre nor circumference; small, and yet great;

earthy, and yet watery; airy, and yet very fire; invisible, yet easily found; soft as down, yet hard above measure; far off, and yet near at hand. That that is inferior, is as that which is superior; and that which is superior is as that which is inferior. Separate the combustible from the incombustible, the earth from the fire, the fluid from the viscous, the hot from the cold, the moist from the dry, the hard from the soft, the subtile from the thick—sweetly, and with a great deal of judgment, *per minima*, in the caverns of the earth—and thou shalt see it ascend to heaven, and descend to earth, and receive the powers of superiors and inferiors. Comprehend this, and be happy! Thou hast discovered the balsam of sulphur, the *humidum radicale* of metals, the sanctuary of nature; and there is little or nothing between thee and the mountain of diamonds, and all the spirits of astromancy, geomancy, and coschinomancy are at your command.

Jolly. Pray, sir, how call you that? That last again!

Mopus. Coschinomancy, sir; that is to say, the most mysterious art of sieve and sheers."

Wilson proceeded to prove how apt a pupil of Ben Jonson he was by bringing out a Roman tragedy, in very stately and correct blank verse, modelled on *Sejanus;* and another comedy of character, *The Projectors*, which was performed in 1664. Wilson then retired from authorship, only to appear once more as a dramatist, with a tragi-comedy in 1690. His work was swept aside by the theatrical wave from France, although it was full of ability, and closer to the best manner of Jonson than that of any of Ben's acknowledged "sons" of the preceding generation. But it possessed neither the sparkle nor the lightness requisite for the stage of Charles II., and Wilson failed where more than one frothier poet succeeded.

After this distinct false start, and after several amateur hands had tried their prentice skill on the new-found drama, it passed into the care of the literary profession. The distinction between literature and the manufacture of plays was not yet conceived, and the Restoration drama owes its importance to the fact that it was the serious occupation of men of letters. Except Marvell and Oldham, every leading writer of the imagination, until the close of the century, was in some degree a constructor of plays. The faults of the drama of the Restoration are conspicuous, but it was at least professional. Composition for the stage was the most lucrative and the most fashionable of all modes of writing, and it was not an unimportant circumstance that the greatest man of letters of the age was also, without exception, its most persistent playwright. Schools of drama were founded, and others took their place. One dramatist only, Dryden, kept the stage all the while, down to 1700. The career of Dryden as a dramatist includes the careers of all his stage companions, only Farquhar being a little later in his main successes. There were several writers who excelled Dryden in single departments of dramatic talent, but on the whole he is the greatest figure here as elsewhere in the literature of the epoch ; and it may be well to glance at the character of his work, to its close, before examining that of any of the subsidiary men who were his fellows.

Dryden had no spontaneous attraction to the stage. He set to work to write plays, after he was thirty, because he was poor, and because this was a ready way to a competence. He took a Spanish plot from a French source, and he produced, in 1663 (not printed till 1669), his comedy of *The Wild Gallant*, a vulgar and unfortunate composition. This was followed in 1664 by *The Rival-Ladies*, a dull tragi-comedy in blank verse, solely remarkable for the preface, in which, among other things, Dryden recommends the use of rhyme in heroic plays. Etheredge, as we shall see later on, immediately acted on this suggestion, and Dryden's third and fourth plays, *The Indian Queen* and *The Indian Emperor*, were examples, bolder than Etheredge's, of the adoption of a new form in English literature—the rhymed serious drama. Dryden's argument in favour of a fashion which he imported from France is worth noting. He said that rhyme, as "that which most regulates the fancy, and gives the judgment its busiest employment, is like to bring forth the richest and clearest thoughts." The English plays written since the reign of Charles I. had been turbid and irregular ; Dryden thought the buskin of dramatic rhyme might give dignity and propriety to the licentious step of the tragedian. The experiment was almost universally accepted for fourteen years, until, in 1678, Dryden himself led the fashion in a return to blank verse, upon which dramatic rhyme suddenly languished. There can be no doubt that the temporary fashion, artificial as it was, had a favourable influence upon versification. The two Mexican tragedies in the first of which Sir Robert Howard (1626-1698) had a share, were eminently successful, and *The Indian Emperor*, in its stilted kind, has a genuine merit. It is true that in such plays as these Dryden laid himself open to the taunt of the Duke of Buckingham, that he looked at his own fancy for inspiration, while Jonson and Fletcher had looked at nature; but in the best examples there was introduced into English literature something of the stately grace of Corneille. In 1667 Dryden achieved an eminent success with *The Maiden Queen*, the only play of his which has been revived in recent times. The comic scenes, which are as sprightly as a galop, were interpreted by a new actress, an orange-girl named Nell Gwyn, who brought down the house, and the king's box with it. This earliest period of Dryden's dramatic activity, not all the productions of which can even be named here, closed with a loose and dull comedy, called *An Evening's Love*, travestied from the French in 1668.

The poet was arrested by the complete failure of this piece, which even contemporary critics allowed had "a foolish plot, and was very profane." Eager to restore his reputation, he took great pains in writing his next drama, the tragedy of *Tyrannic Love*. This play has the fault of almost all Restoration tragedy, namely, that in its scenes "Declamation roars while Passion sleeps"; but it is a particularly careful piece of poetical composition, full of those nervous verses and those affecting apophthegms in which Dryden excels. Although it is, perhaps, his best heroic play, it errs on the side of rant and bombast to such a degree that the poet felt obliged to apologise for this in the prologue, and to pretend that

"Poets, like lovers, should be bold and dare,
Nor spoil their business with an over-care."

In the double tragedy of *Almanzor and Almahide*, commonly

called *The Conquest of Granada* (1672), these tendencies were pushed to a still greater excess, and common sense sank confounded at Dryden's brazen rant. The ringing hyperboles in which the unconquerable Almanzor vaunts his own prowess were very popular at first, but this absurdity did not escape the satire of the Duke of Buckingham, whose Drawcansir is now better remembered than his prototype. Dryden's huge play, with its endless clang of hurtling rhymes, has supplied the language with more proverbial expressions than any other drama of its author's. The peculiar effect of the dramatic record of stupendous passions in regular ringing couplets, the effect which, when heightened by the figure and voice of Betterton, was apt to overwhelm an audience with admiration and pity, may be better understood through an example than through pages of descriptive criticism. The *genre* was bad, and it was to prove ephemeral; but in the hands of such a master as Dryden it was not possible that it should produce no happy results, if only by accident:

> "*Almanzor.* Love is that madness which all lovers have;
> But yet 'tis sweet and pleasing so to rave:
> 'Tis an enchantment, where the reason's bound;
> But Paradise is in the enchanted ground;
> A palace, void of envy, cares and strife,
> Where gentle hours delude so much of life.
> To take those charms away, and set me free,
> Is but to send me into misery;
> And prudence, of whose cure so much you boast,
> Restores those pains which that sweet folly lost.
>   *Lyndaraxa.* I would not, like philosophers, remove,
> But show you a more pleasing shape of love.
> You a sad, sullen, froward love did see;
> I'll show him kind, and full of gaiety.
> In short, Almanzor, it shall be my care
> To show you love; for you but saw despair.
>   *Almanzor.* I, in the shape of love, despair did see;
> You, in his shape, would show inconstancy.
>   *Lyndaraxa.* There's no such thing as constancy you call;
> Faith ties not hearts; 'tis inclination all,
> Some wit deformed, or beauty much decayed,
> First constancy in love a virtue made.

> From friendship they that landmark did remove,
> And falsely placed it on the bounds of love.
> Let the effects of change be only tried;
> Court me, in jest, and call me Almahide;
> But this is only counsel I impart,
> For I, perhaps, should not receive your heart.
>   *Almanzor.* Fair though you are
> As summer mornings, and your eyes more bright
> Than stars that twinkle in a winter's night;
> Though you have eloquence to warm and move
> Cold age and praying hermits, into love;
> Though Almahide with scorn rewards my care,—
> Yet, than to change, 'tis nobler to despair.
> My love's my soul; and that from fate is free;
> 'Tis that unchanged and deathless part of me.
>   *Lyndaraxa.* The fate of constancy your love persue,
> Still to be faithful to what's false to you.
>   [*Turns from him, and goes off angrily.*
>   *Almanzor.* Ye gods, why are not hearts first paired above,
> But some still interfere in others' love?
> Ere each for each by certain marks are known,
> You mould them up in haste, and drop them down;
> And, while we seek what carelessly you sort,
> You sit in state, and make our pains your sport."

The success of *The Rehearsal*, however, whose poisoned arrows found out every crack in the harness of the heroic plays, seems to have checked for the moment Dryden's production of tragedies. His next dramas were his now no longer readable comedies of *Marriage à la Mode* (1672), and the still worse *Assignation*, in 1673. It is needless, in this place, to follow him to still lower depths.

In 1676 he returned to more serious writing, and composed an interesting tragedy in rhyme on a living Indian potentate, the Sultan *Aureng-Zebe*. Mr. Saintsbury has noticed that in this play there is "a great tendency towards *enjambement;* and as soon as this tendency gets the upper hand, a recurrence to blank verse is, in English dramatic writing, tolerably certain." Accordingly the poet admits in the prologue that he

> "Grows weary of his long-loved mistress, Rhyme";

and in his next play, *All for Love, or the World well Lost* (1678), he returns to blank verse. This tragedy is not merely an avowed imitation of the style of Shakespeare—it is almost an adaptation of *Antony and Cleopatra.* For this reason it may be recommended to the student as offering a good opportunity for comparing the tragical manner of the Restoration with that of Elizabeth. This may be done with no injustice to Dryden, since *All for Love* abounds in passages of high poetic beauty. Omitting various efforts of minor importance, we reach the latest play of Dryden's central period, the comedy of *The Spanish Friar* (1681), an amusing story of popular prejudice. This merry attack on the Papists continued to be overrated for at least a century. It can now scarcely be admitted that it ranks as the best of Dryden's comedies.

Occupied with other work, and work that he performed better, Dryden did not return to the stage until he was an old man. Yet his latest plays are far from being his worst. There are passages in his tragedy of *Don Sebastian* which are at least as good as anything of the kind which he ever wrote. In *Amphitryon* he had to compete with rivals no less eminent than Plautus and Molière, yet his version of the ancient story is not immeasurably below theirs. *Cleomenes,* the tragedy of the last of the Spartans, bears the mark upon it of an old man's weakness and weariness, yet contains some noble passages. It is only in his last play, the tragi-comedy of *Love Triumphant,* that we are forced to admit that the natural force of the playwright is wholly abated. When he died, in 1700, Dryden had just been helping Vanbrugh to recast Beaumont and Fletcher's *Pilgrim.* The piece was acted for his benefit; but before it could be printed he was dead. Dryden was engaged, wholly or in part, on twenty-eight (or possibly on thirty) distinct dramatic pieces.

Nothing but need would have spurred Dryden on to the composition of plays—at all events, to that of comic plays. But he had immense literary skill and adroitness, and he concentrated these qualities on the production of comedies on the Spanish plan, where very coarse intrigue and boisterous repartee were combined with stuff almost too serious for such a setting. Reminiscences of Fletcher and Jonson remained with him all through his dramatic career; but though he imitated the French tragedians, he seems never to have recognised the might of French comedy. For Molière, who was nine years his senior, he felt no such veneration as he was ready to express for Corneille, and he never fell under the charm of the new French school. It is Dryden's earliest competitor, Sir George Etheredge, to whom the praise is due of having introduced modern comedy into England. This writer, to whose originality justice has only lately been done, was an idle and dissolute person of quality, whose indolence contrasted with Dryden's workmanlike assiduity. He was born in 1634, spent his youth in Paris, and seems to have remained there at the Restoration, since we hear nothing of him in London until his *Comical Revenge* was acted in 1664. This tragi-comedy was the first play the serious portion of which was written in rhymed heroics. This is interesting; but it is of still greater importance to note that the comic scenes were written by a man who had evidently seen and understood Molière's first great comedies. There was here no busy Spanish intrigue, no extravagant Jonsonian humours; but the mirror was held up to the real, everyday existence of the fop of the period. The success of this play was unprecedented; and four years later Etheredge produced a better comedy, *She Would if She Could;* in 1676 he followed this by a still greater success, *The Man of Mode*. Etheredge wrote no more. He entered the diplomatic service, and went to Constantinople and to Stockholm. In 1685 he was sent as ambassador to Ratisbon, where he stayed till the Revolution turned him out of office. He died about 1691.

The style of Etheredge, in comparison with the rough quality of his predecessors, may be described as having the smoothness of silk, the fragility of porcelain. He produces his effects by brief and graphic touches; light washes of colour leave the picture bright and sunny. Congreve, Goldsmith, and Sheridan are his natural descendants, and his happiest scenes are not unworthy to be classed with the best of theirs. He did not attempt to condemn or correct the manners of his time, and his plays are marred by a deplorable laxity of tone, which soon drove them from the boards when public decency became reawakened. But no one has reflected so accurately as he the motley groups of fashionable London in the reign of Charles II., and some of his figures will always live in literature. His *Man of Mode*, in particular, with all its faults, is one of the leading English comedies. Its Dorimant is the very type of the impudent lady-killer; and its Sir Fopling Flutter the conscientious beau in his meridian:

"*Young Bellair.* See! Sir Fopling is dancing!

Sir Fopling. Prithee, Dorimant, why hast thou not a glass hung up here? A room is the dullest thing without one.

Young Bellair. Here is company to entertain you.

Sir Fopling. But I mean in case of being alone. In a glass a man may entertain himself,——

Dorimant. The shadow of himself indeed.

Sir Fopling. Correct the errors of his motion and his dress.

Medley. I find, Sir Fopling, in your solitude you remember the saying of the wise man, and study yourself!

Sir Fopling. 'Tis the best diversion in our retirement. Dorimant, thou art a pretty fellow, and wearest thy clothes well, but I never saw thee have a handsome cravat. Were they made up like mine, they'd give another air to thy face. Prithee let me send my man to dress thee one day. By heavens, an Englishman cannot tie a ribband.

Dorimant. They are somewhat clumsy-fisted.

Sir Fopling. I have brought over the prettiest fellow that ever spread a toilet; he served me some time under Merille, the greatest *génie* in the world for a *valet de chambre.*

Dorimant. What, he who formerly belonged to the Duke of Candolle?

Sir Fopling. The very same—and got him his immortal reputation.

Dorimant. You've a very fine brandenburgh on, Sir Fopling!

Sir Fopling. It serves to wrap me up after the fatigue of a ball.

Medley. I see you often in it, with your periwig tied up.

Sir Fopling. We should not always be in a set dress; 'tis more *en cavalier* to appear now and then in a *deshabille.*"

In Etheredge the curtain rises for the first time on the frivolous world of the eighteenth century—Strephon bending on one knee to Cloe, who fans the pink blush on her painted cheek, while Momus peeps, with a grimace, through the curtains behind them.

The next dramatist who came to the front was Thomas Shadwell (1640-1692), the son of a royalist gentleman of Norfolk. He, like Etheredge, returned to London from wandering on the Continent, but he had not profited as Etheredge had by his French experience. To his first play, the comedy of *The Sullen Lovers* (1668), Shadwell prefixed an essay in which he announced his passionate admiration for Ben Jonson, and his intention to imitate him, "who never wrote comedy without seven or eight considerable Humours." He himself introduces a morose melancholy man, an airy young gentleman, a foolish positive knight, a conceited poet, a familiar loving coxcomb, and an impudent cowardly hector, while the other personages are merely used to connect the "humours" of these six odd creatures. The play, notwithstanding, has merit, and enjoyed considerable success. Shadwell was encouraged to cultivate the stage, and he produced seventeen long plays, the latest, *The Volunteers*, being posthumous. Shadwell would have passed without much notice among the second-rate writers of his time, if he had not drawn down upon himself the anger of Dryden. As it is, he lives for all time as a black and ridiculous object seen in relief against the blaze of Dryden's wit. The great poet and he had been friends, and had satirised Elkanah Settle in concert in 1674. But Shadwell had become a Whig, and had taunted Dryden in a very coarse and malignant lampoon. Dryden retorted, in 1682, with his immortal satire *MacFlecknoe*. A poetaster named Flecknoe, who had been the butt of all the wits, had lately died, and Dryden represents him as pondering upon his deathbed over the question who should succeed him on the throne of Nonsense. Flecknoe cries at last :

"Shadwell alone my perfect image bears,
Mature in dulness from his tender years;
Shadwell alone of all my sons is he
Who stands confirmed in full stupidity;
The rest to some faint meaning make pretence,
But Shadwell never deviates into sense."

Dull was hardly the true epithet for Shadwell; but he was certainly heavy. He laboured at composition, and produced *The Virtuoso*, it is said, after a prolonged agony of five years. Shadwell's ambition to be ever representing "some natural humour not represented before," his coarseness, his total want of distinction and elevation, have justly deprived him of a high place in literature. But, in spite of Dryden, he was no fool; his comedy of *Epsom Wells* (1676), to name no other, may still be read with pleasure and amusement; and his works are particularly full of matter attractive to antiquaries. There is a rough comicality about such a scene as the following, between a county justice in London and an impudent town lady of fortune:

"*Clodpate.* Come, madam, plain dealing is a jewel. But can you prefer an idle scandalous London life before a pretty innocent housewifely life in the country, to look to your family, and visit your neighbours.

Lucia. To see my ducks and geese fed, and cram my own chickens.

Clodpate. Ay.

Lucia. To have my closet stink like a pothecary's shop with drugs and medicines, to administer to my sick neighbours; and spoil the next quack's practice with the recipe book that belongs to the family.

Clodpate. Very well.

Lucia. And then to have one approved green salve, and dress sore legs with it; and all this to deserve the name of as good a neighbourly body as ever came into Sussex.

Clodpate. Very good.

Lucia. Never to hear a fiddle, but such as sounds worse than the tongs and key, or a gridiron; never to read better poetry than John Hopkins', or Robert Wisdom's vile metre; nor hear better singing than a company of peasants praising God with doleful untuneable hoarse voices, that are only fit to be heard under the gallows.

Clodpate. However you make bold with the country, be not profane. Is not this better than anything in that stinking town?

Lucia. Stinking town! I had rather be Countess of Puddledock, than Queen of Sussex.

Clodpate. Oh foh—but ah, the excellent fresh air upon the Downs.

Lucia. So there's fresh air in a wilderness, if one could be content with bears and wolves for her companions. But, Sir, in short, I am resolved to live at London, and at, or very near the court too.

Clodpate. S'death, the Court? I shall not only be cuckolded, but lose all

my true country interest ; Madam, I beg your pardon, I shall take my leave ;
I am not cut out for a Londoner, or a courtier ; fare you well, good Madam,
though I like your person pretty well, I like not your conditions, I'd not marry
a London cherubin."

At the Revolution, when Dryden would not take the oaths,
and was therefore deprived of the office of poet laureate, he had
the signal annoyance of seeing the laurel placed on the brows of
Shadwell. Over this appointment it has been customary to make
merry, but it would be difficult to point to a Whig of greater
ability to whom it might more fitly have been accorded. Shadwell was extremely stout, and gloried in his supposed resemblance
in this matter to Ben Jonson. Dryden would not let the poor
man enjoy even this small satisfaction. He assured Shadwell
that though he was big in body, that did not prevent him from
carrying but a kilderkin of wit in his tun of flesh.

Sir Charles Sedley (1639-1722) is introduced into Dryden's
Essay of Dramatic Poesy, under the title of Lisideius, as one
who encouraged and defended the imitation of French comedy
in English. Sedley was one of those men who attract the notice
of their contemporaries by their personal magnetism, and who
leave reputations greater than their writings justify. He was
famous for his urbanity, his "prevailing gentle art," and not less
for his wit and judgment. He is remembered in history by his
excuse for his conduct at the Revolution, "that as James II. had
made his daughter a countess, he could do no less than endeavour
to make the king's daughter a queen." He long outlived all these
scandals and turmoils, and died the latest of the early wits of the
Restoration. His first comedy, the *Mulberry Garden* (1668), has
something of the lightness of Etheredge, and his *Bellamira* (1687)
reflects the savage wit of Wycherley. But Sedley, who produced
six plays in all, is no original figure in our drama.

We have now closed the list of the first generation of those
who accompanied Dryden in the foundation of a classic or regular
drama in England. The second, or central group in the drama
of the Restoration contains three leading names, namely, those of

Wycherley, Otway, and Lee, with the subsidiary figures of Mrs. Behn, Settle, Crown, and Buckingham. These are the dramatists who made their appearance, almost simultaneously, early in the seventies, and we proceed to consider them, as before, in chronological order. Mrs. Ayfara or Aphra Behn (1640-1689), whose maiden name was Johnson, took to the trade of literature at the age of thirty, after a youth of singular adventure spent in Guyana and in Holland. She made her debut with a tragi-comedy, *The Forc'd Marriage*, in 1671, and wrote or revised no less than nineteen plays in all. This was only a small portion of her literary work, and in professional energy she exceeded all her male contemporaries, except Dryden. She wrote too fast to write well, and she pandered to the bad taste and bad morals of her age by seasoning her dialogue with such indelicacies as that age required. "The stage how loosely doth Astræa tread," as Pope remarked, Astræa being the pseudonym she adopted. Mrs. Behn's most successful play was her comedy, or brace of comedies, *The Rover* (1677, 1681). Her efforts in serious drama were wretched, but, her lamentable coarseness set aside, she had a certain gift in broad comedy. She is notable as the first Englishwoman who lived by her pen. During her lifetime Mrs. Behn had no female competitor, but during the last decade of the century many women came forward as playwrights. Of these the most successful was Mary Pix, to whom ten published plays are attributed.

Long after the death of William Wycherley (1640-1715) it was reported that he had been wont to say that each of his plays was written much earlier than it was acted or printed. In fact he represented himself as writing his *Love in a Wood* in 1659, although it was not produced until 1672, and his other pieces in the same relative order. If this could be substantiated, it would give to Wycherley, as the inventor of modern English comedy, the precedence over Etheredge. It is difficult to avoid the suspicion that this fact supplies us with the origin of the rumour. Either Wycherley in his old age, or his admirers after his death, were anxious to claim for him an honour which the dates of his pieces belied. He imitates the *Misanthrope* of Molière, moreover, in one of these plays, which, if the fabulous date could be accepted, must have been written before that comedy appeared. Wycherley, who was a Catholic, was brought up in the west of France, and imbibed a sort of military French manner, a swaggering gaiety, that he preserved through life. He was sent to Oxford for a little while, and then passed into the court of Charles II., and into a regiment of guards. While he was sunning himself in the royal favour, he brought out at the King's Theatre two indifferent comedies, and then two others, the *Country Wife* (1675) and the *Plain Dealer* (1677), which have held their place as standard pieces in the drama which is read but not acted. The fine gentlemen and ladies who meet to pull their neighbours to pieces in Olivia's drawing-room in the latter play express their observations with amazing impudence and wit :

"*Novel.* As I was saying, madam, I have been treated to-day with all the ceremony and kindness imaginable at my lady Autumn's. But the nauseous old woman at the upper end of her table——

Olivia. Revives the old Grecian custom, of serving in a death's head with their banquets.

Novel. Ha ! ha ! fine, just, i' faith, nay, and new. 'Tis like eating with the ghost in the *Libertine :* she would frighten a man from her dinner with her hollow invitation, and spoil one's stomach——

Olivia. To meat or women. I detest her hollow cherry cheeks : she looks like an old coach new painted ; affecting an unseemly smugness, whilst she is ready to drop in pieces.

Eliza. You hate detraction, I see, cousin.
[*Apart to Olivia.*

Novel. But the silly old fury, whilst she affects to look like a woman of this age, talks——

Olivia. Like one of the last ; and as passionately as an old courtier who has outlived his office.

Novel. Yes, madam ; but pray let me give you her character. Then she never counts her age by the years, but——

Olivia. By the masques she has lived to see.

Novel. Nay then, madam, then I see you think a little harmless railing too great a pleasure for any but yourself ; and therefore I've done.

Olivia. Nay, faith, you shall tell me who you had there at dinner.

Novel. If you would hear me, madam.

Olivia. Most patiently ; speak, sir.

Novel. Then, we had her daughter——

Olivia. Ay, her daughter ; the very disgrace to good clothes, which she always wears but to heighten her deformity, not mend it : for she is still most splendidly, gallantly ugly, and looks like an ill piece of daubery in a rich frame.

Novel. So ! But have you done with her, madam ? and can you spare her to me a little now ?

Olivia. Ay, ay, sir.

Novel. Then, she is like——

Olivia.—She is, you'd say, like a city bride ; the greater fortune, but not the greater beauty, for her dress.

Novel. Well : yet have you done, madam ? Then she——

Olivia. Then she bestows as unfortunately on her face all the graces in fashion, as the languishing eye, the hanging or pouting lip. But as the fool is never more provoking than when he aims at wit, the ill-favoured of our sex are never more nauseous than when they would be beauties, adding to their natural deformity the artificial ugliness of affectation.

Eliza. So, cousin, I find one may have a collection of all one's acquaintance's pictures as well at your house as at Mr. Lely's. Only the difference is, there we find 'em much handsomer than they are, and like ; here much uglier, and like : and you are the first of the profession of picture-drawing I ever knew without flattery."

The indelicacy of Wycherley's two brilliant comedies has excluded them from the boards for nearly two centuries, except in an extremely modified form. But they contain very vigorous writing, much genuine wit, and sound satire of the fools and rogues whom the author saw about him. Evelyn promised him immortality in a well-turned triplet :

> " As long as men are false, and women vain,
> While gold continues to be virtue's bane,
> In pointed satire Wycherley shall reign."

His style is virile and his wit pungent, but Wycherley has a rough hand in comparison with the velvet touch of Congreve, and a painful cynicism in comparison with Farquhar's good-nature. His gallant adventures, his quarrel with the king, his correspondence in old age with the boyish Pope, and his selfish marriage eleven days before his death, have supplied plenty of material for the collectors of anecdotes. The Squire, Jerry Blackacre, in the *Plain Dealer*, is the ancestor of Tony Lumpkin, and Mr. Pinchwife, in his other comedy, has had many diverting successors. Wycherley was not a poet; as Lord Lansdowne indulgently put it, "he is no master of numbers, but a diamond is not less a diamond for not being polished." The modern reader will be apt to think him clouded as well as rough.

The depressing effect of the intellectual atmosphere of the Restoration is obvious in the cases of poets whose natural gifts were of a serious and sentimental class. There can be no doubt that both Otway and Lee were intended by nature to be tragic writers of a much higher order than contemporary habits of mind and taste permitted them to become. As it is, we owe to one of these men the two best serious plays written in English between the time of Ford and that of Shelley. Thomas Otway (1651-1685) was the only son of a Sussex clergyman. He was educated, in the company of men above his own station in life, at Christ Church College, Oxford. In the long vacation of 1671 he came up to town, and made a very unsuccessful appearance for a single night on the boards of the Duke's Theatre, in one of Mrs. Behn's pieces. He went back to college, but could not forget the stage, and in 1675 contrived to get an heroic tragedy of *Alcibiades* accepted by Betterton. To act in this play, Mrs. Barry, who had made a unsuccessful debut in 1674, was re-engaged, and the part of Druxilla in it opened the celebrated series of her successes as a tragic actress. *Alcibiades* was a poor play, but it was followed in 1676 by *Don Carlos*, one of the best of the declamatory tragedies in rhyme. In this, as in all Otway's plays, the Bettertons and their troupe took the principal parts. The poet fell violently and hopelessly in love with Mrs. Barry, and in 1677 he enlisted in order to sever his acquaintance with her; but after a campaign in Flanders, he returned to the Duke's Theatre, and to his infatuation. This first portion of Otway's career closes with the performance of certain comedies which are below the level even of the age.

In 1680, the decline and death of his rival, the Earl of Rochester, having, it is believed, given a fresh zest to his life, Otway began to write with great vigour. His *Orphan* marks the return to blank verse, and it is, moreover, the first domestic tragedy—that is to say, the first in which royal personages do not hold the leading parts—which had been produced since the days of Elizabeth. It contains the extremely painful story of the result of the love of the same pure and beautiful girl by two brothers, and its legitimately tragical interest is carried so far into the province of anguish that it has ceased to be presentable to a public audience. In this play we find what had seemed a lost quality in English drama since the Commonwealth—tenderness. Over the character of Monimia, the Orphan, probably more tears have been shed than over that of any other stage heroine. Passing by the experiment in which Otway endeavoured to transfer the passion of Romeo and of Juliet to a Latin scene, we come to his second great play, the best tragedy of the Restoration, the *Venice Preserved* of 1682. Here, with a touch still more masculine and direct than in *The Orphan*, Otway employs genuine human passion in the room of the bombastic declamation of the tragedies of his contemporaries, and achieves a success which has never been questioned. The tragedy woven around the sullen wrath of Jaffier and the reasonable sweetness of Belvidera ranks only just below the masterpieces of Shakespeare :

"*Jaffier.* Is this the Roman virtue? this the blood
That boasts its purity with Cato's daughter?
Would she have e'er betrayed her Brutus?
    Belvidera.   No !
For Brutus trusted her : wer't thou so kind,
What would not Belvidera suffer for thee :
    Jaffier. I shall undo myself, and tell thee all.
    Belvidera. Look not upon me, as I am a woman,
But as a bone, thy wife, thy friend ; who long
Has had admission to thy heart, and there
Studied the virtues of thy gallant nature ;
Thy constancy, thy courage, and thy truth,
Have been my daily lesson : I have learnt them,

> Am bold as thou, can suffer or despise
> The worst of fates for thee; and with thee share them.
> *Jaffier.* Oh Thou divinest Power! look down and hear
> My prayers! instruct me to reward this virtue!
> Yet think a little, e'er thou tempt me further:
> Think I've a tale to tell, will shake thy nature,
> Melt all this boasted constancy thou talk'st of
> Into vile tears and despicable sorrows:
> Then if thou should'st betray me!
> *Belvidera.* Shall I swear?
> *Jaffier.* No: do not swear; I would not violate
> Thy tender nature with so rude a bond:
> But as thou hop'st to see me live my days,
> And love thee long, lock this within thy breast;
> I've bound myself by all the strictest sacraments,
> Divine and human——
> *Belvidera.*   Speak!
> *Jaffier.*   To kill thy father—
> *Belvidera.* My father!
> *Jaffier.*   Nay, the throats of the whole Senate
> Shall bleed, my Belvidera: he amongst us
> That spares his father, brother, or his friend,
> So damned: how rich and beauteous will the face
> Of ruin look, when these wide streets run blood;
> I and the glorious partners of my fortune
> Shouting, and striding o'er the prostrate dead;
> Still to new waste; whilst thou, far off in safety
> Smiling, shalt see the wonders of our daring;
> And when night comes, with praise and love receive me."

The author of this play, in fact, seems a sort of prose Shakespeare, a Shakespeare with the romantic charm precipitated. The verse, indeed, is strong and good, but the spirit of the drama is domestic and mundane; there are no flights into the spiritual heavens. The imagination of the dramatist is lucid, rapid, and direct; there is the utmost clearness of statement and reflection; but, although this masterpiece of genius is not obscured, it is certainly toned down by a universal tinge or haze of the commonplace. Otway wrote one more play—a comedy. But he was broken in spirits and resolve, and fell, at the accession of James II., into complete destitution. He spent his last days in a spunging-house on

Tower Hill ; venturing out at the point of starvation, he was given some money by a gentleman of whom he begged, and then died at a baker's shop, being too weak to swallow the first mouthful of bread. He was just thirty-four years of age.

The career of Nathaniel Lee (1655-1692) was as wretched as that of Otway, which in more than one respect it closely resembled. Lee also was a clergyman's son; he was educated at Trinity College, Cambridge, but he came up to London to try to be an actor before he was twenty. Like Otway, he utterly failed on the boards. His first play, *Nero*, came out at the King's Theatre, for which Lee's early dramas were all written, at the same time as Otway's first venture at the Duke's. The impassioned, or rather stilted, fervour of his verse gave satisfaction, and in the next year, 1676, the young poet, not yet of age, produced a *Gloriana* and a *Sophonisba*, both in heroics. These three Roman plays, all in rhyme, possess a certain bombastic merit as poetry, but can only have been saved from failure upon the boards by the admirable acting of Hart and Mohun. Blank verse having once more passed into fashion, Lee came forward with a *Rival Queens* (1677) and a *Mithridates* (1678), which showed a considerable advance in dramatic skill, and that peculiar intensity and excitement in expression which was the charm and the danger of Lee's curious style. The former of these tragedies enjoyed a prodigious success. Here is a fragment of a speech in *Mithridates* :

> " Away, then ! part, for ever part, Semandra !
> Let me alone sustain those ravenous fates
> Which, like two famished tigers, are gone out,
> And leave us in the wind. Death, come upon me !
> Night, and the bloodiest deed of darkness, end me !
> But oh ! for thee, for thee,—if thou must die,
> I beg of heaven this last, this only favour,
> To give thy life a painless dissolution.
> Oh ! may those ravished beauties fall to earth
> Gently, as withered roses leave their stalks !
> May Death be mild to thee, as Love was cruel ! "

This remains within the limits laid down for dramatic poetry.

But Lee's brain was not long under his control, and his fine frenzies overpowered him. In spite of his undoubted ability and his increasing experience, he did not contrive to write one really good play, except, perhaps, *Lucius Junius Brutus* (1681). After producing eleven tragedies, two of them in conjunction with Dryden, Lee, whose intellect had several times threatened to give way, became a raving maniac, and had to be shut up in Bedlam in 1684. After several years' confinement he seemed to be cured, and being set free, produced in 1689 his only attempt at a comedy—*The Princess of Cleve*. His last tragedy, *The Massacre of Paris* (1690), outdid all its predecessors in shrill rant of blank and rhymed verse, and Lee presently went mad once more. He escaped from his keepers out into the streets one night, and perished in some miserable way, at the age of thirty-seven. Lee came very near being a master of sounding blank verse. He was solitary among the dramatists of the age in taking Milton for his model, and even when he is most turgid and most unnatural, there is often a Miltonic swell in his verse which preserves it from complete absurdity. He has often been compared to the early Elizabethans, and he may be called a vulgar Marlowe. His heroic language is often spoiled in its most gorgeous passages by an incidental meanness of expression, as in the famous line where Brutus says to his son—

"I'll *tug* with Teraminta for thy heart."

Lee marks a certain crisis in tragedy. He shrieked so loud that succeeding playwrights gave up the idea of out-screaming so bombastic a writer, and the tendency of tragedy in future was to become sentimental and reflective.

John Crown (1640?-1705?), a writer of mean talent but extraordinary persistence, was a rival of Lee in tragedy and of Dryden in comedy. He was the son of an independent minister in Nova Scotia, and was called, from his prim appearance, "Starch Johnny Crown." We know very little of his life, although, from the appearance of his *Juliana* in 1671 to that of his *Caligula* in

1698, he was constantly before the public as a professional writer. Of the eighteen plays which he printed, the best, beyond question, is the comedy of *Sir Courtly Nice* (1685), adapted at the command of Charles II. from two old Spanish plays. Crown was slow in composition, and, to the author's extreme disappointment, the comedy was only finished in time to be the first new piece acted before James II. In this play, which enjoyed a prolonged success, the humours of the town were amusingly satirised; but Crown as a rule is a dull writer, artificially stirred now and then for a moment into a coarse kind of stage animation. A still more grotesque figure is the Doeg of the second *Absalom and Achitophel*, Elkanah Settle (1648-1724). This absurd creature lives embalmed in the anger of Dryden, but he had a moment of not illegitimate success. He was a young Oxford man, who started as a Whig with a measure of public encouragement. After a somewhat promising tragedy of *Cambyses* in 1670 (printed 1672), he startled Dryden and his compeers out of their decorum by producing in 1673 a tremendous heroic play of *The Empress of Morocco*, on a story which somewhat recalls that of *Hamlet*. This play was smoothly rhymed, and not constructed without ingenuity. In rant it outraved what Lee himself was to achieve. For a moment Settle was at the top of the fashion, but he had neither talent nor principle, and he soon sank into contempt. Of Settle's fifteen plays, the latest was brought out in 1710. Dryden said of him:

"The height of his ambition is, we know,
But to be master of a puppet-show."

Settle fell lower even than this, for he became a mechanic at a puppet-show, and his last public appearances were made within a green dragon of his own invention. The first edition of *The Empress of Morocco* is much sought after on account of the *sculptures* or engravings of scenes in the theatre; it was the earliest illustrated drama in the English language.

The brief success of the heroic plays was proved and summed up by the popularity of the satire upon them, the brilliant

Rehearsal, brought out anonymously in 1672. The principal author of this delightful composite parody was George Villiers, second Duke of Buckingham (1627-1688), of whom it was said that "he inherited from his father the greatest title, and from his mother the greatest estate of any subject in England." Dryden, whom he attacked, painted a severe but just and witty portrait of him in his Zimri, who

> "in the course of one revolving moon,
> Was chymist, fiddler, statesman, and buffoon."

The laugh was turned, but not until it had echoed through London at Dryden's expense. *The Rehearsal* was begun in ridicule of Sir Robert Howard; a certain number of touches were added from a foolish playwright of the name of Stapylton; but it was the series of Dryden's heroic plays in rhyme which were mainly attacked. The hero, Bayes, was a study of Davenant in the first place, but when that poet died the Duke easily altered the portrait to resemble Dryden. It would seem that he worked at the satire, adding ludicrous touches, for eight or ten years. Two critical friends meet Bayes, and ask him to explain the plot of his last play; he declines to satisfy them, but recommends them to come and see his new play in rehearsal. They do this, and find it to consist of an olio of all the most ridiculous points which had ornamented all the heroic plays of the last ten years. In the following extract, from the third act, Sir William Davenant is mainly burlesqued :

"ENTER *Parthenope*.

Smith. Sure, Mr. Bayes, we have lost some jest here, that they laugh at us so.

Bayes. Why did you not observe? He first resolves to go out of town, and then, as he is pulling on his boots, falls in love. Ha, ha, ha.

Smith. O, I did not observe: that, indeed, is a very good jest.

Bayes. Here, now, you shall see a combat betwixt love and honour. An ancient author has made a whole play on't ; but I have despatch'd it all in this scene.

Volscius. How has my passion made me Cupid's scoff !
This hasty boot is on, the other off,

> And sullen lies, with amorous design
> To quit loud fame, and make that Beauty mine.
> My legs, the emblem of my various thought,
> Show to what sad distraction I am brought.
> Sometimes, with stubborn honour, like this boot.
> My mind is guarded, and resolv'd to do't:
> Sometimes, again, that very mind, by love
> Disarmèd, like this other leg does prove.
>
> *Johnson.* What pains Mr. Bayes takes to act this speech himself!
> *Smith.* Ay, the fool, I see, is mightily transported with it.
>
> > *Volscius.* Shall I to honour or to love give way?
> > Go on, cries honour; tender love says, nay:
> > Honour, aloud, commands, Pluck both boots on;
> > But softer love does whisper, Put on none.
> > What shall I do? what conduct shall I find
> > To lead me through this twilight of my mind?
> > For as bright day with black approach of night
> > Contending, makes a doubtful puzzling light;
> > So does my honour and my love together
> > Puzzle me so, I can resolve for neither.
> > [*Exit with one boot on, and the other off.*"

The parody is sometimes so close that the reader hardly knows it from the original; and to read the sparkling pages of *The Rehearsal* is to study the most searching criticism extant on the rhymed tragedies. It is indeed not a little unfortunate for those plays that the parody was a work of real genius, and has practically outlived all the pieces which it was intended to satirise. It was the parent of the various burlesque dramas of the eighteenth century, including the wittiest of them all, *The Critic.* It is, of course, entirely incorrect to say that *The Rehearsal* destroyed or checked the vogue of the heroic plays. Its success was really a symptom of their excessive popularity. Ten years later the Duke put his name to the adaptation of a play of Beaumont and Fletcher, but took no further part in dramatic writing. It should be added that Butler is believed to have had a hand in composing *The Rehearsal.*

The interval of twenty years between the appearance of the large group of dramatists just described and that of the Orange school was marked by the arrival of only one new talent of importance—that of Thomas Southerne (1659-1746), a native of Dublin. He took his first play, the tragedy of *The Loyal Brother* (1682), to Dryden, and asked him to write a prologue to it. For this service the fee had hitherto been five guineas, but Dryden seized this opportunity of beginning to charge ten guineas: "Not out of disrespect to you, young man, but the players have had my goods too cheap." Southerne was a very smart man of business, and he was the first dramatist in England who contrived to make a fortune out of play-writing. He became justly distinguished as a tragic poet. He rebelled against the rant and fustian of the heroic playwrights, and modelled himself upon Otway, whose tenderness is successfully reflected in his scenes, though with some exaggeration. His blank verse runs easily, and owes something to a respectful study of Shakespeare; but we recognise that it is in the process of fossilising into the dead dramatic verse of the succeeding century. Southerne's best plays were produced when the Orange dramatists had completely come to the front, and he answers as a tragic writer to Congreve as a comic one, but with less talent. *The Fatal Marriage* (1694) and *Oroonoko* (1696) are sentimental tragedies, based on the method of Otway's *Orphan*, and cunningly devised to wring tears from distressed and sympathetic audiences. The last scene of *Oroonoko*, a long-drawn agony in melting verses, is a typical specimen of Southerne's powers, which were indubitable, though not of the highest order. Here is a fragment of it:

> "*Oroonoko.* It is not always granted to the great
> To be most happy : if the angry Powers
> Repent their favours, let them take them back :
> The hopes of Empire, which they gave my youth,
> By making me a Prince, I here resign.
> Let 'em quench in me all those glorious fires,
> Which kindled at their beams : that lust of fame,
> That fervour of ambition, restless still,
> And burning with the sacred thirst of sway,
> Which they inspir'd, to qualify my fate,
> And make me fit to govern under them.

> Let them extinguish, I submit myself
> To their high pleasure, and devoted bow
> Yet lower, to continue still a slave ;
> Hopeless of liberty : and if I could
> Live after it, would give up honour too,
> To satisfy their vengeance, to avert
> This only curse, the curse of losing thee.
>   *Imoinda.* If heaven could be appeas'd, these cruel men
> Are not to be entreated, or believ'd :
> O ! think on that, and be no more deceiv'd.
>   *Oroonoko.* What can we do?
>   *Imoinda.* Can I do anything?
>   *Oroonoko.* But we were born to suffer.
>   *Imoinda.* Suffer both,
> Both die, and so prevent them,
>   *Oroonoko.* By thy death !
> O ! let me hunt my travel'd thoughts again ;
> Range the wide waste of desolate despair ;
> Start any hope. Alas ! I lose myself,
> 'Tis pathless, dark, and barren all to me.
> Thou art my only guide, my light of life
> And thou are leaving me ; send out thy beams
> Upon the wing ; let them fly all around,
> Discover every way : Is there a dawn,
> A glimmering of comfort ? the great God,
> That rises on the world, must shine on us."

His comedies are very weak, and stained beyond the custom of the age with cynical indecency. Southerne lived on until long after all the other seventeenth-century dramatists were dead, and survived to receive the homage of Gray.

The name of the Orange dramatists has been given to the group of playwrights who made their appearance at the very close of the century, and who were divided by more than thirty years from the Restoration. Considerable confusion has been caused by neglecting dates in this matter, by not observing that a chasm lies between the contemporaries of Dryden's youth and those friends of his old age. The Orange dramatists of most importance are Congreve, Cibber, Vanbrugh, and Farquhar—all in the main purely comic writers. It may generally be said, that although no improvement of manners or morals was at first observable in these dramatists, their language was much more polished than that of their predecessors. They exchanged mere coarseness of boisterous intrigue for wit and the development of an intricate plot, and they responded to the appeal which had been made by Etheredge, but apparently made in vain, a quarter of a century earlier, for lighter and more brilliant dialogue.

William Congreve (1670-1729) is the most shining figure in literature which the drama of the last half of the seventeenth century presents to us. Voltaire said of him that "he raised the glory of comedy to a greater height than any English writer before or since," and within certain obvious limitations this is still true. There have been comedies better than his, and those of the class in which alone he attempted to excel—that is to say, the non-poetic comedy which holds the mirror up to contemporary manners. But there is no body of comedy left to us by any English writer so brilliantly supported, so sparkling, so distinguished. Some injustice has been done to the memory of Congreve by a passage in *The English Humourists*, where Thackeray, in one of his most imaginative moods, dismisses the great Mr. Congreve as one whose laughing skull lies silent among the ashes and broken wine-jars underneath some desert heap of lava, not to be stirred by modern readers. The student should read this page to admire its author but not to understand its subject. There is no sense in which Congreve can be said to be extinct, or to fear extinction, so long as wit and lucidity and exquisite literary art are appreciated. The main quality of Congreve, and that by which he still holds a place among the great writers of the century, is his wit; in this he is unapproached in modern drama, even in France, where Molière, who excels him in the other branches of dramatic ability, is for once inferior to Congreve. The wittiest of the playwrights of the modern world may not be seriously compared to a skull at Pompeii. While so much must be said in his defence, it has to be added that he neglected other necessary parts of the dramatic scheme in the cultivation of wit. His action is left to wait, cap in hand, on the leisure of his dialogue, and when the former is resumed, the poet has often the air of forgetting whither he intended to proceed with it. His plots are difficult to recollect, and not always very natural in their development. His characters are clearly defined, and often very original; but his conception of them is cynical to a degree which excuses the disfavour into which his comedies have fallen. Congreve is less coarse than Wycherley and Shadwell, but he is scarcely less immoral; and to many readers the varnish of refinement is no extenuation of the ethical result. The drama of Congreve combines, to a singular degree, the very finest literary art with the extreme of what is debased in morals and superficial in sentiment.

Congreve occupied the stage for only six years in his early youth. He was but three-and-twenty when his *Old Bachelor* (1693) appeared, and it had been written two years earlier. It showed a precocious knowledge of the ways of the world, such as was perfectly astounding; the author had written it, by intuition, among the yew-trees of a secluded Berkshire garden. Both Dryden and Southerne touched it up, recommended it, and secured for it a favourable hearing. It was exceedingly successful, and Congreve became the "splendid Phœbus Apollo of the Mall." In the *Old Bachelor* we may trace careful study of the style of Wycherley. There is a certain violence, a certain tendency to pantomime, that are wanting in Congreve's second and much more careful comedy, *The Double Dealer* (1694), which, perhaps for this very reason, found less favour at first with the public. The critics and poets, on the other hand, overwhelmed Congreve with caresses on this occasion, and Dryden, in the best known of his dedicatory addresses, said:

" Heav'n, that but once was prodigal before,
To Shakespeare gave as much, she could not give *him* more."

Such extravagance of praise was excusable, for Congreve was now treading in the very steps of Molière, and that with a fancy and a delicacy of style which were all his own. He proceeded further still in *Love for Love* (1695), his masterpiece, and the most brilliant pure comedy of manners in the English language. The principal personages of this play are drawn with a masterly hand,—Valentine, the scholar-lover, the fine gentleman who half disdains himself for being a man of sense and wit; Tattle, the type of fatuous vanity; Foresight, the pantaloon astrologer; the frivolous and joyous sisters, Frail and Foresight; Ben, in whom we see the earliest example of the stage-sailor; the dignified and passionate Angelica—these crowd the most vivid and the most attractive scene that the multifarious stage of the Restoration has to offer to us. The ravings of Valentine in his pretended madness give excellent examples of Congreve's daring and coruscating wit:

"*Foresight.* This frenzy is very low now, Mr. Scandal.
Scandal. I believe it is a spring-tide.
Foresight. Very likely, truly; you understand these matters;—Mr. Scandal, I shall be very glad to confer with you about these things which he has uttered—his sayings are very mysterious and hieroglyphical.
Valentine. Oh, why would Angelica be absent from my eyes so long?
Jeremy. She's here, sir.
Mrs. Foresight. Now, sister!
Mrs. Frail. O Lord, what must I say?
Scandal. Humour him, madam, by all means.
Valentine. Where is she? oh, I see her;—she comes like riches, health, and liberty at once, to a despairing, starving, and abandoned wretch. Oh welcome, welcome!
Mrs. Frail. How d'ye, sir? Can I serve you?
Valentine. Hark ye—I have a secret to tell you—Endymion and the moon shall meet us upon Mount Latmos, and we'll be married in the dead of night—but say not a word. Hymen shall put his torch into a dark lantern, that it may be secret; and Juno shall give her peacock poppy-water, that he may fold his ogling tail, and Argus's hundred eyes be shut, ha! Nobody shall know but Jeremy.
Mrs. Frail. No, no, we'll keep it secret, it shall be done presently.
Valentine. The sooner the better.—Jeremy, come hither—closer—that none may overhear us—Jeremy, I can tell you news; Angelica is turned nun, and I am turning friar, and yet we'll marry one another in spite of the pope. Get me a cowl and beads, that I may play my part; for she'll meet me two hours hence in black and white, and a long veil to cover the project, and we won't see one another's faces."

In 1697 Congreve produced his solitary tragedy, *The Mourning Bride*. He was too good a poet and too experienced a master of stage effect, to write a play that should not please, and this piece enjoyed an extraordinary success. It has not lacked admirers in recent times, and its first line, " Music has charms to soothe the savage breast," is on every one's lips. In comparison with the other English tragedies of the Orange period it has a merit analagous to that of Crébillon's tragedies in France, and suggests that if Congreve had persisted in tragedy he might have enjoyed the success which attended that writer, who was but two years his junior. But *The Mourning Bride* wants the highest poetic merit; it is monotonous and mechanical; its blank verse, though learned, lacks variety, and its revival in the future is hardly to be expected. Congreve closed his brief and splendid career as a dramatist with his comedy of *The Way of the World* (1700). This play is scarcely inferior, if inferior at all, to *Love for Love*, but it failed to please the public. It has even more wit and less action than Congreve's other comedies, and the town thought its satire ill-natured. Moreover, it immediately followed the brilliant attack made by Jeremy Collier (1650-1726), the non-juror, upon the immorality and profaneness of the English stage. This attack was vehemently resented by Congreve and others, but Dryden bowed to it, and there is no doubt that it met with an instant response from the conscience of the English middle-classes.

Among those favourites of the town whom Collier had the intrepidity to attack, the one who was most open to censure was Captain John Vanbrugh (1672-1726). This very clever and original writer had, indeed, erred by an extraordinary licence, and owes to his coarseness the obscurity into which his plays have fallen. He had, however, great merits; an architect by profession, he carries the art of building into his drama, and constructs his plays with an admirable solidity. Where Congreve is volatile and sparkling, Vanbrugh does not attempt to compete with him, but reserves himself for carefully studied effects, for passages where every touch is marked by the precision and weight of the author's style.

He is perhaps more like Molière than any other English dramatist; he is like him in the abundance of his stage-knowledge, and in the skill he shows in rapid and entertaining changes of situation. At the same time he is English to a fault, saturated with the brutality of the fox-hunting squire of the period. This very coarseness of fibre, added to Vanbrugh's great sincerity as a writer, gives his best scenes a wonderful air of reality. The persons of Congreve's stage are too uniformly brilliant for credence; we are conscious that he is writing, to a great extent, with an ideal before him, and aided by his imagination. Vanbrugh, who is no poet, but a somewhat heavy observer, dowered with occasional flashes of adroitness, presents us only with what he has seen, and often transcribes that with an astonishing fidelity. Vanbrugh made his debut in 1697 with two comedies, *The Relapse* and *The Provoked Wife*, and became famous and prosperous at once. In those days poetical promise was promptly rewarded, and for the merit of his comedies Vanbrugh was made Clarencieux King-at-Arms. He produced ten comedies in all, his later works showing signs of indolence and carelessness. An exception, however, must be made in favour of *The Confederacy* (1705), a most diverting piece, and perhaps, on the whole, its author's best. It is not easy to find a specimen of Vanbrugh's rattling and bustling scene which is sufficiently condensed for quotation. But here is a page from the last-mentioned play in which the two rogues fall out. Brass is pretending to be Dick's *valet-de-chambre*, but when he finds that Dick has struck a vein of special good luck, he feels himself obliged to come to fresh terms:

"*Brass.* Look you, sir, some folks we mistrust, because we don't know 'em: others we mistrust because we do know 'em. And for one of these reasons I desire there may be a bargain before-hand; if not [*raising his voice*] look ye, Dick Amlet——

Dick. Soft, my dear friend and companion. The dog will ruin me [*aside*]. Say, what is't will content thee?

Brass. O ho.

Dick. But how can'st thou be such a barbarian?

Brass. I learnt it at Algier.

Dick. Come, make thy Turkish demand then.

Brass. You know you gave me a bank-bill this morning to receive for you.

Dick. I did so, of fifty pounds, 'tis thine. So, now thou art satisfied ; all's fixed.

Brass. It is not indeed. There's a diamond necklace you robbed your mother of e'en now.

Dick. Ah, you Jew.

Brass. No words.

Dick. My dear Brass !

Brass. I insist.

Dick. My old friend.

Brass. Dick Amlet [*raising his voice*] I insist.

Dick. Ah the cormorant—Well, 'tis thine. But thou'lt never thrive with't.

Brass. When I find it begins to do me mischief, I'll give it you again. But I must have a wedding-suit.

Dick. Well.

Brass. Some good lace.

Dick. Thou shalt.

Brass. A stock of linen.

Dick. Enough.

Brass. Not yet—a silver sword.

Dick. Well thou shalt have that too. Now thou hast everything.

Brass. Gad forgive me, I forgot a ring of remembrance. I would not forget all these favours for the world ; a sparkling diamond will be always playing in my eye, and put me in mind of 'em.

Dick. This unconscionable rogue [*aside*] ! Well, I'll bespeak one for thee.

Brass. Brilliant.

Dick. It shall. But if the thing don't succeed after all ?

Brass. I'm a man of honour, and restore. And so the treaty being finished I strike my flag of defiance, and fall into my respects again.

[*Taking off his hat."*

Vanbrugh left the stage to become the royal architect, and was knighted towards the end of his life. He showed great bitterness in his controversy with Collier, but he could not refute the Puritan's plain statement that all the men of figure in Vanbrugh's plays were professed libertines, and that, nevertheless, he allowed them all to pass off without censure or disappointment. That this charge is true is the fatal objection to all Restoration comedy.

Colley Cibber (1671-1757) is commonly identified with the

dramatic life of the eighteenth century, but his best comedies belong to the seventeenth, and he preceded Vanbrugh in his appeal to the public. He was the son of a Danish sculptor, employed during the youth of the dramatist in beautifying the rooms of Chatsworth. In 1689 Colley Cibber became an actor, and, under the patronage of Congreve, rose early to distinction. His first comedy, *Love's Last Shift* (1696), was imitated or continued by Vanbrugh, in his own first play, *The Relapse*, and this increased Cibber's reputation. In 1697 he published *Woman's Wit*, a piece of inferior merit; but achieved again a popular success with *Love makes a Man*, a very sprightly comedy or long farce, in 1698. *The Careless Husband* (1705) aimed at a higher sort of writing, and ranks as the best of Cibber's works. At least thirty dramatic pieces are attributed to him. Cibber's plays are lighter than thistledown, and mark the rupture between dramatic writing and literature. But they are praiseworthy for their comparative innocence, and for the absence of such cynicism as Collier denounced.

The last great dramatist of the Restoration, the man in whom the flame that Marlowe had kindled was extinguished, George Farquhar (1678-1707), is very far from being the least sympathetic of the series. He was gallant, handsome, and unfortunate, he died in his prime of youth, and all that is recorded of him does credit to his manly gaiety and his courage under disappointment. He was the son of an Irish clergyman of good family, was educated at Trinity College, and went very early on to the Dublin stage. By forgetting to change his sword for a foil, he nearly killed a brother-actor while playing in Dryden's *Indian Emperor*, and the shock gave him a distaste to acting. He entered the army, distinguished himself, and rose to the rank of captain. About 1697 he came to London, and in 1698 brought out his first comedy, *Love and a Bottle*, sprightly with the humours of military life, in which Farquhar excels. Much better in every way, however, was *The Constant Couple* (1700), where the character of a certain Sir Harry Wildair, "an airy gentleman affecting humourous gaity and freedom in his behaviour," gave so much pleasure to the audience at the Theatre-Royal, that in 1701 the poet brought out a second part, to which he gave this hero's name. Farquhar was a smart and handsome fellow, whose empire over the hearts of the ladies was unbounded. One girl, wholly without a dowry, fell in love with him, and secured his hand under the representation that she was wealthy. Farquhar had quitted the army in order to marry her, and was reduced to poverty by her subterfuge, but he had the sweetness of temper never to reproach her. His last and best comedies were *The Recruiting Officer* (1706), and *The Beaux' Stratagem* (1707), the latter composed upon his deathbed. It was understood that the hero of the *Recruiting Officer*, Captain Plume, was Farquhar's portrait of himself:

"*Plume.* A dog, to abuse two such pretty fellows as you ! Look'ee, gentlemen, I love a pretty fellow : I come among you as an officer to list soldiers, not as a kidnapper, to steal slaves.

Pearmain. Mind that, Tummas.

Plume. I desire no man to go with me but as I went myself : I went a volunteer, as you, or you, may do ; for a little time carried a musket, and now I command a company.

Appletree. Mind that, Costar. A sweet gentleman !

Plume. 'Tis true, gentlemen, I might take an advantage of you ; the queen's money was in your pockets, my serjeant was ready to take his oath you were listed ; but I scorn to do a base thing ; you are both of you at your liberty.

Pearmain. Thank you, noble captain. Ecod, I can't find in my heart to leave him, he talks so finely.

Appletree. Ay, Costar, would he always hold in this mind.

Plume. Come, my lads, one thing more I'll tell you : you're both young tight fellows, and the army is the place to make you men for ever : every man has his lot, and you have yours. What think you now of a purse full of French gold out of a monsieur's pocket, after you have dashed out his brains with the butt of your firelock, eh ?

Pearmain. Wauns ! I'll have it, captain—give me a shilling, I'll follow you to the end of the world."

Farquhar possessed a lovable, easy character, full of hasty faults and generous virtues, and he curiously resembled what Fielding was in the ensuing generation.

In a discourse upon comedy which he printed in his miscellany called *Love and Business* (1702), Farquhar hit off a happy definition. "Comedy," he said, "is no more at present than a well-framed tale handsomely told as an agreeable vehicle for counsel or reproof." He meant, no doubt, that of his own drama the motto should be *castigat ridendo mores*, but his natural cheerfulness would break out. His flighty beaux and swaggering cavalry officers too frequently forget to counsel or reprove, but Farquhar succeeds in being always wholesome, even when he cannot persuade himself to be decent. His scenes breathe of the open air, while Congreve's have a heated atmosphere of musk. There is something hopeful and encouraging in finding the crowded and unsatisfactory drama of the Restoration closing, not in inanity and corruption, but in this gay world of Farquhar's, this market-place of life, bright with scarlet tunics and white aprons, loud with drum and bugle, and ringing with peals of laughter and impudent snatches of ballad-music. It is Sergeant Kite, one of Farquhar's heroes, to whom we owe the song of "Over the hills and far away." Farquhar was the last writer who dared to bring the animal riot of the senses face to face with a decent audience, and the best we can say of his morals is that it is more wholesome to laugh with Ariosto in the sunshine than to snigger with Aretine in the shadow. Better than either is to walk in the light of Molière or of Goldsmith.

CHAPTER III

PROSE AFTER THE RESTORATION

THE prose of the last forty years of the seventeenth century is not one of the most attractive sections of literature to the common reader. It is eminently pedestrian in character, unimaginative, level, neutral. It has neither the disordered beauties of the age that preceded it, nor the limpid graces of that which followed it. It is tentative and transitional; and its experiments, like its changes, are in the direction of common sense and conventionality. There is, moreover, a peculiarity about its history which has, doubtless, served to consign it to comparative neglect. Neither of its two greatest names, neither Dryden nor Temple, though both of them men of genius and influence, and one of them a master of English, has left a single volume in prose which is in household use; while its best-known book, if we set aside *The Pilgrim's Progress*, is Locke's *Human Understanding*—a work particularly unengaging in its mere style and delivery. English prose between 1660 and 1700 is exhibited in a great variety of examples, many of them—nay, the majority of them—unimportant to any but an antiquarian reader, and displaying a talent so uniform, that it is not very easy to define the orders of merit. We meet nothing here like the genius with which Hooker or Swift, Bacon or Fielding, towers above all minor contemporaries.

The period, however, is misjudged if we regard its merits as negative merely. It had extraordinary positive qualities. It is notable as the age in which educated Englishmen in the mass began to use their native tongue more or less as we use it now. The interminable sentences which had preserved the awkward forms of the sixteenth century, the affected and excessive use of imagery, the abuse of parenthesis; all these vices of style, which are as marked in Milton as in Ascham and Elyot, fell off from English prose-writing about 1660, and left it a little cold and bare, but terse, sensible, and modern. The change is as distinct as the change from romantic to classical in verse, but the causes of the former are not so easy to explain as those of the latter. Contact with France did much—the neglect of Latin perhaps did more—to strip our prose of needless ornament, while simplifying and defining our grammar. The reform here indicated set in somewhat rapidly, and then, a generation of writers having accepted it to a certain extent, it proceeded very little further for another half century. This arrested modernity will be presently exemplified in the very typical case of Dryden.

It would be to force criticism to pretend to be able to trace a distinct line between the old and new prose, such as may be pretty accurately drawn between the old and new poetry. The two schools blend into one another, and the writers are not, at first, even consistent in their practice. It is convenient to take the date of the Restoration as that at which the prose of our period opens. That date excludes the last of the old prose school, such as Hobbes, Fuller, Harrington, Henry More, and Sir Matthew Hale, who lived beyond it, but who are properly found to be mainly in sympathy with the past. It excludes writers whose production goes on long after that date, such as Izaak Walton and Sir T. Browne, and even writers whose production mainly belongs to a later period, such as Dr. Walter Charleton, the scholastic essayist (1619-1707), when their style shows no influence of a later taste. Arbitrary as this division appears to be, it is found to inconvenience us but little. There is only one great author whom it is difficult to relegate decisively to the one class or to the other, namely, Clarendon; and his historical position has seemed to demand that he should be considered as a product of the earlier age.

The first man in England to write commonly in the new kind of prose was John Wilkins, Bishop of Chester (1614-1672). His great activity after the Restoration, when he became one of the founders of the Royal Society, the main protector of the Nonconformists in the Church of England, and a zealous bishop, may be taken to show that his mind naturally welcomed the new order of things. But his two most interesting books were published long before that date—the *That the Moon may be a World*, in 1638, and *That the Earth may be a Planet*, in 1640. In the first of these curious astronomical treatises he undertakes to prove, in fourteen propositions, that the moon is a habitable world:

"'Twas the fancy of some of the Jews, and more especially of Rabbi Simeon, that the moon was nothing else but a contracted sun, and that both those planets at their first creation, were equal both in light and quantity. For, because God did then call them both great lights, therefore they inferred that they must be both equal in bigness. But a while after (as the tradition goes) the ambitious moon put up her complaint to God against the sun, showing that it was not fit there should be two such great lights in the heavens; a monarchy would best become the place of order and harmony. Upon this, God commanded her to contract herself into a narrower compass; but she being much discontented hereat, replies, What! because I have spoken that which is reason and equity, must I therefore be diminished? This sentence could not choose but much trouble her; and for this reason was she in great distress and grief for a long space. But that her sorrow might be some way pacified, God bid her be of good cheer, because her privileges and charter would be greater than the sun's. He should appear in the day time only, she both in the day and night. But her melancholy being not satisfied with this, she replied again, that that alas was no benefit; for in the day time, she should be either not seen, or not noted. Wherefore God, to comfort her up, promised, that His people the Israelites should celebrate all their feasts and holy days by a computation of her months; but this being not able to content her, she has looked very melancholy ever since; however, she hath still reserved much light of her own."

Wilkins was in strong sympathy with Galileo, who was at that time still alive. In 1641 he published his *Mercury*, a proposition for communicating at great distances by a sort of telegraphy.

Wilkins recurs again and again in his writings to the dream of mechanical flying, by which he is best remembered. In his *Mercury* he says:

"Amongst all possible conveyances through the air, imagination itself cannot conceive any one more useful than the invention of a flying chariot, which I have mentioned elsewhere. By this means a man may have as free a passage as a bird, which is not hindered either by the highest walls or the deepest rivers and trenches or the most watchful sentinels."

The mathematical, scientific, and theological writings of Wilkins were very numerous. But the three little books mentioned above are all that the reader is now likely to meet with. The subjects on which the bishop wrote do not attract us, and his knowledge is trebly superannuated. But his style deserves great praise. His sentences are short, pointed, and exact. He has little or nothing of the redundant languor of his contemporaries; and justice has never yet been done to him as a pioneer in English prose. The praise given to Tillotson belongs properly to Wilkins, for Tillotson lived a generation later, and learned to write English from his study of the Bishop of Chester, whom he enthusiastically admired. The curious reader will find much in the style of Wilkins to remind him of that of Bishop Berkeley.

John Pearson (1612-1686), who succeeded Wilkins as Bishop of Chester, wrote an *Exposition of the Creed* (1659), which has always been considered a sound English classic. It was a series of sermons which he had preached while he was incumbent of the London parish of St. Clement's, Eastcheap. Pearson's style is clear and uniform, rising on rare occasions to positive felicity. The paucity of Pearson's work contrasts with the excessive fecundity of his most distinguished Nonconformist contemporary, Richard Baxter (1615-1691), who published no less than one hundred and sixty-eight treatises, some of them under facetious and even unseemly titles. Jeffries told him that he had written "books enough to load a cart, every one as full of sedition (I might say treason) as an egg is full of meat." Baxter's most popular books were the *Saints' Everlasting Rest* (1650), and *A Call to the Unconverted*

(1657). The autobiography of this pious, useful, irrepressible heresiarch, which appeared posthumously in 1696, is pleasant reading. A third theologian of this period is Ralph Cudworth (1617-1688), the anti-Hobbist and Christian metaphysician. He published, in 1678, a candid and erudite refutation of what then passed for atheism, entitled *The True Intellectual System of the Universe*. The reception of this book, which was too liberal in tone for the fanatics of the age, disgusted him with publicity, and his other works until long after his death remained unpublished. Cudworth's *Intellectual System* is a huge folio of 999 pages. It is called "Part I.," but he completed no more of it. He was successively Master of Clare, and of Christ's College, Cambridge, during nearly half a century.

Towards the close of his life the poet Abraham Cowley came forward with a tract on the *Advancement of Learning* (1661), a *Discourse concerning Oliver Cromwell* (1661), and a collection of eleven *Essays*. This small cluster of prose-writings places him very high among the authors of his time, and while the verse of Cowley has declined in critical estimation, his prose has steadily risen. His style, which owes something to a very intelligent study of Bacon, has a grace and a sweet enthusiasm unusual in writing of the Restoration period. Dr. Johnson excellently remarked that "no author ever kept his verse and his prose at a greater distance from each other." The latter is never tortured, never fantastical, never rhetorical. It is full of delicate reverie, commonly expressed in an unaffected yearning after solitude in nature, and it displays the writer not merely as a very clever, but as a very winning and estimable man. In the eleventh of his Montaigne-like essays, "Of Myself," he gives us some precious reminiscences of the earliest motives of his intellectual life:

"I believe I can tell the particular little chance that filled my head first with such chimes of verse, as have never since left ringing there: for I remember when I began to read, and to take some pleasure in it, there was wont to lie in my mother's parlour (I know not by what accident, for she herself never in her life read any book but of devotion), but there was wont to lie Spenser's works. This I happened to fall upon, and was infinitely delighted with the stories of the knights, and giants, and monsters, and brave houses, which I found everywhere there (though my understanding had little to do with all this), and by degrees with the tinkling of the rhyme and dance of the numbers, so that I think I had read him all over before I was twelve years old, and was thus made a poet as irremediably as a child is made an eunuch. With these affections of mind, and my heart wholly set upon letters, I went to the University; but was soon torn from thence by that violent public storm which would suffer nothing to stand where it did, but rooted up every plant, even from the princely cedars to me the hyssop. Yet I had as good fortune as could have befallen me in such a tempest; for I was cast by it into the family of one of the best persons, and into the court of one of the best princesses in the world."

An interesting little prose work, the preface to his *Poems* of 1656, reveals Cowley to us before he had learned to write in this modern manner. Sprat tells us that his letters were excellent, and that "they always expressed the native tenderness and innocent gaiety of his mind," with "a native clearness and shortness, a domestical plainness, and a peculiar kind of familiarity." It is greatly to be deplored that these letters, of which a large collection once existed, were never printed, and now seem to be hopelessly lost. Cowley's *Essays* should be read by every student of English prose.

John Evelyn (1620-1706) was a man of fortune and a traveller, proficient in all the arts and graceful sciences, and energetic in the pursuit of knowledge. He was early drawn into authorship by his love of letters, and by his desire to communicate his views to the learned world. He wrote with great care, and Waller commended his prose in terms which he usually confined to the best verse of the new school. Of Evelyn's treatises the first which is now remembered is the fifteenth in order of publication, namely, *Sylva*, a most valuable report on the condition of timber in the English dominions, 1664. In the same year he published a discourse on *Architecture*, eventually dedicated to Sir Christopher Wren, and a work on *Gardening*, dedicated to Cowley. He had published a handbook to Engraving, called *Sculptura*, in 1662, and to these he added one on Painting, in 1668. His *Navigation and Commerce* followed in 1674, and his *Terra*, on the arts of cultivation, in 1675. He published twenty-seven volumes in all; the last of them, *Acetaria* (1699), was scarcely worthy of so serious a savant, the subject of it being salads. The vast work on horticulture, entitled *Elysium Britannicum*, on which he worked for forty years, was still unfinished when he died, and has never been published. The literary fame of this dignified and indefatigable man really rests, however, upon a work which he would very probably have disdained to publish, his *Diary* or running autobiography, kept through fifty-six years—1641-1697. This remained in manuscript in the Evelyn library at Wotton until 1818, when it was edited in three large volumes.

The encyclopædic knowledge of Evelyn, and his prodigality in the arrangement and communication of it, justly secured for him the admiration and even the astonishment of the seventeenth and eighteenth centuries. His learning was really extensive, and his taste was so finely trained as to be second to that of no man in England. Whether he discoursed of the decay of oak-trees or of the Arundel marbles, of the making of cider or of the heresy of the Jesuits, there were very few of his listeners, and often none at all, who could assail his erudition. It is difficult to say why, with all this panoply of attainment, he never touched the highest things. The best we can say of him is that he reaches a high average among the prose-writers of his time, and that he is actuated by their most happy instincts, lucidity, candour, the affectionate study of nature. As an example of Evelyn's more familiar style an extract from the *Philosophical Transactions* of the Royal Society may suffice. The winter of 1683 had been excessively severe, and Evelyn was requested to record his observations of the damage done to his own trees at Sayes Court by the cold. He writes on the 14th April 1684:

"As for exotics, I fear my cork trees will hardly recover, but the spring is yet so very backward, even in this warm and dry spot of mine, that I cannot pronounce anything positively, especially of such whose bark is very thick and rugged, such as is the cork, enzina, and divers of the resinous trees. The constantinopolitan, or horse-chestnut, is twigged with buds, and ready to explain its leaf. My cedars. I think, are lost; the ilex and scarlet oak, not so; the arbutus, doubtful; and so are bays, but some will escape, and most of them repullulate and spring afresh, if cut down near the earth at the latter end of the month. The Scotch fir spruce, and white Spanish, which last used to suffer in the tender buds by the spring frost, have received no damage this winter; I cannot say the same of the pine which bears the greater cone, but other Norways and pinasters are fresh; laurel is only discoloured, and some of the woody branches mortified, which being cut to the quick will soon put forth again, it being a succulent plant. Amongst our shrubs, rosemary is entirely lost; and, to my great sorrow, because I had not only beautiful hedges of it, but sufficient to afford me flowers for the making a very considerable quantity of the Queen of Hungary's celebrated water: so universal, I fear, is the destruction of this excellent plant, not only over England, but our neighbour countries more southward, that we must raise our next hopes from the seed. Halimus, or sea purselain, of which I had a pretty hedge, is also perished; and so another of French furzes; the cypress are all of them scorched, and some to death, especially such as were kept shorn in pyramids, but amongst great numbers there will divers escape, after they are well chastised, that is, with a tough hazel or other wand to beat off their dead and dusty leaves, which growing much closer than other shrubs, hinder the air and dews from refreshing the interior parts. This discipline I use to all my tonsile shrubs with good success, as oft as winter parches them."

Yet simple and charming and easy as Evelyn is, we turn to Cowley for a superior simplicity, to Temple for a brighter charm, to Pepys for a more unstudied and congenial ease.

Another of the many Restoration writers of posthumous fame is Colonel Algernon Sydney (1622-1683), one of the most eminent martyrs of the Republic, a "Lucan, by his death approved." Sydney, who was the younger brother of Waller's Sacharissa, and Sir Philip Sydney's grand-nephew, was brought up to be a soldier in the king's army. While a youth, however, he was converted to the most rigid republicanism, became one of Charles I.'s judges, though he did not sign the warrant, and went so far as to protest against Oliver and even Richard Cromwell as tyrants. His life was spent in poverty and exile, until in 1677 he was unwillingly pardoned to please his dying father, the Earl of Leicester. His contumacy, however, was obstinate, and in 1683 the government was glad to include him in the Russell plot, and to murder him without a trace of evidence. His writings are *Discourses concerning Government*, written at Frascati in 1663, but first published in 1698, and letters and memoirs respectively printed in 1742 and 1751. In 1884 a treatise on *Love* was first published from Algernon Sydney's manuscript. Sydney is very diffuse; but the alteration which had come over prose may well be noted by comparing his republican discourses with the totally unreadable reams on the same subject which Harrington had produced in the preceding generation.

Several writers of very high distinction in the world of science must be passed over with almost unbecoming brevity by the historian of style. Among these none could be more distinguished than Robert Boyle (1627-1691), who enjoyed in the reign of Charles II. the same European reputation which Bacon had possessed in that of James I. He wrote on so many subjects, and some of them so trifling, that Swift made fun of him in his *Meditation on a Broomstick;* and his "New Philosophy," his trimming system of natural religion, has gone the way of all intellectual makeshifts. But in the field of physics he was on safer ground, and some of his chemical and pneumatical discoveries have proved of lasting value. His style is wearisome and without elevation. Cudworth, who urged him to translate his voluminous treatises into Latin and destroy the originals, may possibly have been ironical as well as pedantic in so advising. The amiable and indefatigable botanist, John Ray (1628-1705), and the zoologist, Francis Willughby (1635-1672), whose famous busts guard the doorway of Trinity College Library, were men of the same stamp. All these savants, the glory of the new-born Royal Society, wrote in Latin more readily than in English, thought little about their style, and expressed themselves most felicitously when they were describing gardens, the graceful fashion of the day demanding frequent homage to the flower-plots which were then so abundantly laid out. It may be safely said, for instance, that the only page now known to the general reader in all the long-winded writings of Robert Boyle, is that famous passage in which he speaks of seeing tulips and roses bloom together :

"It is so uncommon a thing to see tulips last till roses come to be blown, that the seeing them in this garden grow together, as it deserves my notice, so methinks it should suggest to me some reflection or other on it. And perhaps it may not be an improper one to compare the difference betwixt these two kinds of flowers to the disparity which I have often observed betwixt the fates of those young ladies that are only very handsome, and those that have a less degree of beauty, recompensed by the accession of wit, discretion, and virtue : for tulips, whilst they are fresh, do indeed, by the lustre and vividness of their colours, more delight the eye than roses ; but then they do not alone quickly fade, but, as soon as they have lost that freshness and gaudiness that solely endeared them, they degenerate into things not only undesirable, but distasteful, whereas roses, besides the moderate beauty they disclose to the eye —which is sufficient to please, though not to charm it—do not only keep their colour longer than tulips, but, when that decays, retain a perfumed odour, and divers useful qualities and virtues that survive the spring, and recommend them all the year. Thus those unadvised young ladies, that, because nature has given them beauty enough, despise all other qualities, and even that regular diet which is ordinarily requisite to make beauty itself lasting, not only are wont to decay betimes, but, as soon as they have lost that youthful freshness that alone endeared them, quickly pass from being objects of wonder and love, to be so of pity, if not of scorn ; whereas those that were as solicitous to enrich their minds as to adorn their faces, may not only with a mediocrity of beauty be very desirable whilst that lasts, but, notwithstanding the recess of that and youth, may, by the fragrancy of their reputation, and those virtues and ornaments of the mind that time does but improve, be always sufficiently endeared to those that have merit enough to discern and value such excellences, and whose esteem and friendship is alone worth their being concerned for. In a word, they prove the happiest as well as they are the wisest ladies, that, whilst they possess the desirable qualities that youth is wont to give, neglect not the acquisition of those that age cannot take away."

After passing so many talents in review, we reach at last a genius. John Bunyan, the tinker or brazier of Elstow (1628-1688), is in several respects the most original figure of his time. Merely as a writer, it is extraordinary that, with his utter indifference to literature, he should have contrived to write so remarkably well. As we all know, after a passionate and self-accusing childhood, he became a soldier, and, as on the whole seems probable, in spite of Macaulay, on the royalist side. He returned to his village after a year's fighting, married, and, about the age of twenty-four, was convicted of sin and left the Church of England to communicate with the Baptists. His own account of his conversion, with the evidence it gives of an inborn conscientiousness of almost morbid delicacy, and with the picturesqueness that comes of entire sincerity of expression, is one of the most valuable documents of the period. Even the ringing of bells grew to seem an ungodly pursuit to this strenuous young Puritan:

"Now you must know, that before this I had taken much delight in ringing, but my conscience beginning to be tender, I thought such practice was but vain, and therefore forced myself to leave it; yet my mind hankered, wherefore I would go to the steeple-house and look on, though I durst not ring; but I thought this did not become religion neither; yet I forced myself, and would look on still. But quickly after, I began to think, 'How, if one of the bells should fall?' Then I chose to stand under a main beam that lay overthwart the steeple, from side to side, thinking here I might stand sure; but then I thought again, should the bell fall with a swing, it might first hit the wall, and then rebounding upon me, might kill me for all this beam. This made me stand in the steeple-door; and now, thought I, I am sure enough; for if a bell should then fall, I can slip out behind these thick walls, and so be preserved notwithstanding. So after this I would yet go to see them ring, but would not go any further than the steeple-door; but then it came into my head, 'How, if the steeple itself should fall?' And this thought—it may, for ought I know, when I stood and looked on—did continually so shake my mind, that I durst not stand at the steeple-door any longer, but was forced to flee, for fear the steeple should fall upon my head.

Another thing was my dancing; I was a full year before I could quite leave that. But all this while, when I thought I kept that or this commandment, or did by word or deed anything I thought was good, I had great peace in my conscience; and would think with myself, God cannot choose but be now pleased with me; yea, to relate it in my own way, I thought no man in England could please God better than I. But, poor wretch as I was, I was all this while ignorant of Jesus Christ, and going about to establish my own righteousness; and had perished therein, had not God in His mercy shewed me more of my state by nature."

Bunyan very soon became the most popular preacher in England, and in the winter of 1660 had to be shut up in Bedford Gaol, his intrepidity or obstinacy giving the magistrates no alternative. His captivity, which lasted with intervals until 1672, was a very light and sometimes even nominal one, and gave him full opportunity for reading and composing. He had written several theological tracts before his imprisonment, and in gaol he wrote *Grace Abounding*, which appeared in 1666, and the first and infinitely better part of *Pilgrim's Progress;* he did not print the latter until 1678. In 1684 appeared the second part, and in 1682 *The Holy War*. The didactic story of *The Life and Death of Mr. Badman*, 1680, closes the list of Bunyan's principal works. The end of his career was prosperous and happy. He became by far the most influential of all the nonconformists, and the government, weary with opposing him, or else appreciating his innocent zeal, left him absolutely undisturbed to preach and evangelise. He lost his life by a forced ride through summer rain undertaken to reconcile a father with his son. It may help the conception of this sturdy and original figure to say that, in the age of universal shaved faces and periwigs, Bunyan wore his own red hair and a full moustache. His tall and bony figure and rough features belied the extreme mildness and affability of his manners.

When *The Pilgrim's Progress* was first read to Bunyan's evangelical friends, their opinions were much divided as to whether it ought to be printed or no. A theological work so romantic, so entertaining, nay so humorous as this, was original to the length of being shocking. But when, at last, after some fifteen years, the author plucked up confidence to print it, it was seized by the people with such love and lasting enthusiasm as no other religious book in the language, except the Bible, has awakened. It was, as we all know, an allegory of the journey of the soul of a converted sinner from death to immortality, from darkness to light. Its pictures were drawn partly from Bunyan's daily experience of English rustic life, partly from his recollections of a gorgeous and terrible vision. But the core of it all, the truth on which the allegory rested, was the experience that his own soul and the souls of his Christian friends had gone through. No doubt, the habit of fervent extempore preaching had given Bunyan freedom and rapidity of expression, and had taught him to make his sentences short, picturesque, and pointed. The style of *Pilgrim's Progress* is the very perfection of what the style of such a book should be—homely and yet distinguished, exquisitely simple, yet tuned to music at all its finer moments. The allegory is successful above all other allegories in literature. The abstractions which people it, even when they are mentioned only in one or two lines, never fail to live and stand out vividly as human beings.

Admirers of *The Holy War* have tried to assert as much for that longer and more laborious work. But popular taste has rightly determined that there should be a thousand readers of the first story to ten of the second. There are very fine passages in *The Holy War;* the opening, especially all the first siege of Mansoul, is superbly conceived and executed. But the personages which are introduced are too incongruous, the intrigues of Shaddei and the resistance of Diabolus are too incredible, the contest is too one-sided from the first, to interest us as we are interested in the human adventures of Christian. Bunyan seems powerless to close *The Holy War*, and before he is able to persuade himself to drop the threads, the whole skein of the allegory is hopelessly entangled. *Mr. Badman* is a third work of a totally different character. This is a *conte*, save for its theme, in the French style of the next generation. A realistic story of life misspent in a little country town is told in a dialogue between a Mr. Wiseman and a Mr. Attentive. The hero is a man who "went to school with the Devil, from his childhood to the end of his life." In some ways this neglected book appears to the present writer to possess greater importance than *The Holy War*. It is absolutely original as an attempt at realistic fiction, and it leads through Defoe on to Fielding and the great school of English novels. It is intensely interesting, and as a story, epoch-making. It opens the series of character-romances in England in the same way as *The Roman Bourgeois* of Furetière was doing, at the very same time, in France.

It is hardly necessary to return to *The Pilgrim's Progress* to say that that book does a great deal more than this; it is the matchless and inimitable crystallisation into imaginative art of the whole system of Puritan Protestantism.

The finest professed prose writer of the last forty years of the century is confessedly Sir William Temple (1628-1699), who has nevertheless left no single book which the general reader knows even by name. For all that has been written about him he is still "one of those men whom the world has agreed to praise highly without knowing much" of their claims to reputation. He was the most supple diplomatist of his time, he cultivated a famous orchard, he started the Phalaris controversy, and Swift was his amanuensis; perhaps most reading men have never cared to know much more about Sir William Temple than that. The writings of Temple are inconsiderable in extent, and essentially miscellaneous. When we have mentioned his essay on *The Advancement of Trade in Ireland* (1673), which is sadly wanting in the larger elements of political science, and his *Observations upon the United Provinces* (1672), which show that he could describe what he had seen tersely and picturesquely, his principal literary pretensions are concentrated within one volume, the second of his *Miscellanea* (1692), comprising four essays, "Of Ancient and Modern Learning," "Of the Gardens of Epicurus," "Of Heroic Virtue," and "Of Poetry." To form an estimate of the style of Temple it is needless to go further.

Two short passages will give an idea of his quality. This is how the essay "Of Poetry" opens:

> "The two common shrines to which most men offer up the application of their thoughts and their lives, are profit and pleasure; and by their devotions to either of these, they are vulgarly distinguished into two sects, and called either busy or idle men.
>
> "Whether these terms differ in meaning, or only in sound, I know very well may be disputed, and with appearance enough, since the covetous man takes perhaps as much pleasure in his gains as the voluptuous does in his luxury, and would not pursue his business, unless he were pleased with it, nor would care for the increase of his fortunes, unless he thereby proposed that of

his pleasures too, in one kind or other ; so that pleasure may be said to be his end, whether he will allow to find it in his pursuit or no."

It closes thus :

"I know very well that many, who pretend to be wise by the forms of being grave, are apt to despise both poetry and music as toys and trifles too light for the use or entertainment of serious men : but whoever find themselves wholly insensible to these charms, would, I think, do well to keep their own counsel, for fear of reproaching their own temper, and bringing the goodness of their natures, if not of their understandings, into question : it may be thought at least an ill sign, if not an ill constitution, since some of the fathers went so far, as to esteem the love of music a sign of predestination, as a thing divine, and reserved for the felicities of heaven itself. While this world lasts, I doubt not but the pleasure and requests of these two entertainments will do so too ; and happy those that content themselves with these, or any other so easy and so innocent, and do not trouble the world, or other men, because they cannot be quiet themselves, though nobody hurts them !

"When all is done, human life is, at the greatest and the best, but like a froward child, that must be played with and humoured a little to keep·it quiet till it falls asleep, and then the care is over."

The essays "Of Gardens" and "Of Poetry" are pleasanter than their companions, because less patronising. It is the fault of Temple's discourses that they are too much like popular lectures by a very ignorant man who presumes upon his genteel appearance and elegant delivery. There are no productions which must be read more exclusively for their manner and not for their matter. Temple tells us nothing very agreeably, and then, while we are applauding, he dares to assert that there is no more for us to know. He was not a scholar, nor a critic, nor a geographer, nor even a botanist, and yet scholarship, criticism, geography, and botany are the themes of his four principal essays. His discourse on learning, by a man who could not construe a page of Greek, set Bentley lashing his sides, and woke a din in which the clear falsetto of Temple was entirely drowned.

Nevertheless, Temple is eminently readable. We forgive his parental condescension, his patent ignorance, in the delight and surprise of his modern tone. When he babbles of his oranges and his figs, and says he must leave the flowers to the ladies; when he talks of a friend of his who has a gamekeeper who is a Rosicrucian, and a laundress who is firm in the philosophy of Epicurus; when he laughs and sparkles over his runic nonsense and his Phalaris forgeries like some fine blue-stocking in a Congreve comedy—we feel that English prose has come to the birth, and that here is a man at last who can write about Nothing like a gentleman. If we must not say that Addison was taught by Temple, at least it was Temple who taught the public to be ready for Addison. All this absence of peculiarity, these modern felicities, these lucid sentences without parenthesis, form a shadow of the eighteenth century thrown before, and make the contemporary Clarendons and Charletons seem like old-fashioned squires who have come into the pump-room in boots. We must laugh, with Macaulay, at the empty pretension of what Temple imparts; but when the laugh is over, we should examine his obsolete essays with care to discover what charm of novelty it was, what intuition of the future, what study of the French, that gave his style so accomplished an individuality; and we shall probably come to the conclusion that the tradition of the last century did not err very wildly in considering him the first prose-writer of his age.

Of four theologians who now meet us in our brief survey, but little can be said within such limits as ours. George Fox (1624-1690), the great Quaker, put a strange impressiveness into his *Journal* (1694). The folios of John Flavel (1627-1691) have readers still among the poor. Isaac Barrow (1630-1677) and John Tillotson (1630-1694) were divines of far higher pretensions. The latter practically began his literary career in 1664 with a trimming sermon in the preface of which he called the venerable Hobbes "a dabbler," yet Tillotson was not an illiberal man. In 1689 his treatise *Against the Eternity of Hell Torments* went near to break up his primrose path to the primacy. He grew more genial ever as he rose, and his prelatical apron fluttered so high that at last its fringes covered, so his enemies declared, the Socinians themselves. He was so popular when he died that his widow received 2500 guineas, the largest sum then ever yet paid for an English book, for the copyright of his manuscript sermons. Dryden thought highly of Tillotson's style, and a compliment of his has given the archbishop far too exalted a place in our literary handbooks. Barrow, whose works Tillotson collected and edited, has more vigour and solidity, and was an admirably logical controversialist. Tillotson has the ease of a fluent improvisator; Barrow's sentences fall on the ear with the weight of hammered thought and carefully modulated expression. Few will turn to the works of either of them again for literary pleasure or improvement, and it would only be affectation to treat them as living forces in literature. Barrow (of whom his first biographer quaintly says, that "though he obtained the Mastership of Trinity College, yet that had no bad influence on his morals") was the most eccentric of divines. He used to preach for so long a time, that the organ had to strike up to blow him down, and his dress was so uncouth that once when he appeared in a strange pulpit, half the congregation fled the church. He was, however, esteemed to be easily the deepest and widest scholar of his time.

An admirable writer who had no thought of securing distinction in the world of letters was George Savile, Marquis of Halifax (1630-1695). He was a politician who had a difficult path to pursue across an ocean of battling factions, and who employed his literary skill, usually anonymously, to trim the boat as well as he might. He has been called the founder of the political pamphlet, but this title should perhaps, in justice, be claimed for Sir Roger L'Estrange (1616-1704). Halifax is as simple and as vernacular as Temple, and he has almost as much grace. His *Character of a Trimmer* (1685) is the best known of his essays, and is a piece of brilliant writing which can never become obsolete. Another and more fantastic example of the wit of Halifax is his "Anatomy of an Equivalent." From an admirably sprightly and judicious chain of little essays in *Advice to a Daughter* (1688) we find, under the head of "Diversions," this excellent example of the manner of the Marquis:

"Some ladies are bespoken for merry meetings, as Bessus was for duels. They are engaged in a circle of idleness, where they turn round for the whole year, without the interruption of a serious hour. They all know the players' names, and are intimately acquainted with all the booths in Bartholomew Fair. No soldier is more obedient to the sound of his captain's trumpet, than they are to that which summoneth them to a puppet play or a Monster. The spring that bringeth out flies, and fools, maketh them inhabitants in Hyde Park; in the winter they are an incumbrance to the play house, and the ballast of the drawing room. The streets all this while are so weary of these daily faces, that men's eyes are overlaid with them. The sight is glutted with fine things, as the stomach with sweet ones; and when a fair lady will give too much of herself to the world, she groweth luscious, and oppresses instead of pleasing. The Jolly Ladies do so continually seek diversion, that in a little time they grow into a jest, yet are unwilling to remember, that if they were seldomer seen, they would not be so often laughed at. Besides, they make themselves cheap, than which there cannot be an unkinder word bestowed upon your sex.

"To play sometimes, to entertain company, or to divert yourself, is not to be disallowed; but to do it so often as to be called a gamester, is to be avoided, next to the things that are most criminal. It hath consequences of several kinds not to be endured; it will engage you into a habit of idleness and ill hours, draw you into ill-mixed company, make you neglect your civilities abroad, and your business at home, and impose into your acquaintance such as will do you no credit."

A reprint of the political tracts of Halifax was issued in 1898, and will do much to give popularity to one who is at present little but a name to all except professional students of history.

In prose as in other branches of literature, however, the greatest name throughout the last forty years of the century is that of John Dryden. If he is never quite so exquisite as Temple, or even perhaps as Evelyn, at their best, it is that he had much more to say than they have, and less need to study his manner of saying it. He is the manliest, the most straightforward, the most authoritative prose-writer of the age, and, in his long career of more than thirty years, he surveyed and laid out the whole estate of modern English prose. He was not born with a style. His speech came to him slowly, laboriously, and it was by slow degrees that he threw off the cumbersome robes of his forerunners. Mr. Matthew Arnold has said that "the needful qualities for a fit prose are regularity, uniformity, precision, balance"; these are the very qualities which we meet with in Dryden, and to a like extent in no one before him, when once we have proceeded far enough in his career. It is easy, moreover, to trace his progress, for his prose-works are mainly prefixed or appended to his better known poetical or dramatic productions, and thus more exactly dated than the miscellanies of most of his contemporaries.

The earliest of Dryden's prose treatises is the preface to the *Rival-Ladies* (1664), a short and not very graceful defence of the use of dramatic rhyme, containing, among other things, a valuable statement of the component parts of the new school of English poetry. An essay on the Historical Poem introduces *Annus Mirabilis* (1667), but for many years the critical prefaces of Dryden were affixed only to his plays, of which but few are unprovided in this way. The best known of all his critical writings, the admirable *Essay on Dramatic Poetry*, was an exception, being separately published in 1667. It is a comparison between French classical drama and the old romantic drama of England, carried on in dialogue, under feigned names, by Sedley, Howard, Dorset, and the author. Dryden, whose talents had developed but slowly was now, at thirty-five, just attaining his intellectual manhood. We see him, in this famous piece, not yet entirely at his ease in the construction of his sentences and far less equipped in knowledge and taste than he afterwards became, but already a great force in prose. Such criticism was an absolute novelty in English. *The Essay* was attacked, and to the second, or 1668, edition of *The Indian Emperor* he contributed a "Defence," which is really a supplement to the independent work and should be read with it.

In 1671, in a preface longer than usual, that to *An Evening's Love*, he defended his own practice in comedy, and we feel his hand to be now much lighter, his touch in controversy surer and sharper. The "Essay on Heroic Plays," prefixed to the *Conquest of Granada* (1672), is one of the few writings of the period which we may sincerely wish had been longer; the poet fears he has been tedious in his apology for his strange experiment, but the fact is that he has been tantalisingly brief; at the close of the same play he gives us, however, a "Defence of the Epilogue," in which he is not a little tart in analysing the irregularities of the Elizabethans. Shakespeare himself does not come off unscathed:

> "Shakespeare, who many times has written better than any poet, in any language, is yet so far from writing wit always, or expressing that wit according to the dignity of the subject, that he writes in many places, below—the dullest writer of ours, or of any precedent age. Never did any author precipitate himself from such heights of thought to so low expressions, as he often does. He is the very Janus of poets; he wears, almost everywhere, two faces: and you have scarce began to admire the one, ere you despise the other. Neither is the luxuriance of Fletcher (which his friends have taxed in him), a less fault than the carelessness of Shakespeare. He does not well always, and, when he does, he is a true Englishman; he knows not when to give over. If he wakes in one scene he commonly slumbers in another: and if he pleases you in the first three acts, he is frequently so tired with his labour, that he goes heavily in the fourth, and sinks under his burden in the fifth.
>
> "For Ben Jonson, the most judicious of poets, he always writes properly; and as the character required: and I will not contest farther with my friends who call that wit. It being very certain, that even folly itself, well represented, is wit in a larger signification: and that there is fancy, as well as judgment in it; though not so much or noble: because all poetry being imitation, that of folly is a lower exercise of fancy, though perhaps as difficult as the other; for 'tis a kind of looking downward in the poet; and representing that part of mankind which is below him. In these low characters of vice and folly, lay the excellence of that inimitable writer; who, when at any time, he aimed at wit, in the stricter sense, that is sharpness of conceit, was forced either to borrow from the ancients, as, to my knowledge, he did very much from Plautus: or, when he trusted himself alone, often fell into meanness of expression."

The Assignation (1673) possesses a long dedication to Sedley, in the noblest spirit of panegyric, a little masterpiece in this obsolete species of writing. Not to linger too tediously over these short essays, we must pass by the "Apology for Poetic License" (*The State of Innocence*, 1674), the Montaigne-like dedication to *Aureng-Zebe* (1676), and even the celebrated preface to *All for Love* (1678), in which Dryden rebels against those classical punctilios which he had so long held himself bound to obey. We must note, however, that by this time Dryden is master of every artifice of a sound prose style.

Dryden reached the zenith of his powers as a prose-writer a little after his supremacy as a poet was finally acknowledged. He quitted the peaceful fields of literary criticism in two pamphlets of surpassing vigour, the "Epistle to the Whigs" (prefixed to *The Medal*), 1682, and *The Vindication of the Duke of Guise* (1683). Of these the first displays him as having followed Halifax into political pamphleteering, the latter is sheer polemic. In the first occurs that happy taunt, "If God has not blessed you with the talent of rhyming, make use of my poor stock, and welcome; let your verses run upon my feet; and for the utmost refuge of notorious blockheads, reduced to the last extremity of sense, turn my own lines upon me, and in utter despair of your own satire, make me satirise myself." The second contains the famous pious wish that Shadwell, being "only born for drinking, would let both poetry and prose alone." *The Vindication* was published separately, and was more like a book than any prose-writing which Dryden had hitherto produced. In 1684 he translated Louis Maimbourg's laborious *History of the League*, and added a postscript of fifty pages of his own. He wrote or translated other bulky works of a semi-historical, semi-controversial character, and produced, almost to the day of his death, miscellaneous writings far too numerous to be here named in detail. Last, but not least, among them comes the noble preface to the *Fables* of 1700.

It is almost entirely as a critic that Dryden has left his mark upon English prose. His brief prefaces introduced into our literature an element which it had lacked before, although Hobbes had made one or two efforts in the same direction. Dryden is the earliest of our literary critics, and where his knowledge is not defective he remains still one of the most sympathetic. He owed much to the French in the manner of his analysis, and something in particular to Corneille, who had prefixed prose "examens" to his plays. But Dryden is far more systematic than the French critics of his day, and his gradual revolt against Gallic taste gave him a strength and independence of judgment such as were not to be found in Paris. His delivery is very genial and agreeable, and he has nothing of the unpleasant dictatorial manner of Temple, besides having much more thorough mastery over his subject. He is apparently inconsistent, because of his candour, and because his intellect and taste were developing all through his long career. Sir Walter Scott, who praised Dryden so judiciously, was obliged to lament that "his studies were partial, temporary, and irregular," and this is true. Erudition, in the pedantic sense, was never his forte, but his praise is that he treated literature as a living plant, with a past and a future, not as a mere desert of dead logs. He released us on the one hand from ignorance and indifferentism, and on the other hand from an empirical philosophy of letters. He is not only a fine dramatist and a very lofty poet, but a great pioneer in prose criticism also.

At the close of the century there appeared a philosopher who was destined to revolutionise the entire world of thought, and to exercise on the ensuing age an absolutely tyrannous influence. With no other aid than what Descartes could give him, Locke thrust aside the whole burden of metaphysical speculation which had come down to him, and, with a pure enthusiasm for truth, examined anew every branch of speculation, every foundation of belief. He was not so much desirous to build up a new structure of theory, as to remove all obstacles from about his feet, and to settle his ideas upon a solid basis of fact. He swept away a whole world of the philosophy of the previous age; but the theory which he mainly attacked, or most prominently, was that of the existence of innate ideas, as in itself the source of all philosophic error. That he was not wholly consistent in his attack, or that he left work for his successors, and particularly for Hume to do, does not affect Locke's position as a sceptical and reconstructive genius of the very highest order in philosophy, and as a thinker whose name was paramount through Europe for light and liberty until the full development of German thought a century later.

Yet although John Locke (1632-1704) is so very imposing

a figure in the history of intelligence, he holds but little place in that of pure literature. He has been called "perhaps the greatest, but certainly the most characteristic, of English philosophers"; it might be added, the most innocent of style. He was a resident lecturer at Christ Church, Oxford, until in 1666 he formed the friendship of Shaftesbury (then Lord Ashley), with whom he presently began to reside. He studied medicine under Sydenham (1624-1689), and was introduced to public business by Shaftesbury as his secretary. When his patron fell, in 1673, the post of secretary to the Council of Trade was secured for Locke until 1675. His fortunes rose and subsided with those of Shaftesbury, and in 1684 he was ejected from his college. He resided long in Holland, writing his famous *Essay* at Utrecht. Early in 1690, at an advanced age, he came forward on the first important occasion as an author with this *Essay on the Human Understanding*. The *Two Treatises of Government* belong to the same year, and so does a strictly anonymous *Second Letter concerning Toleration*. The *First Letter*, which was in Latin, had appeared at Gouda, in Holland, in 1689. All the best known and most highly-valued of Locke's writings, therefore, were given to the public within a single twelvemonth, and that when he was nearly sixty years of age. His *Thoughts concerning Education* appeared in 1693, and his theological treatises a little later. His last years, until his health obliged him to retire from business, were largely absorbed by political and official occupations. He was at the Council of Trade again from 1696 to 1700, and fours years later passed peacefully away.

The great *Essay*, like so many other immortal works, produced but little effect at first. It annoyed more than it convinced, and four years passed before a second edition was called for. It gradually grew in esteem, until in the second quarter of the eighteenth century it secured for its author the highest encomiums possible, and in the person of Bishop Berkeley a very illustrious disciple. It is curious to note that of these two philosophers, so nearly allied in intellectual matters, the earlier was the least and the later perhaps the most exquisite writer of English in his generation. As is well known, Locke's central idea is that all our knowledge is derived from experience. His biographer, Professor Fowler, has defined Locke as "the first of modern writers to attempt at once an independent and a complete treatment of the phenomena of the human mind, of their mutual relations, of their causes and limits." Setting apart the extraordinary merits of Locke's contributions to thought, as a mere writer he may be said to exhibit the prose of the Restoration in its most humdrum form. We have now progressed too far into the new period to expect to find the faults of the old lumbering and stately prose, nor are these in the slightest degree the faults of Locke. But his style is prolix, dull, and without elevation; he expresses himself with perfect clearness indeed, but without variety or charm of any kind. He seems to have a contempt for all the arts of literature, and passes on from sentence to sentence, like a man talking aloud in his study, and intent only on making the matter in hand perfectly clear to himself. It is only proper to say that this is not the universal view, and that it is usual to speak of the homespun style of Locke as "forcible," "incisive," and even "ingenious." On this matter the reader must be left to form his own opinion upon personal study, always remembering that the question is one not of substance but exclusively of form. The following passage, which has been selected as a favourable example of Locke's manner, is taken from the *Third Letter of Toleration*, issued in 1692:

"Common sense has satisfied all mankind, that it is above their reach to determine what things, in their own nature indifferent, were fit to be made use of in religion, and would be acceptable to the superior beings in their worship, and therefore they have everywhere thought it necessary to derive that knowledge from the immediate will and dictates of the gods themselves, and have taught that their forms of religion and outward modes of worship were founded upon revelation: nobody daring to do so absurd and insolent a thing, as to take upon him to presume with himself, or to prescribe to others by his own authority, which should in these indifferent and mean things be worthy of the Deity, and make an acceptable part of his worship. Indeed they all agreed in the duties of natural religion, and we find them by common consent owning that piety and virtue, clean hands, and a pure heart not polluted with the breaches of the law of nature, was the best worship of the gods. Reason discovered to them that a good life was the most acceptable thing to the Deity; this the common light of nature put past doubt. But for their ceremonies and outward performances, for them they appeal always to a rule received from the immediate direction of the superior powers themselves, where they made use of, and had need of revelation."

A certain Mr. Samuel Pepys (1633-1703), who was clerk to the Navy and finally secretary to the Admiralty during the last years of the century, left his library to Magdalen College, Cambridge, where it is preserved intact in a handsome building of the age of Queen Anne. Pepys was nearly forgotten, when in 1825 Lord Braybrooke gave to the world a copious diary, kept from 1660 to 1669, nine years and a half, which he had found in shorthand in the Bibliotheca Pepysiana, and had deciphered. In 1879 Mr. Mynors Bright went over the work again, correcting and enlarging the transcript. Lord Braybrooke's task revealed a new author to English readers. This diary, in which Pepys wrote down his experiences, night by night, with extreme artlessness, is unrivalled as a storehouse of gossip and character-painting. When it begins, the author is still young, and freshly come to town to try his fortunes; before it closes the king has greeted him as "another Cicero." It is scarcely literature—that is to say, there is neither art nor effort at construction; but Pepys has extraordinary picturesqueness and great capacity in describing what he has seen in the best and briefest words. Evelyn's diary has a coldness, a dignity, in its ease, that suggest that he conceived that the world might force it into publication. Pepys believed himself absolutely safe behind the veil of his cipher, and he made no effort to paint the lily. How Pepys spent the afternoon and evening of November 5, 1666, may be taken as a typical instance of his precise and garrulous method:

"After dinner and this discourse I took coach, and at the same time find my Lord Hinchingbroke and Mr. John Crew and the Doctor going out to see the ruins of the city; so I took the Doctor into my hackney coach (and he is a very fine sober gentleman), and so through the city. But, Lord!

what pretty and sober observations he made of the city and its desolation; till anon we came to my house, and there I took them upon Tower Hill to show them what houses were pulled down there since the fire; and then to my house, where I treated them with good wine of several sorts, and they took it mighty respectfully, and a fine company of gentlemen they are; but above all I was glad to see my Lord Hinchingbroke drink no wine at all. Here I got them to appoint Wednesday come se'n-night to dine here at my house, and so we broke up and all took coach again, and I carried the Doctor to Chancery Lane, and thence I to White Hall, where I staid walking up and down till night, and then got almost into the play-house, having much mind to go and see the play at Court this night; but fearing how I should get home, because of the bonfires and the lateness of the night to get a coach, I did not stay; but having this evening seen my Lady Jemimah, who is come to town, and looks very well and fat, and heard how Mr. John Pickering is to be married this week, and to a fortune with £5000, and seen a rich necklace of pearl and two pendants of diamonds, which Sir G. Carteret hath presented her with since her coming to town, I home by coach, but met not one bonfire through the whole town in going round by the wall, which is strange, and speaks the melancholy disposition of the city at present, while never more was said of, and feared of, and done against the Papists than just at this time. Home, and there find my wife and her people at cards, and I to my chamber, and there late, and so to supper and to bed."

A memoir so unaffected, drawn up in an age so brutal, might have proved very offensive, but Pepys, though full of human frailty, was a wholesome soul, and undebased by any touch of cynicism. To the humorist and to the antiquarian his faithful Dutch picture of life under Charles II. is invaluable. Pepys was an able administrator in the civil service, and a grave collector of prints, books, maps, and music. In his diary he reveals an emotional side to his character which the world can hardly have suspected.

What we mainly miss in the writers of the Restoration is the higher imaginative quality. We find grace, urbanity, distinction, but we do not find sublimity. An almost unique interest, therefore, attaches to a kind of spiritual or astronomical romance, in which the most glowing fancies are wedded to language of exceptional pomp and splendour. This is *The Sacred Theory of the Earth*, published (in Latin in 1680, in English in 1684) by

THOMAS BURNET

Dr. Thomas Burnet (1635-1715), a Yorkshire divine, who had been brought up under Tillotson at Cambridge, where he spent the greater part of his life until, at the age of fifty, he was elected headmaster of the Charterhouse. It seems a pity that Burnet wrote no more books in his native language, for his gift of sonorous and balanced phrase was very remarkable. He was attacked for the audacity of his speculation, and his last years were disturbed by charges of scepticism, but he lived just long enough to enjoy Addison's enthusiastic praise of *The Theory* in No. 146 of the *Spectator*. As early as 1699 Addison had celebrated *The Sacred Theory* in a Latin ode. The plan of Burnet's famous volume,—which he tells us was suggested to him during a journey across "those wild, vast, and undigested heaps of stones and earth," the Alps,—is an attempt, in all ignorance of geology, to account for the confused horror of the external face of nature. He thinks that the world was created smooth, but suffered from successive cataclysms. His book originally closed with a description of that universal conflagration which is eventually to melt the planet again into polished form, but to this he added a fourth part, describing the Millenium. The imagination of Burnet is often thoroughly Miltonic, and he writes like one possessed with glorious and awful vision. To find a parallel in prose to the more splendid passages of his curious treatise we have to descend to De Quincey. The pages in the third book, which Addison aptly describes as " a funeral oration over this globe," have a singularly majestic cadence, and we may point to Burnet as the founder of that peculiar magniloquence and amplitude of phrase which marked the upper stratum of eighteenth-century prose, and came to their height in the style of Burke :

"The countenance of the heavens will be dark and gloomy; and a veil drawn over the face of the sun. The earth in a disposition everywhere to break into open flames. The tops of the mountains smoking ; the rivers dry, earthquakes in several places, the sea sunk and retired into its deepest channel, and roaring, as against some mighty storm. These things will make the day dead and melancholy; but the night-scenes will have more of horror in them, when the blazing stars appear, like so many Furies, with their lighted torches, threatening to set all on fire. For I do not doubt but the comets will bear a part in this tragedy, and have something extraordinary in them, at that time; either as to number, or bigness, or nearness to the earth. Besides, the air will be full of flaming meteors, of unusual forms and magnitudes; balls of fire rolling in the sky, and pointed lightnings darted against the earth; mixed with claps of thunder, and unusual noises from the clouds. The moon and the stars will be confused and irregular, both in their light and motions; as if the whole frame of the heavens was out of order, and all the laws of Nature were broken or expired."

Compared with the sonorous richness of Thomas Burnet, the ease and grace of Temple seem frivolous, but of course each is admirable in its own way. *The Theory* is, however, to be noted as the sole book of the last forty years of the century which displays in prose the loftier qualities of imagination.

It is generally stated of Robert South (1633-1716) that he is the wittiest of English divines. Steele, writing of him at his death, exclaimed: "Happy genius, he is the better man for being a wit!" To the modern reader the acrimony and petulance of the arch-Tory, the man who sat last on the extreme right of the clerical party, are not wholly pleasing, even now that they are harmless, yet it is easy to see how effective South's vivacity must have been. His style is voluble and nervous; he runs while he talks, and without pausing he snatches, now from one side and now from the other, missiles, ornaments, objects of every description, all of which find their proper places in his motley discourse. He never hesitates to invite virulence, buffoonery, or even downright hateful falsehood to adorn his attacks upon a brother divine, and, as Stillingfleet said, waits in figurative lanes and argumentative narrow passages ready to bespatter his opponents with dirt amid fits of roguish laughter. There is something impish about Dr. South. As a favourable example of his serious manner, the following extract from one of his later sermons may be read with pleasure:

"It is a sad and a poor condition, when there is provision made only for being, not for comfort; for life, not for refreshment. And therefore in the spiritual, as well as in the natural life, there are sublimer fruitions, as well as bare sustenance. For such is the nature of man, that it requires lucid intervals; and the vigour of the mind would flag and decay, should it always jog on at the rate of a common enjoyment, without being sometimes quickened and exalted with the vicissitude of some more refined pleasures. . . . For as in the food that we take into our bodies, it is but very little that passes into nutriment, and so is converted into our substance; so in the greatest affluence of plenty, it is not the mass of the enjoyment, but the elixir or spirit that is derived through it, that gives the comfort."

South's principal antagonists, Dr. Edward Stillingfleet (1635-1699) and Dr. William Sherlock (1641-1707), were men of greater sedateness, but less ability. Stillingfleet ended as Bishop of Worcester; he was a very learned man, but haughty and quarrelsome in disposition. He disputed angrily, not with other divines only, but with Dryden and with Locke; his miscellaneous theological writings, collected in 1710, are exceedingly numerous, and some of them display a real genius for effective polemic. Stillingfleet was so charming in face and figure that he was called "the beauty of holiness." Sherlock, who was Dean of St. Paul's for sixteen years, was, like Stillingfleet, an untiring opponent of the nonconformists. Of his most popular book, his *Practical Treatise on Death*, no less than thirty editions were called for, and Prior expressed the contemporary feeling when he called it "a nation's food." Addison also yielded conspicuous praise to Sherlock, who is nevertheless a writer of no great importance.

Macaulay sought to revive the reputation of Thomas Sprat (1635-1713), Bishop of Rochester, the friend and editor of Cowley. In early life Sprat published Pindaric odes of a very distressing nature. He rose rapidly in church preferment after the Restoration, but never lost his interest in literature and science. In 1667 appeared his *History of the Royal Society*. In 1668 he published Cowley's life, an admirable piece of stately biography, and he is said to have added some touches to *The Rehearsal*. Sprat's theological writings are few and insignificant, and it is hard not to allow that his merits as a prose-writer have been praised with some exaggeration. He is neat, clear, and often dignified, but the epithets "splendid" and "shining" can scarcely be granted to his style without demur.

Gilbert Burnet (1643-1715), Bishop of Salisbury, who is by no means to be confounded with the author of *The Theory*, is another writer whose fame has considerably transcended his merits. G. Burnet, however, for better or for worse, has been a good deal more talked about than Sprat, and must be less briefly dismissed. He was a man born with a genius for success. At the age of twenty-nine he had been offered, and had refused, a choice of four bishoprics. In 1679 he made a great reputation by the first volume of his *History of the Reformation*, still in some sort a standard work. Next year he made capital out of the repentant deathbed of the wicked Earl of Rochester by describing the scene in a pamphlet which enjoyed an astounding popularity. Again a mitre was pressed upon the young divine, but he knew how to wait. Meanwhile he was the most admired preacher in England, and would belabour the pulpit for two whole hours at a time. Burnet, who did not lack courage, took Charles II. to task for his public and private offences, and was discharged from his offices. He went to Holland and schemed for the House of Orange, returning in 1688 as William III.'s confidential chaplain. He was promptly made Bishop of Salisbury, and gave the rest of his life to literature. His famous *Exposition of the Thirty-nine Articles* dates from 1699, and in 1706 he collected his sermons and pamphlets into three thick volumes. In 1724-1734 his best-known work, *The History of My Own Times*, was posthumously issued. This credulous and violent collection of memoirs brings the reader down to 1713. Burnet had been an actor in too many of the political dramas of his time not to possess information which the student of history would be sorry to miss. His gossip is direct and convincing, and he has the gift of bringing a scene plainly before our eyes. Research has made it increasingly certain that he was a conscientious observer, and that his attitude, even in describing his enemies, was accurate and candid. But no one ought to say that Gilbert Burnet is a good writer. He is dry, flat, and particular in a way which becomes common in the eighteenth century, but which had not characterised the writers we have hitherto mentioned. In Burnet, for the first time, we meet with a writer from whose speech the last glimmering reflection of the old enthusiastic style has disappeared. But it is not to be denied that he is wonderfully modern, or that his best character-pieces read very much like leaders in the newspapers of to-day. He is described as "a son of Anak," full of vigour and sap, "black-brow'd and bluff, like Homer's Jupiter."

It will perhaps have been observed that, with the solitary exception of Gilbert Burnet, every one of the authors hitherto dealt with in this chapter was of mature age at the date of the Restoration. Between 1645 and 1675 there was opportunity for plenty of prose-writers to be born, whose work should be a fresh ornament to the seventeenth century. But by a very strange accident these thirty years seemed to add singularly little to prose literature. Defoe, Arbuthnot, Swift, Mandeville, Shaftesbury, Steele, and Addison were all born during that period, and all refrained from publishing prose of any importance until the beginning of the next century. Neither Lewis Atterbury (1656-1731) nor his more famous brother Francis, Bishop of Rochester (1662-1731), each of whom printed sermons, claims more than a bare mention here. Only one new prose-writer of high distinction belongs to the last decade of the seventeenth century, namely, Richard Bentley (1662-1742), the famous Master of Trinity. He was a very great scholar, a man of eminent good sense and vigorous intellectual character, and a personality which set its stamp upon the age. His youth was passed as the domestic tutor of Stillingfleet's son, and his prodigious acquirements were obtained in the Dean's excellent library. When Stillingfleet was made a bishop, Bentley proceeded to Oxford, and there published, in 1691, his *Letter to Dr. Mill*, in Latin, a daring essay in destructive criticism. In 1692 he brought out his *Boyle Lectures*, and through them obtained the friendship and correspondence of Newton. Next year he was appointed King's Librarian. He was now already a famous scholar, on terms of familiar intimacy with such men as Evelyn, Locke, and Sir

Christopher Wren, too famous, indeed, not to excite the petulance of mediocrity. There was much controversy regarding the so-called letters of Phalaris, which Temple had praised in 1692 and Charles Boyle had edited in 1695. Bentley, who knew that he could prove these letters to be spurious, was led into contemptuous controversy about them, and the learned world rang with a very pretty quarrel. Bentley's first essay appeared in 1697, and the rapid exchange of paper bullets went on until 1699. Atterbury, Temple, Garth, Aldrich (even Swift, a little out of date), a host of wits and scholars, were on the one side, and Bentley alone on the other. Yet Bentley eventually conquered all along the line of his foes; nor since 1699 has Phalaris the letter-writer existed. In April 1699 Bentley was made Master of Trinity, and the rest of his career—his insolent struggle for college supremacy, his irregular progress as a scholar, his final victory and repose—belong to the following century. He wrote very little more in English prose, and we are not here concerned to pursue his fascinating adventures any further. The vernacular style of Bentley is rough-hewn, colloquial, shot through with fiery threads of humour, the ideal style for confident and angry polemic. His position as a scholar is summed up in Professor Jebb's statement that his is "the last name of first-rate magnitude which occurs above the point at which Greek and Latin studies begin to diverge." Bishop Stillingfleet is reported to have said that Bentley wanted only modesty to be the most remarkable person in Europe; he was certainly, in the absence of modesty, the most considerable English critic of his time.

CHAPTER IV

POPE

AT the head of a list of "departed relations and friends" which Pope kept, he wrote, "1700 Maji primo obit, semper venerandus, poetarum princeps, Joannes Dryden," although he only saw that poet once, and never knew him. It was the literary relationship that he recognised. King John was dead,—long live King Alexander. Yet between the death of Dryden and the first public appearance of Pope there came an interregnum of nine years, during which any man who was strong enough might have seized the sceptre. But the only pretender was Addison, whose absence of poetic genius is plainly proved by the fact that though Dryden had been ready to recognise him, and though Pope was still a child, he failed, without any lack of will on his own part, to strike a commanding figure on the empty stage. If Addison had never come under the influence of Swift and Steele, he would in all probability never have discovered his true power. He would have gone on writing political copies of verses and academic memoirs on medals, and would have held a very inconspicuous place in the history of literature. At thirty-five Addison had written most of his existing poetry, and was yet, properly speaking, undistinguished.

Joseph Addison (1672-1719) was the son of a Dean of Lichfield, who had written two good books on Morocco. He was educated at the Charterhouse, where he found Steele, and at

Queen's College, Oxford, whence he proceeded to Magdalen and became a fellow. He stayed at Oxford until 1699, cultivating polite literature in a dilettante way. In 1693 Addison came forward with a fluent address *To Mr. Dryden*, and began, under the supervision of that poet, to join the band of young men who were placing the Latin classics in the hands of those who read none but English verse. In April 1694 he produced a brief *Account of the Greatest English Poets*, in verse; the poets were Chaucer and Spenser, at whom he sneered, and Cowley, Milton, Waller, Dryden, and Congreve, whom he praised. In this brief copy of verses there is room for a compliment to "godlike Nassau," which showed the author's Whig bias. In 1695 Addison published a poem *To His Majesty* [William III.], in a strain of grovelling eulogy. He describes noble Nassau as

> "Reeking in blood, and smeared with dust and sweat,
>   Whilst angry gods conspire to make him great."

Meanwhile Addison had been producing a series of very clever mock heroic Latin poems, and a serious one on the Peace of Ryswick. These he published at Oxford in 1699, and so closed his academic career with great applause. Montague, the ideal patron, whose encouragement was to do so much for letters, secured Addison a pension and sent him abroad. In 1701 he wrote to Montague, now Lord Halifax, a *Letter from Italy*, which Mr. Courthope thinks the best of Addison's poems. It is very much in the manner of Waller. He was then writing his cold tragedy of *Cato*, and in 1704 he celebrated Marlborough's victory at Blenheim in *The Campaign*, "a gazette in poetry," as Warton called it; after this he wrote but little verse, except the graceful opera of *Rosamund* in 1706. Addison was totally without lyric gift. He never excelled except in the heroic couplet. As to his versification, it has been considered to mark the transition between Dryden and Pope; but, in the opinion of the present writer, it shows a curious absence of all influence from Dryden; and if it marks any transition at all, it is that between Waller and Pope.

There is no better example of this to be met with than the lines on Marlborough's action at Blenheim :

> ' 'Twas then great Marlborough's mighty soul was proved,
> That in the shock of charging hosts unmoved,
> Amidst confusion, horror, and despair,
> Examined all the dreadful scenes of war ;
> In peaceful thought the field of death surveyed,
> To fainting squadrons sent the timely aid,
> Inspired repulsed battalions to engage,
> And taught the doubtful battle how to rage.
> So when an angel by divine command
> With rising tempests shakes a guilty land,
> Such as of late o'er pale Britannia past,
> Calm and serene he drives the furious blast ;
> And pleased th' Almighty's orders to perform,
> Rides in the whirlwind and directs the storm."

The Campaign might have been written by Waller himself, who, it may be remembered, invented the "gazette in rhyme." In short, the English verse of Addison is the poetry of a scholar and a skilful man of letters, not of a poet.

An unfortunate young clergyman, John Pomfret (1667-1703), possessed more simplicity and a truer poetic instinct than Addison. His *Choice*, in praise of a sequestered life, appeared in 1699, and was a mild herald of the return to nature-study. It was very popular, and was long admired with exaggeration. Here is a specimen of that "old sweet household dream" which Leigh Hunt liked so well, and helped to resuscitate :

> " If Heav'n the grateful liberty would give,
> That I might choose my method how to live,
> And all those hours propitious Fate should lend,
> In blissful ease and satisfaction spend,
> Near some fair town I'd have a private seat,
> Built uniform ; not little, nor too great :
> Better, if on a rising ground it stood ;
> On this side fields, on that a neighb'ring wood.
> It should, within, no other things contain,
> But what were useful, necessary, plain :
> Methinks 'tis nauseous, and I'd ne'er endure
> The needless pomp of gaudy furniture.

> A little garden, grateful to the eye,
> And a cool rivulet run murm'ring by;
> On whose delicious banks a stately row
> Of shady limes, or sycamores should grow;
> At th' end of which a silent study plac'd,
> Should be with all the noblest authors grac'd."

Pomfret was poor, and when at last, in 1703, he obtained a good living, the Bishop of London refused him induction, on account of an ambiguous expression in *The Choice*, and Pomfret died of smallpox and chagrin. The only other name which has a right to detain us in this sterile period is that of John Philips (1676-1708), author, in 1701, of *The Splendid Shilling*, an inimitable piece of mock-heroic blank verse, in the style of *Paradise Lost;* this parody still retains its humour. Philips revolted against the heroic couplet, and wrote only in Miltonic blank verse. In 1705 he published a *Blenheim*, and in 1708 a didactic poem on *Cider* in two books. This last work, otherwise more curious than inspired, is remarkable as introducing exact detail of expression and touches of colour which were outside the fashion of the day. When Philips says—

> ' Let every tree in every garden own
> The Red-streak as supreme, whose pulpous fruit,
> With gold irradiate, and vermillion, shines
> Tempting, not fatal,"

he seems to prophesy of Thomson's *Seasons*. Philips was studying to be a doctor when a life was cut short at thirty-three which promised well for English literature.

The greatest artist in verse, and perhaps the greatest poet, with whom we have to deal in the present volume, Alexander Pope (1688-1744), was born in Lombard Street, May 21, 1688, the son of a Catholic linen-draper. His father retired from business immediately after the poet's birth to a place called Binfield, near Wokingham. Pope, with features carved as if in ivory and with the great melting eyes of an antelope, carried his brilliant head on a deformed and sickly body. Partly for this reason, and partly because of his position as a Catholic, the boy had no regular education. He was taught by the family priest, went to two

schools in short succession, and then returned home to stay at
the age of twelve. The alleys of Windsor Forest now became his
schoolroom. A neighbour, Sir William Trumbull, seems to have
introduced him in 1705 to the aged dramatist Wycherley. But
before this Pope had begun to write, and to devote himself heart
and soul to literature. In 1703, or earlier, he was writing an epic
of *Alcander*, four books of which survived until late in Pope's
life, and were at last reluctantly destroyed, so the poet told
Spence, by Atterbury's advice. In the same year, at the age of
fifteen, he translated the first book of the *Thebais* of Statius.
This still exists, and it is an amazing production. Not merely
is it an extraordinary instance of perseverance to find so young
a boy persisting through an arduous task of nearly nine hundred
lines, but the verse is usually good, and often splendid. Unless
Pope touched it up very much in later years, this translation is a
prodigy. The paraphrases from Chaucer belong to 1704 or 1705,
those from Ovid to 1707. By this time he was launched into
literary society.

Wycherley, with whose talent and career we are already familiar,
was a very odd companion for a home-bred youth. He was approaching
seventy, worn out with a gay life, poor, and deserted
by the polite world. He was perhaps not so stupid as Pope's
biographers have fancied him to be, but quite as disreputable.
Out of the dregs of his brain he was still trying to squeeze some
oozings of poetic fancy, and had in his view the publication of
a " Miscellany " which should redeem his position. He soon
understood how valuable the critical aid of such a brilliant youth
as Pope might be to him, but if he sent the boy his verses to
patch up it must not be forgotten that he gave Pope timely help
on his road to distinction. He introduced him to William Walsh
(1663-1708), a Worcestershire squire, small poet and distinguished
critic, to whom Dryden had, as well as he could, bequeathed his
critical, as to Congreve his dramatic, sceptre. Walsh was a more
useful friend than Wycherley. He was one of the few people
whom Pope sincerely respected, and when Walsh died, too soon

to enjoy his young protégé's earliest triumph, Pope embalmed him as "criticus sagax, amicus et vir bonus." He assures us that Walsh exercised a potent influence on his versification, by telling him that many English poets had been great, but as yet not one correct, and urging this ambition of "correctness" upon him. Pope's first friendship with Wycherley lasted until 1710; there was a quarrel of about a year's duration, and then the oddly-assorted pair were passably friendly again until Wycherley died in 1715. But Pope, by that time, was the first poet in England, and not a little ashamed of the old broken playwright.

Pope's life, partly owing to the tricks he played with the Wycherley correspondence, is not very clear in its details until the beginning of his public literary career. His verses had been handed by the friends already mentioned to such critics as George Granville "the polite" (Lord Lansdowne, 1667-1735), Congreve, Halifax, Cromwell, and Garth. They were felt to be marvellously well-turned, and each polite ingenious reader was glad to contribute his crumb of praise, or offer his touch of complimentary suggestion. In 1704—so Pope asserted—in 1705 at latest, he had written his *Pastorals*, four eclogues on the seasons, in the manner of Virgil. In 1706 Tonson offered to publish them, but from some unknown cause they did not appear until May 1709, when they closed Tonson's *Sixth Miscellany*, Ambrose Philips' *Pastorals* opening it. It is strange that these bucolic performances attracted the notice which they undoubtedly did attract. Walsh deliberately preferred them to Virgil's earlier eclogues. They are singularly sweet in versification, it is true, but tame, artificial, and without a single spark of Theocritean nature:

> " Ye gentle Muses, leave your crystal spring,
> Let Nymphs and Sylvans cypress garlands bring ;
> Ye weeping Loves, the stream with myrtles hide,
> And break your bows, as when Adonis died ;
> And with your golden darts, now useless grown,
> Inscribe a verse on this relenting stone :
> 'Let nature change, let heav'n and earth deplore,
> Fair Daphne's dead, and love is now no more !'"

By the Thames at Windsor white bulls are sacrificed, nymphs bring turtles to the cave of Pan, and grateful clusters swell with floods of wine, in spite of the poet's protestation that he would be severely English and modern. What was praiseworthy in the *Pastorals* was the evidence of painstaking, the strenuous attention to artistic effect, the determination to be what Walsh called "correct." It was not until four years later that the famous pastoral quarrel with Philips took place.

In the meantime Pope, once started, rose to eminence with incredible rapidity. In 1709 he wrote, and, after long polishing, in 1711 published anonymously, his *Essay on Criticism*, a didactic poem in something less than four hundred couplets. It opens with a statement of the rules on which taste is founded, what the limits of dependence on personal judgment are, and where nature must be called in to correct them, and what reverence is due to the rules laid down by the Ancients. It then proceeds to consider what the dangers are which beset the critical path, and to touch on that idle dispute, then still so much in vogue, as to the relative merits of the classical and the modern writer. The laws are laid down by which the critic should regulate his behaviour; he must be candid, modest, open, and well-bred. Instances are then given of critics who, unfortunately, lack these virtues, and we are told that the man who judges should be free to bear attack himself.

"But Appius reddens at each word you speak." Appius was intended for the bearish old critic John Dennis (1657-1734), who had written a tragedy of *Appius and Virginia*. This then is the first, and a very characteristic instance of Pope's peculiar neatness in satiric allusion. We then pass to the history of criticism, and the best critics are reviewed in order. In verse, for which no praise can seem excessive, we are given a portrait of Aristotle:

> " Such once were Critics ; such the happy few,
> Athens and Rome in better ages knew.
> The mighty Stagirite first left the shore,
> Spread all his sails, and durst the deeps explore ;

> He steer'd securely, and discover'd far,
> Led by the light of the Mæonian Star.
> Poets, a race long unconfin'd, and free,
> Still fond and proud of savage liberty,
> Receiv'd his laws; and stood convinc'd 'twas fit,
> Who conquer'd Nature should preside o'er Wit."

This is perhaps the most beautiful passage in the poem, which presently closes with a very fine eulogy of Walsh. There are others scarcely less eloquent, and a number of lines whose curious felicity has given them currency as commonplaces of everyday talk. But there are intervals of flatness as well, and on the whole this is the most uneven of Pope's important works. As the production of a youth of twenty-one it is, in any case, among the historic marvels of precocity.

In 1711 one of Pope's Catholic friends, John Caryll (1655?-1736),—a nephew of the man of the same name who was known as Lord Dartford in the court of the Pretender, and as a small dramatist who had survived from the first Restoration period,—interested Pope in a quarrel then proceeding between Lord Petre and a Miss Arabella Fermor. The former had forcibly cut off a lock of the hair of the latter, and the affair was taking the proportions of a blood feud between the families. Rowe's recent translation of Boileau's *Le Lutrin*, perhaps, suggested to Caryll a similar burlesque on this trivial subject, and he thought Pope might write something which should make this absurd vendetta explode in laughter. A happy reminiscence of Martial—"Nolueram, Polytime, tuos violare capillos"—struck the poet's fancy, and he soon threw himself eagerly upon the task. At first the combatants were flattered, and, with Miss Fermor's permission, *The Rape of the Lock*, in two cantos, appeared in Lintot's *Miscellany* in 1712. It enjoyed great and instant success. Addison hailed it as *merum sal*, and a less conscientious artist than Pope would have been satisfied. But he felt the framework to be too slight, even for such a trifle, and he presently re-wrote the poem, introducing a Rosicrucian "machinery," or supernatural action, of sylphs and gnomes. Thus, much enlarged, he published the poem in five cantos in 1714; but Miss Fermor, who was now married or at the point of marrying, chose to think that by this renewed publication the young poet was intruding too much into her affairs. *The Rape of the Lock* has lately been attacked with great severity by a no less eminent critic than Sir Leslie Stephen, and his authority has been quoted by other writers far less competent to pass a judgment. It seems to me strange that Sir Leslie Stephen should not perceive the unfairness of breaking such an exquisite butterfly of art on the wheel of his analysis, and the inappropriateness on this occasion of grave reproof of Pope's smartness and want of delicacy. When we are told, moreover, that *The Rape of the Lock* is "wearisome" and "effete," there is nothing for it but a direct negation. As well might *Hamlet* be called superficial and *Paradise Lost* flat. In its own class and degree *The Rape of the Lock* is as perfect as these—as entirely successful and satisfactory. Poetic wit was never brighter, verse never more brilliantly polished, the limited field of burlesque never more picturesquely filled, than by this little masterpiece in Dresden china. Its faults, a certain hardness and want of sympathy, are the faults of the age, and mark little more than a submission to the prevalent Congreve ideal of polite manners. Its merits are of the most delicate order, and it was at once recognised that no poem half so good had been produced in England since Dryden's address to the Duchess of Ormond, fourteen years before. Here is the passage where Shock, that "vile Iceland cur," as Dennis called him, acts as his lady's guardian genius :

> " He said : when Shock, who thought she slept too long,
> Leap'd up, and wak'd his mistress with his tongue.
> 'Twas then, Belinda, if report say true,
> Thy eyes first open'd on a billet-doux ;
> Wounds, charms, and ardours were no sooner read,
> But all the vision vanish'd from thy head.
>   And now, unveil'd, the toilet stands display'd,
> Each silver vase in mystic order laid.
> First, rob'd in white, the nymph intent adores,
> With head uncover'd, the cosmetic powers.

> A heav'nly image in the glass appears,
> To that she bends, to that her eyes she rears ;
> Th' inferior Priestess, at her altar's side,
> Trembling begins the sacred rites of pride.
> Unnumber'd treasures ope at once, and here
> The various off'rings of the world appear ;
> From each she nicely culls with curious toil,
> And decks the goddess with the glitt'ring spoil.
> This casket India's glowing gems unlocks,
> And all Arabia breathes from yonder box.
> The tortoise here and elephant unite,
> Transform'd to combs, the speckled, and the white.
> Here files of pins extend their shining rows,
> Puffs, powders, patches, bibles, billet-doux.
> Now awful beauty puts on all its arms ;
> The Fair each moment rises in her charms,
> Repairs her smiles, awakens ev'ry grace,
> And calls forth all the wonders of her face ;
> Sees by degrees a purer blush arise,
> And keener lightenings quicken in her eyes.
> The busy Sylphs surround their darling care,
> These set the head, and those divide the hair,
> Some fold the sleeve, whilst others plait the gown ;
> And Betty's prais'd for labours not her own."

From this time—that is to say, from Pope's twenty-sixth year—we have to think of him as the recognised first poet of his age.

Pope being now launched upon what he called "the dangerous fate of authors," was to discover without loss of time that "the life of a wit is a warfare upon earth." His first adversary was the rugged Dennis, who promptly replied to the sneer about "Appius" in a pamphlet of coarse abuse, describing his young rival's personal disfigurements, and attacking his poetry with violent though occasionally just abuse. Pope's acerbity of temper had as yet hardly made its appearance; as a child he had been an angel of endurance ; and he now sat patient under the torment of Appius. In December a review of his *Essay* in the *Spectator* introduced him to Steele as the editor, and to Addison as the writer of the article, and Pope was courteously invited to contribute to the new and epoch-making gazette. On the 14th of May 1712 the

Spectator contained Pope's *Messiah*, a sacred pastoral in emulation of the *Pollio* of Virgil. Technically this is one of the most faultless of Pope's writings. It is evident that he was studying new effects. This poem is marked by the broken pause and by the use of alexandrines—features which he had hitherto eschewed. The *Messiah* is a dexterous cento of passages from Isaiah, foretelling the advent of Christ. Wordsworth has attacked it with great severity, and it no longer holds its former popularity. When we examine it in detail we find it full of errors against taste and judgment. The way to appreciate it is to read it aloud, and so secure the rhetorical effect which the poet intended. The splendour and fulness of the verse will then bear all objection before them, and the last eighteen lines, at least, will rouse the pulse like a blast from a golden trumpet :

> " See barb'rous nations at thy gates attend,
> Walk in thy light, and in thy temple bend ;
> See thy bright altars throng'd with prostrate kings,
> And heap'd with products of Sabæan springs !
> For thee Idume's spicy forests blow,
> And seeds of gold in Ophir's mountains glow.
> See heav'n its sparkling portals wide display,
> And break upon thee in a flood of day !
> No more the rising sun shall gild the morn,
> Nor ev'ning Cynthia fill her silver horn ;
> But lost, dissolv'd in thy superior rays,
> One tide of glory, one unclouded blaze
> O'erflow thy courts : the light himself shall shine
> Reveal'd, and God's eternal day be thine !
> The seas shall waste, the skies in smoke decay,
> Rocks fall to dust, and mountains melt away ;
> But fix'd his word, his saving power remains ;—
> Thy realm for ever lasts, thy own Messiah reigns ! "

If we persist in applying to classical and rhetorical poetry the tests framed to measure romantic and naturalistic poetry, the result will simply be to exclude ourselves from all possibility of just appreciation of the former. To a critic who argues exclusively from Wordsworth's standpoint, and who dares to be consistent, Dryden must be even as Blackmore and Pope no better than Theobald.

In March 1713, at the desire of Lord Lansdowne, Pope published in folio a pastoral, *Windsor Forest*, the greater part of which he declared that he had written as long ago as 1704. Pope assisted a few weeks later at the first performance of Addison's *Cato*, for which he had written a fine prologue. These two publications are those in which he displays, and that perhaps unwillingly, most of a political bias. His position as a politician, however, was somewhat dubious, for the *Cato* prologue was all on the side of the Whigs, while *Windsor Forest* was applauded by the Tories. Pope, in fact, had no knowledge of statecraft, but possessed a kind of mischievous curiosity which impelled him, as somebody said, to appear in London whenever anything was going on, like a porpoise in stormy weather. *Windsor Forest* is a very promiscuous poem; it seems to contain a little of everything. It is bucolic and anecdotic, political and descriptive, by turns. The boyish work of sixteen does not amalgamate satisfactorily with the manly work of twenty-five. Wordsworth took it under his protection as containing, alone among the poems of its author, "new images of external nature." He was referring doubtless to the exact and highly-coloured catalogue of birds and fishes; but it may be contested that this was the nature-painting of a Weenix or a Hondecoeter, not of a Turner:

> "Our plenteous streams a various race supply,
> The bright-ey'd perch with fins of Tyrian dye.
> The silver eel, in shining volumes roll'd,
> The yellow carp, in scales bedropp'd with gold,
> Swift trouts, diversified with crimson stains,
> And pikes, the tyrants of the wat'ry plains."

This is excellent *genre*, but Wordsworth might have been shown a dozen other instances of Pope's genius for "still life." There is an eloquent recommendation of peace near the end of the poem, intended to convey commendation of the Tory policy. Pope declared that he wrote these lines "soon after the ratification of the Treaty of Utrecht," an event which took place six weeks later than they were published. But this was merely a slip of memory. In March everybody knew that the peace was certain. We may here mention, as closing the first period of Pope's literary career, that in 1715 he was sufficiently ill-advised to publish a paraphrase of Chaucer's *House of Fame*, written when he was twenty-three. Steele saw in it "a thousand thousand beauties," but posterity has come to consider *The Temple of Fame* as one of the poorest and least inspired of its author's productions.

Pope was now twenty-seven, and had published but one work *de longue haleine*. He had become celebrated mainly by what we may call occasional pieces. He was now, however, to come forward with an undertaking of vast proportions. As early as November 1713, Swift, who had made Pope's acquaintance in the spring of that year, was saying aloud in fashionable places that "the best poet in England is Mr. Pope, a Papist, who has begun a translation of Homer into English verse, for which I must have you all subscribe, for the author shall not begin to print till I have a thousand guineas for him." This warmth of friendship with Swift portended a corresponding coolness with Addison, and it is perhaps a mistake to suppose that Addison and Pope had ever, except for a moment about *Cato*, passed the limits of ceremonious acquaintance. In 1714, a year of violent political agitation caused by the death of Anne, Pope was engaged mainly on Homer, and taking very little heed of a birch-rod which Ambrose Philips, for reasons too elaborate to be here dilated on, had hung up for his chastisement at Button's. It has been argued that the anger was confined to Philips, but it is difficult to deny that the whole senate to which Addison gave laws was growing sensibly frigid toward Pope; while the latter poet himself believed that Addison was inciting his friend Thomas Tickell (1686-1740), who was the most gifted of Addison's disciples, to trip him up with a rival translation of Homer. It is true that in June 1715 Pope and Tickell simultaneously obliged the town with a first *Iliad*, but if

Tickell meant to injure Pope he failed egregiously. Indeed, he immediately withdrew, with a gracious compliment to Pope's far greater ability. Pope continued to believe that Addison was moving behind the mask of Tickell and had translated the book. Curiously enough, Steele, who had good opportunities of knowing, and no prejudice thought so too; yet it seems certain that Tickell did the work he signed. It was under the torture of these suspicions that Pope seems to have written the famous portrait of Atticus, the most brilliant individual passage in all his writings, and indeed in all modern satirical literature. These lines were not published until four years after Addison's death (when they appeared in a shabby miscellany called *Cythereia*), and though Pope showed them to such friends as Swift and Lord Burlington, we may console ourselves by knowing that the legend that Addison saw them rests on no evidence, and is against probability. We no longer hold the magnificent Atticus in quite such awe as our fathers did, yet we may fairly be glad to think that he died unconscious of this terrible impeachment.

Pope, slowly perfecting his labours, lingered until his friends the Tories were out of office before his first volume of *The Iliad* appeared. It did not suffer, however, on this account; the subscription lists were of fabulous length and quality, and the poem was adroitly dedicated, not to any politician, but to Congreve. It is estimated that by his entire Homer, spread as it was over eleven years, Pope made clear nine thousand pounds. He admitted in after life that, if he was independent, it was "thanks to Homer." It was allowed that, in spite of Pope's great disadvantages, this success was thoroughly deserved. He did not know Greek well, to be sure, which was no trifling disadvantage; but he was less handicapped by this awkward circumstance than a translator of our own age would be. He did what was perhaps better than making an accurate version of Homer,—he produced the finest, the largest, the most conspicuous poem of the age. Pope's *Homer*, take it all in all, is not approached by any other single poem of the like proportions between *Paradise Lost* and *The Excursion*. It is what English literature has to show of the highest importance in an epical direction throughout the eighteenth century. On this subject the reader may be recommended to Sir Leslie Stephen's excellent pages, as sympathetic and masterly in this instance as we have been obliged to conceive them prejudiced and hasty in their treatment of *The Rape of the Lock.* It is scarcely necessary to remind that reader that Pope wrote, on this as on almost all other occasions, entirely in the heroic couplet.

As early as 1709 Pope had printed, in Lintot's *Miscellany*, a specimen of what he could do as a translator of Homer. This is the "Episode of Sarpedon." Addison, so Pope declared, was the first to urge him to complete the house of which this was the specimen brick. In 1714 he printed other passages; the first volume of *The Iliad* appeared in 1715, and the sixth and last, with its dedication to Congreve, in 1720. It seemed profitable to fulfil the original design, and to present the public with the whole of Homer; but Pope was weary, and could not face the labour of attacking *The Odyssey* unaided. He therefore, in 1723, called in the help of two Cambridge scholars, disciples of his own in verse, Elijah Fenton (1683-1730) and William Broome (1689-1745), whom he paid not illiberally for their share of a task which owed its success to his own name. This *Odyssey* appeared in 1725, with a *Battle of the Frogs and Mice*, contributed by Parnell, who did not live to see it printed. Thus it was Pope's fate "for ten years to comment and translate," and the Homer very nearly absorbed his best powers during the central period of his life; yet the result is such that the student scarcely cares to lament it. Pope explains in a note to *The Dunciad* that he counts these ten years from 1713 to 1725, omitting two years during which, so he pretends, his perfunctory edition of Shakespeare exclusively occupied him.

Meanwhile, in 1717, a collection of his poetical works was called for in quarto and folio, and Pope saw himself a classic at twenty-nine. To this complete edition he added two important poems which had not seen the light, and which it is believed, from internal evidence, he had only just written. These are the *Verses to the Memory of an Unfortunate Lady*, and the *Eloisa to Abelard*. They are unique among Pope's writings as dealing, and that in the most pathetic and luxuriant style, with the passion of love. The poet took all possible pains to mystify his commentators as to the circumstances which led to the composition of these poems. All we can discern is that they belong to that brief period between the abandonment of the house at Binfield, where he had lived since his childhood, and his settlement at Twickenham. In 1717 Pope was with his parents at Chiswick, and this was the year in which he pensioned Teresa Blount, apparently to prevent her from girding at his relations with her sister Martha. These ladies he had known since 1706,[1] and with Martha Blount his connection became more and more intimate until his death. It has even been suspected that they were married. The *Elegy on an Unfortunate Lady* was a mere study in emotional characterisation. It is an expression of impassioned pity for a lady who has destroyed herself to escape from the torture of hopeless love. No poet is obliged to say why he chooses this or the other subject, but Pope, being asked by some silly person who the lady was, saw the opening for a mystification, and set his biographers chasing an *ignis fatuus* for at least a century. The *Elegy* is very short; it only extends to eighty-two lines; but it contains some of Pope's tenderest and most musical verses. The passage beginning—

> "By foreign hands thy dying eyes were closed,
> By foreign hands thy decent limbs composed,
> By foreign hands thy humble grave adorned,
> By strangers honoured, and by strangers mourned!
> What tho' no friends in sable weeds appear,
> Grieve for an hour, perhaps, then mourn a year,
> And bear about the mockery of woe
> To midnight dances, and the public show?
> What tho' no weeping Loves thy ashes grace,
> Nor polish'd marble emulate thy face?

---

[1] I venture to take "the 389th week of the reign of your most serene Majesty," as a more or less literal statement. but indeed the letter of 1714 may be a mere mystification.

> What tho' no sacred earth allow thee room,
> Nor hallow'd dirge be muttered o'er thy tomb?
> Yet shall thy grave with rising flowers be drest,
> And the green turf lie lightly on thy breast:
> There shall the morn her earliest tears bestow;
> There the first roses of the year shall blow;
> While angels with their silver wings o'ershade
> The ground, now sacred by thy reliques made,"

is a fine typical example of Pope's entirely serious manner. The *Eloisa to Abelard* is a very much longer poem, and here the elegiac tone is replaced by an ardour and activity of passion. The riot in the turbulent soul of a woman who loves and has forsworn love, who is torn between earth and heaven, is given with extraordinary psychological skill. It is here that Pope shows most insight into the workings of the human heart, and sets us fancying for a moment, that if he had been born half a century earlier he might have been a dramatist of the same class as Ford. There is no question, however, that the vehicle which Pope used, the polished heroic couplet, is particularly unsuited to subjects of this kind, and gives an artificial air to the most poignant and thrilling passages. We feel that the *Elegy* requires some varied lyric measure, and that the *Eloisa* would move us more if the story of the distracted and impassioned nun were told in stanzas, or in couplets less regularly antithetical. It is only on some such hypothesis that we can account for the fact that these two poems, melodious and fervid as they are, and supplied with every refinement of poetic art, leave us at last a little cold.

Late in 1717 Pope's father died, and during the confusion which ensued, or while his new property at Twickenham was being put in order, he lived for some months at Stanton Harcourt, where he finished the fifth book of *The Iliad*. Then, for the rest of his life, his home was the little classic villa on the north bank of the Thames, where he had his famous grotto, his temple of shells, his five acres of twirled and twisted garden, his sacred groves, and his barge at the foot of a little lawn as smooth as one of his own couplets. Here the frail being, too sickly and nervous to bear the rude shocks of public life, could grow calm and almost happy in solitude. He says:

> "Soon as I enter at my country door
> My mind resumes the thread it dropt before;
> Thoughts, which at Hyde-Park-Corner I forgot,
> Meet and rejoin me in the pensive Grot."

At Twickenham he was to spend a quarter of a century, as an invalid indeed, but one surrounded by friends and admirers, easily first in the only world he valued, the world of letters, and regarded with indulgence and distinction by all that England had to show of what was brightest and best.

Unfortunately the temperament of the poet forbade that he should enjoy the legitimate fruits of his retirement. The independence he had now secured, and the unquestioned eminence to which he had attained, might have lifted him for the rest of his days above all the minor vexations. But he could only breathe in an atmosphere of intrigue, and the physical excitement of anger was the keenest pleasure his nerves could enjoy. At Binfield he had been tolerably peaceful. At Chiswick the great quarrels of his life began—that with Edmund Curll, the publisher, "shameless Curll, the caitiff Vaticide"; that with Colley Cibber, the amiable and voluble comedian; that with Dennis, reawakened by the caricature of Sir Tremendous in the poor farce of *Three Hours after Marriage*, in which three of the wittiest men of the age, Gay, Pope, and Arbuthnot, combined to be dull and offensive. The friendship with Lady Mary Wortley Montagu (1689-1762), prosecuted about this time with extraordinary sprightliness and effusion, contained the seeds of a yet more scandalous feud. In 1723 Pope's flirtation with Judith Cowper, afterwards the aunt of the poet of *The Task*, ended in disappointment and distress. Everything pointed to the path of satire as that along which Pope should now proceed; and Swift, whose influence with Pope was still paramount, was ever urging him to write something worthy a member of that mysterious Scriblerus Club which had been founded to crush the race of scribbling dunces. It cannot be said, however, that Pope was quick in taking advantage of this suggestion. While the Homer proceeded it is quite plain that he had energy for very little else. The first ten years of his life at Twickenham give us but one important independent poem, namely, the lines to Addison, published in Tickell's posthumous edition of 1720. Even these were written, in the earlier time, at Binfield. He was therefore fresh, in 1727, for the composition of a long original work, and he set to with the gusto of a poet who has long been chained to the oar of translation. As early as 1720, it seems, Swift had proposed a general satire to him, and he had sketched a "Progress of Dulness." This design had slumbered until in 1726, after Pope had published his Shakespeare, the errors of that edition were roughly pointed out in a pamphlet by Lewis Theobald (1690?-1744), a busy minor playwright of the period, who eventually, in 1733, himself published a Shakespeare which was far more scholarly than Pope's. Pope immediately pounced upon Theobald (whose name was pronounced Tibbald) as a fit hero for his satire. He took Swift into his confidence, but Swift, who liked satire to be rather general than personal, warned him to "take care that the bad poets do not outwit you."

Gradually the "Progress of Dulness" took the form in which we know it as *The Dunciad*. But Pope worked so slowly that one by one the dunces were dying, and at last it became absolutely necessary to publish the poem at once, if it were to appear at all. There is no more thorny tract of literature than the bibliography of this poem, and we cannot pretend here to give any account of the metamorphoses of *The Dunciad*. It is probable that there was no edition earlier than that of the Owl, published in incomplete form in May 1728. In April 1729 appeared the edition of the Ass laden with Books, which contains the dedication to Swift, the notes and prolegomena, the testimonies of authors, and the indices. This is called the first complete edition, and for twelve years *The Dunciad* ended with the couplet:

> "Enough! enough! the raptur'd Monarch cries;
> And through the Ivory Gate the Vision flies."

But in 1742 *The New Dunciad*, "as it was found in 1741," was published, and this is what forms the fourth and last book of the poem as we hold it now. In 1743, in a final "complete edition," Pope dethroned Theobald, and set up "a more considerable hero," Colley Cibber, thereby greatly injuring the structure of his piece; for though Cibber was a fribble and a light-weight, he was neither dull nor a dunce, while Theobald might justly claim to be the one and the other. Such then is the bare outline of the history of this extraordinary work.

It is not clearly enough recognised that the central figure of this magnificent satire is not any Cibber or Theobald of the moment, but the very deity of Dulness itself incarnate in all the bad writers of the age. We are told about Welsted, Oldmixon, Ward, and the rest, because the animalcules of yesterday are lost beyond recall, and because we must study, while they flash across the microscope for a moment, the insects of to-day. Every hour "ductile Dulness new mæanders takes," but to study them elsewhere than in the present were patent absurdity. This redeems *The Dunciad* from that littleness of purpose which would have soon destroyed a merely personal attack on certain unknown writers. The satire was cruel, was perhaps unworthy of its author's secure and eminent position, but it was exceedingly successful. It has been said—it was suggested to Pope himself—that he really gave immortality to ridiculous names which else would naturally disappear for ever. But what is the immortality which he has given to them? When we meet with the name of Oldmixon, who thinks of the real man, the tiresome old Whig pamphleteer, with his insipid pastorals and his petulant essays? We think of a figure created entirely by Pope; we think of the aged athlete, "in naked majesty," climbing the side of the stranded lighter, to plunge the deeper into the dreadful sluice of mud. Our interest is quickened, indeed, but not created by the consciousness that there was a real Oldmixon, to whom this figment of Pope's imagination must have given exquisite pain. It appears, however, that Pope feared that the work, as it originally stood, might seem to posterity to have too local a bearing. *The New Dunciad* attempts to widen the scope of the satire, to deal with stupidity in education, in philosophy, in the various application of the powers of the mind. Here Pope was far less safe than in dealing with what he thoroughly understood,—literary merit,—and in criticising scholarship and science he made sad blunders. He drew himself together, however, at the close, and the last thirty lines of *The Dunciad*, in which he foretells a kind of Ragnarok of all intelligence, are among the noblest which he has left :

> " In vain, in vain—the all composing hour
> Resistless falls : the Muse obeys the power,
> She comes ! she comes ! the sable throne behold
> Of night primæval and of Chaos old !
> Before her, fancy's gilded clouds decay,
> And all its varying rainbows die away.
> Wit shoots in vain its momentary fires,
> The meteor drops, and in a flash expires.
> As one by one, at dread Medea's strain,
> The sick'ning stars fade off th' ethereal plain ;
> As Argus' eyes by Hermes' wand opprest,
> Clos'd one by one to everlasting rest ;
> Thus at her felt approach, and secret might,
> Art after art goes out, and all is night.
> See skulking Truth to her old cavern fled,
> Mountains of casuistry heap'd o'er her head !
> Philosophy, that lean'd on Heav'n before,
> Shrinks to her second cause, and is no more.
> Physic of metaphysic begs defence,
> And metaphysic calls for aid on sense !
> See mystery to mathematics fly !
> In vain ! they gaze, turn giddy, rave, and die.
> Religion blushing veils her sacred fires,
> And unawares morality expires.
> For public flame, nor private, dares to shine ;
> Nor human spark is left, nor glimpse divine !
> Lo ! thy dread empire, Chaos ! is restor'd ;
> Light dies before thy uncreating word ;
> Thy hand, great Anarch ! lets the curtain fall,
> And universal darkness buries all."

For several years the anger of the Dunces gave Pope enough

to do, and from 1730 to 1737 he edited, more or less perfunctorily, a weekly paper, *The Grub Street Journal*, in which he and his satellites returned the shots which the victims of *The Dunciad* were still sullenly firing. During the same period Pope was at work on those extraordinary devices for getting his own private letters published, which have done his memory more harm with posterity than any other of his unfortunate lapses from the path of honesty. Into this dark and tortuous history we cannot be expected to look in this slight sketch of his poetical career. His next publication was the *Fourth Moral Essay* (December 1731), but it is convenient to leave the consideration of this poem for a moment. By this time a great ethical work, which had occupied Pope's best leisure for two or three years, was almost ready to be given to the public. Bolingbroke had formed a friendship with Pope in 1725, and had laid his scheme of deistical metaphysics before the poet in such a form as to gain his approval. Pope determined to versify Bolingbroke, but he only fulfilled so much of his scheme as is contained in the four books of his *Essay on Man*. Through 1730 and 1731 Pope was deeply engaged in revising and polishing this poem. In 1732-1733 three epistles were published in folio, and a fourth in 1734. They were strictly anonymous at first, and Pope circulated a report that they were written by a well-known divine.

The *Essay on Man* was long supposed to be what Dugald Stewart called it, the "noblest specimen of philosophical poetry which our language affords." It made Pope famous outside his native country, and won him the homage of men like Voltaire and Marmontel. The poet himself took a great pride in this composition, and thought that he had contributed very extensively to philosophical thought. At the present time it takes a lower place. The imagery with which the ethical framework is embroidered is by no means the most brilliant which Pope has produced. There is so great a confusion and want of connection in the system of reasoning that De Quincey is almost justified in his harsh judgment of it as "the realisation of anarchy." The poem contains examples of Pope's worst faults in the awkward construction of sentences and the inversion of words in the search for a rhyme. Nor is this poet's verse itself, in any other work of his maturity, so mechanical or dull. The *Essay on Man* is eloquent and impressive in parts, but it is executed on a plan which was unfavourable to the development of the author's most characteristic powers. It awakened, however, a great curiosity, has been more fruitful than any other of his writings in notes, commentaries, and general discussion, and won to its author's side the great mainstay of his later years, William Warburton, whose famous *Commentary* on the *Essay* first appeared in 1743.

From 1733 to 1738 Pope was very actively engaged on a variety of small works, kindred in manner, and all belonging to the class most congenial to his genius. Ten years earlier Atterbury had tried to persuade him that satire was his true forte, and the success of *The Dunciad* now gave him encouragement to become a didactic satirist. As early as December 1731 he published an epistle to Lord Burlington (*Epistle IV.*), the first of a long series of folio pamphlets. Six weeks later followed the epistle to Lord Bathurst (*Epistle III.*), in February 1733 the epistle to Sir R. Temple (*Epistle I.*), and in February 1735 that to Martha Blount (*Epistle II.*). These pieces, with an old address to Addison on his *Medals*, form the group called since 1743 *Moral Essays*. It has been thought that all this while the poet was scheming a great philosophical poem, of which, not only these epistles, but the *Essay on Man*, and the satirical imitations to be presently noticed, should eventually form part. The second epistle, as it now stands, contains the character of Atossa, which Pope meant for the Duchess of Marlborough, from whom he was accused of receiving the sum of £1000, that it might be suppressed. This is one of those very mysterious incidents, the general effect of which has been to bring great but perhaps exaggerated discredit on the good name of Pope. The third epistle is directed against the abuse of riches, and was written to gratify "that very lively and amiable old nobleman, the late Lord Bathurst." It contains the portrait of the Man of Ross, and is one of the most faultless and attractive of Pope's didactic writings. The fourth epistle continues the subject of the third, and may be referred to for those passages on landscape gardening which, beautiful as they are in themselves, and fine as examples of Pope's stately poetry, are still more important as showing how free Pope was from the worst heresies of the eighteenth century in its attitude towards nature. The episode of Villario, describing Lord Castlemaine's gardens at Wanstead, may be pointed to as an example of the skill which Pope had now attained in the giving maximum fulness of effect and complete artistic satisfaction in the minimum of space and with no apparent effort:

> "Behold Villario's ten years' toil complete;
> His quincunx darkens, his espaliers meet:
> The wood supports the plain, the parts unite,
> And strength of shade contends with strength of light;
> A waving glow the blooming beds display,
> Blushing in bright diversities of day,
> With silver-quivering rills meandered o'er,—
> Enjoy then, you! Villario can no more;
> Tired of the scene pastures and fountains yield,
> He finds at last he better likes a field."

The distinction between the *Moral Essays* and the rest of the ethical and satirical writings of Pope's third period is an entirely perfunctory and Warburtonian one, but it has been thought well to preserve it here on account of its time-honoured place in the arrangement of the poet's works. We must therefore return on our steps to chronicle the publication of one of his miscellaneous satires, that entitled *Satire I.*, brought out ten days after the *First Moral Essay* in February 1733. This is the earliest of the *Imitations of Horace*, undertaken by Pope at Bolingbroke's suggestion, and printed within a fortnight of its composition. It takes the form of a dialogue between the poet and William Fortescue, the lawyer, being a paraphrase of the first satire of the second book of Horace. This poem is a reply to the critics who had charged Pope with malignity in attack, and it professes that nothing but a passion for virtue inspires him. It also contains, alas! for virtue, a really monstrous attack on Lady Mary Wortley Montagu, for whom his early sweetness had long turned to gall.

Several important poems, of a more or less autobiographical character, bear date 1735. Of these the first in date as in value is the celebrated *Epistle to Dr. Arbuthnot*, published on the second day of the year. In this, the most fascinating of Pope's satirical poems, are brought together various fragments into one design, and even the character of Atticus is introduced, although it had already been before the world, in surreptitious form, for twelve years. The whole satire is a splendid apology and a dauntless fresh attack. It is difficult to award the palm to any one of its sections, either to the matchless description with which it opens, to the affecting account of the author's condition "through that long disease, his life," to the Atticus passage, or to the appalling chastisement inflicted, in verse that rings like a whip, on Bufo-Halifax and on Sporus-Harvey. The last of these shall be here selected:

"Let Sporus tremble—*A*. What! that thing of silk,
Sporus, that mere white curd of asses' milk?
Satire or sense, alas! can Sporus feel?
Who breaks a butterfly upon a wheel?
P. Yet let me flap this bug with gilded wings,
This painted child of dirt, that stinks and stings;
Whose buzz the witty and the fair annoys,
Yet wit ne'er tastes, and beauty ne'er enjoys:
So well-bred spaniels civilly delight
In mumbling of the game they dare not bite.
Eternal smiles his emptiness betray,
As shallow streams run dimpling all the way.
Whether in florid impotence he speaks,
And, as the prompter breathes, the puppet squeaks;
Or at the ear of Eve, familiar toad,
Half froth, half venom, spits himself abroad,
In puns, or politics, or tales, or lies,
Or spite, or smut, or rhymes, or blasphemies.
His wit all see-saw, between *that* and *this*,
Now high, now low, now master up, now miss,
And he himself one vile antithesis.
Amphibious thing! that acting either part,
The trifling head or the corrupted heart,

> Fop at the toilet, flatterer at the board,
> Now trips a Lady, and now struts a Lord.
> Eve's tempter thus the Rabbins have exprest,
> A cherub's face, a reptile all the rest;
> Beauty that shocks you, parts that none will trust,
> Wit that can creep, and pride that licks the dust."

In July appeared the *Second Satire*, a somewhat unfortunate discourse on temperance, and in the quarter of the same year two *Satires of Dr. Donne*, one of which had been anonymously printed in 1733. These paraphrases were not successful. Four more *Imitations* were presented to the public, separately, but in rapid succession, in 1737. Of these later satires we can say no more than that the perusal of them reminds the reader of the justice of Dr. Johnson's remark about "the irreconcilable dissimilitude between Roman images and English manners." Of the four the best certainly is the *First Epistle of the Second Book*, addressed to the king as Augustus. It was a very delicate and ambiguous attack on the court, and although it now seems obvious enough that the poet's eulogies were sarcastic, many stupid readers on its first appearance took it in all good faith as a panegyric on the royal party. It is mainly political, as being a manifesto from the Opposition, but it contains also some very interesting passages of literary criticism. Next year, in the summer of 1738, Pope published an epilogue to his satires, under the title *MDCCXXXVIII*. It was finished and brilliant, but the public had become a little weary of this incessant scolding, and Swift, who was now in retirement, expressed a very general feeling when he said that he knew so little of what was passing that he could not fathom the allusions nor fill out the initial letters. Pope wrote a fragment of one more satire, *1740*, but did not publish it. It was long afterwards given to the world by Warton. In 1742 he closed his literary career by the publication of *The New Dunciad*, of which we have already spoken. But his intellectual forces were unabated, and to the last he was polishing his old verses and preparing new editions.

Such a body as his, fretted by such a mind, was not destined for old age. But he was spared a slow decay. He lived on in tolerable ease, balanced between two dear friends of his, who were savage mutual enemies, Warburton and Bolingbroke, until the spring of 1744. He tried to console himself with literary interests for the disappointment of finding his contributions to political warfare politely neglected by his party. He had much to compose and please him; Martha Blount was now entirely with him, smoothing the close of an uneasy life, and in literature his empire was unquestioned. Throughout the month of May he was visibly dying of dropsy and asthma, and on the 30th of that month he passed away very quietly, at the age of fifty-six years and nine days. He was buried in a vault in Twickenham Church.

The amount of attention which has been paid to Pope since his death contrasts curiously with the comparative neglect of his great compeer, Dryden. The reason is, no doubt, that Dryden veiled his own personality in his works, while Pope, more than any other English poet, more even than Byron, impressed himself upon the public in every page he published. Throughout the eighteenth century he was admired with exaggeration; Warburton called him " one of the noblest works of God." Of late years, critics inspired by Wordsworth and De Quincey have no less unduly decried him. His fame reached its nadir in the hands of Mr. Elwin, who undertook to produce a final edition of the most eminent of our classical writers, although his own sympathies were exclusively and fanatically romantic. He was relieved of his task, which had become as painful to himself as to his readers, in 1881, when the volumes began to appear with the name of Mr. W. J. Courthope on the title-page. Mr. Courthope has nobly redeemed the character of the poet, as far as its radical faults would permit him to do so, and his work as an editor is of the first class. It is impossible to deny, and Mr. Courthope does not seek to deny, that since the publication of the Caryll correspondence Pope stands revealed, beyond any hope of justification, as an unscrupulous and intriguing trickster. But this is not the only side to his nature. He had great natural tenderness, extraordinary energy and courage, a passion for pure literature, and a genius second to none in its own class and period. In a sketch like this we may be permitted to insist on those splendid qualities rather than on the faults which he owed, in great measure, to his physical weakness.

The first thing which strikes us on a rapid survey of Pope's writings, is their fragmentary nature. They cannot be called fugitive, because he expended so much elaboration upon them, but none the less is it true that the only important work he completed was *The Rape of the Lock*. Even the Homer he could not finish without calling in foreign help. To the truncated *Dunciad* he gave a false air of completeness by patching on a new piece which does not match. The *Essay on Man*, and all the satires, imitations, and other essays are only disjointed members or scraps of one vast philosophical work which never saw the light. This fragmentary character matters less to us, because it is not his substance or his general effect which we delight in in Pope, but his details. His best poems are bits of mosaic, which we admire the most when we pull them to pieces, tessera by tessera, and analyse their exquisite workmanship. Much has been said, and very vainly said, about his want of originality, his commonplace, his triteness. The fact is that an old truth better said than any one has said it before, is more valuable, is certainly more likely to remain in men's minds, than a new truth awkwardly said. The charm of Pope's best passages, when it does not rest upon his Dutch picturesqueness of touch, is due to the intellectual pleasure given by his adroit and stimulating manner of producing his ideas, and by the astonishing exactitude and propriety of his phrase. When it is all summed up, we may not be much the wiser, but we are sure to be much the brighter and alerter. Hence it is an additional merit that his original writings, in which caustic wit takes so prominent a place, and in which the attention is always kept tensely on the strain, are usually quite short.

It is customary to compare Pope with his great French contemporary or predecessor, Boileau (1636-1711), whose rival Pope was willing to be considered. There are certain points of resemblance between them. Boileau followed La Fontaine, and completed his work in versification, somewhat as Pope followed Dryden. Boileau and Pope each made a very close study of Horace, and became ever more Horatian as they grew older. Each was the first satirist of his time, and each was excessively venomous and personal. Each wrote one very clever and notable mock-heroic poem. Each lifted up his scourge to smite the dunces off Parnassus. But the careful study of Boileau will teach us how much greater the English poet was than the French. Pope was Boileau with the addition of an ear for verse, of an eye for colour and form in *genre*, and of a real imaginative insight into character. What scarcely rose above talent in Boileau was genius in Pope. If, on the other hand, we compare Pope with Dryden, we notice, first of all, the entire absence of that lyrical gift which was so charming in Dryden. Pope's odes and hymns have not been chronicled here, for they are scarcely literature at all. We then notice that, with his superior lightness of intellect, the younger poet has moulded the heroic couplet more thoroughly to his purposes than Dryden ever did, first polishing it to the extreme of mellifluousness, and then teaching it to ring and sparkle with the utmost rapidity and brilliance. Pope's heroics are not only the best in the language, but they are so perfect that it has been impossible, since his day, to use that form—the iambic distich—without seeming intentionally to compete with Pope. He has no romance, no spirituality, no mystery, and the highest regions of poetry he never so much as dreams of; but in the lower provinces there is perhaps no single writer who showers fine things about him with such a prodigality of wit, or dazzles us so much with the mere exercise of his intelligence.

A great deal of other verse was written in the Augustan age, but not very much that can be admitted to be poetry. If this title cannot be conceded to the powerful octosyllabics of Swift, still more resolutely must it be denied to the verses of Defoe and Steele and Mandeville. But there flourished in the lifetime of

Pope one or two writers who deserve to be remembered as "Little Masters" in the art of verse—poets who were far inferior to Pope in intellect, and who yet possessed certain limited gifts in which they were original and in which they managed to surpass him. Of these attendant planets, for they were more than satellites, the three of greatest importance were Prior, Gay, and Parnell. Each of these men had a touch of genius in his composition, and each still holds a certain independence in the world of poetry.

Matthew Prior (1664-1721), except for a brush with Dryden in his youth, published nothing till he had reached middle age. His *Poems* appeared in modest form in 1709, and in a sumptuous folio in 1718. The longest of them is a didactic epic of *Solomon;* this takes the form of three very long sermons, or books, put in the mouth of the wisest of men. The poem has distinct merits; it is perhaps more "correct," in Walsh's sense, than any other in the language; but it cannot be read. This was the case in Prior's own day, and he fretted against the neglect of his masterpiece. *Alma* is also didactic, and also in three books, but here the measure is short and easy, and the poet mingles so much humour with the draught that we drink it willingly. In this poem Prior consciously follows Butler, to whom he pays a fine compliment; but his muse is more graceful, and less wayward. His occasional pieces prove that he had more variety and versatility than Butler, and he not unfrequently obtains an effect which was far above the reach of the author of *Hudibras*. His epigrams are the best we possess in English. He tells a story with unrivalled ease. His lyrics are inimitably gay and audacious. In comparison with Pope's, his epistles and satires are light and careless, but they often possess a great charm. A single stanza gives the very flavour of what is best and most unique in Prior, his gaiety, his unaffected grace, his easy humanity:

> "What I speak, my fair Chloe, and what I write, shows
>   The difference there is betwixt nature and art;
> I court others in verse, but I love thee in prose,
>   And they have my whimsies, but thou hast my heart."

There is a certain relation between Prior and John Gay (1685-1732). Each was successful mainly with the lighter lyre. Gay was perhaps the more important as a man of letters: Prior the more perfect in the work he did best, namely, his *vers de société*. Gay was the friend of all the best writers of his time— an amiable, plump, indolent man, who liked to nestle into warm sinecures in the families of people of quality. Pope used him as a cat's-paw in his quarrel with Ambrose Philips, and Gay's *Shepherd's Week* was published in 1714 to ridicule pastoral writing. But, in its gentle way, it was so excellent that it has survived not as a parody but as veritably the best collection of bucolics produced in the Augustan era, and none the worse for its humour. In 1716 Gay brought out *Trivia*, a sprightly poem on the art of walking the streets of London. In 1727 appeared the first series of his famous *Fables*, in 1728 the no less famous *Beggar's Opera*, suggested by Swift's remark, what "an odd, pretty sort of thing a Newgate pastoral might make," and in 1729 another opera, *Polly*, which enjoyed the advertisement of political persecution, and brought "poor inoffensive Gay" £1200. During these three golden years Gay's reputation, for the moment, almost equalled Pope's. He roused no jealousy, however, and Pope seems to have loved him best and longest among his immediate contemporaries. Gay's finest poetical work is his *Alexander Pope, his safe Return from Troy*, written, in *ottava-rima*, on occasion of Pope's completion of his *Iliad*, but not published till 1776. Here is a fragment of it:

    "Oh, what a concourse swarms on yonder quay!
      The sky re-echoes with new shouts of joy:
    By all this show, I ween, 'tis Lord Mayor's day;
      I hear the voice of trumpet and hautboy.—
    No, now I see them near! Oh, these are they
      Who come in crowds to welcome thee from Troy.
    Hail to the bard whom long as lost we mourn'd,
    From siege, from battle, and from storm return'd!

    Of goodly dames, and courteous knights, I view
      The silken petticoat, and broider'd vest;
    Yea, peers, and mighty dukes, with ribands blue,
      (True blue, fair emblem of unstained breast;)

> Others I see, as noble, and more true,
>   By no court-badge distinguish'd from the rest
> First see I Methuen, of sincerest mind,
> As Arthur brave, as soft as woman-kind.
>
> What lady's that, to whom he gently bends?
>   Who knows her not? ah! those are Wortley's eyes!
> How art thou honour'd, number'd with her friends,
>   For she distinguishes the good and wise.
> The sweet-tongued Murray near her side attends.
>   Now to my heart the glance of Howard flies;
> Now Hervey, fair of face, I mark full well,
> With thee, Youth's youngest daughter, sweet Lepell.
>
> I see two lovely sisters, hand in hand,
>   The fair-hair'd Martha and Teresa brown;
> Madge Bellenden, the tallest of the land;
>   And smiling Mary, soft and fair as down.
> Yonder I see the cheerful Duchess stand,
>   For friendship, zeal, and blithesome humours known:
> Whence that loud shout in such a hearty strain?
> Why all the Hamiltons are in her train!"

"'Twas when the seas were roaring" and "Black-eyed Susan" have placed Gay among British lyrists. He had great humour, and a genuine love of external nature which links him with the romantic writers.

The two last-mentioned poets succeeded best in jocose verse; Thomas Parnell (1679-1718), Archdeacon of Clogher, who also endeavoured to be merry, was best inspired when he was grave or even elegiacal. We know little of his life. Pope discovered him, buried in an Ulster parsonage, and stimulated him to write. Swift brought him up to town, and insisted on presenting him to Harley. Parnell's best pieces all belong to the period between 1713, when he came under Pope's influence, and his early death in 1718. Yet Parnell cannot be called a disciple of Pope; within the narrow range of what he did well there was no poetical writer of his time who showed a greater originality. *The Hermit* is a very perfect piece of sententious narrative work in the heroic couplet, not easily to be matched for polish, elegance, and symmetry. Parnell's remarkable odes, *The Night Piece* and *The Hymn to Contentment*, however, possess more real inspiration. They form a link between Milton on the one hand and Gray and Collins on the other, and their employment of the octosyllabic measure is wonderfully subtle and harmonious. The *Hymn* contains these lines:

> "The silent heart, which grief assails,
> Treads soft and lonesome o'er the vales,
> Sees daisies open, rivers run,
> And seeks, as I have vainly done,
> Amusing thought; but learns to know
> That solitude's the nurse of woe.
> No real happiness is found
> In trailing purple o'er the ground;
> Or in a soul exalted high,
> To range the circuit of the sky,
> Converse with stars above, and know
> All nature in its forms below;
> The rest it seeks, in seeking dies,
> And doubts at last, for knowledge, rise."

It would be easy to sustain the thesis that there is more of imagination, in the purely Wordsworthian sense, more of mystery and spirituality, in Parnell than in any other poet of the time. He was very diffident, and published nothing; but in 1722 Pope collected his posthumous pieces into a volume to which he prefixed a fine dedication, the only fault of which is that it contains too little about the dead Parnell and too much about the living Harley to whom, as the muse "shaded his evening walk with bays," the volume was inscribed.

Among the wits and templars who surrounded Addison many wrote verses, but few wrote them particularly well. Three of his chief friends, however, stand out beyond the rest with some recognised claim to the title of poet. Ambrose Philips (1671-1749) is chiefly remembered on account of his dispute with Pope about the merit of their rival pastorals. Philips wrote, from Copenhagen, an *Epistle to the Earl of Dorset*, which was once admired; and, towards the close of his career, he composed a number of birthday odes to children of quality, in a seven-syllabled measure, which earned him the name of "Namby-Pamby," but which form, in their infantile, or servile, prettiness, his main claim to distinction. Thomas Tickell (1686-1740) is a man of one poem; he composed a really superb elegy, inspired by deep and genuine feeling, on the death of Addison:

> "Can I forget the dismal night, that gave
> My soul's best part for ever to the grave!
> How silent did his old companions tread,
> By mid-night lamps, the mansions of the dead,
> Thro' breathing statues, then unheeded things,
> Thro' rows of warriors, and thro' walks of kings!
> What awe did the slow solemn knell inspire;
> The pealing organ, and the pausing choir;
> The duties by the lawn-robed prelate payed;
> And the last words, that dust to dust conveyed!
> While speechless o'er thy closing grave we bend,
> Accept these tears, thou dear departed friend,
> Oh gone for ever, take this long adieu;
> And sleep in peace, next thy loved Montagu!"

William Somerville (1675-1742) was more interesting as a man than either Tickell or Philips. He was a fox-hunting Warwickshire squire, who used to come up to town periodically to worship Mr. Addison, and who rather late in life ventured upon verse of his own. His chief poem, *The Chase* (1735), is a didactic epic, in four books of blank verse, on the art of hunting with the hounds. He delayed writing it so long that we find his old Addisonian style tempered by the new and freer manner of Thomson. Somerville, in fact, is one of the few transitional figures of the end of this period.

Dr. Samuel Croxall (1680?-1752) published anonymously in 1720 *The Fair Circassian*, a paraphrase of the Canticles. He had previously issued two cantos in imitation of the *Faery Queen*. Croxall was blamed for the voluptuous warmth of his verses, which was indeed something extraordinary from the pen of an embryo canon residentiary. He translated Æsop in 1722. He described his poetical ambition rather too arrogantly, when he said that his aim was "to set off the dry and insipid stuff" of the age by publishing "a whole piece of rich glowing scarlet." Two stanzas from his utterly neglected poetry will show how little Croxall shared the manner of his contemporaries:

> " Unlock the tresses of your burnish'd hair,
>   Loose let your ringlets o'er your shoulders spread ;
> Thus mix'd, we view them more distinctly fair,
>   Like trails of golden wire on ivory laid ;
> So Phœbus o'er the yielding ether streams,
> And streaks the silver clouds with brighter beams.
>
> What rosy odours your soft bosom yields,
>   Heaving and falling gently as you breathe !
> Like hills that rise amidst fair fertile fields,
>   With round smooth tops and flowery vales beneath ;
> So swell the candid Alps with fleecy snow,
> While myrtles bud, and violets bloom below."

The long life of Allan Ramsay (1686-1758), the Edinburgh wig-maker, projects beyond that of Pope at both ends. He gave up the outside of the head for the inside by becoming a bookseller and a publisher; from his shop at the sign of the Mercury he regarded the wits of distant London with almost superstitious reverence. He wrote a great deal of absolute rubbish, but his pastoral drama of *The Gentle Shepherd* (1725) is the best British specimen of its class, and contains some very beautiful passages both of dialogue and of description. Most of Ramsay's original songs were poor, but he preserved the habit of writing in the Doric dialect, and as an editor and collector of national poetry he did thoroughly efficient and valuable work. His two miscellanies, *The Tea-Table* and *The Evergreen*, were not without their direct usefulness in preparing the Scottish ear for Burns.

CHAPTER V

SWIFT AND THE DEISTS

THREE years before the close of the seventeenth century two short works were ready for publication, which a mere accident postponed into the age of Anne. At the darkest moment of English literature, when every branch of original writing except comedy seemed dying or dead, a genius of the very first order was preparing for the press *The Battle of the Books* and *A Tale of a Tub*. It is desirable to remember that these works were complete in 1697, although not published until 1704, since the fact emphasises Swift's precedence of all the other wits of the reign of Anne. It cannot, indeed, be too strongly insisted upon that he was the leader of their chorus. In poetry, Pope, though stimulated and sustained by his sympathy, was quite independent of Swift; but the masters of prose, the great essayists, did not begin to flourish till his mighty spirit had breathed upon them. Swift is the dominant intellectual figure of the first half of the century, as Johnson of the second, and it is hard to deny that he is altogether greater than Johnson. He is original in the first degree. His personal character is such as to illuminate, or else obscure, every other individual that meets him. Swift's love or Swift's hatred colours our conception of every important literary figure of his age. If the *saeva indignatio* which he so adroitly indicated in his own draft of an epitaph has been over-insisted upon, no one can deny or evade the *splendida bilis*. The magnificence of Swift's anger, scintillating with wit, glowing with passion, throws its cometary splendour right across the Augustan heavens. There was an almost superhuman greatness about his cruelty, a feline charm in his caresses, a childishness, like the merriment of a tiger-cub, in his humour; he was irresponsible and terrible; his ambition threw dice with his reckless waggishness, till all was lost and won. He was the most unhappy, the most disappointed man of his age, and yet the greatest and the most illustrious. He is altogether wonderful and inscrutable, a bundle of paradoxes, the object of universal curiosity, the repulsion of the many, the impassioned worship of the few.

Jonathan Swift, "the great Irish patriot," had nothing Irish about him except the accident of being born in Dublin. His father was a Herefordshire man, and his mother was a Leicestershire woman. The elder Jonathan Swift was made steward to the Society of the King's Inns, Dublin, in 1666, and there died about a year afterwards. Some months later his widow bore him a posthumous son, on the 30th of November 1667, and this was the famous writer. His mother was reduced to great poverty, and had to be supported by the charity of her husband's brothers, Godwin and Dryden Swift. As an infant Swift was stolen by his nurse and carried to Whitehaven; his mother, enervated by distress, seems to have acquiesced in this exile for three years, during which time she lodged once more with her relatives in Leicestershire. From 1674 to 1682 Swift was being educated at Kilkenny, the most famous of Irish schools, where Congreve was one of his companions. He was only fourteen when he was removed from Kilkenny to be entered at Trinity College, Dublin, where he stayed until the Revolution of 1688. His college career was not distinguished. He tells us that "he was so discouraged and sunk in his spirits that he neglected his academic studies," and "was stopped of his degree for dulness and insufficiency." He was made a B.A. in 1686, by *special grace*, which he chose to consider a humiliating distinction in such a case as his. Circumstances seem to have made him reckless, and the remainder of his college course is marked by penalty after penalty incurred for riotous behaviour. He read nothing but history and poetry, and probably the crisis of 1688 came only just in time to save him from final expulsion. Destitute and friendless, Swift fled to his only less destitute mother in Leicestershire. This lady remembered that the wealthy and urbane Sir William Temple was her relative, and to him she applied for patronage with success.

Temple accepted the raw young student to read to him and be his amanuensis. But Swift's manners were uncouth, and he had no address which could ingratiate him with the most elegant of living Englishmen. It seems probable that Temple slowly learned to value Swift, but at first his patronage of him must have been merely the observance of a duty claimed by family ties. The young man's health was very bad, and in 1689, after a surfeit of golden pippins, he began to be a sufferer from the mysterious disease of his lifetime, which, as modern science has conjectured, became what is now called a labyrinthine vertigo. After a short visit to Ireland he returned to Temple's service, and on terms more honourable and confidential. Presently the king became aware of his existence, and promised him vague promotion in the army or in the church. When he took his degree of M.A. at Oxford in 1692 he had reputation enough, reflected from the glory of Temple, to meet with a warm reception, and now, at the age of twenty-five, he occasionally versified. His four *Pindaric Odes*, unlucky compositions in the worst manner of Cowley, were his first literary production; with one exception, these did not see the light till a century later, but they were shown to Dryden, who was Swift's relative, and were slain in the cradle by the famous rejoinder, "Cousin Swift, you will never be a poet," or, according to another and more credible report, "a Pindaric poet." In spite of Swift's eager ambition he seems to have written little in these early years, and to have had less desire to print. In the house of Temple he was at the centre of tradition, where anything new, anything not in strict accordance with Gallic taste, must have been contemptuously frowned upon. The fact that

Temple wrote so well and was held to be so fine a literary oracle must in itself have vexed and paralysed a man whose instincts lay in the direction of novel and unlicensed literary forms. In May 1694 he broke the strained cord which bound him to Sir William Temple's household, and returned to Ireland. Eight months later he had taken priest's orders in Dublin, and had obtained the small living of Kilroot in Downshire. While there he met Miss Waring (Varina) at Belfast. He soon became disgusted with solitude at Kilroot, and in May 1696 he went back to Temple's household at Moor Park. Thus a third time the experiment was tried, and now without further vexation. Swift and his patron had learned, if not to love, at least to respect and admire each other. The young clergyman presently resigned his living in favour of a friend, and continued to reside at Moor Park till Temple died in 1699.

This final residence with Temple coincided with Swift's first serious development as a writer. The year 1696-97, the thirtieth of Swift's life, seems to be that in which he first waked up to a consciousness of his original talents. The *Tale of a Tub* has been attributed to an earlier date, but upon no trustworthy evidence, and Swift in 1709 asserted that it was written in 1696 and 1697. That *The Battle of the Books* belongs to the latter year we know, and the resemblance in style between the two works is so close as to suggest that there was no interval between their composition. They seem to be pieces of the self-same mental fabric. To 1697 also belong Swift's earliest characteristic verses, and this year of active production is followed by four of apparent sterility. It seems therefore desirable to discuss the two remarkable prose works which have been just mentioned before proceeding any further with the life of their author, instead of waiting for the date of their publication, in an anonymous octavo volume, in 1704. They were prepared to issue from the press in the winter of 1698, when Temple's illness and death postponed their publication. It is uncertain whether Swift wrote or only proposed to write the other facetious treatises which he announced on the fly-leaf of the

Tale of a Tub. His own phrase is, "Finding my commonplace book fill much slower than I had reason to expect, I have chosen to defer them to another occasion." Probably this means that the sprightly flow of inspiration in 1696-97 dried up for the time being before he had done more than sketch his *General History of Ears*, and his *Critical Essay upon the Art of Canting.*

The very extraordinary treatise called *A Tale of a Tub* is allowed to rank among the first of its author's productions. It displays his finest qualities of imagination and irony when they were in their freshest and most ebullient condition. Swift himself is said to have remarked, at the close of his life, "Good God, what a genius I had when I wrote that book." It is not long, and it is divided into so many varied sections that it seems shorter than it is. The reader is carried along so gaily on this buoyant tide of wit, that he puts the book down with regret to find it ended, when it seemed but just begun. In this, *A Tale of a Tub* forms a surprising contrast to almost all the prose which had preceded it for half a century, the writers of the Restoration, even where they are most correct and graceful, being devoid of this particular sparkle and crispness of phrase. The book is an allegorical romance, but surrounded by so many digressions, one outside the other, like the parts of an ivory puzzle-ball, that scarcely half of it is even nominally narrative. The name is given from the supposed custom of sailors to throw a tub to a whale to prevent him from rolling against their ship; the treatise being a tub for the leviathans of scepticism to sport with, instead of disturbing the orthodox commonwealth. There is an adroit dedication to Lord Somers, and another to the reader, each supposed to be written by the publisher; and then follows the famous and entirely delightful dedication to Prince Posterity, a little masterpiece in Swift's peculiar vein of half humorous, half bitter irony. Part of this address may be selected as a specimen of the style of the book:

"To affirm that our age is altogether unlearned, and devoid of writers in any kind, seems to be an assertion so bold and so false, that I have been sometime thinking the contrary may almost be proved by uncontrollable demonstration. 'Tis true indeed, that although their numbers be vast, and their productions numerous in proportion, yet are they hurried so hastily off the scene, that they escape our memory, and delude our sight. When I first thought of this address, I had prepared a copious list of titles to present your Highness as an undisputed argument for what I affirm. The originals were posted fresh upon all gates and corners of streets; but returning in a few hours to take a review, they were all torn down, and fresh ones in their places; I inquired after them among readers and booksellers, but I inquired in vain, the 'memorial of them was lost among men, their place was no more to be found;' and I was laughed to scorn, for a clown and a pedant, devoid of all taste and refinement, little versed in the course of present affairs, and that knew nothing of what had passed in the best companies of court and town. So that I can only avow in general to your Highness, that we do abound in learning and wit; but to fix upon particulars, is a task too slippery for my slender abilities. If I should venture in a windy day, to affirm to your Highness, that there is a large cloud near the horizon in the form of a bear, another in the zenith with the head of an ass, a third to the westward with claws like a dragon; and your Highness should in a few minutes think fit to examine the truth? 'tis certain, they would be all changed in figure and position, new ones would arise, and all we could agree upon would be, that clouds there were, but that I was grossly mistaken in the zoography and topography of them."

Then we have the author's preface, where the satire is more trenchant, although it is here that Swift quietly regrets that he has "neither a talent nor an inclination for satire"; *A Tale of a Tub* is then introduced, but not until we have been treated to a couple of disquisitions, one on oratorical machines, and the other on the humours of Grub Street. With Section II. the genuine business begins. We have the father who dies, and leaves legacies under a will to his three sons, Peter (the Church of Rome), Martin (the Church of England), and Jack (the Dissenters). The description of these sons, and how they wilfully misinterpreted their father's expressed injunctions, was dangerous ground, and Swift sailed very near the wind. He tried to be discreet in dealing with Martin, and to let him down very gently, but his whole tone was obviously irreverent. As Rivarol says, "L'impiété est une indiscretion," and this Swift found to be true. It was *A Tale of a Tub* which shattered his ambition, and kept him in perpetuity out of the

House of Peers. The whole world laughed over Section IX., but the man who wrote it could hardly be made Bishop of Hereford.

Interspersed between the fragments of the narrative are certain digressions which are delightful reading. Section III. contains the "Digression concerning Critics"; Section V. goes into the silly dispute regarding the relative merits of the ancients and the moderns, as slyly as Sir William Temple's secretary could venture to do; Section IX. is the terrible dissertation on madness, which displays for the first time that strange passion of Swift's for depicting the phenomena of agony and disease, as well as his fondness for mere filth; Section X., somewhat in the tone which Voltaire afterwards adopted in *Candide*, propounds a ridiculous optimism as regards the relation of author to publisher. In later editions than the first, a supplementary history of Martin is added, of inferior merit. It is better to consider the work as closing, as it did in 1704, with the charming little essay in which Swift pretends that he is trying the "experiment very frequent among modern authors, which is to write upon nothing; when the subject is utterly exhausted, to let the pen still move on, by some called the ghost of wit, delighting to walk after the death of its body." This fitly closes a desultory narrative, the central body of which is not very just nor extremely ingenious, but tricked out with every ornament which fancy, humour, invention, and daring could suggest.

In *A Tale of a Tub* the intellectual interest never halts for a moment. There is infinite variety, and the reader is tantalised by the prodigality of wit, never fatigued for a moment by its expression. In pure style Swift never excelled this his first important essay. The polemical and humorous parts are direct and terse beyond anything that had preceded them in English, and when the author permits himself for a moment to be serious, he speaks with the tongue of angels. In the midst of the profane section on the Æolists, there is a page which reaches as far as our language can reach in the direction of dignity and music; and at all times it may be noted that Swift in this work and in *The Battle of the Books* is more picturesque than anywhere else. His admirable style became a little less peculiarly and uniquely his own as he proceeded in life, and as he competed with Addison and Shaftesbury. Hence *Gulliver's Travels*, being a little more in the ordinary language of Swift's later days, strikes us as somewhat less highly-coloured than these earliest treatises, where he is absolutely himself.

The Battle of the Books holds an incidental place in the great Phalaris controversy, although it came somewhat late in the day. It was written to support Temple, who had been rather hard hit by Bentley and by William Wotton (1666-1726) in their *Reflections upon Ancient and Modern Learning*. Swift, as in duty bound, is marshalled in the ranks of the ancients, by Temple's side, and he makes shift to attack literary pretension in the person of a spider, whose castle "is all built with my own hands, and the materials extracted altogether out of my own person." The bee, the lover of antiquity, is "obliged to Heaven alone for my flights and my music." With our present views in criticism, it may seem that the Ancient should have been the spider and the Modern the bee, and Swift is very possibly laughing at his own allies in his sleeve. The narrative, which is what was then called a "travesty," is supposed to be a "full and true account of the battle fought last Friday between the ancient and the modern books in St. James's library," of which Bentley was librarian, and we are to believe that the books themselves, being infected with the controversy raging outside, came to a decisive battle by flying at each other's heads; "but the manuscript, by the injury of fortune or weather, being in several places imperfect,"—a trick of composition which Swift loved to indulge in,—"we cannot learn to which side the victory fell."

There has been litigation between those upper and lower peaks of Parnassus, on which the ancients and moderns respectively reside, and Bentley, a famous warrior among the latter, has vowed to compass the death of two valiant ancients, Phalaris and Æsop.

He is baffled, and retires to his library, where the books range themselves into two ranks, and a new Trojan war breaks out, in which great advantage is gained to the ancients by the defection to their side of Temple, who becomes their champion. Before the battle is described, the apologue of the Spider and the Bee is introduced, illustrating allegory by still subtler allegory. When this is over, Æsop rallies the ancients to the attack; they are gaining the day too easily when the horrible goddess Criticism, in a chariot drawn by geese, arrives at St. James's, and rushes into the fray in the guise of one of Bentley's pamphlets. The battle now becomes Homeric, and great heroes plunge into the fray on either hand; Aristotle lets an arrow fly at Bacon, but misses him and kills Descartes; Homer tramples Davenant in the dirt, and Virgil spares the life of Dryden, while the book closes with the exquisitely diverting episode of Bentley and Wotton. In the 1704 edition, *The Battle of the Books* was followed by the ironical fragment called *The Mechanical Operation of the Spirit*, an exposure of fanaticism which was, to say the least, indiscreet in the mouth of a young ecclesiastic eagerly ambitious to rise in the Church of England. Each of these treatises shows a great freedom from prejudice, a boundless impatience of humbug and pretension, and a savage touch which is all the more brutal because of the delicacy, keenness, and power of sympathy, of which the author shows himself inherently capable upon every page.

With these astonishing productions in his portfolio, Swift went to Ireland in 1699, and after several clerical disappointments, became chaplain to Lord Berkeley in Dublin. In 1700 he received Laracor, and one or two other small livings, upon which he could barely have supported himself had he not retained his Castle chaplaincy; in 1701 Esther Johnson, the famous Stella, joined him in Ireland. For the ladies of Lord Berkeley's family he conceived a great affection, and it was to amuse them that he wrote some of his most delightful trifles, the *Petition of Frances Harris*, in 1700, in verse, and the *Meditation upon a Broomstick*, in 1704, in prose. The second of these, a moral meditation in the style and manner of that eminent philosopher, the Hon. Robert Boyle, opens as follows :

"This single stick, which you now behold ingloriously lying in that neglected corner, I once knew in a flourishing state in a forest. It was full of sap, full of leaves, and full of boughs. But now, in vain does the busy art of man pretend to vie with nature, by tieing that withered bundle of twigs to its sapless trunk. 'Tis now at best but the reverse of what it was, a tree turned upside down, the branches on the earth, and the root in the air. 'Tis now handled by every dirty wench, condemned to do her drudgery, and, by a capricious kind of fate, destined to make other things clean, and to be nasty itself. At length, worn to the stumps in the service of the maids, 'tis either thrown out of doors, or condemned to the last use of kindling a fire. When I beheld this, I sighed, and said to myself, *Surely mortal man is a broom-stick*. Nature sent him into the world strong and lusty, in a thriving condition, wearing his own hair on his head, the proper branches of this reasoning vegetable, till the axe of intemperance has lopped off his green boughs, and left him a withered trunk. He then flies to art, and puts on a periwig, valuing himself upon an unnatural bundle of hairs, all covered with powder, that never grew on his head. But now should this our broomstick pretend to enter the scene, proud of those birchen spoils it never bore, and all covered with dust, though the sweepings of the finest lady's chamber, we should be apt to ridicule and despise its vanity. Partial judges that we are of our own excellencies, and other men's defaults!"

In 1701 Swift spent six months in England, and during that time made his first appearance as an author, at the age of thirty-four, by the publication of his *Contests and Dissensions in Athens and Rome*. This pamphlet was called forth by the impeachment of Lord Somers by the House of Commons; Swift took the side of the Whig peers very strenuously, and during the lull caused by the summer recess published this grave and learned catalogue of instances of factious tyranny by democratic bodies in Greece and Rome. He held his satiric pen under close control, and there is no trace of his peculiar humour until within a page or two of the close. The pamphlet, which was anonymous, was very successful; rumour attributed it confidently to Burnet, but the bishop was prompt in denial, and in 1702 Swift was making no secret of the authorship, which ingratiated him with the Whigs. He was now desirous of gaining political influence, but his position was a little difficult, for he was a Whig and yet at the same time a high-churchman. Going and coming between Laracor and London, he ceases to contribute much to literature until the year 1708; we find him, however, about 1705, and apparently through the good offices of Congreve, becoming acquainted with Addison and his little senate at Will's coffee-house.

In the year 1708, at the age of forty-two, Swift turned seriously to occasional literature as a means of obtaining and exercising political power. He became the greatest of pamphleteers, taking up the line opened by Lord Halifax in the preceding generation, but working it with more vigour and directness. The *Sentiments of a Church of England Man* (1708) is something more than a pamphlet. It is a treatise, in two sections, on the merits of political and religious moderation, and, above all, on the error of advancing opinions merely because those are the opinions of a certain party, as though a party were an order of friars. The argument was clear and admirably grave, but there were certain strictures upon the Dissenters of which the Whig leaders could not approve. In *An Argument against Abolishing Christianity* (1708), Swift gave the reins again to his humour, and pretended to argue gravely against the proposal to laicise the revenues of the Church of England for the purpose of endowing the research of two hundred elegant young sceptics. Swift was never more spirited than in this daring attack upon the Deists:

"If Christianity were once abolished, how could the free-thinkers, the strong reasoners, and the men of profound learning, be able to find another subject so calculated in all points whereon to display their abilities? What wonderful productions of wit should we be deprived of from those whose genius by continual practice hath been wholly turned upon raillery and invectives against religion, and would therefore never be able to shine or distinguish themselves upon any other subject? We are daily complaining of the great decline of wit among us, and would we take away the greatest, perhaps the only topic we have left? Who would ever have suspected Asgill for a wit, or Toland for a philosopher, if the inexhaustible stock of Christianity had not been at hand to provide them with material? What other subject through all art or nature could have produced Tindal for a profound author, or furnished him with readers? It is the wise choice of the subject that alone adorns and distinguishes the writer. For, had a hundred such pens as these been employed on the side of religion, they would have immediately sunk into silence and oblivion."

This sort of irony was perilous stuff, and not a few of the "daggle-tailed parsons" failed to understand that this compromising champion was fighting upon their side. Without laying aside his irony, Swift adopted a loftier tone in his *Project for the Advancement of Religion* (1709). This tract, which was recommended by a charming dedication to Lady Berkeley, is a very powerful indictment of the age for its open and impudent debauchery, and contains a proposal that the Government should appoint a sort of proctors, to subdivide the country between them, and keep guard over the popular morals. Swift denounces society with an obvious sincerity, inspired by a fiery indignation against wickedness, but yet, as the *Tatler* observed, he writes like a gentleman, and not like a vulgar fanatic. He felt, himself, that the wisdom of making the particular reforms he suggested was questionable, but that some sort of remedy was called for by the scandal of the times he pronounced to be absolutely outside discussion. Queen Anne and the Archbishop of York read the tract and were gratified; but nothing was done, either for morality or for Swift.

In the midst of these grave disquisitions, Swift amused himself with the celebrated group of squibs or practical jokes upon the astrologer John Partridge. This man had for thirty years published prophetic almanacs, of the kind not yet wholly extinct. Swift, under the pseudonym of Isaac Bickerstaff, published *Predictions for the year 1708*, which were not vague like those of Partridge, but gave the exact dates at which various interesting persons, among others Louis XIV., would die during that year. Bickerstaff declared himself a sincere astrologer, bent on the exposure of such frauds as the Merlins of the day. He prophesied, incidentally, that Partridge would die on the 29th of March, at about eleven at night. As soon as that date was past, Swift issued another pamphlet giving *An Account of Partridge's Death* in very pathetic terms. The poor astrologer hastened to assure the world that he was still alive, upon which Swift promptly reproved him in a *Vindication of Isaac Bickerstaff* (1709), and in a black-letter *Merlin's Prophecy*. Swift seems to have thrown himself body and soul into this ludicrous and fantastic controversy, and to have summoned contributions to it from Steele, Congreve, Thomas Yalden (1671-1736), and Prior. It raged for two years, and Partridge was reduced to despair; he lived on, however, until 1715. A remote consequence of this astrological absurdity was the foundation of the *Tatler*, produced, as we shall see in the next chapter, under the pseudonym of Isaac Bickerstaff. It has been held of late that the Partridge squibs of Swift are not in good taste, nor very funny. The present writer can only confess to finding them among the most laughable productions in the English language, and to thinking such an impostor as John Partridge only too much honoured by the coruscations of Swift's magnificent facetiousness.

In 1708 Swift prepared a volume of *Miscellanies* for the press, and then abandoned the project. We possess, however, a catalogue of the intended contents, and we find them much the same as those of Morphew's piracy, or half-piracy, in 1711. That volume contained the writings we have mentioned, and, in addition, the *Letter on the Sacramental Test*, of 1708. This celebrated tract, like most of Swift's publications, was anonymous, but in this case the author was particularly anxious to be unknown. He even introduced an allusion to himself and affected to be displeased with it; but the authorship was soon found out, and Swift attributes to the pages of this pamphlet the growing coldness with which the Whigs regarded him. Sir Leslie Stephen has happily summed up Swift's rather puzzling attitude with regard to this *Letter* by saying that "he thought the Whigs scoundrels for not patronising him, and not the less scoundrels because their conduct was consistent with their own scoundrelly principles." The rest of the volume of 1708-1711 is made up of verses, short pedestrian pieces, full of spirit and humour, including, besides what have been already mentioned, the lampoons against Vanbrugh, the architect-dramatist; *The Salamander*, a satire on Lord Cutts; *Baucis and*

Philemon, the most ambitious of Swift's early poems, written in 1706, a very elegant and entertaining imitation of Ovid, rigorously revised by Addison; the compliment to *Mrs. Biddy Floyd*, very gracefully turned; a *Grub Street Elegy on Partridge; A Description of a City Shower*, a marvellously realistic study, in heroics, touched with a pencil which might provoke the envy of M. Zola; and *Sid Hamet's Rod*, a terrible celebration of the mode in which Godolphin broke his treasurer's staff "like naughty lad." Several of the best known of these verses were written for the *Tatler*. In these poems Swift has not the same lightness of touch as certain of his younger contemporaries, but he is splendidly direct, vivid, and vigorous, his lines fall like well-directed blows of the flail, and he gives the octosyllabic measure, which he is accustomed to choose on account of the Hudibrastic opportunities it offers, a character which is entirely his own. It is difficult to quote the most effective passages from Swift's poems, but there is nothing too malodorous for delicate nerves in this page from the *City Shower*:

> "Now in contiguous drops the flood comes down,
> Threatening with deluge this devoted town.
> To shops in crowds the daggled females fly,
> Pretend to cheapen goods, but nothing buy.
> The Templar spruce, while every spout's abroach,
> Stays till 'tis fair, yet seems to call a coach.
> The tuck'd-up sempstress walks with hasty strides,
> While streams run down her oil'd umbrella's sides.
> Here various kinds, by various fortunes led,
> Commence acquaintance underneath a shed.
> Triumphant Tories, and desponding Whigs,
> Forget their feuds, and join to save their wigs.
> Box'd in a chair the Beau impatient sits,
> While spouts run clattering o'er the roof by fits,
> And ever and anon with frightful din
> The leather sounds; he trembles from within.
> So when Troy chairmen bore the wooden steed,
> Pregnant with Greeks impatient to be freed,
> (Those bully Greeks, who, as the moderns do,
> Instead of paying chairmen, ran them through,)
> Laocoon struck the outside with his spear,
> And each imprison'd hero quaked for fear."

With the publication of the *Miscellanies* in 1711, the first period of Swift's strictly literary life closes. He is almost entirely absorbed by politics and by political pamphleteering for the next few years. Over this interesting section of his biography it is necessary that we should pass very hastily in the present sketch.

Two women, as all the world knows, enjoyed the correspondence and the confidential friendship of Swift. "Stella" (Esther Johnson—1681-1728) has been already mentioned. In 1708 he made the acquaintance of "Vanessa" (Hester Vanhomerigh, pronounced Vanummery—1691-1723). The famous *Journal to Stella*, a collection of private documents which throw a marvellous light on the central portion of Swift's history, was kept from September 2, 1710, to June 6, 1713. The world has scarcely seen another so intimate revelation of himself by any man of genius. The result is scarcely literature, but, if it may be said so, something very artless and familiar, which is, for the nonce, rather better than literature. It was begun on the occasion of Swift's visit to London as the confidential solicitor of the Irish bishops, petitioning Queen Anne for first-fruits, a visit which coincided with the fall of the Whig ministry of Somers and Godolphin. This period was the heyday of Swift's personal success as a wire-puller, and during three years he sent Miss Johnson (Stella) a daily chronicle of his minutest doings and sayings. As is well known, though the cause of such reticence is still obscure, Swift was extremely cautious in his relations to women, and caressing as these familiar entries are, they are nominally addressed not to Stella only, but to Miss Dingley, her companion, as well. Much of the *Journal* is written in what the writer calls a "little language"; a sort of lovers' whisper, or sentimental shorthand. Mr. Forster was the first person who dared to give this jargon, the purr of the tiger, verbatim. Here is a passage which looks more than usually formidable, but which may easily be deciphered:

"I came back just by nightfall, cruel cold weather. I have no smell yet, but my cold's something better. Nite dee sollahs, I'll take my reeve. I forget how MD's accounts are. Go, play cards, and be melly, deelest logues, and

Rove Pdfr.—Nite michar MD, FW, oo roves Pdfr.—FW, Lele, lele, ME, ME, MD, MD, MD, MD, MD, MD, MD, FW, FW, FW, ME, ME, FW, FW, FW, FW, ME, ME, ME. The six odd shillings, tell Mrs. B—, are for her New Year's gift. Lele, lele, lele and lele."

A study of the *Journal to Stella* is indispensable to a knowledge of Swift; it exhibits fantastic and tender facets of his character which we should hardly suspect but for its existence; and side by side with these affectionate puerilities are found recorded his gravest thoughts and wildest ambitions. One of the earliest facts which he has to announce to Stella is his introduction to Harley, with whom, and with St. John, he was speedily on terms of intimacy; so that on the 14th of October he was able to boast, that "I stand with the new people ten times better than ever I did with the old, and forty times more caressed." He was now launched on the support of the new Tory party. In November 1710 Swift took up the editorship of the *Examiner*, which had been a Whig paper, and carried it on with extraordinary vehemence and satiric power until June of the following year. His assistance to Harley's administration was immense, and it was the more valued because Swift refused all remuneration for his services. The *Examiner* formed a fortress in which the ministry stood on their isthmus between the old Tories and the Whigs. During this time, and through the years immediately following, Swift seized every opportunity to clinch public feeling by one of his pungent tracts. Of these an immense number exist, and form the political section of his writings. They cannot be enumerated here. The *Conduct of the Allies*, published November 1711, a manifesto from the peace party, is the best known, and now perhaps the most interesting of these. It passed through four editions in a week. At this time Swift was a person of the highest consequence in London society. Bishop Kennett reports that in 1713 "Dr. Swift was the principal man [at Court] of talk and business, and acted as minister of requests."

In May 1712 Swift published a *Proposal for correcting the English Language*. This tract bore his name, and was the earliest of his publications to do so. In April 1713 he got the only piece of preferment he ever secured, the Deanery of St. Patrick's, in Dublin; and the *Journal to Stella* closes with his setting out to take possession. By this time he had gained the affectionate friendship of Gay, Parnell, Berkeley, and particularly Pope, whose *Iliad* he took advantage of his influence with the ministry to commend. During his political greatness Swift was remarkably generous to men of letters. He says, in regard to his success in securing the bishopric of Cloyne for Berkeley (April 12, 1713), "I think I am bound, in honour and conscience, to use all my little credit towards helping forward men of worth in the world." He succeeded in forwarding every one's interest, save only his own. His greatest disappointment had been the refusal of the see of Hereford, in 1712. But the event that sealed the hopelessness of his ambition was the death of Queen Anne; on 1st August 1714 "the party with which Swift had identified himself, in whose success all his hopes and ambitions were bound up, was not so much ruined as annihilated." In September Arbuthnot described Swift as "like a man knocked down, though you may behold him still with a stern countenance aiming a blow at his adversaries." Defiance, however, was now worse than useless, and Swift returned to Dublin in despair.

With the interesting and even romantic events of the next ten years we have nothing to do, for the Dean of St. Patrick's refrained almost entirely from literature. He threw in his lot with the Irish; and having on his first arrival been almost universally shunned and disliked, he ended by being the most popular of patriots. His Irish pamphleteering threw a shadow before in his able and impassioned *Proposal for the Universal Use of Irish Manufactures* (1720); a treatise which brought on its printer a Government prosecution, and, according to Lord Orrery, first turned the tide of Irish popularity in Swift's favour. The *Proposal* is not in Swift's most earnest vein, but it is full of happy turns of irony and paradox, and shows that his wit had not rusted in his long retirement. Of much greater literary importance is the extraordinary series of polemical pamphlets known as the *Drapier's Letters* (1724), in which Swift rises to his highest level as a pure controversialist. The history of these wonderful productions must be given with some minuteness. In 1722 a William Wood, "hardwareman and bankrupt," had secured a patent for supplying Ireland with copper coin to the figure of £108,000. The Irish Houses of Parliament appealed, for it was understood that Wood had carried out his contract in a grossly fraudulent manner; but in the face of violent local opposition Walpole determined to carry out the scheme. Dublin was already in a dangerous ferment when Swift, in July 1724, addressed an anonymous letter on the subject "to the shop-keepers, tradesmen, farmers, and common people of Ireland," signed "M. B., Drapier" (or draper). M. B. professed to be a shrewd Dublin draper, who anticipated personal ruin if Englishmen were allowed to come to his shop and buy his goods in return for sacks full of Wood's brazen rubbish. This first letter produced a great effect; but meanwhile a report of Privy Council recommended the new coinage. On the 4th of August the Drapier produced a second letter, to "Mr. Harding, the Printer"; and a third, to the "nobility and gentry of Ireland," on the 25th of August. Waxing more and more excited, on the 13th of October the Drapier addressed a fourth letter "to the whole people of Ireland." Lord Carteret was now sent over from England, and his first act was to offer a reward of £300 for the discovery of the author of the *Fourth Letter*. The printer was indicted, and Swift thereupon, changing his tactics, was silent for awhile. Events forced from him a fifth letter on the 14th of December, addressed to Lord Molesworth. What is known as the sixth letter, and signed by Swift, was written to Lord Middleton in October 1724, but not printed until 1735. There are other *Drapier's Letters*, but of a later date than the first four. It will be easily admitted that of all political pamphlets in the English language, extracted from their author by the passion of the moment, these on Wood's pence are the most brilliant, and possess, as literature, the most durable interest. They have been much attacked, however, on the score of candour and logic.

Swift's arguments are violent and faulty; he exasperated his antagonists by his deliberate and yet tumultuous misrepresentations. But there is no doubt that he was in downright earnest, that his anger burned white hot, and that he had persuaded himself that the danger was so great and so imminent that he should stick at absolutely no step to prevent it. In the *Drapier's Letters* he talks about the currency in terms so impassioned that we cannot reasonably doubt that he would lightly have committed perjury or even murder if the crime would have given Wood's scheme its final quietus. There is a good deal of monotony about his diatribe; he says, over and over again, in much the same words, "I must confess I look upon it as my duty, so far as God hath enabled me, and as long as I keep within the bonds of truth, of duty, and of decency," but within these bounds he could not keep, "to warn my fellow-subjects, as they value their king, their country, and all that ought or can be dear to them, never to admit this pernicious coin, no, not so much as one single halfpenny"; and driven at last to despair by the obstinacy of the Government, he cries out, "If authority shall see fit to forbid all writings or discourses upon this subject, except such as are in favour of Mr. Wood, I will obey as it becomes me; only, when I am in danger of bursting, I will go and whisper among the reeds, —not any reflexion upon the wisdom of my countrymen,—but only these few words: *Beware of Wood's Halfpence.*" To the same series belongs the brilliant squib, *Wood's Execution* (1724), in which Swift let off some of the bubbling humour which did not befit the *Drapier's Letters*. In connection with these Irish pamphlets should be read two tracts of Swift's later years, the *Vindication of Lord Carteret* (1730), and the *Examination of Certain Abuses* (1732), the former a typical example of the author's irony, and the second of his humour. The *Examination* would rank among the first short examples of purely entertaining literature in the language, if it were not stained with the horrible and gratuitous obscenity which grew on Swift as he became old and reckless. Swift's courageous importunity in 1724 made him the idol of the Dublin citizens, and Walpole shrunk from the task of arresting him in the midst of a bodyguard of the whole population of Ireland. He took no pleasure in this popularity, and when it was at its height talked of dying there "in a rage, like a poisoned rat in a hole." What pleasure in life he could still receive, he seems to have found in his acquaintance with the London wits, and, in particular, with Pope and Arbuthnot. His next and perhaps greatest work sprang out of this pleasant intimacy.

The famous Martinus Scriblerus Club, in which Pope, Swift, and Arbuthnot took the leading parts, was formed, at Pope's suggestion, for the purpose of satirising broadly all literary incompetence. During the latest period of Pope's career the projects of Scriblerus were constantly present to the mind of that poet, and "the great and wonderful work of *The Dunciad*" is the most celebrated of his fragmentary contributions to the labours of the club. Swift, on the other hand, was to exert himself on the creation of a satirical romance, and the first intimation which the world received of this production was a mysterious series of allusions in Pope's *Memoirs of Scriblerus*, in which the four parts of Martin's Travels were rudely sketched. They were to form "very extraordinary voyages, into very extraordinary nations," and to "manifest the most distinguishing marks of a philosopher, a politician, and a legislator." It has been thought that the second part, which is certainly the most genial, was the earliest written; for Vanessa speaks of it in 1722. The whole work, under the title of *Gulliver's Travels*, appeared in the winter of 1726-27. It was anonymous, or rather pseudonymous, for it was supposed to be a relation, by a simple ship's captain of Nottinghamshire, one Lemuel Gulliver, of his adventures in strange lands, and to be edited, for the entertainment of young noblemen, by the cousin of the traveller, Richard Sympson. This editor protested that he had done nothing with the unvarnished narrative, except "strike out innumerable passages relating to the winds and tides," and suchlike marine technicalities. To increase the semblance of genuine geographical pretension, maps of the various countries were inserted, and a portrait of Gulliver.

Critical ingenuity has laboured to discover the sources of the peculiar form taken by this celebrated romance. The author presented the world with one obvious suggestion by stating, in a mock prefatory epistle, that he was the cousin of William Dampier, the famous navigator of the preceding generation. But *Gulliver's Travels* owes most of its external shape to the *Vera Historia* of Lucian, itself a travesty of lost works on geography. The French poet Cyrano de Bergerac (1620-1655) had written a *Voyage à la lune* and a *Histoire comique des états empires du Soleil*, from which Fontenelle had borrowed some hints. Several slight points which Swift used he is said to have taken from a tract by Francis Goodwin, Bishop of Llandaff. There can be no doubt, moreover, that the particular narrative manner of Defoe, whose *Robinson Crusoe* had appeared in 1719, produced an effect upon Swift. All these critical speculations, however, are rather curious than essential. Swift, always among the most original of writers, is nowhere more thoroughly himself than in his enchanting romance of Lemuel Gulliver. Whether we read it, as children do, for the story, or as historians, for the political allusions, or as men of the world, for the satire and philosophy, we have to acknowledge that it is one of the wonderful and unique books of the world's literature.

From internal evidence, it is highly probable that the composition of *Gulliver's Travels* was distributed over a good many years. In the voyages to Lilliput and Brobdingnag there is but little to justify the charges of brutality and cruel violence which are brought against Swift's later satires. They belong to the period of his mental health. The third section of *Gulliver's Travels* is really a miscellany : it has never interested the public so much as the rest of the book ; it deals with speculations with which, it is supposed, Swift could not deal without help from Arbuthnot ; and it holds no very distinct place among the leading works of the writer. The floating island, though described with unusual picturesqueness of phrase, baffles the most willing faith. When he comes to Lagado, Swift flies too modestly beneath the wing of Rabelais. In Glubbdubdrib the reader soon grows like the narrator, and finds that the domestic spectres "give him no emotion at all." Indeed, this portion of *Gulliver's Travels* would hardly live, were it not for the pathetic imagination of the Struldbrugs, a people whose peculiarities appeal to the most secret instincts of mankind. But in all these miscellaneous excursions there is little or nothing which displays to us the darker side of Swift's genius. That side is, however, exemplified to excess in the final part, the Voyage to the Country of the Houyhnhnms. It is difficult not to believe that this was written during the last illness of Stella, when Swift was aware that his best companion was certainly leaving him, and when that remorse which he could not but feel for his conduct to the woman who had so long loved him was turning what milk remained in his nature to gall. In the summer of 1726 the loss of Stella's conversation made him, he tells us, weary of life, and he fled from Ireland in a horror lest he should be a witness of her end. Delany tells us that from the time of her death, and probably from a few months earlier, Swift's character and temper underwent a change. His vertigo became chronic, and so did his misanthropy, and it seems probable that the first literary expression of his rage and despair was the awful satire of the Yahoos. It was with the horrible satisfaction of disease that Swift formed a story which would enable him to describe men as being, though "with some appearance of cunning, and the strongest disposition to mischief, yet the most unteachable of all brutes," and there is something which suggests a brain not wholly under control in the very machinery of this part of the romance. In Lilliput and in Brobdingnag we are struck by the ingenious harmony of the whole design, there being no detail which is not readily credible if we admit the possibility of the scheme; but among the Houyhnhnms probability is ruthlessly sacrificed to the wild pleasure the author takes in trampling human pride in the mire of his sarcasm. Of the horrible foulness of this satire on the Yahoos enough will have been said when it is admitted that it banishes from decent households a fourth part of one of the most brilliant and delightful of English books.

After Stella's death, in January 1728, Swift changed his manner of life in many ways. He never had written constantly or professionally; he now made a practice of neglecting literature. He determined that the lightest things he had written should be "serious philosophical lucubrations" in comparison with what he would now busy himself about. In this mood he fell back again on verse, which he had neglected in middle life, with one or two exceptions. We may retrace our steps for a moment to consider the most important of these exceptions, the longest of Swift's existing poems, *Cadenus and Vanessa* (1713). Cadenus is the Dean himself, *Decanus;* Vanessa is the enthusiastic and unfortunate Miss Vanhomrigh. The poem, in the mocking mythology of the period, tells how a wondrous maid was born under the protection of Venus and Pallas, and how this

> "Vanessa, in her bloom,
> Advanced, like Atalanta's star,
> But rarely seen and seen from far."

She meets Cadenus at last, "declined in health, advanced in years." Cadenus

> "could praise, esteem, approve,
> But understood not what was love";

in short, the history of the singular attachment which existed between those unhappy persons is told with extraordinary fulness and simplicity, in verse that is charmingly arch and gay; but Swift confesses that what really occurred at last, what strange compromise cold friendship made with panting love,

> "Must never to Mankind be told,
> Nor shall the conscious Muse unfold."

Among the poems of his latest period must be mentioned *The Journal of a Modern Lady* (1728); *The Lady's Dressing-Room* (1730), a little masterpiece of a very nasty kind; and *Strephon and Cloe* (1731), which bears the same hall-mark of the Yahoo. *On the Death of Dr. Swift* (1731), in which a maxim of Rochefoucault is expanded in five hundred lines, is an invaluable record of the strangely-compacted temper of the writer, and contains some excellent writing:

> " My female friends, whose tender hearts
> Have better learn'd to act their parts,
> Receive the news in doleful dumps:
> ' The Dean is dead: (Pray what is trumps?)
> Then, Lord have mercy on his soul!
> (Ladies, I'll venture for the vole.)
> Six Deans, they say, must bear the pall:
> (I wish I knew what king to call.)
> Madam, your husband will attend
> The funeral of so good a friend?
> No, madam, 'tis a shocking sight:
> And he's engaged to-morrow night:
> My Lady Club will take it ill,
> If he should fail her at quadrille.
> He loved the Dean—(I lead a heart)
> But dearest friends, they say, must part.
> His time was come: he ran his race;
> We hope he's in a better place.'
> Why do you grieve that friends should die?
> No loss more easy to supply.
> One year is past; a different scene!
> No further mention of the Dean;
> Who now, alas! no more is miss'd,
> Than if he never did exist.
> Where's now this favourite of Apollo?
> Departed:—and his works must follow;
> Must undergo the common fate;
> His kind of wit is out of date.
> Some country Squire to Lintot goes,
> Inquires for ' Swift in Verse and Prose.'
> Says Lintot, ' I have heard the name;
> He died a year ago?'——' The same.'
> He searches all the shop in vain.
> ' Sir, you may find them in Duck Lane;
> I sent them with a load of books,
> Last Monday to the pastry-cook's.

> To fancy they could live a year !
> I find you're but a stranger here.
> The Dean was famous in his time,
> And had a kind of knack at rhyme.
> His way of writing now is past ;
> The town has got a better taste ;
> I keep no antiquated stuff,
> But spick and span I have enough.
> Pray do but give me leave to show 'em ;
> Here's Colly Cibber's birth-day poem ' "—

The Beast's Confession (1732) is a very cynical fable ; *On Poetry, a Rhapsody*, one of the finest of his poetical pieces, dates from 1733, and contains among many other well-known passages, the lines about the fleas "with smaller still to bite 'em." Soon after this Swift's memory and his invention deserted him, but he wrote couplets and epigrams until very late. The lines *On the Death of Dr. Swift* may perhaps be considered as giving, on the whole, the finest impression of Swift's skill and force as a versifier. Of the pieces mentioned above, all are in octosyllabic rhyme.

To the same period preceding his fatal decline belongs the extraordinary farrago of wilfully inane chatter called *The Complete Collection of Genteel and Ingenious Conversation*, better known as *Polite Conversation;* but this, although given to Mrs. Barber for publication in 1738, appears to have been written nine or ten years earlier. The *Polite Conversation*, which pretends to be the result of patient collecting of good things in society, during forty years, by one Simon Wagstaffe, leads off with a very diverting introduction, from which the following passage is taken :

"[This noble art of conversation] is not so easy an acquirement as a few ignorant pretenders may imagine. A footman can swear; but he cannot swear like a lord. He can swear as often, but can he swear with equal delicacy, propriety, and judgment? No, certainly, unless he be a lad of superior parts, of good memory, a diligent observer, one who hath a skilful ear, some knowledge in music, and an exact taste, which hardly fall to the share of one in a thousand among that fraternity, in as high favour as they now stand with their ladies. Neither hath one footman in six so fine a genius as to relish and apply those exalted sentences comprised in this volume which I offer to the world. It is true I cannot see that the same ill consequences would follow from the waiting-woman, who, if she hath been bred to read romances, may have some subaltern or second-hand politeness; and if she constantly attends the tea, and be a good listener, may, in some years, make a tolerable figure, which will serve, perhaps, to draw in the young chaplain or the old steward. But, alas! after all, how can she acquire those hundreds of graces and motions and airs, the whole military management of the fan, the contortions of every muscular motion in the face, the risings and fallings, the quickness and slowness of the voice, with the several turns and cadences the proper junctions of smiling and frowning, how often and how loud to laugh, when to jibe and when to flout, with all the other branches of doctrine and discipline above recited."

A volume of *Miscellanies* saw the light in 1729, which opened with the *Modest Proposal*, a grimly facetious pamphlet recommending that the children of the poor should be killed and distributed as food. A fragment called *Rules for Servants*, of an ironical kind, was written before 1738, but published after the Dean's death. He made his will in 1740, leaving his fortune to found a lunatic asylum in Dublin, "and showed by one satiric touch No nation needed it so much." Almost immediately after this, his mental and physical health was finally submerged. He became furiously insane, until in 1743 this shocking condition was exchanged for one of moody stupor; he died without a struggle on the 19th of October 1745, at the age of nearly seventy-eight. He was privately buried in his own cathedral, the citizens of Dublin vainly desiring to give their patriot a pompous burial. Swift was a tall powerful man, with a rather dull face, illuminated by very singular and flashing azure eyes.

In considering Swift purely as a writer, the factor of his health must always be taken into consideration. At the Tory victory which closed 1711, the highest intellectual honours seemed to be in Swift's hands, but the intolerable vertigo or some other failure of the nervous system stepped in between him and his ambition. It will for ever be a subject of discussion to what extent and in what exact manner Swift's bodily ailments interfered with his intellectual powers. Towards the end, when mental decline was certain, the condition which produced the Yahoos and the *Modest*

Proposal could not be called weakness. His most revolting cynicism was the result, apparently, of physical pain which distressed the nerves and distorted the judgment without weakening the intelligence an iota. Swift's mind, so far as we can observe its action, remained vigorous behind a veil of suffering until it was finally and totally eclipsed. Readers of strong mental digestion are doubtless to be found who would not lose one scrap of what the mighty Dean has left. Others, of more feeble race, will wish that the hideous and monstrous images which crowded upon his dying imagination had found no expression in literature. On this point we need hazard no opinion; enough to say that those images were doubtless the result of disease acting upon a very bold and not over cleanly fancy, and that the most conscientious Swiftean will hardly class them among his best creations.

When we consider the fact that Swift's writings are short and occasional, for the most part, and that he usually adopted such a trifling form as would suit his favourite motto, *vive la bagatelle*, it is impossible not to marvel at the impression of force and importance which these writings present. It is useless to regret that he did not adopt a graver view of the duties of an author. When he tried to be a serious poet, a serious historian, he entirely failed. It is almost absurd to think of so formidable a spirit performing upon the lighter lyre, and yet he scarcely touched any other instrument to the end of his life. As the poor lady put it, Dean Swift could write finely on a broomstick, and not finely merely, but with the most caustic and fatal pungency. In his various works we find one quality almost always predominant—an imperturbable humour, and from this lambent spirit of pleasantry nothing human or divine was safe. To fail to observe the predominance of this humour in Swift's writings is to fail to appreciate their surface; to give this quality too great importance in estimating their character is to mistake the exterior for the actual substance. Swift is not a writer of the first order by merit of his humour or causticity, still less by merit of his coarseness or cynicism; he is a writer of the first order because he moulded language to be the vehicle of a sincerity that has never been surpassed. No author in any language is more vehemently in earnest than Swift, and however unconventional may be the expression of his feelings, however cruel, unclean, and paradoxical, he rivets our attention and commands our respect because we feel him to be essentially and passionately a lover of good things. Under the strangest mask, he is always energising after righteousness. He hates vice so much, that it does not seem merely evil to him, but hideous and ridiculous. He is so utterly and vehemently on the side of purity and liberty and sanity, that he does not mind seeming dirty and unfair and mad. As for his prose style, if the student will carefully read and digest the *Tale of a Tub*, the *Conduct of the Allies*, and the *Vindication of Lord Carteret*, he will be in possession of the typical materials on which to found a judgment in this matter. He will find, perhaps, more brilliant exceptional phrases elsewhere; but in these three short works Swift's manner as a writer will be exhibited to him, his humour, his irony, his rapidity and conciseness, his short bright sentences, "like light dissolved in star-showers," and he will not need to go further to perceive that this was the greatest original intellect in pure literature between Dryden and Wordsworth.

Swift is attended, as a planet by a satellite, by the shadowy reputation of John Arbuthnot (1667-1735). He was a poor Scotch youth, who early settled in London, and took up the medical profession. His first publications were slight scientific pamphlets, among them an *Essay on the Usefulness of Mathematical Learning* (1700). He rose rapidly as a doctor, and in 1705 was appointed Physician Extraordinary to Queen Anne. At the age of forty-five Arbuthnot was still without literary distinction or ambition. In the early part of 1711 he made Swift's acquaintance, and his nature underwent a transformation. He assimilated Swift's peculiar style so rapidly and with such complete success that in 1712 he published two famous pamphlets which were attributed to the greater writer, and might still be so attributed but for Swift's positive statement to Stella. Of these, one is *The Art of Political Lying;* the other, still better known, was issued originally as *Law is a Bottomless Pit,* but reprinted as *The History of John Bull.* Arbuthnot was a leading member of the Scriblerus Club, and the *Memoirs of Martinus Scriblerus,* as they appeared in 1741, are mainly from his pen. He published a solid disquisition on *Ancient Coins* in 1727. In 1731 were printed his *Epitaph on Colonel Chartres,* a piece of splendid invective, and his *Scolding of the Ancients.* Arbuthnot signed nothing, and allowed his papers to be dispersed without a thought for posterity. It is yet undetermined whether certain tracts were written by him or by Swift. His *Miscellanies,* posthumously collected in two volumes in 1751, have many pieces in them which Arbuthnot did not write, and his son repudiated the whole publication. Arbuthnot was a warm-hearted and generous companion, who enjoyed the confidence and intimate friendship of the principal men of letters of his age. Pope addressed to him the finest of his epistles, and Swift said that "his humanity was equal to his wit." He is principally remembered by *The History of John Bull,* designed to strengthen the peace party by laughing at the fallen Duke of Marlborough. It is lively and witty, and would be extremely original in form if the *Tale of a Tub* had not preceded it; it should be added that Arbuthnot has none of Swift's savage violence. The following passage, in which the genius of Handel is whimsically complimented, is taken from Arbuthnot's *Harmony in an Uproar:*

"Frederick Handel, hold up your hand! Know you are here brought to answer to the several following high crimes and misdemeanours, committed upon the wills and understandings, and against the peace, of our sovereign lord the Mobility of Great Britain, particularly this metropolis. To which you shall make true and faithful answer—So help you, Music! Swear him upon the two operas of *Ariadne,* alias *The Cuckoo and the Nightingale.*

"*Imprimis,* you are charged with having bewitched us for the space of twenty years past; nor do we know where your enchantments will end if a timely stop is not put to them, they threatening us with an entire destruction of liberty, and an absolute tyranny in your person over the whole territories of the Haymarket.

"*Secondly*, you have most insolently dared to give us good music and sound harmony, when we wanted and desired bad, to the great encouragement of your operas, and the ruin of our good allies and confederates, the professors of bad music.

"*Thirdly*, you have most feloniously and arrogantly assumed to yourself an uncontrolled property of pleasing us, whether we would or no; and have often been so bold as to charm us, when we were positively resolved to be out of humour.

"Besides these, we can, at convenient time or times, produce and prove five hundred and fifteen articles of lesser consequence, which may, on the whole, at least amount to accumulative treason. How say you, Sir, are you guilty of the said charge or no?

"*Prisoner*. Guilty of the whole charge."

In 1705 a young physician, who had been born in Holland, but early settled in London, Bernard de Mandeville (1670-1733), published a rough poem in octosyllabics, entitled *The Grumbling Hive*. In this fable the style of Swift's verses was imitated, but the manner of the poem was of less importance than the cynical matter, in which it was striven to show that a hive of prosperous vicious bees was ruined by becoming virtuous:

> "To enjoy the world's conveniences,
> Be fam'd in war, yet live in ease,
> Without great vices, is a vain
> Utopia seated in the brain;
> Fraud, luxury, and pride must live,
> Whilst we the benefits receive. . . .
> Do we not owe the growth of wine
> To the dry, shabby, crooked vine,
> Which, while its shoots neglected stood,
> Choked other plants, and ran to wood,
> But blest us with its noble fruit
> As soon as it was tied and cut?
> So vice is beneficial found
> When 'tis by justice lopped and bound."

In 1714 this short piece was reprinted, with a long commentary in prose, under the title of *The Fable of the Bees; or, Private Vices, Public Benefits*. In this form the book made a great scandal, and was prosecuted as a nuisance. Mandeville enlarged his work in successive editions, and he published various other treatises of a similar tendency. He was a paradoxical and truculent writer, with a bluff style, plenty of humour, a homely kind of common sense, and a pronounced taste for vulgarity and vice. His favourite butt was Shaftesbury, whose delicate optimism he detested. Mandeville has much in common with Swift, but never stands on the high moral ground which Swift took so easily and genuinely. He is pregnant, however, with acute observation, and in more than one instance has forestalled modern science in his speculations as to the primitive conditions of society. Sir Leslie Stephen, who has been, of recent critics, the one most indulgent to Mandeville, says that "he gave up to the coffee-houses a penetration meant for loftier purposes." From Mandeville's picturesque tract on *The Causes of the Frequent Executions at Tyburn*, 1725, we take this vignette of a Newgate crowd as a specimen of his style:

"No modern rabble can long subsist without their darling cordial, the good preservation of sloth, geneva,[1] that infallible antidote against care and frugal reflection; which, being repeated, removes all pain of sober thought, and in a little time cures the tormenting sense of the most pressing necessities. The traders who send it among the mob on these occasions are commonly the worst of both sexes, but most of them weather-beaten fellows that have misspent their youth. There stands an old sloven, in a wig actually putrified, squeezed up in a corner, and recommends a dram of it to the goers-by. There another in rags, with several bottles in a basket, stirs about with it where the throng is the thinnest, and tears his throat with crying his commodity; while, further off, you may see the head of a third, who has ventured into the middle of the current, and minds his business as he is fluctuating in the irregular stream. Whilst, higher up, an old decrepit woman sits dreaming with it on a bulk, and over against her in a soldier's coat, her termagant daughter sells the sot's-comfort with great dispatch. The intelligible sounds that are heard among them are oaths and vile expressions, with wishes of damnation at every other word, pronounced promiscuously against themselves, or those they speak to, without the least alteration in the meaning."

The main subject of Mandeville's satire was a writer who had died in early middle age before that unscrupulous satirist became

[1] Gin. Mandeville spells the word "Jeneva."

an adept in controversy. It is doubtful whether, under any circumstances, the graceful Shaftesbury would have measured swords with so rude an opponent. A certain epoch had been marked by the publication, in 1711, of *Characteristics of Men, Manners, Opinions, and Times*, with a preface signed A. A. C. The author was Anthony Ashley Cooper, third Earl of Shaftesbury (1671-1713), and this famous book was a collected edition of his various scattered writings, his "united tracts." The first volume consisted of three treatises, *A Letter concerning Enthusiasm*, originally published in 1708 ; *An Essay on the Freedom of Wit and Humour* (1709); and *Soliloquy, or Advice to an Author* (1710). The second volume contained reprints of Shaftesbury's first publication, *An Inquiry concerning Virtue* (1699[1]), and *The Moralists* (1709). The third volume contained Miscellaneous Reflections, never printed before. Shaftesbury, who had been brought up at the feet of Locke, was the most accomplished Englishman of his day, the man with the widest taste and the most complete culture, while the purity of his personal character matched well with the charm of his intellect. His early treatises were issued half privately, or were even piracies, and they did not make any mark until they were collected as the *Characteristics*. In that form they constituted a solid contribution to the body of English literature, the value of which is nowadays very much underrated. Shaftesbury was a Platonist so far as his sceptical tendencies would permit him to be. For metaphysical philosophy, the teaching of "a sort of moonblind wits," he had a great contempt ; he was a moralist, a sentimentalist, an optimistical theist. He had a profound sense of the harmony of the universe, and this conviction elevated the whole order of his mind. To it we may attribute his most attractive literary quality, the serene stateliness of his style at its best. His influence on the philosophical writers of the succeeding generation was very remarkable, and it is no small praise to Shaftesbury to admit that but for him Pope's *Essay on Man* could never have been written, although Pope, if Warburton may be believed, was a

---

[1] No copy of this edition appears to exist in any public library.

little ashamed of Shaftesbury's ascendancy over him. As a critic Shaftesbury's authority was considerable. He had lived during his youth in the intimacy of some of the leaders of literary and artistic taste in Europe, and he was ready to pronounce with confidence on questions of poetic style and the whole art of rhetoric. It was charged against him that his ideal virtuoso was wholly guided by the laws of æsthetic taste. Shaftesbury did not care to refute such a charge, for he held that " harmony and proportion, in whatever kind," and therefore in less essential matters, " are highly assistant to virtue, which is itself no other than the love of order and beauty in society." He was ready to declare, with Keats, that " Beauty is Truth, Truth Beauty; this is all we know on earth and all we need to know." Two fragments may exemplify the peculiarities of the style of Shaftesbury. The first is taken from his Fourth Miscellany; the second is selected, as an example of his enthusiastic optimism, from the *Inquiry concerning Virtue:*

"Two of this race having been daintily bred, and in high thoughts of what they called pleasure and good living, travelled once in quest of game and rareties, till they came by accident to the sea-side. They saw there, at a distance from the shore, some floating pieces of wreck, which they took a fancy to believe some wonderful rich dainty, richer than ambergreese, or the richest product of the ocean. They could prove it, by their appetite and longing, to be no less than quintessence of the main, ambrosial substance, the repast of marine deities, surpassing all that earth afforded. By these rhetorical arguments, after long reasoning with one another in this florid vein, they proceeded from one extravagance of fancy to another ; till they came at last to this issue. Being unaccustomed to swimming, they would not, it seems, in prudence, venture so far out of their depth as was necessary to reach their imagined prize : but being stout drinkers, they thought with themselves, they might compass to drink all which lay in their way ; even the Sea itself; and that by this method they might shortly bring their goods safe to dry land. To work therefore they went ; and drank till they were both burst. For my own part, I am fully satisfied that there are more sea-drinkers than one or two, to be found among the principal personages of mankind : and that if these dogs of ours were silly curs, many who pass for wise in our own race are little wiser ; and may properly enough be said to have the Sea to drink."

"What tyrant is there, what robber, or open violater of the laws of society, who has not a companion, or some particular set, either of his own kindred, or such as he calls friends; with whom he gladly shares his goods; in whose welfare he delights; and whose joy and satisfaction he makes his own? What person in the world is there, who receives not some impressions from the flattery or kindness of such as are familiar with him? 'Tis to this soothing hope and expectation of friendship, that almost all our actions have some reference. 'Tis this which goes through our whole lives, and mixes itself even with most of our vices. Of this, vanity, ambition, and luxury, have a share; and many other disorders of our life partake. Even the unchastest love borrows largely from this source. So that were pleasure to be computed in the same way as other things commonly are; it might properly be said, that out of these two branches (viz. community or participation in the pleasures of others, and belief of meriting well from others) would arise more than nine-tenths of whatever is enjoyed in life. And thus in the main sum of happiness, there is scarce a single article, but what derives itself from social love, and depends immediately on the natural and kind affections. Now such as causes are, such must be their effects. And therefore as natural affection or social love is perfect, or imperfect; so must be the content and happiness depending on it."

Recent criticism has dealt roughly with what is "flimsy" and "pretentious" in the philosophy of Shaftesbury. The student of pure literature, while lamenting his rhetorical excesses and his tendency to burst into such bastard blank verse as we find in *The Moralists*, should not fail to recognise in him one of the most independent and graceful prose-writers of the age of Anne. He did not live long enough to be influenced by the styles of Swift or Addison, with whom, as a writer, he has but very slight affinity. He is a sort of Ruskin of the Augustan age.

A showy figure, which claimed a much higher literary position than posterity has chosen to relinquish to it, is that of Henry St. John, Viscount Bolingbroke (1678-1751), once so famous for his eloquence that Pitt declared his speeches the most desirable of all the lost fragments of literature. It was after his political misfortunes that Bolingbroke first took to literature as a consolation, and in 1716 wrote his *Reflections upon Exile*, printed in 1735. The most famous of his early writings is a vindication of his conduct towards the Tory party, in a *Letter to Sir William Wyndham* in 1717 (printed 1753). At Fontainebleau he wrote his *Letters on the Study and Use of History* (1735), and his *Letter on the Use of Retirement*. From his house in Battersea he published, in 1749, his *Letters on the Spirit of Patriotism* and his *Idea of a Patriot King*, Pope's treatment of which latter work constitutes one of the famous scandals of the eighteenth century. Mallet published the complete works of Lord Bolingbroke in 1753-4, and it was in reference to this edition that Dr. Johnson said of Bolingbroke, "He was a scoundrel and a coward, a scoundrel for charging a blunderbuss against religion and morality; a coward because he had not resolution to fire it off himself, but left half a crown to a beggarly Scotchman to draw the trigger after his death." The personal magnetism of Bolingbroke must have been very great; he dazzled his own generation, where he merely wearies ours. His boasted style, though unquestionably lucid, is slipshod and full of platitudes, grandiloquent and yet ineffectual. His *Patriot King* is his most pleasing effort; it is a study of an ideal constitutional monarch, intended to justify a sort of paternal right of kings from the standpoint of the Whigs. But criticism now merely smiles at the author's impudent assumption of the airs of a great political philosopher.

At the close of this chapter we may briefly enumerate the most distinguished names in the curious group of acknowledged deists who made their appearance at the beginning of the eighteenth century. The controversy was opened on the orthodox side by Charles Leslie (1650-1722), an Irish non-juror. He darted *A Snake in the Grass* (1696) against the Quakers; but his most famous and effective work was his *Short and easy Method with the Deists* (1697). Twenty-seven treatises are attributed to his fluent and truculent pen. Leslie was a Jacobite, and in 1710 he fled to Bar-le-duc to the Pretender, with whom he resided in extreme discomfort for eleven years. Dr. Matthew Tindal (1656-1733), who attacked the High Church party in *The Rights of the Christian Church* (1706), and *Corah and Moses* (1727), caused a great scandal by the publication of his *Christianity as old as the Creation*, in 1730. Tindal was a Christian, although on the very borders of infidelity. A bolder and less scrupulous deist was Janus Junius Toland (1670-1722); he professed to be a pupil and confidant of Locke, who repudiated the soft impeachment. Toland was said to be the illegitimate son of an Irish priest, and his life was spent in the purlieus of Grub Street. Toland, nevertheless, had great talent; his *Christianity not Mysterious* (1696) is a very original and striking tract, which was received with a howl of indignation. He wrote much more, but nothing so clever as this his first publication. William Wollaston (1659-1724) produced an extremely popular work entitled *The Religion of Nature delineated* (1722), a contribution to constructive deism. Anthony Collins (1676-1729) defended rationalism against the onslaughts of Leslie, but brought down such a storm on his head that he escaped to Holland. His famous *Discourse on Freethinking*, which Swift made fun of, appeared in 1713. These men were not writers of a high genius, and their arguments were timid and often fallacious. But they bear for posterity the charm which is given by persecution, and they prepared the way for bolder and more scientific thinkers. Of their most distinguished opponents we shall speak in the next chapter.

CHAPTER VI

DEFOE AND THE ESSAYISTS

WE proceed to enumerate in the present chapter those miscellaneous figures belonging to the Augustan era which have not been hitherto examined. The oldest of the writers who became greatly distinguished in the reign of Anne was Daniel Defoe (1661 ?-1731), whose baptismal name was Daniel Foe. He was a Londoner, the son of a Nonconformist butcher in the City. He was trained to be a dissenting minister, and was well educated, although, as his enemies never ceased to remind him, "this Man was no Scholar." At four-and-twenty he went into the hosiery business in Cornhill, and seven years later he had to fly from his creditors, owing £17,000. It is believed that he became a pamphleteer long before this, but his biographers have discovered no printed matter indubitably Defoe's earlier than 1691. From 1695 to 1699 he was accountant to the Commissioners of the Glass Duty, and was in prosperous circumstances. His first important tract, the first pamphlet in favour of a *Standing Army*, appeared in 1697, when its author was thirty-six; Defoe became active in supporting William III.'s measures, and published in the king's interest his *Essay on Projects* (1698). Hitherto Defoe had been a pronounced dissenter, but in 1698 he printed an opportunist pamphlet on *Occasional Conformity*. All these exercises, however, amounted to little more than what we should now call journalism. Defoe's first distinct literary success was made in 1701 with his satire in verse, the *True-born Englishman*, in which he ridiculed the popular suspicion of the Dutch in England. He tells us that 80,000 copies of this rough poem were sold in the streets, and the king honoured him for the first time, on this occasion, with an audience. The death of William (March 8, 1702) was a very serious blow to the prospects of his active servant of the pen.

Defoe hailed the advent of Queen Anne with several very poor poems; he was slow to learn that his talents were not those of a versifier. At the close of 1702 he returned to the safer paths of prose with a famous pamphlet, *The Shortest Way with the Dissenters*, a satire upon the High Church Tories, whose extreme tone in private conversation it parodied with daring bluntness. Defoe ironically recommended that "whoever was found at a conventicle should be banished the nation, and the preacher be hanged," and his speech was so plain that while the Highfliers gasped for breath, the Dissenters, on their side, were too much frightened to see the irony. When the truth was perceived, Defoe was prosecuted, and tried in July 1703; he stood for three days in the pillory, but Pope was incorrect in saying that "earless on high stood unabashed Defoe." He was a popular favourite, and admiring crowds wreathed the instrument of his discomfort with garlands of flowers. To the "hieroglyphic state-machine" itself he now addressed a *Hymn*. His punishment in the pillory was succeeded by a long imprisonment in Newgate, and during this latter his tile-works at Tilbury, which were important to his livelihood, failed through his absence from business. He was set free by Harley in the summer of 1704. During his imprisonment he had written *A Collection of Casualties and Disasters*, a bold fancy picture of that famous storm which Addison alluded to in the *Campaign*, "such as of late o'er pale Britannia past." This was undoubtedly issued to a credulous public as veritable history. It was in prison, too, that he started his influential political newspaper, the *Review*, which continued to appear twice a week until February 1705, after which it was published three times a week.

After existing ten years, an extraordinary period for a newspaper in those days, the *Review* expired in June 1713.

Defoe's history after his release is a somewhat perplexing one. He openly pretended to be gagged, and to have promised to write no more polemic for seven years; but in reality he had undertaken an agency for the Government, and presently he went to Scotland, not, it is regretted, so entirely for patriotic purposes as he pretended. He had become, to put it plainly, a paid official spy and secret pamphleteer. He even used his debts as decoys, and as Professor Minto has said, "when he was despatched on secret missions, departed wiping his eyes at the hardship of having to flee from his creditors." The fall of Harley did not deprive Defoe of the Queen's favour; on the contrary, he was immediately sent to Edinburgh on another private errand. Into the history of Defoe's innumerable political writings, one of the vexed questions of bibliography, it is needless to go here. He was exceedingly plausible and adroit, but his personal chronicle, when exposed to the light, has a very unpleasing air of insincerity. He wished, doubtless, to be a patriot, but he could not resist the temptation, as he puts it, of bowing in the house of Rimmon; nor could he conquer his insatiable desire to govern by journalism, to be putting his oar daily and hourly into every species of public business. Among less ephemeral writings of the period may be mentioned *The Apparition of Mrs. Veal* (1706), afterwards constantly republished with a dreary work of divinity by Drelincourt (1595-1669), which the ghost of Mrs. Veal had recommended. This was, it is needless to say, a little piece of realistic romance. In 1709 Defoe printed his *History of the Union*, and in 1715-18 his *Family Instructor*, a solid didactic work which long enjoyed a great popularity.

Defoe was nearly sixty before he began the series of books which have given him the unique place he holds in English literature. Between 1719 and 1728 he composed with extraordinary vigour, rapidity, and fulness, at an age at which the strength of the most ardent writer is usually abated. His undoubted masterpiece, the first part of *Robinson Crusoe*, appeared on the 25th of April 1719; the second followed in August, and in August 1720 was published the third part, being Crusoe's "Serious Reflections." It is scarcely necessary to say that *Robinson Crusoe* is the earliest great English novel, and that in certain respects it has never been surpassed. Crusoe had been the name of one of the author's schoolfellows, and it is plain from many passages in Defoe's works that he had long looked forward to the possibility of exile in distant seas. The story of a certain Alexander Selkirk or Selcraig, who had been left on shore at Juan Fernandez, was the ultimate germ round which the amazing creation of *Robinson Crusoe* took form. The book instantly succeeded, as well it might, and Defoe turned to supply the new demand caused by a fresh sort of literary merchandise. In 1720 he published three romances of no small importance, *Mr. Duncan Campbell*, *Memoirs of a Cavalier*, and *The Life of Captain Singleton*. Of these, the third, a tale of piracy on the southern seas, with its pictures of tropical Africa, has been a main favourite with some lovers of Defoe. In 1722 the indefatigable novelist produced three other notable books, *Moll Flanders*, *The Plague Year*, and *Colonel Jack*. In 1724 were published *The Fortunate Mistress* (*Roxana*), perhaps the best of his novels after *Robinson Crusoe*, and the *Tour through Great Britain*. In 1725 appeared another romance, *The New Voyage round the World*, and *The Complete English Tradesman*, a rather vulgar handbook to the arts of mercantile success. In 1726 he printed *The Political History of the Devil*, and in 1727-28 *The Plan of English Commerce*. When it is said that Mr. William Lee, the most laborious of Defoe students, attributes to the pen of his hero no less than two hundred and fifty-four distinct publications, it will not be a matter for surprise that so few can be mentioned here. Defoe was prosperous during the period we have just described, and installed himself in a handsome house at Stoke Newington, in the company of "three lovely daughters," and two rather scandalous sons. He probably lived beyond his income, for late in 1729 he absconded, and hid himself not far from Greenwich. It has been conjectured, on the other hand, that he may have been insane, and have falsely supposed that it was needful he should fly. In any case he died apart from his family, in a respectable lodging in Ropemaker's Walk, Moorfields, on the 26th of April 1731. It is very difficult to regard the personal character of Defoe with any sympathy. He was dishonest, and yet always prating about honesty. He was writing in a Jacobite newspaper with one hand, while accepting secret money from the Government with the other. He was, as his latest biographer has to admit, "perhaps the greatest liar that ever lived." There is something very sordid about his ambitions, very mean and peddling in his scheme of life. His great genius alone preserves for him a little of our sympathy, and yet, even here, it is probably to Defoe's advantage that his best books make us entirely forget their author.

The secondary novels of Defoe, in this day very little read, belong to the same class as *Robinson Crusoe*, and repeat the manner of that far abler work. When great stress is laid on what has been aptly called Defoe's "absolute command over the carpentry and scaffolding of realism," it should not be forgotten that this realism is seldom antiquarian. The novelist writes of the seventeenth century as if it were the eighteenth. He is reckless with dates, as when we are told that Roxana, a fine lady of the time of Charles II., was born in 1673, and died in the sixty-fifth year of her age, in 1742, that is to say, eighteen or fourteen years, as we choose to compute it, after the date of the publication of the volume. *Moll Flanders* must begin in the year 1613, but the manners are those of 1713. In all these romances the style is the same, that of the publicist. Defoe now writes diurnals no longer; but he sits at home and forges column after column of minute newspaper incidents. The mode is almost always that of autobiography, and no very palpable advance in narrative has been made since Meriton Latroon told his own adventures in *The English Rogue*, 1665-1680, of Richard Head (1630?-1678). The type is still that of the Spanish Picaroon novel of adventure, and Defoe moves forward much less decidedly towards the romance of manners than did his great French contemporary, Lesage, whose *Gil Blas*, the English student should remember, had begun to appear in 1715. But Defoe's observation of character is blunt indeed, and totally unimaginative, when compared with what it superficially resembles, the insight of Lesage. In this class of Defoe's novels *Roxana* may be mentioned first. It is the history of a beautiful French refugee, from her cradle in Poictiers to her grave in Amsterdam; it is also the history of a more sympathetic figure, Amy, her maid. The heroine's real name is Mdlle. de Beleau; she receives the name of Roxana half way through the book, because she happens to perform in a Turkish drama. She is a handsome and brazen adventuress, and the book is a minute study of the "splendeurs des courtisanes." The "misères" are the subject of *Moll Flanders*, a Newgate prostitute and thief, who is transported to Virginia, but lives to return and die a penitent. Each book is written, with a coarse morality, to show "où mènent les mauvais chemins." *Moll Flanders* is a sort of English version of *Manon Lescaut*, but there is no comparison between them as works of art and passion; from this point of view Defoe is as crude as Prèvost on this one occasion, was subtle and exquisite.

Captain Singleton is an attempt to conjure with the same staff that created *Robinson Crusoe;* this book has had its enthusiastic admirers, but they have been few and perhaps paradoxical. *Colonel Jack* is more readable; his adventures are indeed not those which are set forth, as outside a strolling booth, on the title-page, but they are sufficiently surprising and diverting in their way. The hero is a pickpocket, and the book is full, even beyond Defoe's wont, of little peddling details of a kind to be appreciated by small tradesmen. Like Moll Flanders, Jack is shipped to the plantations after a long career of crime, is penitent, of course, and after a world of vicissitudes, winds up as a virtuous and wealthy Virginian planter. Defoe is even more pitiless to female than to male obliquity. The *Memoirs of a Cavalier* must not be omitted in this catalogue of Defoe's secondary romances. They pretend to give an historical account of affairs in Germany and England between 1632 and 1648; the hero is a Shropshire gentleman, a zealous fighter in the royal cause. It is well known that of all Defoe's attempts at forged history this was the most successful in deceiving; a list of illustrious persons, among them the great Lord Chatham, are mentioned as believing the memoirs to be genuine and contemporary. Of the personages which animate these rough novels of Defoe's, Charles Lamb, the most humane of critics, confessed that they "can never again hope to be popular with a much higher class of readers than that of the servant-maid or the sailor." Macaulay went further, and was utterly extravagant in his dispraise of these books. Yet the quality in them which he found so particularly nauseous, the realism, the unvarnished attention to minute fact, is just what preserves their interest, and may, one of these days, possibly lead to their revival. Defoe, in these novels, is more like M. Zola than any other English writer, and it seems probable that a generation which accepts the author of *Au Bonheur des Dames* may open its arms once more to the laureate of the British tradesman. In all these romances Defoe shows little humour and no pathos, and his study of human nature is exclusively from the outside. Of the following passages the first is taken from *Roxana*, the second from *The Political History of the Devil:*

"In less than half an hour I returned, dressed in the habit of a Turkish princess; the habit I got at Leghorn, when my foreign prince bought me a Turkish slave, as I have said. The Maltese man-of-war had, it seems, taken a Turkish vessel going from Constantinople to Alexandria, in which were some ladies bound for Grand Cairo in Egypt; and, as the ladies were made slaves, so their fine clothes were thus exposed, and with this Turkish slave I bought rich clothes too. The dress was extraordinary fine indeed; I had bought it as a curiosity, having never seen the like. The robe was a fine Persian or Indian damask, the ground white, and the flowers blue and gold, and the train held five yards. The dress under it was a vest of the same, embroidered with gold, and set with some pearl in the work, and some turquoise stones. To the vest was a girdle five or six inches wide, after the Turkish mode; and on both ends, where it joined or hooked, was set with diamonds for eight inches either way, only they were not true diamonds,—but nobody knew that but myself.

"The turban, or headdress, had a pinnacle on the top, but not above five inches, with a piece of loose sarcenet hanging from it; and, on the front, just over the forehead, was a good jewel, which I had added to it.

"This habit, as above, cost me about sixty pistoles in Italy, but cost much more in the country from whence it came; and little did I think, when I bought it, that I should put it to such a use as this, though I had dressed myself many times by the help of my little Turk, and afterwards between Amy and I, only to see how I looked in it. I had sent her up before to get it ready, and when I came up I had nothing to do but slip it on, and was down in my drawing-room in a little more than a quarter of an hour. When I came there, the room was full of company, but I ordered the folding-doors to be shut for a minute or two, till I had received the compliments of the ladies that were in the room, and had given them a full view of my dress."

"I happened to be at an eminent place of God's most devout worship the other day, with a gentleman of my acquaintance, who, I observed, minded very little the business he ought to have come about. First I saw him busy staring about him, and bowing this way and that way. Nay! he made two or three bows and scrapes when he was repeating the responses to the Ten Commandments, and, I assure you, he made it correspond strangely, so that the harmony was not so broken in upon as you would expect it should. Thus: *Lord*—and a bow to a fine lady, just come up to her seat—*have mercy upon us;*—Three bows to a throng of ladies that came into the next pew all together—*and incline*—then stopped to make a great scrape to my lord,—*our hearts*—just then the hearts of all the church were gone off from the subject, for the response was over, so he huddled up the rest in whisper, for God A'mighty could hear him well enough, he said, nay as well as if he had spoken as loud as his neighbours did.

"After we were come home, I asked him what he meant by all this, and what he thought of it.

"'How could I help it?' said he; 'I must not be rude.'

"'What?' says I, 'rude to who?'

"'Why,' says he, 'there came in so many she-devils, I could not help it.'

"'What?' said I, 'could you not help bowing when you were saying your prayers?'

"'O, Sir,' says he, 'the ladies would have thought I had slighted them; I could not avoid it.'

"'*Ladies!*' said I; 'I thought you called them *devils* just now?'

"'Ay, ay, devils,' said he, 'little charming devils; but I must not be rude to them, however.'

"Very well,' said I, 'then you would be rude to God Almighty, because you could not be rude to the Devil?'"

Defoe lives, and will ever live, by *Robinson Crusoe*, the most thrilling boy's book ever written. In 1704 a Scotch buccaneer, Alexander Selkirk of Largo, sailing with Dampier's fleet in the Pacific, was left by his own choice on the desolate island of Juan Fernandez. He stayed there, without seeing a human face, for four years and four months. When he returned to England he became a nine days' wonder, and he was "interviewed" by Steele. Captain Dampier, in his *Voyage round the World*, said, in 1712, that "it would be no difficult matter to embellish a narrative with many romantic incidents" taken from Selkirk's adventures. This is precisely what Defoe did, and Selkirk's story formed much more than the germ of *Robinson Crusoe*. It is the darkest side of Defoe's character, and one that militates strongly against even the mere literary value of his books, that he seldom issued them as works of the imagination, but as narratives actually intended to deceive the public. He declares that *Roxana* is "not a story, but a history," and he asserts of *Robinson Crusoe* that it is "a just history of fact, neither is there any appearance of fiction in it." Nor did he blush to stoop to tricks which were deliberately fraudulent and clandestine, such as dating the last-mentioned narrative 1704, in order to make his Crusoe seem to have preceded Selkirk. These artifices matter little to the reader, who now would rather that Defoe should have written fiction than reported fact, but they throw light on the intellectual character of the author. Defoe had no ambition; he worked as blindly and as restlessly as a mole, and his contemporaries, who saw his writing everywhere, knew nothing of the man himself. He did not wish to win personal distinction; he would have been the first to tell us that he wrote out of zeal for public morality, and to make money. By dint of incessant journalistic work he had attained great skill and fluency in writing, and he had been storing up details in his capacious memory all his life. When his apoplexy withdrew him a little from the hurly-burly, he turned his restless pen to a new sort of trade; and while his hand was still vigorous there was thrown in his way the matchless collection of facts about the solitary man, marooned on the blossoming island, and subduing nature to his wants. The result was that, rather by accident than art, this prosaic and unimpassioned hack produced one of the most beautiful of the world's romances, and tried time after time to repeat his great success, without ever rising again much above mediocrity. Defoe had extraordinary talents, and he retains a not unimportant niche in the history of literature; but it can scarcely be denied that his character exhibits, almost to excess, some of the least pleasing qualities of the eighteenth-century mind and morals.

John Dennis (1657-1734), the critic, was the son of a city saddler. He was educated at Caius College, Cambridge, but was ejected for stabbing a fellow-student. He went over to Trinity Hall, where he proceeded to his M.A. in 1683. He inherited a small fortune, and after travelling on the Continent, settled in London during the last decade of the century as the companion of Dryden, Wycherley, and Congreve. Of his very numerous early productions there may be mentioned, *Remarks on Prince Arthur* (1696), *The Advancement of Poetry* (1701), *The Grounds of Criticism* (1704). These volumes contain much sound sense, and are particularly notable for their fervent and judicious eulogy of Milton. There is nothing in them of that jealous, carping tone for which Dennis afterwards became noted. Dennis fell into reduced circumstances, and he had the impression that younger authors, Addison and Steele in particular, slighted him. About 1710 he began to be extremely ferocious in attacking the new school, and Pope especially irritated him. In 1711 Dennis published *Reflections on an Essay upon Criticism*, in which he called Pope a "stupid and impotent hunch-backed toad," which "surprised people sleeping" that it might "fasten its teeth and its claws" upon them. The vicious temper of Dennis has become proverbial, but his early writings in criticism deserve respectful attention. He published a large number of poems and plays, but these are destitute of all merit. He outlived his annuities and died in extreme penury, an object of charity to those whom he had slandered.

We have now to speak of the famous friends whose careers are inextricably woven into one another and into the intellectual texture of the age of Queen Anne—Steele and Addison. Richard Steele (1672-1729) is now believed to have been born in March 1672; that is to say, about six weeks earlier than his great companion. Like Swift, he was an Englishman born in Dublin. One of the most touching passages in his writings, the 181st *Tatler*, tells us that he lost his father at the age of five, and gives us this memorable sketch of his mother:

"The first sense of sorrow I ever knew was upon the death of my father, at which time I was not quite five years of age; but was rather amazed at what all the house meant, than possessed with a real understanding why nobody was willing to play with me. I remember I went into the room where his body lay, and my mother sat weeping alone by it. I had my battledore in my hand, and fell a beating the coffin, and calling Papa; for, I know not how, I had some slight idea that he was locked up there. My mother catched me in her arms, and, transported beyond all patience of the silent grief she was before in, she almost smothered me in her embraces; and told me in a flood of tears, 'Papa could not hear me, and would play with me no more, for they were going to put him under ground, whence he could never come to us again.' She was a very beautiful woman, of a noble spirit, and there was a dignity in her grief amidst all the wildness of her transport; which, methought, struck me with an instinct of sorrow, that, before I was sensible of what it was to grieve, seized my very soul, and has made pity the weakness of my heart ever since. The mind in infancy is, methinks, like the body in embryo, and receives impressions so forcible, that they are as hard to be removed by reason, as any mark with which a child is born is to be taken away by any future application. Hence it is, that good nature in me is no merit; but having been so frequently overwhelmed with her tears before I knew the cause of any affliction, or could draw defences from my own judgment, I imbibed commiseration, remorse, and an unmanly gentleness of mind, which has since insnared me into ten thousand calamities; and from whence I can reap no advantage, except it be, that, in such a humour as I am now in, I can the better indulge myself in the softnesses of humanity, and enjoy that sweet anxiety which arises from the memory of past afflictions."

Steele and Addison were at school together at Charterhouse, but at Oxford they parted, the former proceeding to Christ Church and the latter to Magdalen. In 1695 Steele, who had removed to Merton, enlisted as a trooper in the Life Guards, and almost immediately afterwards published his first work, a poem called *The Procession*, on Queen Mary's funeral. This was dedicated to Lord Cutts, who sought out the author, and gave him a commission in his own regiment. For the next few years we know little of Steele except that he became a captain. In 1701 he published *The Christian Hero*, a short manual of religious ethics, which passed through many editions, but which was very poorly relished by Steele's fast military associates. "From being thought no undelightful companion, I was now reckoned a disagreeable fellow," he tells us. "To enliven his character," he brought out in the same year his first comedy, *The Funeral*, printed in 1702, which was successful. In 1703 he issued another comedy, *The Lying Lover*, which was "damned for its piety," and in 1705 *The Tender Husband* enjoyed the same fate at Drury Lane. We may pass on to mention the only other play which Steele produced, *The Conscious Lovers* of 1722. Steele's four comedies mark the return of the comic stage to decency. They are comparable, as literary productions, not to the plays of the great Orange period, but to the best of what Cibber and Mrs. Centlivre were bringing out at the same time. Of them all, *The Tender Husband*, in its mild way, is perhaps the most amusing.

Steele became one of the earliest members of the famous Kit-Cat Club, founded by Jacob Tonson (1656-1736). In May 1707 Arthur Maynwaring obtained for him from Harley the appointment of Gazetteer, his duties being to keep the official newspaper "very innocent and very insipid." In the following September he married for the second time. His new wife, "my adorable Molly," was the lady to whom were addressed the very curious and interesting series of letters which we possess, first printed in 1787. The year 1707 is that in which Steele probably came first into regular communication with Swift, who had been a friend of Addison's, certainly since 1705. We may now return to Addison, whose early poetry has been considered in a previous chapter, and who had helped Steele in composing *The Tender Husband*. He was henceforth to be engaged in very close companionship with both Steele and Swift. It was, indeed, the sympathetic genius of the latter which, applied to the characters of the other two, seems to have set them both on fire at the somewhat advanced age of thirty-seven. When Addison published his *Remarks on Several Parts of Italy* he presented a copy of it to Swift with the words, "to the most agreeable companion, the truest friend, and the greatest genius of his age." The three men were presently identified in the popular opinion in the publication of a very remarkable work, *Mr. Bickerstaff's Lucubrations.*

The name of Isaac Bickerstaff had been borrowed from a shop-front by Swift as a pseudònym under which to tease Partridge the almanac-maker; and when Steele, on the 12th of April 1709, issued the first number of the *Tatler*, he also adopted it. This famous newspaper, printed in one folio sheet of "tobacco-paper," with "scurvy letter," ran to 271 numbers, and abruptly ceased to appear in January 1711. It enjoyed an unprecedented success, for, indeed, nothing that approached it had ever before been issued from the periodical press in England. The division of its contents was thus arranged by the editor: "All accounts of gallantry, pleasure, and entertainment shall be under the article of White's Chocolate House; poetry under that of Will's Coffee-House; learning under the title of Grecian; foreign and domestic news you will have from St. James's Coffee-House; and what else I shall on any other subject offer shall be dated from my own apartment." The political news gradually ceased to appear. It is pretended that Addison himself did not suspect Steele's authorship of the new paper until the fifth number, and the eighteenth is certainly the first which came from Addison's hand. Of the 271 *Tatlers*, 188 were written by Steele, 42 by Addison, and 36 by both conjointly. Three were from the pen of John Hughes (1677-1720), a graceful minor writer, author of the very successful tragedy of *The Siege of Damascus* (1720). These, at least, are the numbers usually given, but the evidence on which they are based is slight. It rests mainly upon the indications given by Steele to Tickell when the latter was preparing his edition of Addison's *Works*. The conjecture may be hazarded that there were not a few *Tatlers* written by Addison which he was not anxious to claim as his particular property.

In 1710 Swift's relations with Steele began to grow strained. Swift declares that the latter is "the worst company in the world till he has a bottle of wine in his head." Addison, however, remained Steele's firm friend, and less than two months after the cessation of the *Tatler* there appeared the first number of a still more famous common enterprise, the *Spectator*, on the 1st of March 1711. It was announced to appear daily, and was to be composed of the reflections and actions of the members of an imaginary club, formed around "Mr. Spectator." In this club the most familiar figure is the Worcestershire Knight, Sir Roger de Coverley, the peculiar property of Addison. Here is the outline of one of the lesser figures in the Spectator club traced by the delicate pencil of Addison :

"Will Wimble is younger brother to a baronet, and descended of the ancient family of the Wimbles. He is now between forty and fifty; but being bred to no business and born to no estate, he generally lives with his elder brother as superintendent of his game. He hunts a pack of dogs better than any man in the county, and is very famous for finding out a hare. He is extremely well versed in all the little handicrafts of an idle man. He makes a May-fly to a miracle ; and furnishes the whole country with angle-rods. As he is a good-natured officious fellow, and very much esteemed on account of his family, he is a welcome guest at every house, and keeps up a good correspondence among all the gentlemen round about him. He carries a tulip-root in his pocket from one to another, or exchanges a puppy between a couple of friends that live perhaps in opposite sides of the county. Will is a particular favourite of all the young heirs, whom he frequently obliges with a net that he has weaved, or a setting-dog that he has 'made' himself. He now and then presents a pair of garters of his own knitting to their mothers or sisters ; and raises a great deal of mirth among them, by inquiring as often as he meets them, 'How they wear?' These gentleman-like manufactures and obliging little humours make Will the darling of the county."

The *Spectator* continued to appear daily until December 1712. It consisted of 555 numbers, of which Addison wrote 274, Steele 236, Hughes 19, and Pope 1 (*The Messiah*, *Spectator* 378). Another contributor was Eustace Budgell (1685-1736), Addison's cousin, who afterwards drowned himself under London Bridge. His essays were considerably modified by the pen of Addison. The *Spectator* enjoyed so very unequivocal a success that it has puzzled historians to account for its discontinuance. In No. 517 Addison killed Sir Roger de Coverley, "that nobody else might murder him." This shows a voluntary intention to stop the publication, which the Stamp Act itself had not been able to do by force.

On the 13th of April 1713 Addison's famous tragedy of *Cato*, partly written some twelve years before, was performed amid great public enthusiasm. Whigs and Tories united to applaud this stately and conventional drama, with its prologue by Pope and its epilogue by Garth. It was deliberately executed in the French taste, and the author was rewarded by the unmeasured praise of the foreign critics. Modern readers have grown colder and colder in their attitude towards this famous tragedy, but there are lines in it, and a single scene, which still live in literature. Steele, meanwhile, had started another newspaper. The *Guardian* began to appear on the 12th of March 1713. It ran to 176 numbers, about 82 of which are Steele's; the other contributors were Addison, Berkeley, Pope, Tickell, Budgell, Hughes, and perhaps Gay and Parnell. During the publication of the *Guardian* Steele and Swift became finally estranged. The former plunged deeper and deeper into politics, presently left the newspaper to be conducted by Addison and Berkeley, and entered Parliament as member for Stockbridge. In September his pamphlet on *The Importance of Dunkirk* appeared, and on the 1st of October the *Guardian* was terminated, to be reissued within a week as the *Englishman*. This paper, in 57 numbers, mainly political, was written entirely by Steele, with help from William Moore. After publishing one or two polemical tracts Steele was, in March 1714, ejected from the House of Commons, his troubles being envenomed by the vivacity of Swift's hatred. His next newspapers, the *Lover* and the *Reader*, soon failed. Swift cruelly but pointedly remarked that Steele was obliging "his party with a very awkward

Pamphleteer in the room of an excellent Droll," so completely did he seem in the field of politics to have forgotten his early cunning of hand. For the moment Addison stood aside from the heat of party, and was occupied in 1713 on a work concerning *The Evidences of Christianity*. In the autumn of 1714 he added to the seven volumes of the *Spectator* an eighth. Meanwhile the Tories had fallen, and the Whigs clustered in triumph around the new king, George I. Addison was immediately appointed Chief Secretary for Ireland in the new Government.

Steele's turn also had arrived, and he was made Supervisor of Drury Lane Theatre early in 1715. He was presently elected M.P. for Boroughbridge, and in April was knighted by the king. In March 1715 he brought out at Drury Lane Addison's comedy of *The Drummer*, a play adorned by some smartness of dialogue, but in other respects one of the weakest of its author's productions. Addison's short-lived greatness in the political world had come to an end when the Duke of Shrewsbury resigned in August 1715. In December of that year Addison started his newspaper of the *Freeholder*, which lasted, in 55 numbers, until June 1716. The essays in this periodical mainly dealt with questions concerning the situation of political affairs at the moment, and Steele, who thought himself the better politician, compared the voice of Addison to a lute and his own to a trumpet. The "lute" was rewarded by a Commissionership for Trade and the Colonies; and Addison presently married an old flame of his, the Countess of Warwick. In 1717, with Sunderland's triumph, Addison came into office again; but we find Steele writing, "I ask no favour of Mr. Secretary Addison." The latter retired with a pension in 1718. In 1719 the tension between the two old friends became very sharp, and amounted almost to a quarrel—a state of things which the generous heart of Steele bitterly lamented, when, on the 17th of June of that year, Addison died prematurely of dropsy. His body lay in state in Jerusalem Chamber, and was buried by lamplight in the Abbey. Tickell bewailed him in an immortal strain of melody and pathos.

Steele survived his friend by ten years, but his literary work during that time was scrappy and unimportant. He started fresh newspapers, the *Theatre*, the *Spinster* (concerning the woollen trade, and not maiden ladies), and in 1722 brought out at Drury Lane his Terentian comedy of *The Conscious Lovers*. Two other plays, *The School of Action* and *The Gentleman*, begun about this time, were never finished; their fragmentary scenes first saw the light in 1809. In 1723, broken in health and with his affairs in hopeless confusion, Steele left London, never, it is believed, to return. The rest of his life he spent obscurely, partly at Hereford, partly at Carmarthen. In the latter town he died on the 1st of September 1729.

The time has probably gone by when either Addison or Steele could be placed at the summit of the literary life of their time. Swift and Pope, each in his own way, distinctly surpassed them. Nor, if their essays in periodical form are put out of sight, can their other writings claim any very lively immortality. But the *Tatler* and the *Spectator* hold an extraordinary place in the affections of Englishmen, and form a body of literature which is in its own way unique. They endeavoured, as Addison put it in the 10th *Spectator*, "to enliven morality with wit, and to temper wit with morality," by introducing to the public a kind of reading such as had never come in its way before. In considering the conduct of these periodicals it is useless to continue the vague discussion whether Addison or Steele was the more skilful. If Steele was a little more ready than his friend to take the initiative, Addison was a little more capable of arresting the interest of the reader unaided. The *Freeholder* has better things in it, no doubt, than either the *Lover* or the *Reader*. The great proof of the power of these two friends is found in the fact that, although it is comparatively so easy to imitate a discovery, there was no tolerable successor to the *Guardian* for nearly forty years, nor could the *Rambler* be held to follow the *Spectator* otherwise than, as Lady Mary Wortley Montagu said, "a pack-horse would follow a hunter."

It is difficult in a short summary of facts to give any impression of the influence exercised on the mind and feelings of his country by Addison. It was out of proportion with the mere outcome of his literary genius. It was the result of character almost more than of intellect, of goodness and reasonableness almost more than of wit. His qualities of mind, however, if not of the very loftiest order, were relatively harmonised to an astonishing degree, so that the general impression of Addison is of a larger man than the close contemplation of any one side of his genius reveals him as being. He has all the moral ornaments of the literary character; as a writer he is urbane, cheerful, charming, and well-mannered to a degree which has scarcely been surpassed in the history of the world. His wit is as penetrating as a perfume; his irony presupposes a little circle of the best and most cultivated listeners; his fancy is so well tempered by judgment and observation that it passes with us for imagination. We delight in his company so greatly that we do not pause to reflect that the inventor of Sir Roger de Coverley and Will Honeycomb had not half of the real comic force of Farquhar or Vanbrugh, nor so much as that of the flashing wit of Congreve. Human nature, however, is superior to the rules, and Addison stands higher than those more original writers by merit of the reasonableness, the good sense, the wholesome humanity that animates his work. He is classic, while they are always a little way over on the barbaric side of perfection.

The style of Addison is superior to his matter, and holds a good many flies in its exquisite amber. It did not reach its highest quality until Addison had become acquainted with *A Tale of a Tub*, but it grew to be a finer thing, though not a greater, than the style of Swift. Addison was excessively fastidious in his choice of words, laboriously polishing and balancing his phrases until they represented the finest literary art at his disposal, until the rhythm was perfect, the sentence as light and bright as possible, and the air of good breeding at which he always aimed successfully caught. He was probably the earliest English author of prose, except, perhaps, Sir Thomas Browne, who aimed deliberately at beauty of execution, and treated the pedestrian form with as much respect as though it had been verse. It does not seem to be known to what extent Addison was influenced by French models. The great Frenchmen of the preceding generation had been observers, "Spectators," like himself: La Rochefoucauld, with his clean and unadorned simplicity of style; La Bruyère, with his irony and common sense. The latter, as was sure to be the case, was soon recognised as an intellectual kinsman of Addison's, whose limpid, graceful style not a little resembles his. Addison was probably familiar with the *Caractères*, which were published in 1687, when he was a lad. Addison's share in completing the development of our language was very considerable; he smoothed down English phraseology to an almost perilous extent, and Swift, who admitted that the *Spectator* was very pretty, thought that Addison's tendency was too feminine. He vastly enlarged the field of the English author by directly addressing the women, and was the first secular writer whose productions formed part of the tea-equipage of the virtuous fine lady.

With some modification, what has been said of Addison may be repeated of Steele, whose fame has been steadily growing while the exaggerated reputation of Addison has been declining. The character of Steele, with his chivalry and his derelictions, his high ideal and his broken resolves, has been a favourite one with recent biographers, who prefer his rough address to the excessive and meticulous civility of Addison. It is permissible to love them both, and to see in each the complement of the other. It is proved that writers like Macaulay and even Thackeray have overcharged the picture of Steele's delinquencies, and have exaggerated the amount of Addison's patronage of his friend. But nothing can explain away Steele's carelessness in money matters or his inconsistency in questions of moral detail. He was very quick, warm-hearted, and impulsive, while Addison had the advantage of a cold and phlegmatic constitution. Against the many eulogists of the younger man we may place Leigh Hunt's sentence, "I prefer open-hearted Steele with all his faults to Addison with all his essays." His style presents less material for study than that of Addison, because it is itself unstudied. When Addison was so delicately weighing and polishing his sentences, Steele was pouring out what he saw or what he felt. He is very incorrect, sometimes downright ungrammatical. When he preaches, as he is very apt to do, we fall to nodding in his face. But we wake again when he returns to the subject he knows best, the shifting pictures of human life, with its hopes and disappointments, its laughter and its tears. When he talks to us about the beauty of virtuous women, the loneliness of orphan children, the innocent conversation of old men, any of the single human topics which literature had so long time thought below her dignity, we are fascinated and bewitched; his style takes fire, "the motion doth dilate the flame," and Steele becomes a great writer. Of his humour Mr. Austin Dobson has well said that " it has little of practised art or perceptive delicacy; but it is uniformly kindly, genial, indulgent." The most famous phrase which Steele has bequeathed to posterity is to be found in the 49th *Tatler*, where he nobly says of Lady Elizabeth Hastings that "to love her is a liberal education."

The professional theologians of the age of Anne possess little charm for a modern student of literature. Even Dr. Samuel Clarke (1675-1729), the most eminent of the divines during his own age, is now but little read or regarded. He was educated at Caius College, Cambridge, and was one of the first who embraced the discoveries of Sir Isaac Newton, to whom he affected, throughout his career, to stand in the relation of a theological knight-errant. His publications were very numerous; of especial interest are the Boyle Lectures, given in 1704 and 1705, on *The Being and Attributes of God* and on *The Evidences of Natural and Revealed Religion*. In these books he takes up a central position between orthodoxy and deism, and stands forth as the representative of what were known as Low Church views. His acceptation of the doctrine of the Trinity was far from sound, and in 1712 his tract on this subject was arraigned before Convocation. Clarke was plunged into violent controversy; from this cause, perhaps, he never received the promotion in the Church to which his gifts entitled him. In 1717 he published a correspondence, on philosophy and religion, which had passed between himself and Leibnitz (1646-1716). He is a clear, cold writer, who seems to arrange his ideas in the form of mathematical diagrams.

Dr. Benjamin Hoadly (1676-1761) desired to be known as the "Friend of Clarke," whose works he edited. He was a man of incomparable ardour and restlessness of mind, an uncompromising Whig of the school of Locke. Hoadly was excessively unpopular; the poets hated him, and his sympathies for the dissenters made him distrusted by his own class. He was tainted with heterodoxy even to a greater extent than Clarke, and was far more reckless in the statement of his opinions. As a writer, he is both furious and tiresome, and almost the only purely literary interest we have in him centres around his friendship for Steele. In spite of his unpopularity he was early raised to the see of Bangor, where his famous sermon on *The Nature of the Kingdom of Christ*, 1717, involved him in the noisy and prolonged dispute known as the Bangorian Controversy. Sir Leslie Stephen says, that "in his pachydermatous fashion Hoadly did some service, by helping to trample down certain relics of the old spirit of bigotry." In the course of his very long life Hoadly not only rose to be successively Bishop of Hereford, Salisbury, and Winchester, but even outlived the enmity of his literary contemporaries, and Akenside greets him thus in his last years:

> "We attend thy reverend length of days
> With benediction and with praise;
> We hail thee in the public ways,
> Like some great spirit famed in ages old!"

Hoadly, although so tough and rugged, was all his life a cripple, and used to kneel in the pulpit when he preached.

Thomas Sherlock (1678-1761) was a sort of theological lawyer, eminent for the clear masculine good sense of his sermons. He is remembered as the author of a *Letter* on the earthquakes of 1750, of which no fewer than 100,000 copies were sold. His style in this treatise is dignified and vigorous.

The most prominent figure in philosophy between Locke and Hume is George Berkeley (1685-1753), the most acute of English metaphysicians, and the most polished writer of his age. This extraordinary man was born in a cottage near Dysert Castle, in the county of Kilkenny; his parents were Irish people of English descent. In 1696 he was sent to the Irish Eton, Kilkenny School, where Congreve and Swift had preceded him. Four years later he matriculated at Dublin. From 1700 to 1713 he was a resident of Trinity College, where, as early as 1705, and apparently without external influence of any kind, he formed that theory of the non-existence of matter which was to be the central idea of his future philosophy. It is probable that Berkeley's mind was early prejudiced against the deists by Dr. Peter Browne (1660?-1735), the metaphysical opponent of Toland, as Browne was at that time Provost of Trinity. In 1707 Berkeley became M.A., and fellow and tutor of his college. To these offices he presently added those of Greek lecturer and junior dean. He took orders in 1709, but it was not until twenty years later that he began to engage in clerical duty. In 1707 he published anonymously two Latin tracts on mathematics, and was all this time jotting down the entries in that invaluable *Commonplace Book*, which Dr. Campbell Fraser first published in 1871. This enables us, as its editor says, "to watch Berkeley when he was awakening into intellectual life, in company with Locke and Descartes and Malebranche." It was from Locke that Berkeley immediately started; his views of spiritual things being, moreover, tinctured in later life by the study of Plato. On this basis he built the structure of his phenomenalism—his theory that what we see and touch is only a symbol of what is spiritual and eternal; that nothing is, but only seems to be. Berkeley's first attempt to convert the world to a belief in the non-existence of matter is found in the *Essay towards a New Theory of Vision*, published in 1709. This treatise is intended to show that sight affords us knowledge, which our experience hastens to translate into the language of touch, so that sight is really foresight, and the action of the eyes has no reality until it is transformed into a mental condition, an experience of visual suggestions. His hypothesis is supported, even in this youthful essay, with great beauty of illustration and charm of delivery, but the author did not for the present attempt to pass beyond his proof of the existence of an artificial world of visual ideas. He followed it, however, in 1710, with a *Treatise concerning the Principles of Human Knowledge*, of which only a fragment was ever published. In this Berkeley endeavoured to extend his theory from the phenomena of sight to those of the whole world of sense. He complained that the philosophical dust which philosophers had hitherto raised in the consideration of matter had "blocked up the way to knowledge." He proposed to clear away materialism altogether, in order that Man might clearly and simply come into contact with the Eternal Spirit. He believed that the objects which we think we see around us exist only as a harmonious chain of appearances founded by a mind, and appealing directly to the spiritual consciousness.

This abstruse and novel theory of metaphysics was at first received with ridicule by those who did not take the trouble to understand it. A man of higher stamp and more philosophical training, Dr. Samuel Clarke, recognised Berkeley as "an extraordinary genius," but rejected his theory, and oddly enough thought that he had mistaken his direction in taking up metaphysics. Berkeley spent the next years in further developing his philosophical views, and published in 1713 his beautiful little volume of Platonic dialogues, entitled *Hylas and Philonous*. The object of this treatise was to establish still further the incorporeal nature of the Soul, and to prove, by wielding his theory against the deists, that it was a weapon which could only be used in the service of revealed religion. In this work Berkeley first displayed his wonderful skill as a manipulator of the English language, which had never been employed for the discussion of philosophical ideas with anything like so much grace and refinement. He now laid down with complete courage his axiom that "no idea can exist out of the mind"; and he thought that the recognition of this metaphysical fact was "a direct and immediate demonstration of God's existence, and a short method of crushing scepticism." In these dialogues Hylas is the objector, and his difficulties are ingeniously solved by Philonous, the champion of the phenomenal theory of the world. In order to print his dialogues in London, Berkeley made, in January 1713, his first journey to England, and arrived just in time to take his place in the brilliant world of letters that has received its name from Queen Anne. He was welcomed in London literary society by Steele, who immediately secured him to write a series of bright essays against the freethinkers in the pages of the *Guardian*.

Swift immediately perceived the merit of Berkeley, and writes to Stella on his first meeting that this is a great philosopher—one whom he will favour as much as he can. Berkeley was received on terms of equality, too, by Addison, Pope, and Arbuthnot, and sat in Addison's box at the first performance of *Cato*. His beauty of person, his unaffected grace of manner, and an indescribable air of goodness and candour which emanated from him, combined to make him a universal favourite. Pope protested that there had been given "to Berkeley every virtue under heaven"; and the grim Atterbury confessed that "so much understanding, so much knowledge, so much innocence, and such humility, I did not think had been the portion of any but angels, till I saw this gentleman." In the autumn of 1713, by Swift's help, he obtained a chaplaincy to the Earl of Peterborough, which enabled him to spend ten months in Sicily, Italy, and France, under auspices of a peculiarly brilliant kind; and in Paris he met Malebranche. From 1716 to 1720 he was again in Italy. Legend asserts that a heated conversation with Malebranche, on the subject of the non-existence of matter, led to the death of the Frenchman. Dates, however, are against this story, which is picturesque, but foreign to the gracious character of Berkeley. A *Natural History of Sicily*, which the philosopher is supposed to have written in 1719, has been lost. In 1720 he competed for a prize offered by the French Academy for a Latin dissertation, *De Motu*, but the prize was allotted to Crousaz, the Swiss logician. With this production the philosophical work of Berkeley's early life closes.

On his return to England he threw himself into the discussion of social problems, and published in 1721 an *Essay towards preventing the Ruin of Great Britain*, which was called forth by the misery ensuing on the collapse of the South Sea speculation. It is a plea for stoic simplicity of life. He then went back, after an absence of eight years, to his college life at Dublin. In May 1724 he was made Dean of Derry, the richest deanery in Ireland; but it was with no intention of settling in a rich living that he accepted it. His mind had long been dwelling on the fact that, as he puts it in his solitary poem,

"Westward the course of Empire takes its way."

He was planning an ideal university in the Bermuda Islands—a scheme which had been encouraged by the fact that Swift's Vanessa (Hester Vanhomrigh) had just left him half her considerable fortune, although Berkeley was not aware that she had ever seen him. The Bermuda project, furthered by Berkeley's pure passion and irresistible fascination, succeeded to an amazing degree, and a vote for a public grant of £20,000 to endow the Bermuda University was actually carried through both Houses of Parliament. Berkeley meanwhile was idolised in England, and he carried captive admirers so unlike one another as Voltaire and Queen Caroline. It was not, however, until late in 1728 that he succeeded in starting for America; and then not for Bermuda but for Rhode Island. In January 1729 he landed near Newport, with a newly married wife, and there bought an inland farm and built a house. The plan for an endowed university never came to anything, for Walpole took care to wreck it. Berkeley settled down to the composition of his *Alciphron*, which is reported to have been written in a cave on the shore of Rhode Island. It is said that Berkeley was one of the early benefactors of Yale College. This strange philosophic exile in America—a period of great calm and happiness in his life—closed, after three years, at the end of 1731. He settled, not at Derry, of which he still was dean, but in London.

As John Stuart Mill has remarked, the leading purpose of Berkeley as a philosopher was to vanquish the freethinkers. He pushed this polemical intention a little too far in his next work, *Alciphron, or the Minute Philosopher*, 1732, in which his main attack is upon Shaftesbury and Mandeville. This is the longest of Berkeley's books, and perhaps the most easy for the outsider to understand; philosophers have condemned it as the least valuable. The scene of the book is laid in Rhode Island, and the form is that of the Platonic dialogue, in its most polished and graceful shape. The dialogues are seven, and there is a slight setting of landscape to each, with a hint of woods and gardens, and the distant hallo of the fox-hunter. *Alciphron* was abundantly attacked, and the doctrine of immaterialism proved doubly unwelcome when it was seen to be used as an argument against atheism, whose genteel professors the author sneered at as "minute philosophers."

"I can easily comprehend that no man upon earth ought to prize anodynes for the spleen more than a man of fashion and pleasure. An ancient sage, speaking of one of that character, saith, He is made wretched by disappointments and appetites. And if this was true of the Greeks, who lived in the sun, and had so much spirit, I am apt to think it still more so of our modern English. Something there is in our climate and complexion that makes idleness nowhere so much its own punishment as in England, where an uneducated fine gentleman pays for his momentary pleasures with long and cruel intervals of spleen. . . . There is a cast of thought in the complexion of an Englishman, which renders him the most unsuccessful rake in the world. He is, as Aristotle expresseth it, at variance with himself. He is neither brute enough to enjoy his appetites, nor man enough to govern them. He knows and feels that what he pursues is not his true good, his reflection only serving to show him that misery which his habitual sloth and indolence will not suffer him to remedy. At length, being grown odious to himself, and abhorring his own company, he runs into every idle assembly, not from the hopes of pleasure, but merely to respite the pain of his own mind. Listless and uneasy at the present, he hath no delight in reflecting on what is past, or in the prospect of anything to come. This man of pleasure, when after a wretched scene of vanity and woe his animal nature is worn to the stumps, wishes for and dreads Death by turns, and is sick of living, without having ever tried or known the true life of man."

For some time Berkeley was fully engaged in controversy, and then in the spring of 1734 he returned to Ireland, as Bishop of Cloyne—a little town which was to be his home for the next eighteen years. In the palace at Cloyne he presently set up a distillery of tar-water—a medicine which had long attracted him, from its supposed quality of being charged with "pure invisible fire, the most subtle and elastic of bodies." Finally, in 1744, he published his extraordinary book called *Siris*, a chain of philosophical reflections and inquiries concerning tar-water. In this treatise Berkeley originates a phrase often attributed to Cowper, and describes tar-water as a beverage which "cheers but not inebriates." A single passage can give but little impression of the strange crossed warp and woof of the book :

"The balsam or essential oil of vegetables contains a spirit, wherein consist the specific qualities, the smell and taste of the plant. Boerhave holds the native presiding spirit to be neither oil, salt, earth, nor water, but somewhat too fine and subtle to be caught alone and rendered visible to the eye. This, when suffered to fly off, for instance, from the oil of rosemary, leaves it destitute of all flavour. This spark of life, this spirit or soul, if we may so say, of the vegetable departs without any sensible diminution of the oil or water wherein it was lodged.

"It should seem that the forms, souls, or principles of vegetable life subsist in the light or solar emanation, which in respect to the macrocosm is what the animal spirit is to the microcosm,—the interior tegument, the subtle instrument and vehicle of power. No wonder, then, that the *ens primum* or *scintilla spirituosa*, as it is called, of plants should be a thing so fine and fugacious as to escape our nicest search. It is evident that nature at the sun's approach vegetates, and languishes at his recess ; this terrestrial globe seeming only a matrix disposed and prepared to receive life from his light. . . . The luminous spark which is the form or life of a plant, from whence its differences and properties flow, is somewhat extremely volatile."

BERKELEY'S "SIRIS"

Siris is a most curious amalgam of hints for the manufacture and use of the author's panacea, and of magnificent flights into Platonic regions of pure intellect. Of late Berkeley had been studying the Greek metaphysicians with especial earnestness, and in *Siris* his thought is etherealised and his style kindled by contact with the light and fire of ancient thought. In no other part of his writings does Berkeley reach the brilliant and audacious subtlety of the best passages in *Siris*.

In 1752 Berkeley determined to resign Cloyne and to settle in Oxford; but George II., while desiring him to live where he pleased, vowed that he should die a bishop. He published one or two tracts while he was at Oxford, but his stay there was brief; without positive illness, he grew weaker and weaker. On the 14th of January 1753 he died peacefully, while sleeping on a sofa, and was buried in Christ Church Cathedral. He lived just long enough to be praised by Hume, though it does not appear that Berkeley became aware of the existence of the young man who was destined to be our next great philosopher. In this place no attempt can be made to sketch Berkeley's contributions to thought. We have only to deal with him as a writer. In this capacity we may note that the abstruse nature of his contributions to literature has unduly concealed the fact that Berkeley is one of the most exquisite of all writers of English prose. Among the authors who will find a place in the present volume, it may perhaps be said that there is not one who is quite his equal in style; his prose is distinguished as well for dignity and fulness of phrase, without pomposity, as for splendour and delicacy of diction, without effeminacy.

William Law (1686-1761) was a Christian mystic whose name was first rescued from obscurity by the pious care of Gibbon, whose father he had taught in early youth; Law had afterwards resided in the historian's family. Law spent the rest of his life in a sort of cloister in his native village of King's Cliff, where certain pious ladies clustered round him and formed a little spiritual community. For their use, in the first instance, he wrote his remarkable Evangelical treatise, *A Serious Call to a Devout and Holy Life*, 1729, —a volume that is composed in an enthusiastic and exalted spirit which is almost an anomaly in the prosaic eighteenth century. Law was a High Churchman, and he enjoined upon his readers an unflinching asceticism, denouncing every species of carnal pleasure with the fervour of a Tertullian. Although the Wesleyans in the succeeding generation owed a good deal to his teaching, neither they nor any section of the Church of England could be said to be his disciples. He is, in fact, a solitary philosophic mystic, of very unusual literary gift. Certain of his treatises contain sketches somewhat in the manner of La Bruyère, of typical men and women of the world, drawn with a great deal of wit and fancy. Wesley was at first an admirer of Law, but he broke with him in 1738, and in 1756 Wesley severely and publicly attacked his old friend's mysticism. Yet late on in life Wesley found himself obliged to speak of the *Serious Call* as "a treatise which will hardly be excelled in the English tongue either for beauty of expression or for justice and depth of thought."

The two women who wrote most cleverly during the reign of Anne were unlucky enough to secure a pre-eminence in coarseness of language, a quality which would have enabled them to graduate with success in the school of Charles II. It has never been suggested to question the ability of Lady Mary Wortley Montagu (1689-1762), the eldest daughter of Evelyn Pierrepont, Duke of Kingston, though she is now perhaps best remembered by her unseemly squabbles with Pope. Lady Mary was educated under Bishop Burnet, who early instilled into her a passionate love of literature. For him, at the age of twenty, she translated the *Enchiridion* of Epictetus. At eight years old she was the toast of the Kit-Cat Club, her face already giving promise of the splendid beauty of her maturity. When she was six-and-twenty, her husband, Edward Wortley Montagu, was appointed ambassador to the Porte, and Lady Mary had the advantage, for two or three years, of studying Eastern manners under unusually favourable circumstances. From 1739 to 1761 she resided principally in

Italy. It was her habit, during her long periods of exile from England, to write copiously to friends at home, and when a selection from these letters was published in 1763 Lady Mary was recognised at once as having been one of the wittiest of English letter-writers. She took pains to introduce into this country in 1717 the Turkish practice of inoculation for the smallpox, and it is in a letter to Miss Sarah Chiswell, from Adrianople, on 1st April of that year, that she first mentions this subject, in the following terms:

"I am going to tell you a thing that I am sure will make you wish yourself here. The small-pox, so fatal and so general amongst us, is here entirely harmless by the invention of *ingrafting*, which is the term they give it. There is a set of old women who make it their business to perform the operation every autumn, in the month of September, when the great heat is abated. People send to one another to know if any of their family has a mind to have the small-pox; they make parties for this purpose, and when they are met (commonly fifteen or sixteen together), the old woman comes with a nut-shell full of the matter of the best sort of small-pox, and asks what veins you please to have opened. She immediately rips open that you offer to her with a large needle (which gives you no more pain than a common scratch), and puts into the vein as much venom as can lie upon the head of her needle, and after binds up the little wound with a hollow bit of shell; and in this manner opens four or five veins. The Grecians have commonly the superstition of opening one in the middle of the forehead, in each arm, and on the breast, to mark the sign of the cross; but this has a very ill effect, all these wounds leaving little scars, and is not done by those who are not superstitious, who choose to have them in the legs, or that part of the arm that is concealed. . . . Every year thousands undergo this operation, and the French ambassador says, pleasantly, that they take the small-pox here by way of diversion, as they take the waters in other countries."

In many respects, though hard and mannish in temper, Lady Mary was eminent for width of view and for a mind open to the whole intellectual horizon. Her *Town Eclogues*, printed in 1716 in heroic verse, are so rich and sparkling that they almost place Lady Mary among the poets, but they are of astounding freedom of thought and language.

A muse more draggle-tailed than Lady Mary's now claims our attention for a moment. Delarivière Manley (1672-1724) was born in Guernsey, of which island her father was governor. She was early left an orphan, was seduced and basely abandoned by a relative, and during the remainder of her unhappy life never succeeded in making peace with society. She set herself to write for the stage, and produced two plays in 1696, a tragedy of *The Royal Mischief* and a comedy of *The Lost Lover*, both of which enjoyed a considerable success. Her later dramas were less brilliant and less fortunate. She fell into poverty and distress, and revenged herself upon the town in 1709 by publishing the four volumes of that "cornucopia of scandal" *The New Atalantis*, in which almost every public character of the day had his or her niche. This scurrilous book passed through a great number of editions; it amused Swift, who determined to make use of the author. He described Mrs. Manley to Stella as having "very generous principles for one of her sort, and a great deal of good sense and invention;" although Steele, after she had attacked him, professed to find her "a bubble to his mind." She continued her prolific *Secret Memoirs*, and presently slipped into journalism. In June 1711 Swift gave up into her hands the editorship of the *Examiner*. She held it until the beginning of 1713. Mrs. Manley's scandalous pamphlets are now dispersed, in many cases beyond recognition. Mr. Austin Dobson believes that she wrote the famous Toby *Character of Richard St—le* in 1713. She grew to be very fat and homely, but she found an admirer in Alderman Barber, who lifted her from the drudgery of Grub Street and gave her a home in his house until she died. We would willingly give a page from *The New Atalantis*, but unfortunately it is precisely where Mrs. Manley is most picturesque that it is least possible to quote from her.

CHAPTER VII

THE DAWN OF NATURALISM IN POETRY

TOWARDS the close of Pope's career, a distinct change began to come over the face of English poetry. When the prestige of Pope was at its height, and the execution of his verse most highly admired, the strongest among the younger poets began to cease to follow him, partly, perhaps, because they despaired of surpassing him in his peculiar excellences—partly, no doubt, in response to an alteration in popular taste. Pope himself, by his *Eloisa to Abelard*, had hinted at the possibility of reintroducing poetry of a very serious and romantic type, which should deal with questions of moral passion in solemn numbers. The work of the group of poets which was then presently to be in the ascendant proved to be pitched mainly in this key, to which Pope never recurred, although he received the productions of the first romantic poets with sympathy, and even, it is said, with the hand and eye of a benignant technical master. The imitation of Pope was revived a generation later, and also, of course, existed widely throughout the period of which we are now speaking; but it is not always clearly enough recognised that the Augustan spirit had remarkably little part in suggesting what was best in the poetry of the second section of the eighteenth century.

During the twenty-five years from the publication of Thomson's *Winter* in 1726 to that of Gray's *Elegy* in 1751, the nine or ten leading poems or collections of verse which appeared were all of a new type, sombre, as a rule, certainly stately, romantic in tone to the extreme, prepared to return, ignorantly indeed, but with respect, to what was "Gothic" in manners, architecture, and language, all showing a more or less vague aspiration towards the study of nature, and not one composed in the heroic couplet hitherto so rigorously imposed on serious verse. *The Seasons*, *Night Thoughts*, and *The Grave* are written in blank verse, *The Castle of Indolence* and *The Schoolmistress* in Spenserian stanza, *The Spleen* and *Grongar Hill* in octosyllabics (in the latter case very loosely strung), while the early odes of Gray and those of Collins are composed in a great variety of simple but novel lyric measures. The later elaborate odes of Gray, published in 1754, come outside our limit of date, and form in their turn a link with the nineteenth century.

This group of poets, then, containing one great man of letters, Gray, and at least two poets of very high rank, Thomson and Collins, possesses an historical importance out of proportion with its popularity at the present moment. After having enjoyed a reputation considerably in excess of their merits, certain of these romantic moralists of the second quarter of the eighteenth century are now scarcely read at all. Their names, nevertheless, are still familiar to every educated person, and they live in tradition and anecdote. They mark the faint glow of the coming naturalism much more clearly than do the poets of the succeeding age, where the darkness was most solid just before the dawn. In their pomp of style and crepuscular moral splendour they appeal to a taste which is not of to-day; but a careful and sympathetic study of their writings may be urged upon the student of literature as indispensable to a proper comprehension of one very characteristic side of the intellectual development of the eighteenth century.

The study of nature which is marked in the writings of this group of poets received considerable encouragement from the newly-fostered appetite for ballads and loosely-kilted Scottish songs. Allan Ramsay, in his *Scots Songs* of 1719, and still more in his *Tea-Table Miscellany* and *Evergreen* of 1724, had responded to the nascent curiosity regarding the simpler lyric literature of an earlier age. His own ballads were artless, but he had encouraged the publication of those very remarkable lyrics, *The Braes of Yarrow* of Hamilton of Bangour (1704-1754) and the *William and Margaret* of David Mallet. The former of these poems contains such stanzas as the following, which, with their strange fugitive melody, must have sounded with extraordinary freshness on the ears of the subjects of Queen Anne:

> " Sweet smells the birk, green grows, green grows the grass
>   Yellow upon Yarrow bank the gowan,
> Fair hangs the apple frae the rock,
>   Sweet the wave of Yarrow flowin'.
>
> " Flows Yarrow sweet? as sweet, as sweet flows Tweed,
>   As green its grass, its gowan as yellow,
> As sweet smells on its braes the birk,
>   The apple frae the rock as mellow.
>
> " Fair was thy love, fair, fair indeed thy love;
>   In flowery bonds thou him didst fetter;
> Though he was fair and weil beloved again
>   Than me he never loved thee better.
>
> " Busk ye, then busk, my bonny, bonny bride;
>   Busk ye, busk ye, my winsome marrow,
> Busk ye, and love me on the banks of Tweed,
>   And think nae mair on the braes of Yarrow.'

Although the sedateness of the style of Thomson and his school shows little superficial influence from these pathetic ballads, the simplicity of the latter and their direct appeal to nature were not without a marked effect upon the poetry of the generation.

The connecting link between this group of poets and their predecessors of the Augustan age is found in the works of Edward Young (1683-1765), who was considerably older than Pope and Gay, but who did not develop his poetical genius till very late in life. Young published nothing until his thirtieth year. In 1741, at the mature age of fifty-eight, he superintended the collection of his "poetical works," in two volumes, which, however, interesting now to the student of his career, contained no single page which, had Young written no more, would call for his mention in such a volume as this. It was during his old age that he composed and published those works which have given him so prominent a literary position.

Young was educated at Oxford, where he became a lay fellow of All Souls in 1708; he remained at the university, fretting against obscurity, until middle life. In 1721 he attempted to enter Parliament, but was defeated, and finally, when nearly fifty years of age, he took holy orders, and sought promotion in the Church, since he could find it nowhere else. He was made chaplain to the king in 1728, and accepted the college living of Welwyn in 1730, but here his ecclesiastical preferments ended. For the next thirty-five years, in various tones of angry protest or murmuring persuasion, he endeavoured, but in vain, to draw attention to his want of a mitre. He closed his long career, rich indeed through his marriage with the Earl of Lichfield's daughter, Lady Elizabeth Lee, but petulant, proud, and solitary. The insatiable ambition of Young has been the theme of many moralists, and the tendency of his personal character was indubitably parasitic; but it would be easy to show, on the other hand, that he really was, to an eminent degree, what Hobbes calls an "episcopable" person, and that his talents, his address, his loyalty, and his moral force were qualities which not only might, but for the honour of the English Church should, have been publicly acknowledged by preferment. When he saw men like Sherlock and Secker (1693-1768), as a reward for "running a race for the old ladies," bounding into the padded ease of bishops' thrones, Young, sitting alone in the light of his austere intellect, may be forgiven if he displayed some angry indiscretion.

Towards the middle of the Queen Anne period Young appeared with his first important poem, *The Last Day*, printed at Oxford in 1713; part of it had already been seen in the *Guardian*. It is a sombre essay in the heroic couplet, and in three books, on the end of the world; and, in spite of some coarse imagery and a good deal of needless bombast, it possesses considerable gloomy force. The final book is the best, and the address of the lost soul to God, beginning—

> " Father of mercies ! why from silent earth
> Didst thou awake, and curse me into birth ? "

if of dubious piety, is not equalled for poetic felicity elsewhere in Young's writings outside *Night Thoughts*. This piece was succeeded in 1714 by *The Force of Religion*, a short poem in two books; the first containing a very commonplace account, abruptly introduced, of the feelings of Lady Jane Gray on being separated from Guildford; and the second, a relation of their meeting. There is no other point to this crude poem than the introduction of compliments to Lady Salisbury. Young's next effort was made in the direction of the theatre. He attempted to conquer distinction as a tragedian. His *Busiris* succeeded at Drury Lane in 1719. In this blank-verse tragedy there is very little about Busiris; the interest centres around the violent and lawless passion of Myron for the gentle Mandane. There is a perilous scene of dumb show between Mandane and Memnon, in the fourth act, which might be so played as to be very effective. But the verse and language have the violence, with some of the tragic glow, of Lee, whom Young seems to have taken as a model. *The Revenge* (1721), though generally admitted to be a better play, was not so successful as its predecessor. This also is in the taste and style of the Restoration, and turns upon the colossal passions and magnificent indignation of a Moor, Zanga, who talks very eloquently, and like the future poet of the *Night Thoughts*; it is to Young's credit that he treats a story much resembling that treated by Shakespeare, without inevitably reminding us of *Othello*. His third tragedy, *The Brothers*, was not performed until 1753. Young was too rhetorical to be a successful dramatist, and the lamp he affected to use while composing—a candle stuck into a human skull—failed to inspire him satisfactorily. In 1725 he began, and in 1728 concluded, the publication of his series of seven satires, *Love of Fame, the Universal Passion*, for which he received £3000. These pieces preceded Pope's essays in the same direction, and though Swift justly complained that they should have been either more merry or more angry to be good satires, they pleased the town. They were smooth and brilliant, though very carelessly rhymed; they were really witty, though they always lacked the last polish; and, until Pope threw them into the shade by the lustre of his own, they passed as very light and sparkling satires in the Latin manner. The fifth, on Woman, is much the brightest and liveliest; the second contains the famous eulogy upon Chesterfield. These satires are so entirely unlike Young's earlier and later writings in character and versification as to show the extreme danger of dogmatising upon questions of dubious authorship on the sole evidence of internal style. Young now sank to extraordinary depths of failure in a variety of lyrical experiments. He had less of the singing gift in his composition than almost any other poet of equal magnitude on record, and his Odes called *Ocean* (1728), *Imperium Pelagi* (1729), *Sea-Piece* (1733), and *The Foreign Address* (1734), read like intentional burlesques, or the patter-songs in some screaming nautical vaudeville. Hardly less unfortunate is the lyric volume of his extreme old age, *Resignation*, printed in 1762.

It is by *The Complaint, or Night Thoughts* (1742-44), a poem of about ten thousand lines of blank verse in nine books, that Young holds his rank among the British poets, and the general reader may totally ignore all else that he has written. The first book of *Night Thoughts*, with its famous opening line, its rich note of romantic despair, its exquisite episodes, its sustained magnificence of phrase, is one of the lesser treasures of the English language. In form, it is Miltonic, without exaggeration, and, save for an unfortunate tendency to crystallise in abrupt self-contained single lines, its versification is of a rare dignity and harmony. This first book is studded with peculiar beauties, and it is to its successors, where the argument counts for more and the mere ornament for less, that we must look for the general characteristics of the poem. We find there that the poet is occupied, night after night, during his fits of sleepless dejection, in vindicating orthodoxy against an infidel lay-figure named Lorenzo, who is for ever being knocked over and then placed on his feet again. The whole didactic edifice is completed by the addition of a book of *Consolation*, "addressed to the Deity, and humbly inscribed to His Grace the Duke of Newcastle," in which the starry orrery of the nightly heavens is reviewed and commended. The extraordinary vogue of *Night Thoughts*, which lasted for a century, has succumbed to a series of vigorous attacks in our own age, and Young is now in danger of being underrated. His faults are volubility, inequality of workmanship, excessive fondness for a hollow kind of brazen rhetoric, and an atrabilious view of the duties as well as the pleasures of life. His merits are wit, great quickness, and ingenuity of fancy, dignity of expression and a power, obtained through emulation with Thomson, of spinning off reams of correct and harmonious blank verse. Many of his single lines, such as—

" And quite unparadise the realms of light,"

or

" The worm to riot on that rose so red "—

show the beginning of a return to the fuller music of the seventeenth century. The following passages may be given as exemplifying the peculiarities of Young's style :

" Death ! great proprietor of all ! 'tis thine
To tread out empire ; and to quench the stars.
The sun himself by thy permission shines ;
And, one day, thou shalt pluck him from his sphere.
Amid such mighty plunder, why exhaust
Thy partial quiver on a mark so mean ?
Why thy peculiar rancour wreak'd on me ?
Insatiate archer ! could not one suffice ?
Thy shaft flew thrice ; and thrice my peace was slain ;
And thrice, ere thrice yon moon had fill'd her horn."

" The sprightly lark's shrill matin wakes the morn ;
Grief's sharpest thorn hard pressing on my breast,
I strive, with wakeful melody, to cheer
The sullen gloom, sweet Philomel ! like thee,

And call the stars to listen; every star
Is deaf to mine, enamour'd of thy lay.
Yet be not vain; there are, who thine excel,
And charm through distant ages: wrapt in shade,
Pris'ner of darkness! to the silent hours,
How often I repeat their rage divine,
To lull my griefs, and steal my heart from woe!
I roll their raptures, but not catch their fire.
Dark, though not blind, like thee, Mæonides!
Or, Milton! thee; ah, could I reach your strain!
Or his, who made Mæonides our own.
Man too he sung: immortal man I sing;
Oft bursts the song beyond the bounds of life;
What, now, but immortality can please?
O had he press'd his theme, pursu'd the track,
Which opens out of darkness into day!
O had he, mounted on his wing of fire,
Soar'd where I sink, and sung immortal man!
How had it blest mankind, and rescu'd me!"

Two poets, who carried but a light weight, and whose work was mainly put forth posthumously, claim, nevertheless, a brief notice as taking part in the general return to a more natural treatment of verse. John Byrom (1692-1763) was a Manchester man, who became a fellow of Trinity College, Cambridge, and fell in love with the daughter of the great Bentley. A melodious *Pastoral*, celebrating that lady under the name of Phebe, was printed in the 605th *Spectator*, and is the best known of Byrom's writings. He became a physician, and then a professional stenographer, liking to describe himself as "Inventor of the Universal English Short-hand," and a votary of the "Tachygraphic Goddess." Late in life he became deeply impressed by the views of the religious mystic, Law, and in 1751 he versified the views of that apostle in an essay in heroic rhyme, entitled *Enthusiasm*. The poems of Byrom were first published after his death, in two volumes, printed at Manchester in 1773; his *Journals* first saw the light in 1854-57. His verse is of a highly miscellaneous character; the bulk of it is religious, and even polemical; the remainder is made up of apologues, epigrams, epistles, pastoral songs, dialogues in Lancashire dialect, tales and descriptions. Here are some of his pastoral stanzas:

> "Sweet music went with us both all the wood through,
> The lark, linnet, throstle, and nightingale too;
> Winds over us whisper'd, flocks by us did bleat,
> And chirp went the grasshopper under our feet.
> But now she is absent, though still they sing on;
> The woods are but lonely, the melody's gone:
> Her voice in the concert, as now I have found,
> Gave ev'rything else its agreeable sound."

> "Rose, what is become of thy delicate hue?
> And where is the violet's beautiful blue?
> Does aught of its sweetness the blossom beguile?
> That meadow, those daisies, why do they not smile?
> Ah! Rivals, I see what it was that you drest,
> And made yourselves fine for—a place on her breast:
> You put on your colours to pleasure her eye,
> To be pluckt by her hand, on her bosom to die."

> "How slowly time creeps, till my Phebe return!
> Whilst amidst the soft zephyr's cool breezes I burn;
> Methinks if I knew whereabouts he would tread,
> I could breathe on his wings, and 'twould melt down the lead.
> Fly swifter, ye minutes, bring hither my Dear,
> And rest so much longer for 't when she is here.
> Ah, Colin! old Time is full of delay,
> Nor will budge one foot faster for all thou canst say."

Byrom delights in the anapæstic tetrameter, which he wields very smoothly, and employs on the most extraordinary occasions, as when he is discussing Biblical criticism—

> "Dismissing the doubt, which a querist had got.
> If the Baptist did eat animalcules, or not,
> 'God forbid!' says the Father, 'a thing so absurd!
> The summit of plants is the sense of the word.'"

Occasionally Byrom drops his characteristic or typical eighteenth century manner, and writes quaint lyrics which seem inspired by Nicholas Breton. He is one of the most interesting provincial figures of the time.

An old bachelor named Matthew Green (1696-1737), who had

been all his life a clerk in the Customs, left behind him a poem of some eight hundred lines—*The Spleen*—which "Mr. C. J.," the friend for whose amusement it had been written, published in 1737, and so practically introduced Green's name to the public. This poem was an epistle in octosyllabic verse, recommending a quiet life and sensible manners as the best remedy against dejection or "the vapours." In the seventeenth century this metre had been used for lyrical and pastoral verse, Butler and Swift had successively employed it, with modifications, for purposes of satire, but Green was quite independent of these his predecessors. In style and temper he was astonishingly like his French contemporary, J. B. L. Gresset (1709-1777), whose poems, first printed in 1734, it is needless to say Green had never heard of. He is a master of refined philosophic wit and gentle persiflage; his delicate raillery is without the least element of rancour; he addresses a little circle of private friends, and is charming because so easy, natural, and sincere:

> "Here stillness, height, and solemn shade
> Invite, and contemplation aid:
> Here nymphs from hollow oaks relate
> The dark decrees and will of fate,
> And dreams beneath the spreading beech
> Inspire, and docile fancy teach;
> While soft as breezy breath of wind,
> Impulses rustle through the mind:
> Here Dryads, scorning Phœbus' ray,
> While Pan melodious pipes away,
> In measur'd motions frisk about,
> Till old Silenus puts them out:
> There see the clover, pea, and bean,
> Vie in variety of green;
> Fresh pastures speckl'd o'er with sheep;
> Brown fields their fallow sabbaths keep;
> Plump Ceres golden tresses wear,
> And poppy-topknots deck her hair;
> And silver stream through meadows stray,
> And Naiads on the margin play;
> And lesser nymphs on side of hills
> From plaything urns pour down the rills."

It calls forth the reader's surprise to note how wide a range of reflection Green's little poem moves across, yet whatever his witty muse touches she adorns. The originality of Matthew Green, the fact that he never wastes a line by repeating a commonplace, together with his fine cheerfulness as of an Agur, desiring neither poverty nor riches, make us regret that he left so little behind him, and so narrowly escaped the poppy of oblivion.

The world has become familiar with the misfortunes and adventures of Richard Savage (1698-1743) through the captivating biography of him written by Dr. Johnson. There is now no question, however, that Johnson was biassed in his judgment of this person by the partiality of friendship, and the life is full of obvious errors of date and fact. Savage ostentatiously described himself on his title-pages as "Son of the late Earl Rivers," but it is more than doubtful whether this unwise son knew his own father. It is needful here only to dwell on the fact that at the age of about thirty Savage displayed for two or three years some genuine poetical talent, and published three vigorous works in heroic measure. *The Bastard* (1728), written in real or feigned indignation against his supposed mother, the Countess of Macclesfield, enjoyed a success of scandal; it is short, terse, and effective. In *The Wanderer* (1729) Savage made a very different effort to subdue the public, with a long and serious poem in five books. Dr. Johnson, naturally attracted to the moral parts of this work, gives a totally false idea of its character. It is really a kind of prototype of Goldsmith's *Traveller*, to which it bears the sort of relation that Dryden is conventionally supposed to bear to Pope. What is mainly noticeable in *The Wanderer*, which describes the flight over Europe of a man who has been bereaved of one Olympia, is the influence of Thomson, enlarging the range of poetic observation, and encouraging an exacter portraiture of natural objects. The last book of Savage's poem is remarkably full of brilliant if often crude colour, and the reader is startled to meet with such attempts to give new landscape-features as the following:

> " There blue-veil'd yellow, thro' a sky serene,
>   In swelling mixture forms a floating green ;
>   Streaked thro' white clouds a mild vermilion shines,
>   And the breeze freshens, as the heat declines."

In 1730 Savage published in folio certain very mellifluous *Verses on Viscountess Tyrconnel's Recovery*, and then sank, for the rest of his life, into a merely perfunctory versifier.

A brilliant but obscure metaphysical and scientific poem, entitled *Universal Beauty*, was published in no fewer than six anonymous folio instalments in the course of 1735, and is now very rarely met with complete. It was from the pen of an Irish squire, Henry Brooke (1703-1783), long afterwards author of an unimportant sentimental novel, *The Fool of Quality*. His poem deserves attention. It is written in very musical couplets, with, however, too frequent indulgence in the alexandrine. It is manifestly inspired by the optimistic philosophy of Shaftesbury. The following passage gives an idea of Brooke's mode of approaching the most intractable natural phenomena :

> " Recluse, th' interior sap, and vapour dwells
>   In nice transparence of minutest cells ;
>   From whence, through pores or transmigrating veins,
>   Sublim'd, the liquid correspondence drains,
>   Their pithy mansions quit, the neighb'ring choose,
>   And subtle, thro' th' adjacent pouches ooze ;
>   Refin'd, expansive, or regressive pass,
>   Transmitted through the horizontal mass ;
>   Compress'd, the ligneous fibres now assail,
>   And, ent'ring, thence the essential sap exhale,
>   Or lively with effusive vigour spring,
>   And form the circle of the annual ring ;
>   The branch implicit, of embow'ring trees ;
>   And foliage, whisp'ring to the vernal breeze ;
>   While zephyr tun'd, with gentle cadence blows,
>   And lull'd to rest consenting eyelids close."

The third part of *Universal Beauty* deals with the vegetable kingdom in detail, and in a style which irresistibly reminds the reader of Erasmus Darwin's verses half a century later. Brooke never fulfilled the promise of this remarkable first poem.

A friend of Savage and Thomson, of whose early career little is known, was the Welshman John Dyer (1699-1758), to whom, by some accident of fortune, rather more than his share of credit has habitually been given by the critics. No doubt Dyer was very early in the field with his *Grongar Hill*, a kind of descriptive ode, published in 1726, the year of Thomson's *Winter*. It is rash to deny genius to a poet whom Gray and Wordsworth have extravagantly praised, and Dyer, who was a painter by profession, had a delicate eye for landscape. The closing lines of the poem are, undeniably, very charming:

> "Be full, ye courts, be great who will;
> Search for Peace with all your skill :
> Open wide the lofty door,
> Seek her on the marble floor,
> In vain you search, she is not there;
> In vain ye search the domes of care !
> Grass and flowers Quiet treads,
> On the meads, and mountain-heads,
> Along with Pleasure, close allied,
> Ever by each other's side :
> And often, by the murmuring rill,
> Hears the thrush, while all is still,
> Within the groves of Grongar Hill."

It seems odd that the extreme awkwardness of the opening lines of *Grongar Hill*, and a certain grammatical laxity running through the work of Dyer, should have been treated with so much lenity by critic after critic. His later didactic poems, in blank verse which owes its existence still more to Milton than to Thomson, are *The Ruins of Rome* (1740) and *The Fleece* (1757). Dyer's Welsh landscapes, with their yellow sun, purple groves, and pale blue distance, remind us of the simple drawings of the earliest English masters of water-colour, and his precise mode of treating outdoor subjects, without pedantry, but with a cold succession of details, connects him with the lesser Augustans through Somerville

As the gentleman predicted, Dyer is buried in the "woollen" of his too-laborious *Fleece*.

In 1728 a young Scotch minister, Robert Blair (1699-1746), printed an elegy in *Memory of William Law*. He then began to sketch a poem of a more ambitious character, on the terrors of death. In 1731 he was appointed to the living of Athelstaneford, where he polished and slowly completed his poem. In 1743, Young having in the meanwhile started his *Night Thoughts*, Blair finally published *The Grave*, a didactic piece in something less than eight hundred lines of blank verse. He wrote nothing else, and died still young. Blair was isolated from all his chief English contemporaries, but he follows the same moral and romantic aims as they. In his celebration of the ghastly solitude of the tomb, and all the grim circumstances of death and bereavement, he seems to stretch out his hands to Otway on the one side and to Crabbe on the other. His poem is less ornate, but more vivid and concentrated than Young's, and has the advantage of being a great deal shorter. Blair was evidently acquainted with the Elizabethan tragic poets, and his iambics are more easy and varied than even those of Thomson :

> " Tell us, ye dead ! will none of you, in pity
> To those you left behind, disclose the secret ?
> Oh ! that some courteous ghost would blab it out,—
> What 'tis you are, and we must shortly be.
> I've heard that souls departed have sometimes
> Forewarn'd men of their death. 'Twas kindly done
> To knock, and give the alarum. But what means
> This stinted charity ? 'Tis but lame kindness
> That does its work by halves. Why might you not
> Tell us what 'tis to die ? Do the strict laws
> Of your society forbid your speaking
> Upon a point so nice ? I'll ask no more :
> Sullen, like lamps in sepulchres, your shine
> Enlightens but yourselves. Well, 'tis no matter ;
> A very little time will clear up all
> And make us learn'd as you are, and as close."

> " Oft, in the lone church-yard at night I've seen,
> By glimpse of moonlight chequering thro' the trees,

> The schoolboy with his satchel in his hand,
> Whistling aloud to bear his courage up,
> And lightly tripping o'er the long, flat stones
> (With nettles skirted, and with moss o'ergrown),
> That tell in homely phrase who lies below.
> Sudden he starts ! and hears, or thinks he hears,
> The sound of something purring at his heels ;
> Full fast he flies, and dares not look behind him,
> Till out of breath he overtakes his fellows ;
> Who gather round, and wonder at the tale
> Of horrid apparition, tall and ghastly,
> That walks at dead of night, or takes his stand
> O'er some new-open'd grave, and, strange to tell !
> Evanishes at crowing of the cock."

Among the single didactic poems of a gloomy cast, of which so many were produced during the eighteenth century, *The Grave* stands highest in point of execution, and is the least overweighted with mere rhetoric and commonplace. It was Blair who first spoke of "visits, like those of angels, short and far between," and the rough felspar of his style flashes with sudden felicities that resemble these heavenly interviews.

The poets whom we have hitherto mentioned, however meritorious, were distinctly of the second order, and not one of them could be named as a leader or pioneer. Very different was the position of James Thomson (1700-1748), in whom we meet with the most original and influential poetic figure which exists between Pope and Gray. There was hardly one verse-writer of any eminence, from 1725 to 1750, who was not in some measure guided or biassed by Thomson, whose genius is to this day fertile in English literature. If his influence had been as broad as it was potent, and his originality as versatile as it was genuine, Thomson might have been one of the six or seven greatest English poets. As it is, within his restricted limits he is as exquisite, as sincerely inspired, as any poet needs be, and his function in recalling English men of letters to an imaginative study of external nature is of the highest historical importance.

Thomson was born of genteel parents, at Ednam, on the Scottish border. His childhood was spent in a romantic part of Roxburghshire, surrounded by all the elements of local superstition and natural mystery. He was educated at Edinburgh, where, as a student of divinity, he began, at the age of twenty, to write verses, which, like the piece beginning "When from the opening chambers of the east," however crude in execution, showed a marvellous fondness for such unfashionable themes as the labour of plaided herdsmen and the sights and sounds of village life. Early in 1725 Thomson came up to London to seek his fortune, and while in great straits from poverty wrote his poem of *Winter* in the autumn of that year. He was at this time in correspondence with other young poets, with Dyer, with Savage, and with David Mallet or Malloch (1702?-1765), whose ballad of *William and Margaret* had in some sort inaugurated the new romantic school in 1724. Mallet afterwards became a pronounced imitator of the blank verse of the *Seasons*, but, though afterwards only too notorious in the worlds of politics and letters, he never fulfilled the lyric promise of his early youth.

Thomson, whose genius seems to have struck every one who met him, soon found patrons, and in March 1726 *Winter* was published in folio. Mallet took a copy of it to Aaron Hill (1685-1750), a poetaster and small dramatist of very considerable pretensions at that time, who affected to be a rival *censor elegantiarum* to Pope. Hill sounded the praises of the new descriptive poem through London, and Thomson's success was complete. In 1727, after publishing a poem to *The Memory of Sir Isaac Newton*, he produced *Summer; Spring* followed in 1728, and in 1730 the completed *Seasons* appeared, including *Autumn* and a final *Hymn* to Nature. As this celebrated series of poems now stands, it contains about 5500 lines, but it was much shorter in its original form. To the close of his life the poet was incessantly altering and adding to it, introducing allusions to dead friends, and modifying the episodes. A variorum edition of the *Seasons*, a task often promised but never fulfilled, would be a boon to students of English literature. In its present form *Winter*, which was the earliest, is also the shortest and the freshest of the sections. The author paints what by experience he knows so well, the horrors of a Cheviot December. It cannot, perhaps, be said that *Winter* is so imaginative, in the special Wordsworthian sense, as some later writings of Thomson became, but it is peculiarly delightful as the outpouring of a picturesque memory, exactly stored with all those beautiful trifling incidents of life and nature which most men see only to forget. Such vignettes as those of the redbreast helping himself to crumbs, the family waiting anxiously for the man who is perishing in the snow, the goblin-story told to a ring of pale faces round the farm-house fire,—these have a sharpness of outline, an impassioned simplicity and truth, which the poet never surpassed. In *Spring* there is less incessant verbal felicity, but more imagination; the poet has read more and thought more, and while the scene of the fisherman angling for trout has scarcely less brightness than its forerunners, the final panegyric on nuptial love displays higher intellectual powers than *Winter* had revealed. *Summer* is very much longer than the other three sections, and presents a different character. It is somewhat over-burdened with narrative episodes, that of Celadon and Amelia, that of Damon and Musidora, which are graceful in themselves, but a little out of keeping with the rest; while several hundred lines are expanded in a most elaborate but second-hand description of the various modes in which men are affected by the torrid agonies of the tropic summer. Yet, even in *Summer*, and specially in the beautiful picture of the washing and shearing of sheep, we find Thomson, as ever, when he deals with what he has himself known and seen, glowing and felicitous. *Autumn*, with the lengthy episode of Lavinia, and its vivid sketches of hunting and harvesting, follows with no sense of loss; and the *Hymn* at the close, with the rolling organ-harmony of its Pantheism, rounds the whole poem off with splendid effect. It is from the *Hymn* that we may here pause to give an example of Thomson's most serious manner:

"Nature, attend! join every living soul,
Beneath the spacious temple of the sky,
In adoration join; and, ardent, raise

> One general song! To Him, ye vocal gales,
> Breathe soft, whose spirit in your freshness breathes :
> Oh! talk of Him in solitary glooms,
> Where, o'er the rock, the scarcely waving pine
> Fills the brown shade with a religious awe.
> And ye, whose bolder note is heard afar,
> Who shake the astonished world, lift high to Heaven
> The impetuous song, and say from whom you rage.
> His praise, ye brooks, attune, ye trembling rills ;
> And let me catch it as I muse along.
> Ye headlong torrents, rapid and profound ;
> Ye softer floods, that lead the humid maze
> Along the vale ; and thou, majestic main,
> A secret world of wonders in thyself,
> Sound His stupendous praise, whose greater voice
> Or bids you roar, or bids your roarings fall.
> Soft-roll your incense, herbs, and fruits, and flowers,
> In mingled clouds to Him, whose sun exalts,
> Whose breath perfumes you, and whose pencil paints.
> Ye forests bend, ye harvests wave, to Him ;
> Breathe your still song into the reaper's heart,
> As home he goes beneath the joyous moon.
> Ye that keep watch in Heaven, as earth asleep
> Unconscious lies, effuse your mildest beams,
> Ye constellations, while your angels strike,
> Amid the spangled sky, the silver lyre.
> Great source of day! best image here below
> Of thy Creator, ever pouring wide,
> From world to world, the vital ocean round,
> On nature write with every beam His praise.
> The thunder rolls : be hushed the prostrate world ;
> While cloud to cloud returns the solemn hymn."

At the age of thirty, therefore, Thomson found himself the leading poet of the younger generation, and the heir-apparent to the throne of Pope. But instead of rising to fresh triumphs, he began to decline, and although he still wrote abundantly, a kind of sterility, a blight of dulness, fell upon his verses. Immediately after the publication of the completed *Seasons* he enjoyed the advantage of travelling for nearly two years in France and Italy, as governor to the son of the Solicitor-General, and this experience of the South of Europe inspired the descriptive passages of his poem of *Liberty*, which appeared in five separate folio instalments between 1734 and 1736. This poem, which, when completed, consisted of rather more than three thousand lines of blank verse, proved a great disappointment to Thomson's admirers. Aaron Hill, indeed, declared that he looked "upon this mighty work as the last stretched blaze of our expiring genius"; but no one else was able to read it, and the most devoted of all Thomsonians, Lord Lyttelton himself, thought it an act of piety to reduce and popularise it. The poet now gave his attention, with moderate and temporary success, to the stage, and produced the tragedies of *Sophonisba* (1730), *Agamemnon* (1738), *Edward and Eleanora* (which was suppressed on account of its flattering allusions to Frederick, Prince of Wales), 1739, *Tancred and Sigismunda* (1745), and the posthumous *Coriolanus*. On the 1st of August 1740, moreover, there was performed at Clifden the masque of *Alfred*, by Thomson and Mallet, in the second act of which "Rule Britannia" first occurred. The first edition of *Alfred*, an octavo of 1740, is anonymous, but the lyric was afterwards published with Thomson's initials, without remonstrance from Mallet, and was no doubt the composition of the former.

In May 1748 was printed the most exquisite of Thomson's productions, the famous poem in Spenserian stanza entitled *The Castle of Indolence*. From a letter to Paterson it appears that this poem was begun as early as 1733, and if Thomson had died at that time his poetical works might be as rich although much less copious than they now are, for *The Castle of Indolence* is of a very different quality from the leaden *Liberty* and the stolid bombastic dramas. The opening stanzas are more like the work of Keats than any other verse which the eighteenth century has given us, and in their music there is less of the dull undertone of the conventional manner of the age than anywhere else, except in the finest lines of Gray and Collins. The poem is in two cantos—the first describing the embowered castle of the false enchanter, Indolence, and all the lotus-eating captives that it harboured; while the second recounts the conquest of this wicked one by a certain Knight of Arts and Industry. The poem is a curious mixture of romantic melancholy and slippered mirth, of descriptive passages which rise into a clear Æolian melody, and portraits of real people sketched in the laughter of gentle caricature. Over the whole lies a blue atmosphere of vagueness, an opium-cloud, a vapour of dreams from the land of echoes, and the total effect is one of elaborate unreality, as of a finely-proportioned piece of architecture built in mirage :

> " Joined to the prattle of the purling rills
> Were heard the lowing herds along the vale,
> And flocks loud bleating from the distant hills,
> And vacant shepherds piping in the dale :
> And, now and then, sweet Philomel would wail,
> Or stock-doves plain amid the forest deep,
> That drowsy rustled to the sighing gale ;
> And still a coil the grasshopper did keep ;
> Yet all these sounds yblent, inclined all to sleep.
>
> " Full in the passage of the vale, above,
> A sable, silent, solemn forest stood ;
> Where nought but shadowy forms was seen to move,
> As Idlesse fancied in her dreaming mood :
> And up the hills, on either side, a wood
> Of blackening pines, ay waving to and fro,
> Sent forth a sleepy horror through the blood ;
> And where this valley winded out, below,
> The murmuring main was heard, and scarcely heard, to flow.
>
> " A pleasing land of drowsy-hed it was,
> Of dreams that wane before the half-shut eye ;
> And of gay castles in the clouds that pass,
> Forever flushing round a summer-sky :
> There eke the soft delights, that witchingly
> Instil a wanton sweetness through the breast,
> And the calm pleasures always hovered nigh ;
> But whate'er smacked of noyance, or unrest,
> Was far, far off expelled from this delicious nest."

There can be no doubt that *The Castle of Indolence* had a marked influence in determining certain phases of the work of Shelley.

Thomson was a very indolent man, "more fat than bard beseems," but unselfish, singularly loyal as a friend, and devoid of all mean vices. "That right friendly bard, Mr. Thomson," as Shenstone calls him, was a universal favourite, and every Muse in England went into mourning when, in consequence of a neglected cold, he died suddenly on the 27th of August 1748, having but a little while outlived Pope and Swift. The mode in which the most dissimilar persons unite to speak of "our old, tried, amiable, open, and honest-hearted Thomson," shows us that the heavy, silent little man, with his mixture of shyness and laziness, exerted an irradiating influence over which he had no conscious control, and prepares us to find him surrounded and followed by a cloud of more or less distinguished disciples. Of these the most prominent, in their personal relation to the master, were Armstrong and Lyttelton. In both these writers we see very plainly the defects of the poetic system of Thomson, with its excess of redundant phraseology and its pompous Latin phrases and neologisms. John Armstrong (1709-1779) was, like Thomson, a Roxburghshire man. He became a London physician, and had the indiscretion to admit being the author of a didactic poem, *The Economy of Love* (1736), the publication of which was justly considered a breach of professional etiquette. He tried to "drug the memory of that insolence" by producing a very grave poem, also in blank verse, on *The Art of Preserving Health* (1744), divided into four books, on air, diet, exercise, and the passions. This was a very difficult subject, but it was treated with unexpected grace and vigour. Armstrong also contributed four medical stanzas to *The Castle of Indolence*. His epistles, *Benevolence* (1751) and *Taste* (1753), are in heroic rhyme, in which none of the Thomsonians excelled, and no one will ever read either Armstrong's tragedy, *The Forced Marriage* (1754), or the would-be sprightly prose essays which he published in 1758 under the pseudonym of Lancelot Temple. He collected his works in two pretty volumes of *Miscellanies* in 1770. Armstrong's diction was absurdly tumid; he calls a wild briar-rose "a cynorrhodon," and a cold bath "a gelid cistern." But his merits of dignity and melody are at present underrated. The structure of Armstrong's blank verse is excellent, and though founded upon Thomson's, has a certain independent stateliness.

If we desire to name a personage as typical of what was best in the ordinary man of cultivation in the eighteenth century, we can do no better than point to George Lyttelton of Hagley, first Lord Lyttelton (1709-1773). He was a virtuous politician, who rose to be Chancellor of the Exchequer; he was the founder of a house that has never ceased to hold a respectable place in the country; he was the friend of great poets and divines, and something of a divine and a poet himself, while his life comprised all that was elegant and amiable in man. Cruel sceptics, like Gibbon, have not failed to point out that his works are "not illuminated by a ray of genius." But his heart has spoken once or twice, in the loosely-strung Pindaric *Monody* to his wife, and in the elegiac prologue to *Coriolanus*, Thomson's posthumous tragedy.

Another and more ambitious Thomsonian was Richard Glover (1712-1785), a politician whom indignation against Walpole hurried into copious blank verse. There must be few men now alive who can boast a more than fragmentary acquaintance with the epics of Glover. *Leonidas* (in nine books, afterwards enlarged), 1737, begins his poetical career, and *The Athenaid* (positively in thirty books), 1788, closed it. Glover is only remembered by his extremely spirited ballad of *Admiral Hosier's Ghost*, which, however, he might have improved by shortening to five syllables the last line of each octett.

The increased lightness of touch and command over the resources of language which were secured by the practice of the Augustan age, encouraged the production of rapid and polished epigrammatic or burlesque verse in the period we have now reached. Lord Chesterfield's exquisite impromptu to Miss Ambrose is one example of the exercise of this new power; another is the "Live while you live" of Dr. Philip Doddridge (1702-1751):

> " Say, lovely Tory, why the jest
> Of wearing orange on thy breast,
> When that same breast, betraying, shows
> The whiteness of the rebel rose?"

> " 'Live while you live'—the epicure would say,
> 'And seize the pleasure of the present day;'
> 'Live while you live'—the sacred preacher cries,
> 'And give to God each moment as it flies.'
> Lord! in my views let both united be;
> I live in pleasure when I live to Thee!"

Isaac Hawkins Browne (1706-1760) was master of this easy brightness; in 1736 he published an amusing set of parodies—*The Pipe of Tobacco*, long afterwards imitated by the authors of *Rejected Addresses*. The epigrams of Robert Craggs, Lord Nugent (1709-1788), may still be read with entertainment; and David Garrick (1716-1779), although he affected to call himself "a poor player and still poorer bard," was vain of his accomplishments upon the lighter lyre. There is a touch of genuine pathos in his clever epitaph on Quin the actor:

> " That tongue which set the table on a roar,
> And charm'd the public ear, is heard no more!
> Clos'd are those eyes, the harbingers of wit
> Which spoke, before the tongue, what Shakespeare writ;
> Cold are those hands, which, living, were stretched forth
> At friendship's call to succour modest worth.
> Here lies James Quin! deign reader to be taught
> (Whate'er thy strength of body, force of thought,
> In nature's happiest mould however cast),
> To this complexion thou must come at last."

Among all these butterflies of song, Sir Charles Hanbury Williams (1709-1759) takes the place of a wasp, if not of a veritable hornet. He was the Pasquin of his age, and a master of violent stinging invective in hard verse. In his own age no one dared to collect the savage lyrics of Williams, which were first presented to the world in 1822. Dr. Alexander Webster's (1707-1784) epigram or address to his wife recalls us to humanity, and displays the fragile porcelain beauty of eighteenth-century verse in its tenderest light.

From among the multitude of minor poets, we may select three very dissimilar names for brief special notice. In a family of distinguished rhyming divines, Charles Wesley (1708-1788) was the one who rose nearest to the purely secular standard of a poet. He was the younger brother of the great founder of the Methodists, with whom he was associated as a hymn-writer. There can be little question that the sacred songs of Charles Wesley, most of them what are called "hymns of experience," reach at their noblest the highest level of Protestant religious poetry in this country since George Herbert. His *Wrestling Jacob* is his masterpiece, and is inspired by a genuine dramatic passion. It opens thus :

> "Come, O thou traveller unknown,
>   Whom still I hold, but cannot see;
> My company before is gone,
>   And I am left alone with thee;
> With thee all night I mean to stay,
> And wrestle till the break of day.
>
> "I need not tell thee who I am,
>   My misery or sin declare;
> Thyself hast called me by my name,
>   Look on thy hands, and read it there!
> But who, I ask thee, who art thou?
> Tell me thy name, and tell me now."

The hymns of the eighteenth century are so interesting from what we may call the philosophical standpoint that we may be in danger of overrating their positive literary value, which is apt to be small. William Shenstone (1714-1763), the bard of the Leasowes, has been called "our principal master of the artificial-natural style in poetry." His *Pastoral Ballad* (1743), in four sections, is written in the lightest of anapæsts, and has all the pink and silver grace of a Watteau. In 1742, when Thomson had written, but not circulated, his *Castle of Indolence*, Shenstone issued *The Schoolmistress*, a short but very happy study in some thirty-five half-burlesque Spenserian stanzas. He takes his place in the rapid transition of style as a definite link between Thomson and Goldsmith. His bachelor ideal of life is very neatly summed up in the ingenious stanzas, *Written in an Inn at Henley:*

> " To thee, fair freedom ! I retire
>   From flattery, cards, and dice, and din ;
> Nor art thou found in mansions higher
>   Than the low cot or humble inn.
>
> " 'Tis here with boundless power I reign ;
>   And every health which I begin
> Converts dull port to bright champagne,—
>   Such freedom crowns it, at an inn.
>
> " I fly from pomp, I fly from plate !
>   I fly from falsehood's specious grin ;
> Freedom I love, and form I hate,
>   And choose my lodgings at an inn.
>
> " Here, waiter, take my sordid ore,
>   Which lacqueys else might hope to win !
> It buys, what courts have not in store,
>   It buys me—freedom at an inn.
>
> " Whoe'er has travelled life's dull round,
>   Where'er his stages may have been,
> May sigh to think he still has found
>   The warmest welcome—at an inn."

Still more artificial, still more mild and colourless, are the productions of William Whitehead (1715-1785), the laureate, who, nevertheless, has some indefinite claim to be called a poet. His epistles on *The Danger of Writing Verse* (1741) and *Ridicule* (1743) were incessantly scoffed at by Churchhill; his little epitaphs, "similes," fables, and songs are often happier in their simplicity.

Two very noble lyrical poets closed this period of our literature, and preserved it from expiring in feebleness and insipidity. It may be convenient to consider first the younger of these, William Collins (1721-1759), whose career practically closed before the end of the half century, and before Gray came prominently before the public. Collins was the son of a hatter in Chichester. His early verses are lost, though one copy of them was actually published, it is believed, in 1734. He was educated at Winchester and at Magdalen College, Oxford. While he was an undergraduate he printed a volume of *Persian Eclogues* (1742), and a brief *Epistle to Sir Thomas Hanmer* (1743), both works now extremely scarce. He proposed to enter the army, and then the Church, but was prevented in each case by indolence, as it is said,—more probably by a nervous irresolution of character, which foreshadowed his future calamity. Collins came to London with "many projects in his head." In 1747 (December 1746) he printed his famous *Odes*, a thin pamphlet of three and a half sheets. The book failed to sell, and Collins destroyed the remainder of the edition. The young poet now formed the friendship of the genial and affectionate Thomson, on whose death, in 1748, he wrote the exquisite elegy (or "ode"), beginning, "In yonder grave a Druid lies." In 1749, after a brief acquaintanceship with the Rev. John Home (1724-1808), afterwards popular as the author of the tragedy of *Douglas*, Collins addressed this friend in an ode, the longest of his existing works, *On the Popular Superstitions of the Highlands*. An uncle in this year left the poet a small fortune, and feeling his nervousness grow upon him, Collins retired to Chichester. He was at this time only twenty-eight years of age, but no further writings of his have been preserved. In 1750 he wrote an *Ode on the Music of the Grecian Theatre*, which he invited the Oxford composer, William Hayes (1707-1777), to set to music. Unfortunately this and *The Bell of Arragon*, the latest of the odes of Collins, have never been recovered. Their immediate predecessor, in a mutilated condition, was printed in 1788. Collins's debilitated state of health gradually settled into absolute melancholia; in 1753 he went to France and Flanders to avert the coming horror, if possible, but returned worse than he went; and in 1754, during a visit to Oxford, had to be removed to a lunatic asylum. He lived in his sister's house in Chichester, hopelessly insane, and was released at last by death on the 12th of

June 1759, neglected by the world and scarcely remembered by his friends.

There are very few poets from whose wheat so little chaff has been winnowed as from that of Collins. His entire existing work does not extend to much more than fifteen hundred lines, at least two-thirds of which must live with the best poetry of the century. Collins has the touch of a sculptor; his verse is clearly-cut and direct; it is marble-pure, but also marble-cold. Each phrase is a wonder of felicitous workmanship, without emphasis, without sense of strain. His best strophes possess an extraordinary quiet melody, a soft harmonious smoothness as of some divine and aerial creature singing in artless, perfect numbers for its own delight. The *Ode to Simplicity* and the *Ode written in 1746* perhaps present this delicate art of melody in its directest form:

> " How sleep the brave who sink to rest,
> By all their country's wishes blest!
> When Spring, with dewy fingers cold,
> Returns to deck their hallowed mould,
> She there shall dress a sweeter sod
> Than fancy's feet have ever trod.
>
> " By fairy hands their knell is rung;
> By forms unseen their dirge is sung;
> There honour comes, a pilgrim gray,
> To bless the turf that wraps their clay;
> And freedom shall awhile repair,
> To dwell, a weeping hermit, there!"

Essentially a lyric poet, Collins is not happy in a long flight, and his two lengthiest odes, *To Liberty*, and *On Popular Superstitions*, though they contain what are perhaps his noblest passages, are far from being noble throughout. The most popular of his lyrics have been the *Ode to Evening* and *The Passions*. The first of these displays a sustained power of painting landscape effects which Collins does not repeat elsewhere. Mr. Swinburne has made a very interesting comparison between this poem and the paintings of the school of Corot and Théodore Rousseau. *The Passions* suffers from the disadvantage of having been made a stock-exercise for elocutionists in successive generations. Its language is often exceedingly brilliant and effective, but the continuity of thought is broken, and simplicity is sacrificed to the desire of covering too large a canvas. Of the twelve odes of which the famous little volume of 1747 is composed, five have now been mentioned. The *Ode to Pity* has a pathetic flute-like melody, and some pleasant note of that other unhappy Sussex poet, Otway:

> " But wherefore need I wander wide
>   To old Ilissus' distant side,
>   Deserted stream and mute?
>   Wild Arun, too, has heard thy strains,
>   And Echo, 'midst my native plains,
>   Been soothed by Pity's lute."

The *Ode on the Poetical Character* is inferior to Gray's analogous ode, with which it is impossible not to compare it. *The Manners* achieves with perfect ease and grace what the Whiteheads and Nugents of the age were for ever attempting to perform. Among the posthumous poems, the *Popular Superstitions*, especially in its ninth and subsequent strophes, reaches a height of pure lyric elevation and rapture, which makes us deeply regret the loss of what may have been the masterpiece of Collins, his ode on the *Music of the Grecian Theatre*. His latest lyrics, especially the *Dirge in Cymbeline*, prove to us that up to the moment when he laid down his pen in unconquerable physical lassitude, the genius of Collins was advancing in precision and delicacy. This is the marvellous ninth strophe of the *Popular Superstitions:*

> " Unbounded is thy range; with varied style
>   Thy muse may, like those feathery tribes which spring
>   From their rude rocks, extend her skirting wing
> Round the moist marge of each cold Hebrid isle,
>   To that hoar pile, which still its ruin shows;
> In whose small vaults a pigmy-folk is found,
>   Whose bones the delver with his spade upthrows,
> And culls them, wondering, from the hallowed ground!
>   Or thither, where, beneath the showery west,
> The mighty kings of three fair realms are laid;
>   Once foes, perhaps, together now they rest,

> No slaves revere them and no wars invade;
> Yet frequent now, at midnight's solemn hour,
> The rifted mounds their yawning cells unfold,
>   And forth the monarchs stalk with sovereign power,
> In pageant robes, and wreathed with sheeny gold,
> And on their twilight tombs aerial council hold."

The intellectual quality of Collins is not so strongly marked as his pure and polished art; but he had sympathy with fine things unpopular in his own lifetime. He was a republican and a Hellenist and a collector of black-letter poetry, in an age that equally despised what was Greek and what was Gothic. It may perhaps be allowed to be an almost infallible criterion of a man's taste for the highest forms of poetic art to inquire whether he has or has not a genuine love for the verses of William Collins.

It seems scarcely generous to say of a writer, whom we must all admit to be a much greater man of letters, that what has just been said is not true in his case, yet certainly no such special training or native capacity is needful for the appreciation of much that is obviously delightful in the poetry of Thomas Gray (1716-1771). Gray and Collins, distinct enough in character to the careful critical inspector, have to the outward eye a curious similarity. They were contemporaries; they wrote very little, and that mostly in the form of odes; they both affected personation and allegorical address to a very unusual extent; both studied effects which were Greek in their precision and delicacy; both were learned and exact students of periods of literature now reinstated in critical authority, but in their day neglected. Yet, while Gray was the greater intellectual figure of the two, the more significant as a man and a writer, Collins possessed something more thrilling, more spontaneous, as a purely lyrical poet. When they are closely examined, their supposed similarity fades away; and, without depreciating either, we discover that each was typical of a class— that Collins was the type of the poet who sings, as the birds do, because he must; and Gray of the artist in verse, who has learned everything which the most consummate attention to workmanship can teach him, when added to the native faculty of a singularly delicate ear. Each has his separate charm, but we must not stultify our own enjoyment of either by pushing too far a parallelism which, though strongly marked, turns out to be mainly superficial.

Gray, the most important poetical figure in our literature between Pope and Wordsworth, was born in London on the 26th of December 1716. He was educated at Eton, where his principal friends were Horace Walpole and Richard West (1717-1742), the "Favonius" of his correspondence, a lad of some tender elegiac promise. From Eton Gray proceeded in 1734 to Cambridge, which was henceforth to be his main domicile. He was admitted to Pembroke, but presently went over as a fellow-commoner to Peterhouse. While he was an undergraduate Gray began to publish Latin verses, and in 1738 to translate classical passages into excellent English verse. In 1739 he accompanied Horace Walpole to France and Italy in a tour which occupied three memorable years, and it was on first crossing the Alps that Gray became impressed with the noble beauty of mountain scenery, which had hitherto been regarded, even by poets, with more horror than admiration. In a letter to West (November 16, 1739) he uses the now famous phrase, describing the Alps, "not a precipice, not a torrent, not a cliff, but is pregnant with religion and poetry." In 1741 Gray and Walpole, who had been too long in exclusive mutual companionship, quarrelled, and each proceeded home alone; but in 1744 this breach was amicably healed. On the death of his father, which happened two months after the poet's return from Italy, he found the affairs of his family disordered, and in the winter of 1742 he returned to reside at Cambridge. This year, 1742, was that in which he began to be an original English poet. He wrote a fragment of a Thomsonian tragedy, *Agrippina*, his odes *On Spring*, *On a Distant Prospect of Eton College*, and *On Adversity*, the *Sonnet on the Death of West*, and began the *Elegy in a Country Churchyard*. To this fertile year succeeded five of almost entire poetic stagnation, during which Gray, a victim to dejection, buried himself among the classics in his rooms at Peterhouse. In 1747 he published, in pamphlet form, his *Eton College* ode, which attracted no attention whatever. About this time Gray wrote that delicious trifle *The Ode on the Death of a favourite Cat*. Next year he formed the acquaintance of William Mason (1725-1797), then a scholar of St. John's, his imitator and future biographer, and from this time forward Gray never again endured the same solitary wretchedness that he had first suffered at Cambridge. Three of Gray's odes, printed in Dodsley's *Miscellany* in 1748, introduced his work, though still not his name, to the public, and in the winter of 1749 he continued, and in the summer of 1750 finished, his *Elegy in a Country Churchyard*. This was anonymously published in the spring of 1751. In 1753 *Six Poems by Mr. T. Gray*, including, besides those already mentioned, *A Long Story*, written in 1751, were published as a luxurious folio, with full-page illustrations by Richard Bentley, son of the Master of Trinity. Many of these poems were identified with the rustic village of Stoke Pogis, in Bucks, where several of Gray's female relations resided, and where his mother died and was buried in 1753.

The first period of Gray's literary career now closes. In 1754 he opened a second by finishing a very important poem, a resonant ode on *The Progress of Poesy*, composed in competition with the triumphal *epinikia* of Pindar, in very elaborate stanza-form. A second Pindaric ode on *The Liberty of Genius* was planned about the same time, but of this there exists only a fragment of the argument. A third effort in the same direction, *The Bard*, begun in the winter of 1754, was completed in the summer of 1757. Meanwhile Gray, dissatisfied with the want of notice taken by the Peterhouse authorities of a rude practical joke played upon him by some undergraduates, moved over to Pembroke in 1756. In this latter college he was among personal friends, and this remained his home until he died. He never held a fellowship or any college office. In 1757 he printed at Strawberry Hill the two Pindaric poems under the title of *Odes*. They were instantly and decisively successful; Gray was acknowledged to be the leading poet of the day, and a few months later he was offered, and declined, the office of poet-laureate at the death of Colley Cibber. The remainder of his life was very uneventful. In 1760 and 1761 he was mainly giving his attention to early English poetry, of which he intended to write a history; and in the latter year his study of Icelandic and Celtic verse led to the composition of his Eddaic poems, *The Fatal Sisters* and *The Descent of Odin*. Henceforward the main events in Gray's life were his enthusiastic friendships with younger men, such as Nicholls and Bonstetten, and his summer excursions in search of romantic scenery. In 1768 he collected his *Poems* in the first general edition, and was appointed Professor of Modern History and Modern Languages at the University of Cambridge; he delivered no lectures. In 1769 Gray's latest poem, the *Installation Ode*, was published, and in the autumn of that year he took his famous journey among the English lakes, the *Journal* of which was posthumously published in 1775, and is the most finished of his prose writings. Gray died, in his rooms at Pembroke College, on the 30th of July 1771, and was buried, beside the body of his mother, in the romantic churchyard of Stoke Pogis. Some stanzas may here be quoted from one of the least hackneyed of Gray's poems, the beautiful fragmentary *Ode on Vicissitude:*

> " Now the golden morn aloft
>   Waves her dew-bespangled wing,
> With vermeil cheek and whisper soft
>   She woos the tardy spring;
> Till April starts, and calls around
> The sleeping fragrance from the ground;
> And lightly o'er the living scene
> Scatters his freshest, tenderest green.
>
> " Newborn flocks, in rustic dance,
>   Frisking ply their feeble feet;
> Forgetful of their wintry trance,
>   The birds his presence greet:
> But, chief, the sky-lark warbles high
> His trembling, thrilling ecstasy;
> And, lessening from the dazzled sight,
> Melts into air and liquid light.

> " Yesterday the sullen year
>   Saw the snowy whirlwind fly ;
>   Mute was the music of the air,
>   The herd stood drooping by ;
>   Their raptures now that wildly flow,
>   No yesterday, nor morrow know ;
>   'Tis Man alone that joy descries
>   With forward and reverted eyes.
>
> " See the wretch, that long has tossed
>   On the thorny bed of pain,
>   At length repair his vigour lost,
>   And breathe and walk again ;
>   The meanest flowret of the vale,
>   The simplest note that swells the gale,
>   The common sun, the air, the skies,
>   To him are opening Paradise."

Against the right of Gray to be considered one of the leading English men of letters no more stringent argument has been produced than is founded upon the paucity of his published work. It has fairly been said that the springs of originality in the brain of a great inventive genius are bound to bubble up more continuously and in fuller volume than could be confined within the narrow bounds of the poetry of Gray. But the sterility of the age, the east wind of discouragement steadily blowing across the poet's path, had much to do with this apparent want of fecundity, and it would be an error to insist too strongly on a general feature of the century in this individual case. When we turn to what Gray actually wrote, although the bulk of it is small, we are amazed at the originality and variety, the freshness and vigour of the mind that worked thus tardily and in miniature. As a poet Gray closes the period we have been discussing in the present chapter, and then passes beyond it. His metrical work steadily advances : we have the somewhat cold and timid odes of his youth ; we proceed to the superb *Elegy*, in which the Thomsonian school reaches its apex, and expires ; we cross over to the elaborate Pindaric odes, in which Gray throws off the last shackles of Augustan versification, and prepares the way for Shelley ; and lastly, we have the purely romantic fragments of the close of his life, those lyrics inspired by the Edda and by Ossian, in which we step out of the eighteenth century altogether, and find ourselves in the full stream of romanticism.

In no sketch of the genius of Gray, however slight, can we afford to ignore the range and singular fulness of his intellectual acquirements. He was described by one well qualified to judge as being in his time "perhaps the most learned man in Europe." His knowledge of Greek literature, and especially Greek poetry, was as deep as it was subtle; he was equally keen in his study of all that suited his own peculiar habits of mind in the authors of modern Europe, and when he was already advanced in life he mastered Icelandic, at that time a language almost unknown even in continental Scandinavia. His tendency of mind was to be habitually dejected; he was solitary, and a hypochondriac. Against this constitutional melancholy, intellectual activity was his great resource, and his favourite saying was, "to be employed is to be happy." We are fortunately able to follow the development of this exquisite and sequestered mind in the copious series of his letters to his private friends, first imperfectly collected in 1775; in this remarkable correspondence, which yields to none in the language in brightness and elegance, we observe the movements of the fastidious brain and melancholy conscience, illuminated and gilded by the light of such spontaneous humour as the sprightlier poems of the writer ought to have prepared us for.

Among the writings of Gray it is unquestionable that the *Churchyard Elegy* stands first. In other poems he has during brief passages displayed higher qualities than are illustrated here, but in no second work is the noble tone of tenderness and distinction preserved at such a uniform level of perfection. By credit of this single piece Gray stands easily at the head of all the English elegiac poets, and, as Mr. Swinburne puts it, "holds for all ages to come his unassailable and sovereign station." Encrusted as it is with layers upon layers of eulogy, bibliography, and criticism, we have but to scrape these away to find the immortal poem beneath as fresh, as melodious, as inspiring as ever. With regard to the two great Pindaric odes, criticism has by no means spoken with the same unanimity. The contemporaries of Gray found these elaborate pieces difficult to the verge of unintelligibility. Later critics, who have not pretended to find them unmeaning, have yet objected to their overblown magnificence, their excess of allegorical apparatus, and their too manifest metrical artifice. That they do not belong to the school of simplicity may be freely admitted, but there are certain themes, suggestively described by De Quincey, in the treatment of which simplicity is out of place. The Progress of Poesy and the prophetic raptures of a dying bard may be recognised as belonging to the same class of subjects as Belshazzar's Feast. The qualities rather to be regarded in these elaborate pieces of poetic art are their originality of structure, the varied music of their balanced strophes, as of majestic antiphonal choruses answering one another in some antique temple, and the extraordinary skill with which the evolution of the theme is observed and restrained. It is in this latter characteristic that Gray shows himself, as an artist, to be far superior to Collins. The student will not fail, in some of Gray's minor writings, in the sonorous *Stanzas to Mr. Bentley*, in the thrilling flute-like tones and nature-sketches of the fragmentary *Ode on Vicissitude*, in the Gothic picturesqueness of *The Descent of Odin*, to detect notes and phrases of a more delicate originality than are to be found even in his more famous writings, and will dwell with peculiar pleasure on those passages in which Gray freed himself of the trammels of an artificial and conventional taste, and prophesied of the new romantic age that was coming. The faults of Gray's poetry are obvious, especially in his earlier writing; they are the results of an exaggerated taste for rhetoric and for allegory. But the main features of his work are such that we may frankly acknowledge him to have succeeded when he tells us that "the style I have aimed at is extreme conciseness of expression, yet pure, perspicuous, and musical."

CHAPTER VIII

THE NOVELISTS

THERE is nothing offensive to the dignity of literary history in acknowledging that the most prominent piece of work effected by literature in England during the eighteenth century is the creation, for it can be styled nothing less, of the modern novel. In the seventeenth century there had been a very considerable movement in the direction of prose fiction. The pastoral romances of the Elizabethans had continued to circulate; France had set an example in the heroic stories of D'Urfé and La Calprenède, which English imitators and translators had been quick to follow, even as early as 1647. The *Francion* of Sorel and the *Roman Bourgeois* of Furetière (the latter, published in 1666, of especial interest to students of the English novel) had prepared the way for the exact opposite to the heroic romance, namely, the realistic story of everyday life. Bunyan and Richard Head, Mrs. Behn and Defoe—each had marked a stage in the development of English fiction. Two noble forerunners of the modern novel, *Robinson Crusoe* and *Gulliver's Travels*, had inflamed the curiosity and awakened the appetite of British readers; but, although there were already great satires and great romances in the language, the first quarter of the eighteenth century passed away without revealing any domestic genius in prose fiction, any master of the workings of the human heart. Meanwhile the drama had decayed. The audiences which had attended the poetic plays of the beginning and the comedies of close of the seventeenth century now found nothing on the boards of the theatre to satisfy their craving after intellectual excitement. The descendants of the men and women who had gone out to welcome the poetry of Shakespeare and the wit of Congreve were now rather readers than playgoers, and were most ready to enjoy an appeal to their feelings when that appeal reached them in book form. In the playhouse, they came to expect bustle and pantomine rather than literature. This decline in theatrical habits prepared a domestic audience for the novelists, and accounts for that feverish and apparently excessive anxiety with which the earliest great novels were awaited and received.

Meanwhile, the part taken by Addison and Steele in preparing for this change of taste must not be overlooked, and the direct link between Addison, as a picturesque narrative essayist, and Richardson, as the first great English novelist, is to be found in Pierre de Marivaux (1688-1763), who imitated the *Spectator*, and who is often assumed, though somewhat too rashly, to have suggested the tone of *Pamela*. Into this latter question we shall presently have need to inquire again. It is enough to point out here that when the English novel did suddenly and irresistibly make its appearance, it had little in common with the rococo and coquettish work which had immediately preceded it in France, and which at first, even to judges so penetrating as the poet Gray, was apt to seem more excellent, because more subtle and refined. The rapidity with which the novel became domiciled amongst us, and the short space of time within which the principal masterpieces of the novelists were produced, are not more remarkable than the lassitude which fell upon English fiction as soon as the first great generation had passed away. The flourishing period of the eighteenth-century novel lasted exactly twenty-five years, during which time we have to record the publication of no less than fifteen eminent works of fiction. These fifteen are naturally divided into three groups. The first contains *Pamela*, *Joseph Andrews*, *David Simple*, and *Jonathan Wild*. In these books the art is still somewhat crude, and the science of fiction incompletely understood. After a silence of five years we reach the second and greatest section of this central period, during which there appeared, in quick succession, *Clarissa*, *Roderick Random*, *Tom Jones*, *Peregrine Pickle*, *Amelia*, and *Sir Charles Grandison*. As though invention had been exhausted by the publication of this incomparable series of masterpieces, there followed another silence of five years, and then were issued, each on the heels of the other, *Tristram Shandy*, *Rasselas*, *Chrysal*, *The Castle of Otranto*, and *The Vicar of Wakefield*. Five years later still, a book born out of due time, appeared *Humphrey Clinker*, and then, with one or two such exceptions as *Evelina* and *Caleb Williams*, no great novel appeared again in England for forty years, until, in 1811, the new school of fiction was inaugurated by *Sense and Sensibility*. The English novel, therefore, in its first great development, should be considered as comprised within the dates 1740 and 1766; and it may not be uninstructive, before entering into any critical examination of the separate authors, to glance at this chronological list of the first fifteen great works of English fiction.

The novels contained in the catalogue just given, however widely they differed from one another in detail, had this in common, that they dealt with mental and moral phenomena. Before 1740 we possessed romances, tales, prose fiction of various sorts, but in none of these was essayed any careful analysis of character or any profound delineation of emotion. In Defoe, where the record of imaginary fact was carried on with so much ingenuity and knowledge, the qualities we have just mentioned are notably absent; nor can it be said that we find them in any prose-writer of fiction earlier than Richardson, except in some very slight and imperfect degree in Aphra Behn, especially in her Rousseauish novel of *Oroonoko*. Before, indeed, we begin to chronicle the feats of the novelists, we have to deal with the last of the old school of romance-writers, whose solitary work appeared when Richardson, Fielding, and Smollett were in the midst of their successes. This was Robert Paltock (1697?-1767?) of Clement's Inn, of whom nothing is certainly known, save that, in

1751, he published, in two volumes, *The Life and Adventures of Peter Wilkins*, a sailor who was shipwrecked near the South Pole, and who fell in with a wonderful winged race of Glums and Gawries, one of whom, the beautiful Youwarkee, he found fainting outside his hut, and afterwards married. On taking her up,

"I found she had a sort of brown chaplet, like lace, round her head, under and about which her hair was tucked up and twined; and she seemed to me to be clothed in a thin hair-coloured silk garment, which, upon trying to raise her, I found to be quite warm, and therefore hoped there was life in the body it contained."

This book is not so skilfully imagined as *Robinson Crusoe*, to which it owes not a little; but the strange people, winged with graundees or throbbing crimson robes of their own skin, are described with a charming fancy, and *Peter Wilkins* will never want admirers. It belongs, however, to the old school, and was probably written before the publication of *Pamela*.

The first great English novelist, Samuel Richardson (1689-1761), was born and bred in Derbyshire. He records of himself that when still a little boy he had two peculiarities—he loved the society of women best, and he delighted in letter-writing. Indeed, before he was eleven, he wrote a long epistle to a widow of fifty, rebuking her for unbecoming conduct. The girls of the neighbourhood soon discovered his insight into the human heart, and his skill in correspondence, and they employed the boy to write their love-letters for them. In 1706 Richardson was apprenticed to a London printer, served a diligent apprenticeship, and worked as a compositor until he rose, late in life, to be Master of the Stationers' Company. He was fifty years of age before he showed symptoms of any higher ambition than that of printing correctly Acts of Parliament and new editions of law-books. In 1739 the publishers, Rivington and Osborne, urged him to compose for them a volume of *Familiar Letters*, afterwards actually produced as an aid to illiterate persons in their correspondence. Richardson set about this work, gave it a moral flavour, and at last began to write what would serve as a caution to young serving-women who were exposed to temptation. At this point he recollected a story he had heard long before, of a beautiful and virtuous maid-servant who succeeded in marrying her master; and then, laying the original design aside, Richardson, working rapidly, wrote in three months his famous story of *Pamela*.

All Richardson's novels are written in what Mrs. Barbauld has ingeniously described as "the most natural and the least probable way of telling a story," namely, in consecutive letters. The famous heroine of his first book is a young girl, Pamela Andrews, who describes in letters to her father and mother what goes on in the house of a lady with whom she had lived as maid, and who is just dead when the story opens. The son of Pamela's late mistress, a Mr. B. (it was Fielding who wickedly enlarged the name to Booby) becomes enamoured of her charms, and takes every mean advantage of her defenceless position; but, fortunately, Pamela is not more virtuous than astute, and after various agonies, which culminate in her thinking of drowning herself in a pond, she brings her admirer to terms, and is discovered to us at last as the rapturous though still humble Mrs. B. There are all sorts of faults to be found with this crude book. The hero is a rascal, who comes to a good end, not because he has deserved to do so, but because his clever wife has angled for him with her beauty, and has landed him at last, like an exhausted salmon. So long as Pamela is merely innocent and frightened, she is charming, but her character ceases to be sympathetic as she grows conscious of the value of her charms, and even the lax morality of the day was shocked at the craft of her latest manœuvres. But all the world went mad with pleasure over the book. What we now regard as tedious and prolix was looked upon as so much linkèd sweetness long drawn out. The fat printer had invented a new thing, and inaugurated a fresh order of genius. For the first time, the public was invited, by a master of the movements of the heart, to be present at the dissection of that fascinating organ, and the operator could not be leisurely enough, could not be minute enough, for his breathless and enraptured audience. In France, for some ten years past, there had been writers,—Crébillon, Marivaux, Prévost,—who had essayed this delicate analysis of emotion, but these men were the first to admit the superiority of their rough English rival. In *Marianne*, where the heroine tells her own story, which somewhat resembles that of Pamela, the French novelist produced a very refined study of emotion, which will probably be one day more largely read than it now is, and which should be looked through by every student of the English novel. This book is prolix and languid in form, and undoubtedly bears a curious resemblance to Richardson's novel. The English printer, however, could not read French,[1] and there is sufficient evidence to show that he was independent of any influences save those which he took from real life. None the less, of course, Marivaux, who has a name for affectation which his writings scarcely deserve, has an interest for us as a harbinger of the modern novel. *Pamela* was published in two volumes in 1740. The author was sufficiently ill-advised to add two more in 1741. In this latter instalment Mrs. B. was represented as a dignified matron, stately and sweet under a burden of marital infidelity. But this continuation is hardly worthy to be counted among the works of Richardson.

The novelist showed great wisdom in not attempting to repeat too quickly the success of his first work. He allowed the romances of Henry and Sarah Fielding, the latter as grateful to him as the former were repugnant, to produce their effect upon the public, and it was to an audience more able to criticise fiction that Richardson addressed his next budget from the mail-bag. *Clarissa, or The History of a Young Lady*, appeared, in instalments, but in seven volumes in all, in 1748, with critical prefaces prefixed to the first and fourth volumes. In this book, the novelist put his original crude essay completely into the shade, and added one to the masterpieces of the world. Released from the accident which induced him in the pages of *Pamela* to make his heroine a servant girl, in *Clarissa* Richardson depicted a lady, yet not of so lofty a rank as to be beyond the range of his own

[1] It is, however, now certain that there existed an English version of *Marianne*.

observation. The story is again told entirely in letters; it is the history of the abduction and violation of a young lady by a finished scoundrel, and ends in the death of both characters. To enable the novelist to proceed, each personage has a confidant. The beautiful and unhappy Clarissa Harlowe corresponds with the vivacious Miss Howe; Robert Lovelace addresses his friend and quondam fellow-reveller, John Belford. The character of Clarissa is summed up in these terms by her creator:—" A young Lady of great Delicacy, Mistress of all the Accomplishments, natural and acquired, that adorn the Sex, having the strictest Notions of filial Duty." Her piety and purity, in fact, are the two lode-stars of her moral nature, and the pursuit of each leads her life to shipwreck.

By the universal acknowledgment of novel-readers, Clarissa is one of the most sympathetic, as she is one of the most lifelike, of all the women in literature, and Richardson has conducted her story with so much art and tact, that her very faults canonise her, and her weakness crowns the triumph of her chastity. In depicting the character of Lovelace, the novelist had a difficult task, for to have made him a mere ruffian would have been to ruin the whole purpose of the piece. He is represented as witty, versatile, and adroit, the very type of the unscrupulous gentleman of fashion of the period. He expiates his crimes, at the close of a capital duel, by the hands of Colonel Morden, a relative of the Harlowe family, who has seen Clarissa die. The success of *Clarissa*, both here and in France, was extraordinary. As the successive volumes appeared, and readers were held in suspense as to the fate of the exquisite heroine, Richardson was deluged with letters entreating him to have mercy. The women of England knelt sobbing round his knees, and addressed him as though he possessed the power of life and death.

The slow and cumbrous form of *Clarissa* has tended to lessen the number of its students, but there is probably no one who reads at all widely who has not at one time or another come under the spell of this extraordinary book. In France its reputation has always stood very high. Diderot said that it placed Richardson with Homer and Euripides, Rousseau openly imitated it, and Alfred de Musset has styled it the best novel in the world. To those who love to see the passions taught to move at the command of sentiment, and who are not wearied by the excessively minute scale, as of a moral miniature painter, on which the author designs his work, there can scarcely be recommended a more thrilling and affecting book. The author is entirely inexorable, and the reader must not hope to escape until he is thoroughly purged with terror and pity.

After the further development of Fielding's genius, and after the advent of a new luminary in Smollett, Richardson once more presented to the public an elaborate and ceremonious novel of extreme prolixity. The *History of Sir Charles Grandison*, in seven (and six) volumes, appeared in the spring of 1754, after having been pirated in Dublin during the preceding winter. Richardson's object in this new adventure was, having already painted the portraits of two virtuous young women—the one fortunate, the other a martyr—to produce this time a virtuous hero, and to depict "the character and actions of a man of true honour," as before, in a series of familiar letters. There is more movement, more plot in this novel than in the previous ones; the hero is now in Italy, now in England, and there is much more attempt than either in *Pamela* or *Clarissa* to give the impression of a sphere in which a man of the world may move. Grandison is, however, a slightly ludicrous hero. His perfections are those of a prig and an egoist, and he passes like the sun itself over his parterre of adoring worshippers. The ladies who are devoted to Sir Charles Grandison are, indeed, very numerous, but the reader's interest centres in three of them—the mild and estimable Harriet Byron, the impassioned Italian Clementina della Porretta, and the ingenuous ward Emily Jervois. The excuse for all this is that this paragon of manly virtue has "the most delicate of human minds," and that women are irresistibly attracted to him by his splendid perfections of character. But posterity has admitted that the portrait is insufferably overdrawn, and that Grandison is absurd. The finest scenes in this interesting but defective novel are those in which the madness of Clementina is dwelt upon in that long-drawn patient manner of which Richardson was a master. The book is much too long.

Happy in the fame which "the three daughters" of his pen had brought him, and enjoying prosperous circumstances, Richardson's life closed in a sort of perpetual tea-party, in which he, the only male, sat surrounded by bevies of adoring ladies. He died in London, of apoplexy, on the 4th of July 1761. His manners were marked by the same ceremonious stiffness which gives his writing an air of belonging to a far earlier period than that of Fielding or Smollett; but his gravity and sentimental earnestness only helped to endear him to the women. Of the style of Richardson there is little to be said; the reader never thinks of it. If he forces himself to regard it, he sees that it is apt to be slipshod, although so trim and systematic. Richardson was a man of unquestionable genius, dowered with extraordinary insight into female character, and possessing the power to express it; but he had little humour, no rapidity of mind, and his speech was so ductile and so elaborate that he can scarcely compete with later and sharper talents. It should be no small praise to him, however, that he is able, in the course of his lengthy and wiredrawn productions, to preserve the general proportions of a scheme better than either Fielding or Smollett. He was a plump man, very gracious and gentle, but painfully afflicted with nervous tremor, and a hypochondriac all his life. As an example of Richardson, we may give part of one of the letters addressed to Miss Howe by Miss Harlowe:

"I have been frighted out of my wits. Still am in a manner out of breath. Thus occasioned—I went down, under the usual pretence, in hopes to find something from you. Concerned at my disappointment, I was returning from the woodhouse, when I heard a rustling, as of somebody behind a stack of wood. I was extremely surprised, but still more to behold a man coming from behind the furthermost stack. O! thought I, at that moment, the sin of a prohibited correspondence!

"In the same point of time that I saw him, he besought me not to be frighted, and, still nearer approaching me, threw open a horseman's coat; and, who should it be but Mr. Lovelace! I could not scream out (yet attempted to scream the moment I saw a man, and again when I saw who it was), for I had no voice; and had I not caught hold of a prop, which suppörted the old roof, I should have sunk.

"I had hitherto, as you know, kept him at distance, and now, as I recovered myself, judge of my emotions when I recollected his character from every mouth of my family, his enterprising temper, and found myself alone with him, in a place so near a bye-lane, and so remote from the house. But his respectful behaviour soon dissipated those fears, and gave me others, lest we should be seen together, and information of it given to my brother; the consequences of which, I could readily think, would be, if not further mischief, an imputed assignation, a stricter confinement, a forfeited correspondence with you, my dearest friend, and a pretence for the most violent compulsion; and neither the one set of reflections, nor the other, acquitted him to me for his bold intrusion."

The greatest of English novelists, Henry Fielding (1707-1754), was descended from a younger branch of the Denbigh family. He was born at Sharpham Park, in Somersetshire; he was educated at Eton and at Leyden, and appeared in London, as a very fine strapping fellow of over six feet, with enormous capacity for enjoyment, and no obvious opportunity of securing it, in 1728. He began to earn a living by writing for the stage, and by publishing lampoons in verse. There are attributed to him, in all, some twenty-eight dramas, mostly comedies and farces, mainly produced before 1737. One of his burlesques, *The Tragedy of Tragedies* (1730), an impassioned piece of parody in honour of Tom Thumb, has lived in dramatic literature, but the rest of Fielding's plays are remembered only by the curious. It is believed that, discovering that he could no longer live by the stage, Fielding determined about 1737 to revert to his original study of the law, and meanwhile supported himself by much anonymous writing. In 1740 he was called to the Bar, and in November of that year was awakened to his true vocation by the publication of *Pamela*. Fielding was not one of the admirers of Richardson's method of rewarding virtue in long-drawn epistolary fiction. All that was tame and priggish and sordid in that very imperfect book appealed to Fielding at once as deserving sharp and condign punishment. He determined to parody *Pamela*, and to take a brother of that heroine as the central figure of his burlesque. Hence it is that at the opening of Fielding's first novel, Joseph Andrews is discovered modestly rebuffing the advances of an unscrupulous lady of fashion. After progressing a little way, however,—some five chapters comprise all the parody of Richardson,—Fielding became fascinated by his own characters, invested them with genuine human interest, and on a foundation of rough burlesque built that beautiful structure of pure comedy which we know as *The History of Joseph Andrews*, published early in 1742.

On the title-page of the novel composed in this half-accidental way the author has stated that it is "written in imitation of the manner of Cervantes," and in the preface he has defined *Joseph Andrews* as "a comic epic poem in prose." He was evidently conscious that the book was formed of somewhat heterogeneous materials, and he was anxious to cover his inconsistencies by emphasising the fact that it was all a burlesque. In this Fielding did himself an injustice; *Joseph Andrews* is comic, no doubt, but it is a work of far higher artistic value than any mere burlesque of a novel like *Pamela* could be. It is not its author's best constructed book, and Fielding was never, as we have remarked, so good an architect of his work as Richardson was. There are episodes, such as that of Leonora and Bellarmine, which break the thread of the narrative and leave the reader in suspense for pages and pages. But the characters, and the bustle and intrigue in which they exhibit themselves, are of the purest comedy, while Parson Abraham Adams, alone, would be a contribution to English letters. This simple and learned clergyman, with his goodness of heart and his eccentric manners, is really the hero of the novel, the somewhat insipid loves of Joseph and Fanny forming little more than an excuse for the journeys of Parson Adams. Mrs. Slipslop and Mrs. Towwouse, Trulliber and Peter Pounce, make excellent minor figures in this most facetious genre-piece, while at the end the author recurs to the old satire on Richardson, and introduces Squire Booby (the Mr. B. of *Pamela*) and his wife in the very triumph of her "strange conjunction of purity and precaution." Joseph, however, by a touch of final satire, is proved not to be Pamela's brother after all, but the child of "persons of much greater circumstances" than Gaffer Andrews and his wife. Richardson bitterly resented all this rude intrusion into his moral garden, and never ceased to regard Fielding with open aversion.

Fourteen months after the publication of his first novel, Fielding collected his scattered writings, or a certain portion of them, in three volumes of *Miscellanies* (1743). The first volume comprised his occasional poems of the last fifteen years, and several essays in prose. The second contained, beside two dramas, the Lucianic history called *A Journey from this World to the Next;* this begins with a very sprightly satire, culminating in the author's entrance into Elysium; unhappily, when in a charming vein, he meets Julian the Apostate, who soliloquises, not always very amusingly, for one hundred and forty pages. Julian relinquishes his position to Anne Boleyn, and the fragment presently closes. There are some exceedingly fine passages in this shapeless work. The third volume of the *Miscellanies* is entirely occupied by the novel of *Mr. Jonathan Wild the Great.* This has never been a favourite among Fielding's readers, because of its caustic cynicism and the unbroken gloom of its tone, but it is equal to the best he has left us in force and originality. It is the history of an unmitigated ruffian, from his baptism by Titus Oates to his death at Newgate on "the Tree of Glory." The story is intended to mock those relations in which biographers lose themselves in pompous eulogies of their subjects, for their "greatness," without consideration of any "goodness," by showing that it is possible to write the history of a gallows-bird in exactly the same style of inflated gusto. The inexorable irony which is sustained all through, even when the most detestable acts of the hero are described, forms rather a strain at last upon the reader's nerves, and no one would turn to *Jonathan Wild* for mere amusement. But it shows a marvellous knowledge of the seamy side of life, the author proving himself in it to be as familiar with thieves and their prisons as in *Joseph Andrews* he had been with stage-coaches and wayside taverns; while nothing could be more picturesque than some of the scenes with Blueskin and his gang, or than the Petronian passages on board ship. It may be noted that there had been a real Jonathan Wild hanged at Tyburn in 1725. Mr. Austin Dobson has suggested that this novel, which certainly shows little sign of the new tendencies in fiction, was written earlier than *Joseph Andrews*.

It now becomes very difficult to trace Fielding for several years. He was poor, his health had declined, and his fortitude was assailed by a multitude of calamities. In 1744 he prefixed to the second edition of Sarah Fielding's novel of *David Simple*, which had been attributed to him, a long and very interesting preface, in which he speaks of himself as having no leisure for writing. We cannot guess what can thus have absorbed his time, unless he was working as a barrister. A little later he was certainly engaged in political journalism, and had gained the friendship of Lord Lyttelton. By the help of this enlightened patron, Fielding was at the close of 1748 raised above the fear of want by being appointed a Justice of the Peace for Westminster. It is further to Lyttelton, it appears, that we owe the next and greatest of Fielding's works, since *Tom Jones* was begun at his suggestion, and since he supported the novelist during great part of its composition. This famous book, which many critics have not hesitated to style the greatest novel ever published, appeared in six volumes, under the title of *The History of Tom Jones, a Foundling*, in February 1749. The very form of this book showed that the author, who stated when the work was only half through that it had already employed "some thousands of hours," had shirked no pains to make it a work of art; it opened with a dignified but somewhat pathetic dedication to Lord Lyttelton, and consisted of eighteen books, each preceded by a "prolegomenous" chapter which was an essay, usually of a bantering kind, on some favourite theme of the author's. Fielding took great pains in composing these essays, which were imitated by Thackeray and by George Eliot, and a perusal of them, isolated from the novel itself, gives us perhaps the most favourable impression of Fielding as a prose writer. It is from the introduction of the Fourth Book of *Tom Jones* that we select our specimen of Fielding's style :

"I am convinced that awful magistrate my Lord Mayor contracts a good deal of that reverence which attends him through the year, by the several pageants which precede his pomp. Nay, I must confess, that even I myself, who am not remarkably liable to be captivated with show, have yielded not a little to the impressions of much preceding state. When I have seen a man strutting in a procession after others whose business hath been only to walk before him, I have conceived a higher notion of his dignity than I have felt on seeing him in a common situation. But there is one instance which comes exactly up to my purpose. This is the custom of sending on a basket-woman, who is to precede the pomp at a coronation, and to strew the stage with flowers, before the great personages begin their procession. The Ancients would certainly have invoked the Goddess Flora for this purpose, and it would have been no difficulty for their priests or politicians to have persuaded the people of the real presence of the deity, though a plain mortal had personated her and performed her office. But we have no such design of imposing on our reader, and therefore those who object to the heathen mythology may, if they please, change our goddess into the above-mentioned basket-woman. Our intention, in short, is to introduce our heroine with the utmost solemnity in our power, with an elevation of style, and all other circumstances proper to raise the veneration of our reader. Indeed, for certain cases, we would advise those of our male readers who have any hearts to read no further, were we not well assured that how amiable soever the picture of our Heroine will appear, as it is really a copy from nature, many of our fair countrywomen will be found worthy to satisfy any passion, and to answer any idea of female perfection, which our pencil will be able to raise."

When we come to the story itself, it is to find ourselves moving among the healthiest company ever devised by a human brain. The winds of heaven blow along the pages, the stage is filled with persons whose cheeks are ruddy with the freshest health, whose simplicity and unaffectedness are nature itself, and whose voices are so gay and wholesome that we hardly can bring ourselves to be offended when some of them speak a little too coarsely in their old-world accents. There is Mr. Allworthy, with his "good heart and no family," who finds so mysteriously in his bed, on his return from London, a new-born infant, needless to say, the full-blooded hero of the story. There is that typical roaring foxhunter, Squire Western, there is the timid and unfortunate Partridge, there are the pedants Square and Thwackum, there is the impossible little prig Blifil, whom only a generous mind could have created. All these, and a host of other clearly-defined characters, all drawn standing out in the sunlight, dance attendance on the gallant, handsome, but too-human Tom, and the bright Sophia. Any sketch of the plot of a book which every one ought to have read, would be entirely out of place here. We are all still echoing the "ne plus ultra" of Lady Mary Wortley Montagu. It is only critical, however, to admit that there are spots on the sun. Fielding's unfortunate love of episodes leads him astray here as elsewhere. In the tenth chapter of the eighth book the plot is caught in the web of a dreadful spider called "the Man of the Hill," and is held there for six mortal chapters. In the eleventh book there is a great deal more than the reader cares for about Mrs. Fitzpatrick, and in the fourteenth book about Mrs. Miller, which ladies, however, have more claim to our attention than the Man on the Hill has. It is also obvious, surely, that the last volume is hurried, as though the author were tired, and did not care to draw his threads together neatly. But there is remarkably little to cavil at, and so long as wit and wholesomeness, manly writing and generous thinking, with a genial appreciation of all that makes life worth enjoying, are welcome among us, this truly sunny book will never lack its admirers.

His gout and his active labours as a magistrate made Fielding's life for the next few years no bed of roses. He was suggesting plans for checking the increase of robbers, he was recommending the new-found waters of Glastonbury. Finally, in the last week of 1751 appeared his latest novel, *Amelia*, in four volumes. It might be separated from *Tom Jones* by twenty years, instead of two, so obvious is the sense of failing health, so ripe and melancholy the fulness of experience. When we speak of the proofs of failing health, we refer to no decline in force or genius, but to lessened animal spirits, to a quieter and sadder ideal of life. There is far more shadow and less sunshine in *Amelia* than in *Tom Jones*, while in some respects it is certainly much more humane and tender. Those who have preferred *Amelia* to its predecessors must, we think, have been overenchanted by the character of its patient and saintly heroine, without whom the book would fall in pieces. Her husband, Captain Booth, on whom it can scarcely be doubted that the world has unjustly built its conception of Fielding himself, is very natural and human, but unstable to the last degree, and noticeably stupid. Many of the incidents are crudely introduced, being no doubt actual history which the novelist did not take the trouble to work into his picture. *Amelia* was not popular in its own day, but rose into favour at the beginning of the present century; and Thackeray, who did not wholly appreciate the morals of *Tom Jones* or *Joseph Andrews*, found those of Fielding's latest novel entirely to his taste. On the other hand, it is, surely, what they certainly are not, a little dull.

Indeed the end was near, and the Atlantean novelist, who had squandered the rich treasure of his youth, was already bowed under the orb of his fate. He still struggled manfully to be a faithful servant to the public, and his pamphlets of 1752 and 1753 testify to his vigilance as a magistrate and his anxiety to befriend the poor. At length, in the summer of the latter year, the physicians insisted on his retirement to Bath, but he soon came back to break up, for the Government, a notorious gang of street robbers. He could scarcely drag himself about, so feeble was he with gout, asthma, and jaundice, and in the summer of 1754 he was obliged, as a last chance, to try the voyage to Portugal. He lingered for two months at Lisbon, where he died on the 8th of October, and where

"Beneath the green Estrella trees,
No Artist merely, but a Man,
Wrought on our noblest island-plan,
Sleeps with the alien Portuguese."

His *Journal of the Voyage*, his last book, appeared in 1755. There are few figures in our literary history which inspire so much sympathy as Fielding. His character was full of superficial faults, but he was pre-eminently honest, good, and manly. These qualities are reflected in his work, which is not always clean, but always breezy and healthy. Fielding was a much more careful writer, in spite of his easy air, than either Richardson or Smollett; his intellect was better trained than that of either, and he is as much more grammatical than the first as he is more graceful than the second. His constructive power as a novelist was perhaps less than Richardson's, and he certainly had not so refined an insight into the character of women. But he knew men ten times better than the creator of Sir Charles Grandison, and his place in the fiction of manners is broader as well as higher than Richardson's can ever be. The extraordinary variety of his four great books, inspired respectively by indignant humour, by irony, by geniality, and by tenderness, puts him easily above Smollett, who might otherwise at one or two points seem to compete with Fielding successfully.

Richardson was an elderly man, Fielding in the ripeness of manhood, and Smollett quite young, when each flourished as a novelist; and hence, though more than thirty years separated the birth of the first from that of the third, they are to be considered as contemporaries—*Roderick Random*, indeed, being exactly contemporaneous with *Clarissa*, and a little older than *Tom Jones*. Tobias George Smollett (1721-1771) was brought up in a beautiful valley of Dumbartonshire by his grandfather, Sir James Smollett of Bonhill, whose death in 1740 left the youth with no other provision than an excellent education. He was already something of a poet, and had come up to London in 1739 with a very bad tragedy, *The Regicide*, which Garrick refused. Smollett was obliged to become surgeon's mate on board a man-of-war, and served in the affair of Carthagena. He left the fleet and settled in the West Indies, somewhat longer than Roderick Random did. In Jamaica he married one who at least had seemed to be an heiress, Miss Nancy Lascelles. After a world of adventures he found himself in London again in 1744, trying to combine the professions of medicine and literature, and scourging the follies of the age from a garret. In January 1748 Smollett published, in two volumes, his first novel, *The Adventures of Roderick Random*. This book is a good instance of his method, and exemplifies the merits as well as the defects of his style. It takes the form of an autobiography; the hero is a Scotchman who is singularly like Smollett himself in the nature of his adventures. He is even shipped off to the West Indies as a surgeon, and there can be no doubt that the author was mainly repeating, but also, one hopes, exaggerating, what he himself had seen and experienced. *Roderick Random* is intentionally modelled on the plan of Lesage, and here, as elsewhere, Smollett shows himself less original than either Richardson or Fielding. He can hardly be said to invent or to construct; he simply reports. He does this with infinite spirit and variety. Comedy and tragedy, piety and farce, follow one another in bewildering alternation. But although he dazzles and entertains us, he does not charm. The book is ferocious to a strange degree, and so foul as to be fit only for a very well-seasoned reader. The hero, in whom Smollett complacently could see nothing but a picture of "modest merit struggling with every difficulty," is a selfish bully, whose faults it is exasperating to find condoned. The book, of course, is full of good things. The hero is three separate times hurried off to sea, and the scenes of rough sailor-life, though often disgusting, are wonderfully graphic. Tom Bowling, Jack Rattlin, and the proud Mr. Morgan are not merely immortal among salt-sea worthies, but practically the first of a long line of sailors of fiction. There is, moreover, the meek and gentle Strap, so ungenerously treated by the hero, that we almost throw the book from us in anger, when at last Random is permitted, on the last page, to crown his own ill-gotten gains with the fortune of the lovely Narcissa.

The same inconsistent qualities, mingled, however, with considerably greater breadth and freedom, go to make up the four volumes of *The Adventures of Peregrine Pickle* (1751), which is not a better novel than its predecessor, but possesses finer passages. This is, indeed, a very difficult book to criticise, so great is the inequality of its execution. The first volume is in Smollett's best style, displaying his faults of coarseness and satiric ferocity to the full, but concise, brisk, and exquisitely humorous. The second, which is mainly occupied with the French and Flemish passages, is vivacious, but to a much less degree, and by fits and starts. Two-thirds of the third volume are taken up by the nauseous and impertinent "Memoirs of a Lady of Quality," a fungoid growth of episode. The fourth is weighted through its first half by Smollett's passion for elaborate social satire, but wakes up again into pure and lively fiction towards the close. Here, as in *Roderick Random*, the personal unloveliness of the hero's character is annoying. Peregrine is a handsome, swaggering swashbuckler, ungenerous and untrustworthy to the highest degree, with hardly any virtue but that of brute courage. Smollett, nevertheless, smiles at him all through, and seems to be assuring us that he is only sowing his wild oats. The extraordinary violence of the characters, which is more marked here than in any other book of the author's, becomes fatiguing at length. The internecine animosities of Mrs. Trunnion and Mrs. Pickle, the bitter inhumanity of almost everybody in the book, leave us at first exasperated and then incredulous. It is difficult to say why a novel so very disagreeable and so full of faults does, nevertheless, impress the reader as a work of genius. The humours of Commodore Trunnion and Lieutenant Jack Hatchway are still unsurpassed in their kind, though they have inspired so many later hands. The long and stately comedy of the Roman dinner is still a masterpiece of elaborate, learned fooling. Nor are the treasures of the author's studied and artificial humour anywhere scattered with more careless profusion than over the earlier pages of this unequal book.

Smollett was not happily inspired in his next novel. *The Adventures of Ferdinand, Count Fathom* (1753), is more serious than its predecessors; the author's intentions seem to have been romantic. But the hero, once more, and more than ever, is a repulsive scoundrel, and the forest-scenes, which have been praised for their poetical force, appear to us to be simply brutal when they are not bombastic. The public, at all events, rejected *Count Fathom*, and Smollett turned to other branches of literature. He translated *Don Quixote* (1755); he started the *Critical Review*, a newspaper, mainly consisting of short notices of books, which Smollett edited, and partly wrote, with the help of a staff of six or seven hacks. He had an old grudge against one of the Carthagena admirals, and he used the *Critical Review* as a vehicle for censuring this man anonymously in terms which went beyond all possible endurance. Smollett acknowledged the authorship of the article, and was imprisoned as well as fined for the libel. While he was in gaol, he amused himself by imitating Cervantes in a novel in two volumes, *The Adventures of Sir Lancelot Greaves*, printed in 1761, an absurd and exaggerated satire which added nothing to his fame.

Emulous of the success which was attending his countrymen, the Scotch historians, Smollett undertook to write a *Complete History of England*, from Julius Cæsar down to the year 1748; this he afterwards continued to the year 1765. The first edition of this perfunctory work appeared in 1758; Smollett was no born historian, but he wrote with verve and confidence, and when he approached the events of his own age, he prepared himself to treat them with the vivacity of a novelist. If he did not lift his style to a level with that of Hume or Robertson, he easily surpassed the Guthries and Campbells of his day; and from this period we have to think of him as famous. Unfortunately, with success in authorship came the utter ruin of his health, and the loss of his only child, a charming daughter. Smollett was ordered to Italy by his doctors, and he spent two years on the continent of Europe in desultory travel, out of sympathy with what he saw, and ignorantly prejudiced against all customs that clashed in any degree with British habit. He was the original of Smelfungus, who "set out with the spleen and jaundice, and every object he passed by was discoloured and distorted." Sterne, who did not err from want of sympathy, wittily says of Smollett's opinions of the works of art in Italy, that they should have been reserved for his physician. The *Travels in France and Italy*, which he published in 1766, throw more light upon the author than upon the countries he traversed.

Smollett, indeed, was now a wreck; he enjoyed a slight respite in the village of his birth by his native lake, which suited him far better than Bolsena or Garda. His praises of Leven Water, in *Humphrey Clinker*, both in prose, and in his graceful ode, are among the best specimens we possess of his descriptive powers, and show that he could be deeply moved by landscape, when its associations assisted the impression. Any return to cheerfulness or ease, however, was but temporary. The angry and tortured spirit produced in 1769 a fantastic story in two volumes, *The Adventures of an Atom*, one of the foulest and most distressing works ever published, in which the firebrands of indiscriminate satire are hurled hither and thither without aim or purpose. The only part of this Japanese monstrosity which is worth remembering is the attack on Yak-strot, the Earl of Bute. Smollett certainly possessed, with his own Jan-ki-dtzin, "the art of making balls of filth, which were famous for sticking and stinking." This dreadful book was the last that he wrote in England. Utterly shattered and exhausted, he went abroad again, and settled in a villa near Leghorn, under the care of the amiable poet-physician Armstrong. And now a miracle took place, almost unparalleled in literature. For ten years the imaginative powers of Smollett had shown signs of steady decline, and had in his last novel sunk below toleration. What he wrote had long been dull and vindictive, the outcome of a dying mind that sought in filth and peevishness a counter-irritant to its exhaustion. But at Leghorn, during the last year of his life, all the wasted powers of the brain appeared to flicker up in a last flame, and it was almost on his deathbed that Smollett wrote the best of all his books, that masterpiece of wit and frolic, the inimitable *Expedition of Humphrey Clinker*, published in three volumes, in 1771, a few weeks before he died.

It may, perhaps, be questioned whether certain isolated passages of *Peregrine Pickle* do not surpass, in graphic power, any one page of *Humphrey Clinker;* but no critic can well question that the latter is the best sustained, the most complete, and the least disagreeable of Smollett's novels. It is written in the form of letters; it should more properly be called the Expedition of Matthew Bramble, for Humphrey is merely a Methodist postilion picked up by the family of that gentleman near the end of the first volume, and no very prominent character anywhere. The adventures of Mr. Bramble, who sallies forth in search of health at Bath, in London, at Harrogate, at Scarborough, in the Scottish Highlands, at Buxton, and at Gloucester, are no doubt mainly those of Smollett himself, and the only disagreeable parts of the book are the pages in which the old gentleman dwells with the gusto of an invalid on the symptoms of himself or of his fellow-patients. Mr. Bramble is accompanied, however, by his sister Tabitha, a treasure, and by his excellent niece and nephew; it is the letters of all these persons, with those of their servants, that make up the tale. There is a pretty love-intrigue going on all the time between the niece Lydia and a mysterious stranger; but as a rule the novel is distinctly comic in tone, yet with none of the ferocity, the tendency to scourge society, which is so marked elsewhere in Smollett. There is noticeable, moreover, for the first time, in *Humphrey Clinker*, a power of creating characters which are not caricatures, and a sympathy for average human nature. In short, this swan-song of the novelist is in the highest degree tantalising as showing us what he could have done throughout his life if he had cared to cultivate the best part of his genius. If we had more examples of the gaiety that presided at the birth of Winifred Jenkins and Tabitha Bramble we should not doubt, as we now do, whether we are justified in naming Smollett in the same breath with Richardson and Fielding. Looking at his work, however, from the broadest point of view, and acknowledging all its imperfections as well as its imitative quality, we have also to acknowledge that it bears upon it the stamp of a vigorous individuality, and that it has extended no little fascination to later masters of English fiction. Without Smollett Dickens would no more be what he is than Thackeray would be without Fielding. Here is a page from *Peregrine Pickle* :

"The next enterprise in which this triumvirate engaged was a scheme to frighten Trunnion with an apparition, which they prepared and exhibited in this manner. To the hide of a large ox Pipes fitted a leathern vizor of a most terrible appearance, stretched on the jaws of a shark which he had brought from sea, and accommodated with a couple of broad glasses instead of eyes. On the inside of these he placed two rush-lights, and with a composition of sulphur and saltpetre made a pretty large fuse, which he fixed between two rows of his teeth. This equipage being finished, he, one dark night chosen for the purpose, put it on, and following the commodore into a long passage in which he was preceded by Perry with a light in his hand, kindled his firework with a match, and began to bellow like a bull. The boy, as it was concerted, looking behind him, screamed aloud and dropped the light, which was extinguished in the fall; when Trunnion, alarmed at his nephew's consternation, exclaimed, 'Zounds! what's the matter?' And turning about to see the cause of his dismay, beheld a hideous phantom vomiting blue flame, which aggravated the horrors of its aspect. He was instantly seized with an agony of fear, which divested him of his reason; nevertheless, he, as it were mechanically, raised his trusty supporter in his own defence, and the apparition advancing towards him, aimed it at the dreadful annoyance with such a convulsive exertion of strength, that, had not the blow chanced to light upon one of the horns, Mr. Pipes would have had no cause to value himself upon his invention. Misapplied as it was, he did not fail to stagger at the shock, and dreading another such salutation, closed with the commodore, and having tripped up his heels, retreated with great expedition."

Before we leave the great period we must spare a word for Sarah Fielding (1710[1]-1768), the pale moon who attended these three main luminaries. Her *David Simple*, published in 1742, in

---

[1] Not 1714, as usually stated on the authority of her monument at Bath.

two volumes, is not a great, but it is certainly an unduly neglected, book. Not only does its rank in time, as the third English novel, give it interest, but it displays a certain prim grace of construction, and a considerable refinement in the analysis of character. It takes a place midway between the work of Richardson and that of her brother, less morbid than the former, less gusty than the latter, and of course much feebler than either. The sedate wavering of David Simple between the rival passions of Camilla and Cynthia might, it may be suggested, have served Richardson as a hint for the conduct of Sir Charles Grandison. Sarah Fielding, it is to be regretted, made no further serious effort in fiction; perhaps her brother's genius dazzled her. But she had a genuine talent of her own. It is thus that *David Simple* closes:

> "If every man who is possessed of a greater share of wit than is common, instead of insulting and satirising others, would make use of his talents for the advantage and pleasures of the society to which he happens more particularly to belong; and if they, instead of hating him for his superior parts, would, in return for the entertainment he affords them, exert all the abilities nature has given them for his use, in common with themselves, what happiness would mankind enjoy, and who could complain of being miserable? It was this care, tenderness and benevolence to each other which made David and his amiable company happy, who, quite contrary to the rest of the world, for every trifling frailty blamed themselves, whilst it was the business of all the rest to lessen, instead of aggravating, their faults. In short, it is this tenderness and benevolence which alone can give any real pleasure, and which I most sincerely wish to all my readers."

There was born between the dates of Fielding's and Smollett's births a writer whose position in literature is anomalous, but whom we may for convenience sake treat among the novelists. He was in all things the very antidote to Smollett, whose excess of ferocity was a symptom of retrograde movement in literary civilisation which perhaps needed to be balanced by an equal excess in effeminate tenderness. Laurence Sterne (1713-1768) was born at Clonmel, the third of a long line of the feeble children born to a soldier and his wife during their incessant hurrying from camp to camp. His childhood was spent in the fatiguing and demoralising life of a wandering regiment, until, in 1723, he went to school at Halifax. His weary father was at last run through the body in a duel about a goose, in Jamaica, and died in 1731. Next year his cousin sent Sterne to Jesus College, Cambridge, where he formed a lifelong friendship for the witty and disreputable versifier John Hall Stevenson (1715-1785). Sterne was at the university for three years, and then went into the Church, the profession for which, in all probability, he was less fitted than for any other. Nothing is more curious than the fact that this singularly original and ebullient character was content for no less than twenty-three years, from 1736 to 1759, to be no more than a silent country clergyman. In 1738 he became vicar of Sutton-in-the-Forest; in 1741 he married Miss Elizabeth Lumley, who brought him the extraordinary wedding-portion of an extra living, that of Stillington; he painted and fiddled and shot, he joked with Stevenson at Skelton Castle; and he indulged to excess, and to the rapid destruction of his domestic peace, in what he calls "a course of small, quiet attentions" to a succession of ladies. He was a prebendary, and a speculative farmer, and the first of flirts; but he passed middle life without showing any signs of becoming an author. At last, in the beginning of 1759, at the age of forty-six, he began to write a heterogeneous sort of humorous memoirs, the form of which seemed to depend on the whim of the writer, and his perseverance in pursuing his task. Two volumes of this book, called *The Life and Opinions of Tristram Shandy, Gent.*, were published at York on the 1st of January 1760, and the unknown country parson began his real life, the seven years of celebrity and social triumph allotted to him before his death.

The first volume of *Tristram Shandy* introduced to a delighted if faintly scandalised public the immortal Rabelaisian figures of Slop and Yorick, Uncle Toby knocking the ashes out of his tobacco-pipe, and that exemplary couple Walter and Elizabeth Shandy. It also propounded the new religion of philandering, "that tender and delicious sentiment which ever mixes in friendship where there is a difference of sex." But the general effect of the first volume, unaided and undeveloped, must have been rather bewildering; it was annotated, as it were, by the second volume, which certainly shows more brilliant literary ability, and in which the great figures of the brothers Shandy and that of Corporal Trim stand out with extraordinary force. The public was enchanted, and Sterne hurried up to town to be the lion of the season; "the honours paid me were the greatest," he complacently writes, "that were ever known from the great"; and he hastened next year to publish a collection of rather commonplace *Sermons of Mr. Yorick.* In January 1761 had followed two more volumes of *Tristram Shandy.* In the third volume Sterne gets his hero off his hands, and writes a preface; unhappily, too, he gets afloat upon the dreary subjects of Noses and Slawkenbergius, and indulges in a great deal of fantastic cursing, in the Rabelais vein. The early part of vol. iv., "Slawkenbergius's Tale," is sheer Rabelais, but we come out of it into the most delightful sunshine of humour; then follows the bedroom scene, and we sit, hushed with delight, while Mr. Shandy, holding fast his forefinger between his finger and thumb, reasons with my Uncle Toby as he sits in the old fringed chair, valenced round with parti-coloured worsted bobs.

Unhappily, Sterne's health began to fail just as he became famous; vol. iv. closes with a reference to his "vile cough." In his letters he talks of lying down and dying, though next moment he will be "as merry as a monkey and forget it all." Early in 1762 he was obliged to set out for the South of Europe, and lived for more than a year at Toulouse, with his wife, and Lydia his only daughter. Before starting he saw the fifth and sixth volumes of *Tristram Shandy* out of the printer's hands (December 1761). These were less popular than their predecessors; vol. v., indeed, is not remarkable; but vi. should have instantly pleased, for it contains the story of Le Fevre, and, what is even better than that famous episode, the admirable curtain dialogue between Mr. and Mrs. Shandy on the question whether Tristram should be breeched or no. In 1764 Sterne came back to England; some notes of French travel were worked up for publication, and then put aside to serve for *Tristram Shandy*. They now form vol. vii., which with vol. viii., introducing the Widow Wadman, saw the light in January 1765. Both of these are charming; the first prepares us for the lighter touch and more exquisite style of the *Sentimental Journey*; in the second the long-drawn answers of Uncle Toby begin to fascinate us, and have not yet time to weary us. In 1766 followed a second and a much livelier collection of *Sermons*, in which, as Gray said, you often see Sterne "tottering on the verge of laughter, and ready to throw his periwig in the face of the audience." These sermons may be taken as forming a sort of Sunday edition of *Tristram Shandy*, for family use. To conclude the history of the latter work, its last and ninth volume appeared in January 1767.

Sterne's second visit to the South of Europe began in the autumn of 1765 and closed in the summer of 1766. He returned to enter upon the most celebrated of his Platonic flirtations, that with Mrs. Draper, the Eliza of his correspondence, although the wretched state of his health should alone have warned him against such exhausting frivolities. He was writing in 1767 a new book, which was to be in four volumes, describing his latest adventures in France and Italy, and while composing this, he says: "I have torn my whole frame into pieces by my feelings." He came to London when the MS. of two small volumes was finished, and in February 1768 appeared *A Sentimental Journey through France and Italy; by Mr. Yorick*. No more was to be written. Sterne was lodging over a silk-bag shop in Old Bond Street, and there, on the 18th of March 1768, he rather suddenly died, in the presence of none but servants, and they strangers. It is asserted that the body was snatched from its grave, and was dissected in the surgery of a Cambridge professor of anatomy—a grim anecdote which seems to round off Sterne's odd career as he himself might have desired. He did not live quite long enough to enjoy the success of his latest book, a success which was almost unbounded, whether in this country or in France. These passages are taken, the first from *Tristram Shandy*, the second from *A Sentimental Journey*:

"Though my father persisted in not going on with the discourse, yet he could not get my Uncle Toby's smoke-jack out of his head. Piqued as he was at first with it, there was something in the comparison at the bottom which hit his fancy; for which purpose, resting his elbow upon the table, and reclining the right side of his head upon the palm of his hand, but looking first steadfastly in the fire, he began to commune with himself and philosophise about it. But his spirits being wore out with the fatigues of investigating new tracts, and the constant exertion of his faculties upon that variety of subjects which had taken their turn in the discourse, the idea of the smoke-jack soon turned all his ideas upside down, so that he fell asleep almost before he knew what he was about.

"As for my Uncle Toby, his smoke-jack had not made a dozen revolutions before he fell asleep also. Peace be with them both! Dr. Slop is above stairs: Trim is busy in turning an old pair of jack-boots into a couple of mortars to be employed in the siege of Messina next summer, and is this instant boring the touch-holes with the point of a hot poker: all my heroes are off my hands; 'tis the first time I have had a moment to spare, and I'll make use of it, and write my preface."

"When we had got within half a league of Moulins, at a little opening in the road leading to a thicket, I discovered poor Maria sitting under a poplar; she was sitting with her elbow in her lap, and her head leaning on one side within her hand; a small brook ran at the foot of the tree.

"I bid the postilion go on with the chaise to Moulins, and La Fleur to bespeak my supper; and that I would walk after him.

"She was dress'd in white, and much as my friend described her, except that her hair hung loose, which before was twisted within a silk net. She had, superadded likewise to her jacket, a pale green ribband which fell across her shoulder to the waist; at the end of which hung her pipe. Her goat had been as faithless as her lover; and she had got a little dog in lieu of him, which she had kept tied by a string to her girdle; as I looked at her dog, she drew him towards her with the string. 'Thou shalt not leave me, Sylvio!' she said. I looked in Maria's eyes, and saw she was thinking more of her father than of her lover or her little goat; for as she uttered them the tears trickled down her cheeks."

The present writer is obliged to record an opinion at variance with what is usual among critics when he confesses a great preference for the *Sentimental Journey* over *Tristram Shandy*. In the earlier book, no doubt, the humour, which is sometimes worthy of Shakespeare, is superlatively fine, where it makes itself felt; but this is at intervals, through splendid oases in what is now little better than a desert of oddity, dulness, and indelicacy. In the *Sentimental Journey* the wit is perhaps less brilliant, but it is more evenly distributed, and there is not a dull page in the book. There is an extraordinary completeness of impression here, a delicacy of light and colour, an artistic reserve, which were totally wanting, perhaps wilfully excluded, from *Tristram Shandy*. Sentiment, it may be said, has gained on humour, and few English critics have any patience with Sterne's sentiment. It is, however, the very blood in the veins of his style, and to disregard it seriously is to fail to comprehend the author. There is no writer with whom it is more necessary to be in intellectual sympathy than Sterne. We must think of him as he was, with his thirst for enjoyment, for colour, for mental and physical sunlight, bound down to the proprieties by his cassock of an English clergyman, standing, as he says, "at the window in my dusty black coat, and looking through the glass to see the world in yellow, blue, and green, running at the ring of pleasure." He is much more himself, much happier and more inimitable, when he is surveying French life in this wistful and indulgent humour, than when he is riding the hobby-horses of his crotchets, and boring us with Slawkenbergius. In his latest work the theme is slight enough, but the absence of cant, the apparent artlessness, the freaky and childish oscillation between laughter and tears, the quickness of observation in little things, in which last quality Sterne is absolutely unrivalled, combine to delight all who are not too solemn to be pleased.

The style of Sterne is more strongly marked than that of any of his contemporaries. In such examples as the episode of Nameth (in *Tristram Shandy*), and the story of Maria, it is a sort of essence evidently distilled word by word, phrase by phrase, with infinite attention to artistic beauty and melody.

In other cases he seems to be so unaffected as to aim at no style at all, but the careful reader will generally suspect this artlessness to be the result of labour. He had evidently studied the French writers of the age very carefully, and had adopted many of their roseate graces. It has to be added, in the briefest sketch of this very difficult writer, that his extraordinary originality did not guard him against that snare of the indolent, plagiarism, in which he was a terrible sinner; that his delicacy of style and feeling do not prevent his being, not indeed gross like Smollett, but scandalously prurient; like Aretino, *il ricane dans l'ombre;* and finally, that his sentimentality is commonly only skin-deep, and adopted more for purposes of intellectual self-indulgence than for philanthropy. Critics of the present day, however, are scarcely ready enough to perceive how civilising a thing this conscious tenderness was in an age and country that were still in many ways brutally barbaric. It is easy in analysing Sterne to point out faults and shortcomings; it is harder to give a suggestion of his marvellous charm as an artist, and of the enduring beauty of his pathetic humour.

The success of the great masters of realistic fiction created a demand for novels, and a great number were produced by minor hands only to be forgotten. The solitary instance in which anything like reputation was gained by one of these imitators was in the case of Charles Johnstone (1719?-1800), whose *Chrysal, or the Adventures of a Guinea*, originally in two volumes, attracted great attention in 1760. This savage and gloomy book, which, perhaps, took its form from a reminiscence of Addison's "Adventures of a Shilling," in the *Tatler*, was a very clever following of Smollett in his most satiric mood. It was several times reprinted before the author completed it by publishing two volumes more in 1765. In 1759 Dr. Samuel Johnson produced his didactic romance, *Rasselas*. A little later, in 1764, Horace Walpole inaugurated the mediæval school of fiction, which was to culminate in Walter Scott, with his *Castle of Otranto*. In 1766 appeared Henry Brooke's *Fool of Quality*, and that ever fresh and ever charming masterpiece, Goldsmith's *Vicar of Wakefield*. Henry Mackenzie, inspired by Sterne, opened his series of melancholy romances with *The Man of Feeling* in 1771, the year of Smollett's death. We shall speak of the most important of these works in dealing with their respective authors; several of them still hold a prominent place in literature. But they are merely satellites in attendance on the three great lights of eighteenth-century fiction, on Richardson, Fielding, and Smollett, and when the third of these departed, the art of novel-writing ceased to progress, in any large sense, until it was taken up forty years afterwards by Jane Austen and Sir Walter Scott.

CHAPTER IX

JOHNSON AND THE PHILOSOPHERS

A CRITIC who is certainly unprejudiced has called Bishop Butler "the most patient, original, and candid of philosophical writers." The second quarter of the eighteenth century was not rich in contributions to religious literature, but it is to the glory of the Church of England that it possessed this singularly interesting man. The enthusiasm and direct ardent rhetoric of the seventeenth century were now things of the past. The very struggle between orthodoxy and the Deists was no longer novel; in the prosaic and mathematical theology of Clarke, stuck full of intellectual diagrams, it had ceased to be a spirit of warmth or movement. It is difficult to be convinced that on one side or the other there had been of late any great doctrinal fervour of faith or disbelief. The last of the genuine old Deists was Thomas Chubb (1680-1747), the tallow-chandler, a writer of little dignity. The orthodox theologians, in spite of their indignant and perpetual protestations, had really resigned so much that the creed of the English Church was becoming unnerved. The proper stimulant required by the religious mind of the country was given on one side by the new Puritans, by Law and Wesley and Whitefield, and on the other by an Anglican philosopher of extraordinary force and genius. So much had gradually been admitted to be doubtful that the scribbling bishops were ready to let Pilate's question pass virtually unanswered; Butler came, and revealed a man who, as he himself says, made "the search after truth the business of his life."

Joseph Butler (1692-1752) was the son of a dissenting linen-draper in Wantage. He was educated at a nonconformist school at Tewkesbury, where it is curious that three future bishops of the Church of England were taught at the same time. In 1713 Butler, although past the age of twenty-one, was still at this college, for it was from Tewkesbury that he sent his famous letters to Clarke, then the acknowledged intellectual head of the English Church, putting forward certain metaphysical objections which had occurred to him in the study of Clarke's writings. Clarke thought so highly of these letters that he appended them to his own letters and published them in 1716. In 1714 Butler entered the English Church, and proceeded to Oriel College, Oxford. He was ordained in 1718, and next year we find him appointed Preacher at the Rolls Chapel, to which was presently added the rectory of Haughton-le-Skerne in Durham; this was exchanged in 1725 for the "golden rectory" of Stanhope, in the same county.

In 1726 Butler published his first book, a selection of fifteen *Sermons* preached at the Rolls Chapel. The first three, on human nature, are, in fact, sections of one essay, on the constitution of the instincts of humanity; in which an effort is made to inquire into the meaning of morality. There follow sermons on certain of the passions, as Benevolence, Anger, Compassion, and Love to God. More lively than Butler usually cares to be is the sermon on "The Government of the Tongue." This volume attracted a moderate degree of notice, but the author of it was soon temporarily forgotten. Secker, who had courtlier ways, but whose affection for his old schoolfellow was unbounded, took occasion at last to mention him one day to Queen Caroline, who was known to have read the *Rolls Sermons* with profit. She replied that she thought Mr. Butler had been dead. "No, madam, but buried!" another friend, Archdeacon Blackburne, answered. Butler was soon digged out of his Durham grave to be Clerk of the Queen's Closet.

In 1736 Butler emerged into fame by the publication of a

work on which he had been engaged for seven years, *The Analogy of Religion, Natural and Revealed, to the Constitution and Course of Nature.* In 1738 he was made Bishop of Bristol, in 1740 Dean of St. Paul's, and in 1747 was offered the Primacy. This he refused, saying, in his melancholy way, that "it was too late for him to try to support a falling church." In 1750, however, he consented, after some demur, to exchange the see of Bristol for Durham. He had become prematurely old, and of venerable appearance, with long white hair. Two years later he died. Butler's temperament was silent and retiring; he did not shine in conversation, though some very striking remarks of his are recorded. He had no love for female society, but preserved very loyally his old companionships with friends, such as Secker. His writings show no interest whatever in any form of literature, except theological controversy, nor is it recorded of him that he had any love of books. But he cultivated the fine arts, and in particular had a sort of passion for architecture. His taste for what would a century later have been called Puseyite decorations is well known.

The *Analogy* is an isolated work. Even in its own age, when polemical pamphleteering was in fashion, though it was read, it was neither attacked nor defended. It does not refer to any theological movement that preceded it, and it is not the precursor of any subsequent literature. It stands alone, original, inexorably honest and veracious, but unsympathetic, like its silent and unexpansive author. The germ of the *Analogy* has been traced to the fifteenth of the *Rolls Sermons*, that on the Ignorance of Man. The design of the entire work is, while taking for proved that there is an intelligent Author of Nature and natural Governor of the world, to apply to the subject of religion "the analogy of nature,"—that is to say, the laws and phenomena of the external world. Butler's central idea is the majesty and authority of the conscience, placed in the centre of the human instincts as the representative of the divine will. Of late years a great many thinkers of various schools have held that Butler, although so fervent a believer himself, has furnished in the *Analogy* a philosophical persuasion to atheism.

His debt to the views of Shaftesbury has been dwelt upon, and he has been charged with exalting morality at the expense of faith. Into these questions it is impossible to enter here. No serious mind, however, can deny the greatness of Butler. His work, with all its peculiarities, is marked by extreme intellectual candour, by the purity of thought which disdains to conceal a weakness through any subterfuge of style, and by a passion for truth which must always affect the unbiassed reader.

Some words must be given to the subject of Butler's style, on which critics have been curiously at disagreement. The question was early raised; even the Bishop's dearest friend, Secker, thought that somewhat was lacking to this expression of his thoughts. Later admirers have combated the criticism, and have found no fault with the lucidity of his diction. All must agree that Butler's style is studiously unadorned. But the source of a considerable difference of opinion among critics may perhaps be traced to the bishop's own inequality. The pure and eloquent sentences of the sermon on "Love to God" are scarcely to be recognised as by the same hand as parts of the *Analogy*. An enthusiast who is impatient of any condemnation of Butler's style may, however, be confronted with the famous passage about the microscope and the staff, for instance:

"Thus a man determines that he will look at such an object through a microscope, or, being lame, supposes that he will walk to such a place with a staff a week hence. His eyes and his feet no more determine in these cases than the microscope and the staff. Nor is there any ground to think they any more put the determination in practice, or that his eyes are the seers or his feet the movers in any other sense than as the microscope and the staff are. Upon the whole then our organs of sense and our limbs are certainly instruments which the living persons ourselves make use of to perceive and move with: there is not any probability that they are any more, nor, consequently, that we have any other kind of relation to them than what we may have to any other foreign matter formed into instruments of perception and motion, suppose into a microscope or a staff (I say any other kind of relation, for I am not speaking of the degree of it), nor consequently is there any probability that the alienation or dissolution of these instruments is the destruction of the perceiving and moving agent."

These involved and clumsy clauses creep along like the steps of a man floundering in deep sand. The author struggles with his thoughts, gets entangled in contingent sentences, repeats the same word with awkward persistence; and all from an intense and scrupulous desire to say nothing but what he means. Yet it must be recollected that Berkeley, saying also nothing but what he means, says it in language that is all fire and crystal. The best apology that can be made for Butler at his driest, is to admit that he is seldom quite so wooden as Locke. His method in argument has been ingeniously compared to that of a chess-player.

Much more obviously related to Shaftesbury than Butler was the Scottish metaphysician Francis Hutcheson (1694-1746), who was born at a village in Ulster. Like Butler, he early corresponded with the amiable Dr. Clarke on religious philosophy. In 1725 he published the first of a group of four anonymous pamphlets, his *Inquiry concerning Beauty*. He was then residing as a schoolmaster in Dublin, which city he left on his election in 1729 to fill the chair of moral philosophy at Glasgow. He published a good deal, and after his death there appeared, in 1755, his *System of Moral Philosophy*. Hutcheson is principally remembered by those essays in which he expands and illustrates the æsthetic system of Shaftesbury, and accentuates the analogy between virtue and beauty. He is a link between the author of the *Characteristics* and Adam Smith, who worked under him at Glasgow. Hutcheson's manner as a writer is clear and elegant. Here is a graceful fragment from the *Inquiry concerning Beauty*:

"The beauty of trees, their cool shades, and their aptness to conceal from observation, have made groves and woods the usual retreat to those who love solitude, especially to the religious, the pensive, the melancholy, and the amorous. And do we not find that we have so joined the ideas of these dispositions of mind with those external objects, that they always occur to us along with them? The cunning of the heathen priests might make such obscure places the scene of the fictitious appearances of their Deities; and hence we join ideas of something divine to them. We know the like effect in the ideas of our churches, from the perpetual use of them only in religious exercises. The faint light in Gothic buildings has had the same association of a very foreign idea, which our poet shows in his epithet—'a dim religious light.' In like manner it is known that often all the circumstances of actions, or places, or dresses of persons, or voice, or song, which have occurred at any time together, when we were strongly affected by any passion, will be so connected that any one of these will make all the rest recur. And this is often the occasion both of great pleasure and pain, delight and aversion to many objects, which of themselves might have been perfectly indifferent to us. But these approbations or distastes are remote from the ideas of beauty, being plainly different ideas."

The learned and caustic librarian of Cambridge University, Conyers Middleton (1683-1750), has a niche in anecdote as the personal opponent of Bentley, and in literature as a traitor in the camp of orthodoxy, or, more favourably, as the author of a too idolatrous, but eloquent and highly polished *Life of Cicero*, in 1741. It has been considered that Middleton's covert attacks upon the credibility of miracles and other matters of Protestant creed, marked the beginning of a new tide of critical religious speculation in England. His *Free Inquiry into Miraculous Powers* caused quite a sensation when it appeared in 1747. The arguments of Middleton were ridiculed by Wesley, and scandalised Gray, but they strengthened the hands of Hume, and they helped to mould the conscience of Gibbon. His writings were collected in 1752.

A queer writer whose work long possessed a peculiar attraction for the public, and who is now less read than he deserves, is Thomas Amory (1691-1788), who would have been a novelist had he been born a generation later. As it is, his somewhat crazy books hover about the borderland of regular fiction, and have some relation, though no similarity, to those of Sterne. Amory was an ardent Unitarian, and in his volumes all the virtuous characters belong to this persuasion. He published nothing until he had passed his sixtieth year. In 1755 he sent out from his house in the Barbican *Memoirs of several Ladies of Great Britain*, which purports to describe English country life in the years 1739 and 1740. This was followed by a most eccentric romance, *The Life of John Buncle, Esq.* (1756-66). Buncle marries seven successive wives, all of them Socinians. These books are excessively long-winded and full of miscellaneous information, quaintly, but often humorously, imparted, for Amory's aim was to compose an olio of universal entertainment. His descriptive passages are charming, and his pages are redolent of the *pot-pourri* of the eighteenth century. He desired that his epitaph should be " Here lies an Odd Man." It is difficult to know what Hazlitt meant when he said that the spirit of Rabelais had entered into Amory, for there seems no sort of relation between the two, except a taste for rambling on from one theme to another. As a specimen of Amory at his best, we may quote from *John Buncle* the description of the grotto (the book is full of grottos, mostly decorated with shells) in which the hero discovered the charming Azora:

" It was a large cavern at the bottom of a marble mountain, and, without, was covered round with ivy, that clung about some aged oaks, on either side the entrance, that seemed coeval with the earth on which they grew. Abundance of large laurel trees, in clumps, adorned an extensive area before the door ; and saffron, and hyacinth, and flowers of many colours, covered in confused spots the carpet green. The beautiful ground refreshed the sight, and purified the air ; and to enhance the beauties of the spot, a clear and cold stream gushed from a neighbouring rock, which watered the trees and plants, and seemed to combat with the earth, whether of them most contributed to their growth and preservation. It was a sweet rural scene. For charms and solitude the place was equally to be admired.

" The inside of this grotto was a beautiful green marble, extremely bright, and even approaching to the appearance of the emerald. It was thick set with shells, and those not small ones, but some of the largest and finest kinds ; many of them seemed, as it were, squeezed together by the marble so as to show the edges only ; but more were to be seen at large, and filled with the purest spar. The whole had a fine effect, and as the cave had been divided by art into six fine apartments, and had doors and chimneys most ingeniously contrived, both the mansion and its situation charmed me in a high degree."

Amory's span of life, which covered nearly a hundred years, touched the careers of Dryden and of Byron.

Another pleasant worthy was William Oldys, the antiquary (1696-1761), one of the earliest of our bibliographical writers. He published, in a miscellany, in 1732, the admirable anacreontic beginning, "Busy, curious, thirsty Fly"; and, on quite another scale, a very eloquent and heroic *Life of Sir Walter Raleigh*, in 1736. Oldys was a lifelong collector of literary curiosities, and in 1755 his industry was rewarded, after a period of great poverty, and two years spent in the Fleet Prison, by his being made Norroy King-at-Arms. From 1744 to 1746 Oldys was engaged on the mighty task of editing the eight volumes of the *Harleian Miscellany*. But perhaps the best literary work he performed is to be found in the numerous biographies he contributed between 1747 and 1760 to the original edition of *The Biographia Britannica*. Several copies of Langbaine's *Lives of the Dramatic Poets*, containing copious MS. notes by Oldys, still exist, and are much sought after by collectors.

In 1774 appeared a collection of the *Letters* of Philip Dormer Stanhope, fourth Earl of Chesterfield (1694-1773), addressed to his natural son, Philip Stanhope, and this correspondence excited a great deal of curiosity. It has been the misfortune of Chesterfield to be seen through the coloured glass of a much greater man's anger. Few now read the letters, but every one knows that Johnson said that "they teach the morals of a ———, and the manners of a dancing-master," and of their author, "This man, I thought, had been a lord among wits, but I find he is only a wit among lords." It was on the 7th of February 1735 that Johnson addressed to Chesterfield his terrible and celebrated invective about the *Dictionary*. The *Letters*, however, were read with eagerness, and deserved to be read. If they were Machiavelian, they were full of good sense expressed in pure English, and full also of unaffected grace and fine breeding. It is curious that the man who in all England desired most, during his lifetime, to be considered polite, is mainly remembered for one breach of manners, which was very probably due to the neglect of a servant. A writer of less brilliant rank than Lord Chesterfield, but, like him, the darling of society, was the psychologist and critic Henry Home, Lord Kames (1696-1782), a Scotch law lord, who, starting from Shaftesbury, found himself violently affected by Butler. His *Art of Thinking* (1761), and *Elements of Criticism* (1762), especially the latter, were widely read in that age of universal metaphysical curiosity. Lord Kames managed a county estate with vigour, and wrote a practical work, *The Gentleman Farmer* (1771), which was long esteemed. In the present day, if Lord Kames is read at all, it is for his ingenious and acute speculation into the sources of æsthetic pleasure.

It was the conviction of William Warburton, Bishop of Gloucester (1698-1779), that he would hold in the eyes of posterity much the same pre-eminence and isolated greatness that Samuel Johnson actually maintains. He cultivated the majestic airs of a tyrant in literature; he argued, he denounced, he patronised the orthodox, and he bellowed like a bull at the recalcitrant. He was so completely certain of his own intellectual supremacy, that the modern reader feels almost guilty in being able to feel but scant interest in him and in his writings. Sir Leslie Stephen remarks that "for many years together Warburton led the life of a terrier in a rat-pit, worrying all theological vermin." In 1736 he published his *Alliance between Church and State*, in 1738 three books of his once famous *Divine Legation*, in 1741 three books more. In 1738 he took up the cudgels in defence of Pope's orthodoxy, and lived in ever-deepening intimacy with that poet until Pope's death in 1744. He slowly rose in the Church, attaining the see of Gloucester in 1760, after which he published little except his *Doctrine of Grace*, in 1762. Warburton was very learned, but so headstrong, arrogant, and boisterous, that he stuns the reader, and those who now examine the vast pile of his writings are not likely to be gratified. What he might gain by his vigour he more than loses by his coarseness, and the student sickens of his ostentation and his paradox. His disciple, Dr. Richard Hurd (1720-1808), Bishop of Worcester, tried to continue the influence of Warburton, whose remains he edited in 1788. Hurd was a cold and "correct" writer, no less arrogant than his master, little less learned, and if anything even more vapid and perverted as a would-be leader of literary taste; in style he seems a kind of ice-bound Addison. The *Correspondence* of these two portentous divines appeared in 1809.

All that Warburton fancied himself to be, Dr. Samuel Johnson (1709-1784) was. In the person of this ever-fascinating hero of the world of books we find the dictator of letters, the tyrant over the consciences of readers, that the militant bishop of Gloucester was too ready to conceive himself to be. Johnson holds a place in some respects unique in literature. Other writers, however sympathetic or entertaining their personal characters may have been, live mainly in their works; we read about them with delight, because we have studied what they wrote. But with Johnson it is not so. If we knew nothing about his career or character, if we had to judge him solely by the works he published, our interest in him would shrink to very moderate proportions. Swift and Pope, Berkeley and Gray, Burke and Fielding, have contributed more than Johnson to the mere edifice of English literature. But, with the exception of Swift, there is no one in the eighteenth century who can pretend to hold so high a place as a man of letters. The happy accident by which he secured the best of all biographers is commonly taken to account for this fact, but the character, the wit, the vigour, must have first existed to stimulate a Boswell and to entrance generation after generation. The fact is that Johnson's indolence and the painful weight of his physical temperament prevented his literary powers from being fully expressed in the usual way; but they were there, and they found a vehicle in speech at the dinner-table or from his tavern-throne. He talked superb literature freely for thirty years, and all England listened; he grew to be the centre of literary opinion, and he was so majestic in intellect, so honest in purpose, so kind and pure in heart, so full of humour and reasonable sweetness, and yet so trenchant, and at need so grim, that he never sank to be the figure-head of a clique, nor ever lost the balance of sympathy with readers of every rank and age. His influence was so wide, and withal so wholesome, that literary life in this country has never been since his day what it was before it. He has made the more sordid parts of its weakness shameful, and he has raised a standard of personal conduct that every one admits. He was a gruff old bear, "Ursa Major," but it would surely be hard to find the man or woman, whose opinion is worth having, who does not love almost more than revere the memory of Sam Johnson.

On the 18th of September 1709 a son was born at Lichfield to a local bookseller and his wife, Michael and Sara Johnson. From his birth Samuel Johnson was afflicted with the scrofulous complaint known as the king's evil, and when he was three years old his mother took him up to London to be touched by Queen Anne. He attended the Lichfield grammar-school, and then read a great deal in a desultory fashion at home. In the autumn of 1728 he went up to Oxford, to Pembroke College, where he seems to have resided only about fourteen months, though he returned again for a very short time in 1731. At the close of that year, Johnson's father died, and left his affairs in so embarrassed a condition that his family was reduced to poverty. For the next five years Johnson's career is very obscure to us. We gather that he made several efforts to get work as an usher, and was for a short time tutor at Heywood; in 1735 he performed a piece of hack-work for a Birmingham bookseller, *A Voyage to Abyssinia*, from a French abridgment of Father Lobo's Portuguese travels. The anonymous preface to this translation is Johnson's earliest original publication. This preface is written in a very characteristic style, though not, as has been carelessly stated, in his more pompous manner. We give an example of it:

"The reader will here find no regions cursed with irremediable barrenness, or blessed with spontaneous fecundity, no perpetual gloom or unceasing sunshine; nor are the nations here described either devoid of all sense of humanity, or consummate in all private and social virtues. Here are no Hottentots without religion, policy or articulate language, no Chinese perfectly polite, and completely skilled in all sciences. He will discover, what will always be discovered by a diligent and impartial inquirer, that wherever human nature is to be found, there is a mixture of vice and virtue, a contest of passion and reason, and that the Creator doth not appear partial in His distributions, but has balanced in most countries their particular inconveniences by particular favours."

From this time, for twenty years, Johnson was more or less dependent for support on the labours of his pen, and the iron entered deeply into his soul. He suffered from a physical inability to prolong the effort of writing, and he absolutely required leisurely intervals of repose and meditation. Hence, even when employment was abundant, he often failed to take full advantage of it, and not less often the work he did gave dissatisfaction to his stupid taskmasters. As a schoolmaster he had already failed because he had "the character of being a very haughty, ill-natured gent, and had such a way of distorting his face" that it frightened the lads. It was at this moment that he married a wife twenty-one years older than himself, whose little fortune was presently sunk in a school near Lichfield. Johnson was now forced to try the tender mercies of Grub Street.

In the spring of 1737, with twopence-halfpenny in his pocket, and in company with one of his late pupils, David Garrick, who had three-halfpence in his, Johnson arrived in London. It is not clear how he lived at first, but later on in the year he entered the service of Edward Cave (1691-1754) the publisher, who, in 1732, had started *The Gentleman's Magazine*, an admirable periodical, which still survives. Cave had a large staff of literary hacks at work on his magazine, which had by this time secured an important position, and in 1738 Johnson was installed as one of these regular writers. In May of that year S. J. published, in folio, an imitation of the Third Satire of Juvenal, under the title *London*, for which he received ten guineas. This poem, though to be somewhat eclipsed by a later success, enjoyed the favour of the town. It was a vigorous but certainly not an inspired study in heroic couplets in the manner of Pope, who was still before the public as a living force, one of whose satires appeared on the very same day as *London*. The latter poem is not always marked by the author's later seriousness of purpose; Johnson affects in it to scorn and puff away the city which he had really learned to find already indispensable, and which he was presently to love with passion. After the thirty-fourth line the sentiments of *London* are placed in the mouth of "indignant Thales," in whom the person of Steele has been usually recognised; he is represented as seeking retirement in Wales. There is pathos in the nervous lines in which the poet expresses the misery of those who, poor and enlightened, are obliged to endure the insolence of blockheads; Johnson, here at least, speaks from the heart, and not less when he asks the question, "When can starving merit find a home?" The Orgilis passage is the best in the poem, which only extends to about two hundred and sixty lines.

Two trifling publications belong to the year 1739, *The Complete Vindication*, an ironical defence of the licensers for suppressing Brooke's tragedy of *Gustavus Vasa*, and a satire, *Marmor Norfolciense*, for which latter it was absurdly rumoured afterwards that Johnson suffered a state prosecution. For the next four years he was busy in writing out the reports of the parliamentary debates for *The Gentleman's Magazine*, under the transparent disguise of "Debates in Magna Lilliputia." He was now working in companionship with Savage and with Dr. John Hawkesworth (1715?-1773), who acquired an extraordinary skill in counterfeiting Johnson's style, to the dismay of the future editors of the latter. At this time Johnson seems to have admired Savage as much as Hawkesworth admired Johnson; and when the unhappy poet died in 1743, the latter set to work to write his memoir. *The Account of the Life of Mr. Richard Savage* appeared in 1744; it is the longest and most elaborate of Johnson's essays in biography, and may still be read with great pleasure, in spite of various patent faults. It recounted, with all detail, a scandal, into the truth of which Johnson had not taken the pains to inquire; it was but careless in the statement of facts which lay easily within the writer's circle of experience; and it treated with extreme indulgence a character which, in a stranger, would have called down the moralist's sternest reproof. The critical passages now escape censure only because so few in the present day read the works examined. But the little book was undeniably lively; it contained several anecdotes admirably narrated, and its graver parts displayed the development of Johnson's studied magnificence of language. Good biography was still rare in England, and *The Account of Savage* attracted a great deal of notice.

It again becomes difficult at this point to trace Johnson's career very closely. In 1745 he printed a pamphlet on *Macbeth*, and in 1747 the prospectus of a vast scheme which he had formed, that of an English Dictionary, on a scale hitherto unattempted. He dedicated his *Plan of a Dictionary* to Lord Chesterfield, who sent him ten pounds, and then took no further interest in the matter, to his own lasting misfortune. For eight years no more was heard of this projected work. In 1748 Johnson spent a short holiday at Hampstead, where he wrote his longest and best poem, *The Vanity of Human Wishes*, published in 1749. This is a study in heroic verse, like *London*, but it extends to another hundred lines, and is, moreover, a much finer and more accomplished production. It is an imitation of the Tenth Satire of Juvenal, and is written in a very grave and even melancholy vein, though without unseemly bitterness. It was not much liked when it appeared; Garrick declared it was "as hard as Greek." The public had become accustomed to a thinner and smarter kind of satire, to the lucid snip-snap of the immediate followers of Pope, and *The Vanity of Human Wishes* was voted obscure. It is certainly weighted with thought, and the closeness with which the Latin original is followed gives a certain tightness of phrase, the result of a meritorious concentration. But it is perhaps the most Roman poem in the language, the one which best reflects the moral grandeur of Latin feeling and reflection; and it has contributed more familiar quotations to the language than any other work of Johnson's. Such a passage as the following gives a very favourable notion of Johnson as a didactic poet:

> "On what foundation stands the warrior's pride,
> How just his hopes, let Swedish Charles decide;
> A frame of adamant, a soul of fire,
> No dangers fright him and no labours tire;
> O'er love, o'er fear, extends his wide domain,
> Unconquer'd Lord of passion and of pain;

>   No joys to him pacific sceptres yield,
>   War sounds the trump, he rushes to the field ;
>   Behold surrounding kings their power combine,
>   And one capitulate, and one resign ;
>   Peace courts his hand, but spreads her charms in vain,
>   ' Think nothing gained,' he cries, ' till nought remain ;—
>   On Moscow's walls till Gothic standards fly,
>   And all be mine beneath the polar sky.'
>   The march begins in military state,
>   And nations on his eye suspended wait ;
>   Stern Famine guards the solitary coast,
>   And Winter barricades the realms of Frost ;
>   He comes, nor want nor cold his course delay,—
>   Hide, blushing glory, hide Pultowa's day."

A pleasing incident now broke into the monotony of Johnson's gray and laborious existence. His old pupil, David Garrick, had risen into success more rapidly than Johnson had, and was now manager of Drury Lane Theatre. When he was keeping school at Edial Hall, in 1736, Johnson had written a blank verse tragedy on a Turkish subject, but had vainly attempted, in later years, to get it acted. Garrick loyally determined that he would produce it, and after some obstinate struggles with the author, who could not be brought to yield willingly to any stage requirements, *Mahomet and Irene* was acted on the 6th February 1749. Johnson was present, and did not, on this occasion, "suspend the soft solicitudes of dress." He gained nearly £300 by the play, which, however, did not run for more than nine nights, and was never revived. Garrick had introduced the incident of Irene's being strangled on the stage, and to Johnson's mingled mortification and satisfaction, the audience hissed and called out "Murder! murder!" In future, on the stage, as in the printed play, the heroine was forced out by the mutes, crying for mercy, and was seen no more. The tragedy was presently published under the title of *Irene*. Johnson's solitary play labours under the disadvantage of being perfectly uninteresting. It was founded on a tragedy, by one Charles Goring, that had been acted at Drury Lane forty years before ; there was no plot worth mentioning, no development of characters, no bustle or intrigue. The conduct of the speeches and the versification is closely modelled on that of the sentimental tragic poet Rowe, whose plays had been popular in Johnson's early youth; what Johnson said of Rowe's plays, long afterwards, might be repeated almost verbally as a criticism of *Irene*. The most amusing thing about the whole incident of this play is Johnson's odd remark to Garrick about the silk stockings of the actresses.

Posterity is more ready to realise the Sage in the character of "a majestic teacher of moral and religious wisdom" than as one whose scarlet waistcoat fluttered the dove-cotes of Drury Lane. Since the days of Addison and Steele, or since, to be more exact, the *Guardian* of 1713, there had been made many attempts to rival the great social newspapers of the reign of Anne. But none of these had been successful, and Johnson, finding himself now moderately famous, determined to issue a new periodical. It was difficult to find a name; but one night he sat down on his bed, and determined not to go to sleep till he had thought of a title. The *Rambler* occurred to him at last, and he sank to rest contented. On the 20th of March 1750 the first number of this little newspaper appeared, and it closed on the 14th of March 1752. The death of his wife, a few days after the latter date, has been given as the cause of Johnson's discontinuance of a periodical of which he was probably weary. He wrote the *Rambler* unaided, with the exception of five numbers—of these one was written by Richardson; two by Elizabeth Carter (1717-1806), the translator of Epictetus; one by Hester Mulso, better known as Mrs. Chapone (1727-1801); and one by Catherine Talbot (1720-1770). These ladies deserve mention, not merely as dear and lifelong friends of Johnson, but as apt disciples of his moral manner. Johnson's authorship was at first kept secret, but his style was now familiar to careful readers, and was promptly recognised. The publisher complained that "the encouragement as to sale" was not in proportion "to the raptures expressed by the few that did read it." The *Rambler* is "too wordy," as the author confessed; he tried to be a little lighter in manner in the twenty-nine papers he contributed in 1752 and 1753 to Hawkesworth's *Adventurer*, and somewhat later we shall be called, in describing the *Idler*, to speak of him as a periodical writer at his best.

Meanwhile the mighty *Dictionary* had been slowly progressing, and in April 1755 it was published in two folio volumes. It hardly belongs to literature, except in connection with two short essays, in which Johnson shows himself at his best as a prose-writer, namely, the dignified and pathetic preface, which can scarcely be read to the close without emotion, and the astonishing letter, on the subject of a patron's duties, which he addressed to Chesterfield on the 7th of February 1755. In these two short compositions, in each of which the author is singularly moved, his English, though always stately and formal, is lifted out of the sesquipedalian affectation of magnificence which has amused the world so much, and which was beyond question a serious fault of Johnson's style. Here, and especially in the letter to Chesterfield, he is simple, terse, and thrilling, and, as the occasion was a private one, we may take it that in the extraordinary fire and pungency of the sentences we have something like a specimen of that marvellous power in conversation which made Johnson the wonder of his age. What, in all literature, indeed, is more splendid than such restrained and suggested invective as this:

"Seven years, my lord. have now passed since I waited in your outward rooms, or was repulsed from your door; during which time I have been pushing on my work through difficulties, of which it is useless to complain, and have brought it, at last, to the verge of publication, without one act of assistance, one word of encouragement, or one smile of favour. Such treatment I did not expect, for I never had a patron before.

"The shepherd in Virgil grew at last acquainted with Love, and found him a native of the rocks.

"Is not a patron, my lord, one who looks with unconcern on a man struggling for life in the water, and when he has reached ground encumbers him with help? The notice which you have been pleased to take of my labours, had it been early, had been kind; but it has been delayed till I am indifferent, and cannot enjoy it; till I am solitary, and cannot impart it; till I am known, and do not want it. I hope it is no very cynical asperity not to confess obligations where no benefit has been received, or to be unwilling that the public should consider me as owing that to a patron, which Providence has enabled me to do for myself."

There is something of the same brightness and ease in the papers of the *Idler*, a series of essays published by Johnson from the 15th of April 1758 to the 5th of April 1760 in a newspaper called the *Universal Chronicle*. He took less trouble with his *Idlers* than with his *Ramblers*, and the result is more pleasing. Johnson as an essayist is most happy when he analyses a character, in the manner of La Bruyère, mingling criticism with narrative; the best example is the sketch of Dick Minim. He possessed shrewdness, judgment, singular knowledge of human nature, and plentiful wit; somehow all these qualities, though fused by his literary genius, did not quite produce a great essayist.

Perhaps it might be said that the best of Johnson's *Idlers* was the long apologue which appeared in book form while he was publishing his shorter weekly essays. The agreeable story of *The Prince of Abyssinia* (known from the seventh edition onwards by the name of its hero, *Rasselas*) was composed in the evenings of one week, to defray the expenses of his mother's funeral and to pay her debts. He received one hundred pounds as the first payment for this book, which appeared in April 1759, about three weeks after Voltaire's *Candide*. Johnson was interested in this latter fact, and said that "If they had not been published so closely one after the other . . . it would have been in vain to deny that the scheme of that which came latest was taken from the other." The resemblance, however, appears somewhat slight to a modern reader; Johnson has all the advantage in health and profundity, Voltaire in wit and intellectual daring. *Rasselas* is not a brilliant romance; the artless young person who flies to it as a story of African adventure will be sadly disappointed. It is a description in measured and elegant prose of how Rasselas became discontented in his Happy Valley, how he fled from it, in company with his sister Nekayah, under the guidance of an old man of infinite resource named Imlac, and how, after some mild and incredible incidents, they resolved to return to Abyssinia. The charm of the book is its humanity, the sweetness and wholesomeness of the long melancholy episodes, the wisdom of the moral reflections and disquisitions; nor is there wanting here and there the gentle sunshine of a sort of half-suppressed humour. *Rasselas* enjoyed an instant success, and was reprinted seven or eight times before Johnson died.

The toilsome part of Johnson's life closed with the publication of the Dictionary; and with his acceptance of a pension of £300 from the king a few years later he attained positive ease. He had now passed the age of fifty, and for the rest of his life he was glad to sit in his arm-chair and genially to tyrannise over the literary world. In 1763 he had the signal good fortune to have presented to him James Boswell, a young Scotchman of some quality, who rewarded Johnson's fatherly friendship by writing after his death a more perfect biography than has hitherto been composed about any other human being. Boswell was always taking "minutes of what passed," and from this time onward the smallest incidents of Johnson's career, his phrases, his jokes, his gestures, all are known to every educated reader, far better known indeed than any fragment of his literary works. In 1764 the "Club" was created; among its original members were—besides Johnson—Reynolds, Burke, Goldsmith, and Hawkins. Garrick, C. J. Fox, and Boswell were soon added. To Johnson his semi-presidential chair at the Club was, as he said, "the throne of human felicity," and it was from this social palace that his edicts went forth to the world. He was no longer anxious to write. He loitered for nine years over a very perfunctory edition of Shakespeare, which finally appeared in 1765. For five years more he was silent, until in 1770 he contributed to the Wilkes controversy a tract, *The False Alarm*, on the Tory side. Having once plunged into the giddy waters of political pamphleteering, the old Tory veteran could not induce himself to withdraw. He published in 1771 *Thoughts on the late Transactions respecting the Falkland Islands*, which was geographical as well as polemical.

In 1774 he attempted to stem the tide then flowing against the court party by a tract entitled *The Patriot*, and in 1775 he took the wrong side about America in *Taxation no Tyranny*. In 1776 these four treatises were issued in one volume, as *Political Tracts*, by S. J. It may be noticed that Johnson's full name seldom appeared on a title-page during his lifetime. Of the political pamphlets it may be said that they were forcible, but entirely without historical breadth or sympathy.

As Johnson approached his sixtieth year his health and spirits improved, and the lifelong weariness of his physical nature, which had made him seem indolent and sometimes irritable, abated. He even began to think that he could venture upon what was, in those days, a heroic adventure—no less than a journey to the Scottish Highlands and Hebrides. Boswell was extremely anxious that this apparently impossible scheme should be carried out, and in August 1773 the sage positively started for Edinburgh. Here his younger friend joined him, and they passed up the east coast of Scotland, crossed by Inverness, visited most of the inner Hebrides, and returned by Boswell's home at Auchinleck to Edinburgh. Johnson was away from London three months and a half, and justly desired to be praised for his "resolution and perseverance." The day after his return he wrote to Boswell that he was "ready to begin a new journey"; and accordingly in the autumn of 1774 he made a tour in North Wales. He gallantly complained that there was nothing adventurous in travelling in Wales. Late in the year appeared his *Journey to the Western Islands*, which is not to be compared for interest with Boswell's later work on the same theme. It was, however, read with curiosity and respect, for Johnson's reputation was now in its full splendour. In 1775 Oxford made her old disciple an LL.D., and Johnson a few months later entered into controversy with the "foolish and impudent" James Macpherson, whose version of Ossian he regarded with contempt. Johnson properly mistrusted the literary honesty of Macpherson, and openly told him that his book was an imposture in a letter only less famous than the Chesterfield specimen.

Johnson's literary work now seemed to be wellnigh ended, but in 1777 he undertook a labour of biography and criticism, which was perhaps, had he considered his responsibilities, the most arduous he had ever thought of. This is the book usually reprinted as *Lives of the English Poets*, but published in 1779-1781 as *Prefaces, biographical and critical, to the most eminent of the English Poets*. The life of Savage, though too long for the system of the book, was worked in, and so were other lives that Johnson had already written. The poets themselves appeared in sixty-eight volumes, and Johnson's *Lives* in a special edition of four volumes. The selection was arbitrary, although there was no intention of throwing scorn on Chaucer and Spenser by opening the roll of fame with Cowley. This was done merely to suit the convenience of the publisher. The *Lives* are of very various interest and value. Some of the worst are those in which Johnson deals with great men, such as Milton and Gray; some of the best are those in which he allows himself to meditate around very little men, as in the case of Edmund Smith. A very beautiful passage, from the last-mentioned life, fairly represents the style of Johnson at its ripest and best:

"Of Gilbert Walmsley, thus presented to my mind, let me indulge myself in the remembrance. I knew him very early; he was one of the first friends that literature procured me, and I hope that at least my gratitude made me worthy of his notice.

"He was of advanced age, and I was only not a boy; yet he never received my notions with contempt. He was a Whig, with all the virulence and malevolence of his party; yet difference of opinion did not keep us apart. I honoured him, and he endured me.

"He had mingled with the gay world, without exemption from its vices or its follies, but had never neglected the cultivation of his mind; his belief of Revelation was unshaken; his learning preserved his principles; he grew first regular, and then pious.

"His studies had been so various that I am not able to name a man of equal knowledge. His acquaintance with books was great; and what he did not immediately know, he could at least tell where to find. Such was his amplitude of learning, and such his copiousness of communication, that it may be doubted whether a day now passes in which I have not some advantage from his friendship.

"At this man's table I enjoyed many cheerful and instructive hours, with companions such as are not often found; with one who has lengthened, and one who has gladdened life; with Dr. James, whose skill in physic will be long remembered; and with David Garrick, whom I hoped to have gratified with this character of our common friend. But what are the hopes of man! I am disappointed by that stroke of death which has eclipsed the gaiety of nations, and impoverished the public stock of harmless pleasure."

The book is full of wit and thought, but although a charming companion it is one of the worst of guides. Johnson was a competent critic only within a certain sharply-defined groove.

In 1782 the death of his old dependant, the "useful and companionable" Robert Levett, called forth what is certainly the most tender, and towards its close the most admirable of Johnson's minor poems:

> "His virtues walked their narrow round,
>   Nor made a pause, nor left a void;
> And sure the Eternal Master found
>   The single talent well employed.
>
> "The busy day, the peaceful night,
>   Unfelt, uncounted, glided by;
> His frame was firm, his powers were bright,
>   Though now his eightieth year was nigh.
>
> "Then with no fiery throbbing pain,
>   No cold gradations of decay,
> Death broke at once the vital chain,
>   And freed his soul the nearest way."

These stanzas might have been signed by Matthew Arnold, so modern are they in their workmanship.

Johnson was now himself approaching his end, and more illustrious friends than Levett were dropping away from his side. His last two years were melancholy, and somewhat lonely. On the 13th of December 1784, tended by many whom he loved, he passed away at his house in Bolt Court. George III. had lost the most famous of his subjects. After Johnson's death every scrap of his manuscript that could be found was printed, his *Prayers and Meditations* in 1785, his *Sermons* in 1788-89, his

Diary in North Wales in 1816; and in 1791 Boswell set the topstone to the edifice of Johnson's glory by his immortal biography.

Philosophical speculation occupied the pens of so many men of letters in the middle of the eighteenth century, that it is impossible here to do more than name the most original of the thinkers by profession. David Hartley (1705-1757) was the founder of associational psychology. He was a Yorkshire man, a fellow of Jesus College, Cambridge, and eventually a country physician. His life was wholly without incident; he had poor health, but great cheerfulness and benevolence. Hartley is in the highest sense of the phrase a man of one book, which he began to write before he was twenty-five, published when he was forty-four, and continued to revise until his death. This is his *Observations on Man, His Frame, Duty, and Expectations* (1749). He defined his own contribution to moral philosophy in these words: "I take it to be proved from the doctrine of association, that there is, and must be, such a thing as pure disinterested benevolence; also a just account of the origin and nature of it." A side doctrine of his which was much discussed is the theory of vibrations, and of man as a cluster of "vibratiuncles." Hartley's ideas were afterwards taken up and expanded by James Mill (1773-1836). Another founder of a school, though a thinker of less force than Hartley, was Thomas Reid (1710-1796), the philosopher of common-sense applied to moral questions. The works of Reid, from his *Enquiry into the Human Mind* (1763), to his *Active Powers of Man* (1788), show a great clearness of intellect and a strictly logical habit, but no great enthusiasm or originality. His philosophy has been defined as a combination of the views of Clarke and Shaftesbury.

By far the greatest philosophical writer who had appeared since Berkeley was revealed, however, in David Hume (1711-1776), the leader of the utilitarians, and one of the greatest critics of thought who have ever lived. Hume occupies our attention in many ways, as an essayist, as an historian, and as a philosopher, in all three durably eminent. He was born, of Berwickshire parents, in Edinburgh; from his earliest infancy he was strongly inclined to books, but he was not prominent as a scholar, and his opening steps in life were somewhat vacillating. Some physical crisis occurred in him at the age of twenty, and woke him into genius. He spent three years with the Jesuits at La Flèche, and there he began to plan his first work, an essay on moral philosophy, which appeared at length, early in 1739, in two volumes, under the title of a *Treatise of Human Nature*. It was not successful, though Hume probably exaggerates in describing it as stillborn from the press. At all events a third volume appeared next year. Hume was now beginning to attract notice; Hutcheson was interested in him, and introduced him to his brilliant young scholar, Adam Smith. In 1741 and 1742 appeared anonymously the two volumes of his *Essays, Moral and Political*, which were very warmly received. Here as elsewhere Hume shows himself, though so modern in speculation, an aristocrat in politics, and from the first a sincere enemy to popular government. In the essay on the origin of government, he states his view of the limited responsibilities of the people with his accustomed calm lucidity:

"Man, born in a family, is compelled to maintain society from necessity, from natural inclination, and from habit. The same creature, in his further progress, is engaged to establish political society, in order to administer justice, without which there can be no peace among them, nor safety, nor mutual intercourse. We are therefore to look upon all the vast apparatus of our government, as having ultimately no other object or purpose but the distribution of justice, or in other words, the support of the Twelve Judges. Kings and parliaments, fleets and armies, officers of the court and revenue, ambassadors, ministers and privy councillors, are all subordinate in their end to this part of administration. Even the clergy, as their duty leads them to inculcate morality, may justly be thought, so far as regards this world, to have no other useful object of their institution."

He loses no opportunity of exposing the evil results of "villainous seditions" and "Whig strokes." His home all this time was his mother's farmhouse at Ninewells, on the border of Berwickshire, where he was content to live very quietly among his books.

He roused himself from this retirement in 1745, when he undertook to take charge of a wretched young nobleman, the Marquis of Annandale; this irksome business soon came to an end. Hume's friends saw that his talents were not appreciated, and that he was in danger of yielding to indolence; they gained him a secretary's office on the absurd expedition of General St. Clair; a little later, under the same commander, at Turin and then at Vienna, the philosopher cased his now very unwieldy person in scarlet, which made him look "like a grocer of the train-bands." He was in London again, glad to return to his library, in 1749. While he was away from England, in 1748, a publisher reproduced his first work, in abridged form, as *Philosophical Essays Concerning the Human Understanding*, but again without attracting public attention.

Retiring once more to Ninewells, Hume buried himself again in literature, and produced in rapid succession three of his most important books, his *Dialogues on Natural Religion* in 1750 (not published till long afterwards), his *Principles of Morals* in 1751, and his *Political Discourses* in 1752. The last of these was as happy in increasing the reputation of the author as it has been influential in pointing the road for all future students of political economy. He had by this time, through strict economy, arrived at a competence, and he removed his residence to Edinburgh, where, in 1752, he became the Advocates' Librarian, a post which was greatly envied for its opportunities, although the salary was paltry. It had already been discovered that Hume was unsound in doctrine, but though his election was bitterly opposed on the ground of his deism, it was enthusiastically carried by his friends. In 1753 Hume thus described to a friend his condition in his Edinburgh home :

"I shall exult and triumph to you a little that I have now at last—being turned of forty, to my own honour, to that of learning, and to that of the present age—arrived at the dignity of being a householder.

"About seven months ago, I got a house of my own, and completed a regular family, consisting of a head, viz. myself, and two inferior members, a maid and a cat. My sister has since joined me, and keeps me company.

With frugality, I can reach, I find, cleanliness, warmth, light, plenty and contentment? What would you have more? Independence? I have it in a supreme degree. Honour? That is not altogether wanting. Grace? That will come in time. A wife? That is none of the indispensable requisites of life. Books? That *is* one of them; and I have more than I can use. In short, I cannot find any pleasure of consequence which I am not possessed of in a greater or less degree; and, without any great effort of philosophy, I may be easy and satisfied. As there is no happiness without occupation, I have begun a work which will occupy me several years, and which yields me much satisfaction."

This was the famous *History of Great Britain* (*James I., Charles I.*), the first volume of which appeared in 1754. To his great chagrin this famous work failed to please any class of readers. He tells us: "I was assailed by one cry of reproach, disapprobation, and even detestation. . . . I scarcely heard of one man in the three kingdoms, considerable for rank or letters, that could endure the book." In the first anguish of disappointment, he talked of changing his name, and becoming a citizen of France. Further volumes, however, of the *History* appeared in 1756, 1759, and 1762, and the merits of the work gradually commended themselves to the general public. The methods of the recent school of history have discredited Hume, whose first aim was to amuse, or at least to please, whose researches were superficial, and whose statements were anything but authoritative. It is almost laughable to compare Hume's treatment of any incident, or still more, of any crisis, with S. R. Gardiner's treatment of the same. But Hume's style, which had always been easy and lucid, was now at its best, and in an age which did not demand scientific accuracy from its historians he passed for a chronicler of genius. His slavish regard for royal authority is a worse fault than his want of exact information; the reader seeks in his pages in vain for an expression of enthusiasm for British liberty or of indignation at Stuart tyranny. Hence the philosophic attitude which is so adroitly adopted ceases presently to deceive the reader, and at last exasperates him. Nevertheless, when we compare this polished and elegant compendium, in all its dignity and sober beauty, with such crude histories as those of Carte, Bower, and Guthrie, which preceded or accompanied it, we are ready to grow enthusiastic over its signal excellence.

While this great book was passing through the press, Hume's indomitable industry found occasion for the publication of other important work. In 1757 appeared the *Natural History of Religion*, which completed the statement of his sceptical philosophy. In 1763, having completed the *History*, Hume went to reside in France, a country where he found himself particularly happy, and where his literary reputation stood remarkably high. For more than three years he was secretary to the English embassy in Paris. He returned to England to hold office as Under-Secretary of State until 1769. The rest of his life was spent in comparative affluence, always as a bachelor, in his house at Edinburgh, where he died on the 25th of August 1776.

Hume's place in literature is not, at the present moment, adequate to what we know of his powers of intellect or to his originality as a thinker. He is acknowledged to be a great man, but he is very little read. His *History*, in fragments, and his *Essay on Miracles*, which still enjoys a kind of success of scandal, are all that the general reader knows of Hume. If we deplore this fact, it must be admitted that his cool and unimpassioned criticism of belief, his perpetual return to the destructive standpoint, yet without vivacity, as one who undermines rather than attacks an opposing body, his colourless grace, the monotony of his balanced and faultless sentences, offer to us qualities which demand respect but scarcely awaken zeal, and, in short, that Hume although a real is a somewhat uninspiring classic. His great merit as a writer is his lucidity, his perfectly straightforward and competent expression of the particular thing he has it on his mind to say. To demand from him the fire of Berkeley or the splendour of Gibbon would be to expect from an essentially frigid writer an effect which he does not even desire to produce. It is only right to add that several distinguished critics of the present century have expressed for the style of Hume an admiration which we cannot help believing to be a little in excess of its merits. A good example of Hume's sententious manner is to be found in his remarks on the character of Elizabeth:

"So dark a cloud overcast the evening of that day which had shone out with a mighty lustre in the eyes of all Europe. There are few great personages in history who have been more exposed to the calumny of enemies and the adulation of friends than Queen Elizabeth; and yet there is scarcely any whose reputation has been more certainly determined by the unanimous consent of posterity. The unusual length of her administration, and the strong features of her character, were able to overcome all prejudices; and, obliging her detractors to abate much of their invectives, and her admirers somewhat of their panegyrics, have at last, in spite of political factions, and, what is more, of religious animosities, produced a uniform judgment with regard to her conduct. Her vigour, her constancy, her magnanimity, her penetration, vigilance and address, are allowed to merit the highest praises, and appear not to have been surpassed by any person that ever filled a throne. A conduct less rigorous, less imperious, more sincere, more indulgent to her people, would have been requisite to form a perfect character. By the force of her mind she controlled all her more active and stronger qualities, and prevented them from running into excess; her heroism was exempt from temerity, her frugality from avarice, her friendship from partiality, her active temper from turbulency and a vain ambition; she guarded not herself with equal care or equal success from lesser infirmities, the rivalship of beauty, the desire of admiration, the jealousy of love, and the sallies of anger."

That most whimsical of triflers and wittiest of fops, Horace Walpole, Earl of Orford (1717-1797), in 1757 set up a private printing-press at Strawberry Hill, and had no choice but to become an author. He had previously published some easy pamphlets and had contributed essays in 1753 to *The World*. His *Catalogue of Royal and Noble Authors* appeared early in 1758, in a private edition, and was so much sought after that the delighted amateur was forced to develop into a professional writer against his will. His book was very successful; but faults were justly found with it, and Walpole suffered the agonies of criticism until he was "sick of the character of author." He was not so sick, however, as to refrain from printing a volume of his *Fugitive Pieces* in 1758, and three volumes of *Anecdotes of Painting* in 1761. In 1765 (December 1764) there was published, under circumstances of thrilling secrecy, an anonymous romance, *The Castle of Otranto*, which was promptly fathered upon Horace Walpole. This Gothic novel positively frightened grown-up people to the extent of making them unwilling to seek their beds, and was pronounced a "masterpiece" by so grave a critic as Warburton. In his *Historic Doubts* (1766), Walpole attempted to whitewash the character of Richard III., and awakened an agreeable controversy. In 1768 he produced a clever buckram tragedy, *The Mysterious Mother*. Besides all these and other miscellaneous works, Horace Walpole is the author of what gives him a far higher place than he would otherwise hold, the marvellously sprightly and charming series of letters first given to the world in 1798, and added to in successive instalments down to 1847.

The critics of the eighteenth century were very unwilling to take Horace Walpole seriously, and his frivolity, foppery, and artificiality gave them an excellent excuse. He was the prince of *petits maîtres*, and everything which proceeded from his pen showed an affectation of writing carelessly, like a fine gentleman. But his natural gifts were very brilliant, and if he had been poor or a Frenchman he would probably have made a great name for himself in literature. He catches and reflects, in his correspondence, the physiognomy of the middle of the century to a degree which points to something little short of genius. The social seductions of the age, its rose-coloured affectations, the very *frou-frou* of the fans of its great ladies, live and will live for ever in his easy pages. Horace Walpole's letters, long cast aside contemptuously by criticism as malicious and ephemeral, are now reasserting their right to exist, in virtue of the enchantment of their delicacy. Nor is his work in other departments of literature wholly contemptible. *The Castle of Otranto*, which pretended to be a reprint of a black-letter publication of 1529, would impose on no one now as an antique, but it is decidedly interesting as a story, in its mild moonlight horror. It is still more important as the first specimen in English of the narrative of mediæval romance which was presently to culminate in the novels of Walter Scott, and which was, for a time, to sweep every other species of fiction before it. This was part of Horace Walpole's ignorant but instinctive love of Gothic ornament and mediæval architecture, neither of which he understood, however, nearly so well as the less ambitious Gray, who had science enough to laugh at the stucco and the gilded gimcracks of Strawberry Hill. *The Castle of Otranto* is now seldom printed except in company with its earliest imitator, *The Old English Baron* of Clara Reeve (1725-1803), published in 1777. A certain relation or parallelism may not uninstructively be drawn between Walpole and his French contemporary, the Comte de Caylus (1692-1765). Each was an amateur in archeology, art, and literature, and each did not a little to prepare the way for serious professional labour in all those departments.

In 1759 the popular Scottish rhetorician, Dr. Hugh Blair (1718-1800), began a series of discourses on the cultivation of taste by the study of polite literature, which, wanting as they are in all that constitutes sound criticism, demand notice because of the authority which they exercised for at least half a century, and because of their influence upon contemporary style. Blair was vain and empty, insipid and loquacious, and his lectures have not even the sincerity of the dry essays of Kames. Towards the end of the century Blair achieved reputation and emolument by publishing successive volumes of his sermons, in which he applied to theology the same vague platitudinising rhetoric that he had before given to literature. In these sermons the manner introduced by Shaftesbury reaches its final debasement. Blair had the presumption to blame the style of Johnson; but as the reputation of that great man rose, his Scottish critic found himself supple enough to become one of the closest of Johnson's superficial imitators. Johnson himself, and others only less than he, thought that they found something to praise in Blair's bucket of warm water; but the modern reader seeks there in vain for any solid profit to the intellect or the taste.

A whole literature of delightful books was inaugurated by the Rev. Gilbert White (1720-1793) in his immortal *Natural History of Selborne*, which appeared in 1789, but was the collection of a lifetime. White was educated with the Wartons at Basingstoke, and proceeded to Oriel College, Oxford; he took orders in 1747, and as early as 1751 became curate of Selborne, a beautiful sylvan parish in Hampshire, where he had been born. He came back to Oriel the following year, and served the university as proctor; in 1755, however, he returned to Selborne, and remained there for the rest of his life. He declined living after living that he might remain in his beloved birthplace, accepting first one or two college-curacies, and then a Northamptonshire vicarage, but all as sinecures. Gilbert White was deeply in love with Hester Mulso, afterwards known as Mrs. Chapone; she declined his hand, and he never offered it to any one again. He corresponded with two of the most active naturalists of the period, Thomas Pennant (1726-1796), and the Hon. Daines Barrington (1727-1800), to both of whom he was abundantly useful in his observations. In 1767 Gilbert White began to write down the natural history of his native parish, and in 1771 we find that the idea of publication had crossed his mind; three years later he talks of a possible "moderate volume." He was hampered, however, by every species of scruple and timidity, and the handsome quarto did not leave the printers' hands until the spring of 1789. The book is written in the form of letters to friends; a shorter second part, with a new title-page, deals with *The Antiquities of Selborne* in the same manner. It is the earlier part which is the favourite; after the appearance of hundreds of volumes describing the natural history of various parts of England, Gilbert White's book still preserves its unfailing charm and the bloom of its pristine freshness. It is one of the most delightful legacies which the eighteenth century has bequeathed to us. On every page some trace of original observation arrests us:

"Herons seem encumbered with too much sail for their light bodies; but these vast hollow wings are necessary in carrying burdens, such as large fishes and the like. Pigeons, and particularly the sort called *smiters*, have a way of clashing their wings the one against the other over their backs with a loud snap; another variety called *tumblers* turn themselves over in the air. Some birds have movements peculiar to the season of love; thus ring-doves, though strong and rapid at other times, yet in the spring hang about on the wing in a toying and playful manner; thus the cock-snipe, while breeding, forgetting his former flight, fans the wind like the wind-hover; and the greenfinch in particular exhibits such languishing and faltering gestures as to appear like a wounded and dying bird. The king-fisher darts along like an arrow; fern-owls, or goat-suckers, glance in the dusk over the tops of trees like a meteor. Starlings, as it were, swim along, while missel-thrushes use a wild and desultory flight. Swallows sweep over the surface of the ground and water, and distinguish themselves by rapid turns and quick evolutions; swifts dash round in circles; and the bank-martin moves with frequent vacillations like a butterfly. Most of the small birds fly by jerks, rising and falling as they advance."

Without aiming at a style, Gilbert White is picturesque, precise, and vivid to a very brilliant degree; and there are few novelists who sustain the reader's interest so successfully.

Hume's work as a historian was continued by a very accomplished writer, who, without being an imitator of Hume, possessed to a singular extent the same habits of mind, the same merits, and the same faults. William Robertson (1721-1793) was a native of Midlothian, and entered the Scottish Church in 1743. He took a prominent and spirited part in the public life of Edinburgh, and in 1758 became suddenly famous by the publication of his *History of Scotland*. He was rewarded for this excellent work by being made Principal of Edinburgh University and Historiographer for Scotland. In 1769 he issued the three volumes of his *History of the Reign of Charles V.*, one of the best paid pieces of literary labour ever undertaken by a human pen, and this was followed by several historical works of minor importance. Robertson was not more impressed than Hume with the necessity of close, independent, and impartial research, but he was no less graceful in style, and he diffused over his best work an even milder radiance of philosophic reflection. Hume and Robertson are strangely alike as historians. Neither descends the hill to survey the country at his feet, but each has exceedingly long sight, and the power of taking wide and harmonious Pisgah-views from his self-adopted eminence. Robertson, however, is certainly superior to Hume in his skill in making general estimates of history. It is not the least of Robertson's claims to our consideration that the opening chapters of his *Charles V.* had the effect of awakening a historic sense in the childhood of Carlyle, supplying him with "new worlds of knowledge, vistas in all directions." Robertson describes the discovery of America with peculiar gusto, lingering with delight over every gorgeous detail :

> " As the sun arose, all their boats were manned and armed. They rowed toward the island with their colours displayed, with warlike music, and other martial pomp. As they approached the coast, they saw it covered with a multitude of people, whom the novelty of the spectacle had drawn together, whose attitudes and gestures expressed wonder and astonishment at the strange objects which presented themselves to their view. Columbus was the first European who set foot on the new world which he had discovered. He landed in a rich dress, and with a naked sword in his hand. His men followed, and kneeling down, they all kissed the ground which they had so long desired to see. They next erected a crucifix, and prostrating themselves before it, returned thanks to God for conducting their voyage to such a happy issue. They then took solemn possession of the country for the crown of Castile and Leon, with all the formalities which the Portuguese were accustomed to observe in acts of this kind in their new discoveries."

Various streams of philosophical tendency from Hutcheson, Hume, and Hartley met in the brilliant Adam Smith (1723-1790), a Kirkcaldy youth, educated at Balliol College, Oxford, and called early in life to be the disciple and then the successor of Hutcheson at Glasgow. His two books are the *Theory of Moral Sentiments* (1759), and the *Inquiry into the Nature and Causes of the Wealth of Nations* (1776), both originally delivered as courses of lectures at Glasgow. The former of these was highly popular; it presented with dignity and felicity the favourite optimistic theories of the age, the cheerful system of man as a beautiful specimen of celestial clock-work which needs but to be undisturbed to go on merrily till it runs down. None of the philosophers, except Butler, seem to have retained the seventeenth-century conviction of the inherent badness of human nature, or of its tendency to moral decay. Smith's second book is vastly superior to his first. He had been to France in the meantime, and had come into personal relations with the great French economists Quesnay (1694-1774) and Turgot (1727-1781). His mind was eminently receptive, and in an element of extreme tranquillity he worked out his theories slowly to their last results. The chief merit of the *Wealth of Nations*, and that which enables it still to hold its place at the head of the politico-economic literature of the world, is not any very great originality in detail, but an extraordinary grasp of all parts of the subject, and a marvellous ability in illustrating theoretical propositions by apt instances from practical life. Adam Smith is usually spoken of as the first prophet of Free Trade; it would be nearer the truth, remarks Sir Leslie Stephen, "to say that he was the first writer who succeeded in so presenting that doctrine as to convince statesmen" in its favour. To the purely literary student, desirous of an example of Adam Smith's style, which is always lucid and correct, no better specimen can be recommended than the letter he wrote to Strahan, describing his last interview with the dying Hume:

"He said that when he was reading, a few days before, Lucian's Dialogues of the Dead, among all the excuses which are alleged to Charon for not entering readily into his boat, he could not find one that fitted him; for he had no house to finish, he had no daughter to provide for, he had no enemies upon whom he wished to revenge himself. 'I could not well imagine,' said he, 'what excuse I could make to Charon in order to obtain a little delay. I have done everything of consequence which I ever meant to do; and I could at no time expect to leave my relations and friends in a better situation than that in which I am now likely to leave them. I therefore have all reason to die contented.' He then diverted himself with inventing several jocular excuses, which he supposed he might make to Charon, and with imagining the very surly answers which it might suit the character of Charon to return to them. 'Upon further consideration,' said he, 'I thought I might say to him "Good Charon, I have been correcting my works for a new edition. Allow me a little time, that I may see how the public receives the alterations." But Charon would answer, "When you have seen the effect of these, you will be for making other alterations. There will be no end of such excuses: so, honest friend, please step into the boat." But I might still urge, "Have a little patience, good Charon; I have been endeavouring to open the eyes of the public. If I live a few years longer, I may have the satisfaction of seeing the downfall of some of the prevailing systems of superstition." But Charon would then lose all temper and decency. "You loitering rogue, that will not happen those many hundred years. Do you fancy I will grant you a lease for so long a term? Get into the boat this instant, you lazy loitering rogue."'"

Several of the pioneers of science in the eighteenth century, the great technical teachers, were far from disdaining the arts of graceful expression. There is no more interesting example of this fact than Sir William Blackstone (1723-1780), who contrived to make one of the most readable of books out of a compendium of jurisprudence. Blackstone began life as a poet. His copy of octosyllabics, entitled *The Lawyer's Farewell to his Muse*, is one of the best minor poems of the time, and suggests that so skilful a versifier might have taken his place with the professional lyrists. In one hundred lines it describes the charms of poetry, the obligation of the author to quit the Muse, and the solemn enthusiasm with which he will devote himself to another mistress, and, absorbed in the study of "Britannia's laws,"

> " Observe how parts with parts unite
> In one harmonious rule of right;
> See countless wheels distinctly tend
> By various laws to one great end."

These lines are usually attributed to the year 1741, when Blackstone entered himself at the Middle Temple; but they seem too vigorous and too polished to be the work of a lad of eighteen, and it may be suggested, as more probable, that they were written in 1746, when the author was called to the bar. Until 1766 Blackstone remained identified with Oxford, successively as undergraduate at Pembroke, as fellow and bursar of All Souls, as principal of New Inn Hall, and as first Vinerian professor. In 1765-69 he published his *Commentaries on the Laws of England*, in four quarto volumes. By this work he made about

£15,000. Although the *Commentaries* had faults which have since been abundantly pointed out, their merits were obvious alike to lawyers and to the public, and no legal work has ever enjoyed or deserved so eminent a popular success. Blackstone writes easily and brightly, though few critics of to-day would endorse Fox's enthusiastic dictum that the Vinerian Professor was the best prose-writer of his day, "far more correct than Hume and less studied than Robertson."

The earliest art-criticisms of any value published in this country were contained in the annual and biennial *Discourses* which Sir Joshua Reynolds, P.R.A. (1723-1792), delivered from January 1759 to his retirement in December 1790. They were issued year by year, and collected after his death. The popularity of these essays has been steadily maintained, and Reynolds can now be omitted in no catalogue of the leading writers of the second half of the century. His periods are full and eloquent, and he mingles with his æsthetic philosophy, which he borrowed mainly from the French, a practical knowledge due to his own technical experience. He is often enthusiastic and always singularly sympathetic as a teacher, while the best proof of the value of his discourses is that they are still in constant demand, and eagerly consulted by professional artists. It is in the course of his Fourteenth Discourse that the President pauses to make his touching reference to the recent death of his rival Gainsborough :

"It may not be improper to make mention of some of the customs and habits of this extraordinary man ; points which come more within the reach of an observer : I, however, mean only such as are connected with his art, and indeed were, as I apprehend, the causes of his arriving to that high degree of excellence which we see and acknowledge in his work. Of these causes we must state, as the fundamental, the love which he had to his art; to which, indeed, his whole mind seems to have been devoted, and to which everything was referred ; and this we may fairly conclude from various circumstances of his life, which were known to his intimate friends. Among others, he had a habit of continually remarking to those who happened to be about him, whatever peculiarity of countenance, whatever accidental combination of figures, or happy effects of light and shadow, occurred in prospects, in the sky, in walking the streets, or in company. If, in his walks, he found a character that he liked, and whose attendance was to be obtained, he ordered him to his house: and from the fields he brought into his painting-room stumps of trees, weeds, and animals of various kinds; and designed them, not from memory, but immediately from the objects. He even framed a kind of model of landscapes on his table, composed of broken stones, dried herbs, and pieces of looking-glass, which he magnified and improved into rocks, trees, and water. How far this latter practice may be useful in giving hints, the professors of landscape can best determine."

It was, doubtless, through his lifelong companionship with Johnson, Burke, and Goldsmith that Reynolds learned to write in the English language only a little less brilliantly than they.

CHAPTER X

THE POETS OF THE DECADENCE

THERE is no section of our national poetry so sterile, so unstimulating, as that which we have now reached, the poetry of the third quarter of the eighteenth century. Compared even with the period which immediately preceded it, although that was not greatly inspired, it is singularly dull, mechanical, and dusty. There is nothing here so majestic as the odes of Gray or so tender as those of Collins—nothing to challenge comparison with the frank nature-study of Thomson. Names there are in plenty, names of poets not yet utterly discrowned, but on whose brows the laurel is growing very thin and brittle. The greatest of the group is a noble prose-writer, who wrote graceful verses. The rest are either survivals, or else men with the light of the next age already dimly reflected in their faces. The most characteristic of them is scarcely a poet at all, but a versifier, who without charm or imagination, summed up all that the mere tradition of poetic art in the eighteenth century could teach an extremely clever artisan. In the verses of Erasmus Darwin the classic style found itself unsurpassed, and, in that direction, fortunately unsurpassable. As the century approached its close, a newer and a nobler choir of true poetic voices began to be heard, not always to be distinguished at the outset from the hard see-saw of the older generation, yet for ears attuned bringing real music in the *Village* of Crabbe, and the *Poetical Sketches* of Blake, both in 1783, the *Table-Talk* of Cowper

(1785), and Burns's Kilmarnock volume of 1786. But the pleasant task of touching this revival is left to my successor.

How very rapidly what was living and organic in Collins and Gray became fossilised may be seen by examining the frigid work in verse of the physician, Mark Akenside (1721-1770). This writer was the son of a butcher in Newcastle-on-Tyne, where, at the age of sixteen, and still at school, he published *The Virtuoso*, a poem in Spenserian stanza, which preceded in publicity both Thomson's and Shenstone's efforts in that form, the honour of reviving which should therefore rest with Akenside. In 1744, on his way from Edinburgh to complete his medical studies in Holland, he published his *Pleasures of Imagination* in London; his *Odes* appeared in 1745; and in 1746 his *Hymn to the Naiads*. He was at the latter date only in his twenty-fifth year, but he wrote no more poetry of importance, and is to be classed with those in whom the lyric vein is early stanched. Akenside became a distinguished member of the Royal Society, a writer of valuable physiological treatises, and a leading hospital physician. The first edition of the *Pleasures of the Imagination* was anonymous, and in three books of cold and stately blank verse. In the prose "design," Akenside mentioned Addison, from whom he had borrowed much, but not Shaftesbury, to whom he owed his entire philosophical groundwork. Akenside thought that "the separation of the works of imagination from philosophy" was a very undesirable thing, and he determined to unite the theories of the *Characteristics* with his own strenuous verse. The result was not wholly unlucky, but the world has preferred to take its Shaftesbury undiluted with blank verse; Akenside afterwards re-wrote his poem, without improving it. His odes are icy-cold, and full of elegance rather than beauty; his *Hymn to the Naiads* is usually held, and with good cause, to be his best poem, the most graceful, the most sculpturesque specimen of his blank verse. It closes thus:

"He, perchance, the gifts
Of young Lyæus, and the dread exploits,
May sing in aptest numbers: he the fate

> Of sober Pentheus, he the Paphian rites,
> And naked Mars with Cytherea chained,
> And strong Alcides in the spinster's robes,
> May celebrate, applauded. But with you,
> O Naiads, far from that unhallowed rout,
> Must dwell the man whoe'er to praisèd themes
> Invokes the immortal Muse. The immortal Muse
> To your calm habitations, to the cave
> Corycian, or the Delphic mount, will guide
> His footsteps; and with your unsullied streams
> His lips will bathe: whether the eternal lore
> Of Themis, or the majesty of Jove,
> To mortals he reveal; or teach his lyre
> The unenvied guerdon of the patriot's toils,
> In those unfading islands of the blessed,
> Where sacred bards abide. Hail, honoured Nymphs!
> Thrice hail! For you the Cyrenaic shell,
> Behold, I touch, revering. To my songs
> Be present ye, with favourable feet;
> And all profaner audience far remove."

Akenside was not without influence on poetic style, and he possessed a direct disciple in the early writings of T. L. Peacock. At his very best Akenside is sometimes like a sort of frozen Keats. Two exact contemporaries of Akenside claim mention here only on the strength of one fine lyric apiece—James Grainger (1721-1766), a didactic West Indian sugar-planting physician, having published in 1755 an *Ode to Solitude*, before he began to sing of canes and swains in tedious couplets; and Francis Fawkes (1721-1777), being the author of "The Brown Jug," printed among his *Original Poems* of 1761:

> "Dear Tom, this brown jug that now foams with mild ale
> (In which I will drink to sweet Nan of the Vale)
> Was once Toby Fillpot, a thirsty old soul
> As e'er drank a bottle, or fathom'd a bowl;
> In boosing about 'twas his praise to excel,
> And among jolly topers he bore off the bell.
>
> "It chanc'd as in dog-days he sat at his ease
> In his flower-woven arbour as gay as you please,

With a friend and a pipe puffing sorrows away,
And with honest old stingo was soaking his clay,
His breath-doors of life on a sudden were shut,
And he died full as big as a Dorchester butt.

" His body, when long in the ground it had lain,
And time into clay had resolv'd it again,
A potter found out in its covert so snug,
And with part of fat Toby he form'd this brown jug,
Now sacred to friendship, and mirth, and mild ale ;
So here's to my lovely sweet Nan of the Vale."

Fawkes was distinguished as a translator of the classics, and he had the complaisance to render into English the Latin poems of his friend Christopher Smart (1722-1770). Throughout his own century, Smart received no other honours, and his forlorn reputation has only very recently been lifted out of the limbo where it was lying with that of the Langhornes and the Merricks. In no existing history of literature does Smart receive anything like his due meed of attention, as being, in a dreary age of versifiers, a very original, if somewhat crazy and unbalanced poet. He went to Pembroke College, Cambridge, in 1738, and remained there until 1754, when he lost his fellowship through the fact of his marriage having been discovered. Of his eccentric and disreputable ways in college we find traces in the letters of Gray, who was resident with him for a long time at Pembroke, and who describes him as graduating for Bedlam or a jail. After having tested the merits of either kind of asylum, however, in 1752 Smart pulled himself together, and published a collection of his *Poems*, a handsome quarto, containing, besides some sixteen odes in following of Gray, a didactic *Hop-Garden*, in two books of Thomsonian blank verse, a masque, and some miscellaneous ballads. These pieces are all mediocre, although illuminated here and there with flashes of gorgeous phraseology. In 1753 Smart published *The Hilliad*, a conceited satire on Dr. John Hill, who had somewhat severely reviewed Smart's odes. This poem is chiefly notable as having probably suggested the form and the title of the much more famous *Rolliad* (1785) of Lawrence and

Fitzpatrick. About 1754 Smart let himself out on a lease for ninety-nine years, to work for a bookseller, and in 1761 he became violently insane once more. Dr. Johnson went to see him in the madhouse, and his account of the visit is well known. "I did not think," said the lexicographer, "that he ought to be shut up. His infirmities were not noxious to society. He insisted on people praying with him; and I'd as lief pray with Kit Smart as with any one else. Another charge was that he did not love clean linen; and I have no passion for it." While in Bedlam, Smart wrote his famous *Song to David*, published in 1763. Worn out with drunkenness and depressed with debt, the unhappy poet sank in 1770.

It is difficult to describe and impossible to analyse the *Song to David*, a lyric in 516 lines, many of which evade any literal paraphrase in prose. It is obviously the work of an intellect which is partially unhinged, but the removal of self-criticism seems to have withdrawn at the same time many of the conventional scruples of the hide-bound eighteenth-century writer, and to have unsealed the fountains of poetic language. What Smart means may occasionally be doubtful, but no one can fail to recognise that his Biblical fancy is steeped in all the flush and bloom of Eden:

> "For adoration ripening canes
> And cocoa's purest milk detains
>   The western pilgrim's staff;
> Where rain in clasping boughs inclos'd,
> And vines with oranges dispos'd,
>   Embower the social laugh.
>
> "Now labour his reward receives,
> For adoration counts his sheaves
>   To peace, her bounteous prince;
> The nectarine his strong tint imbibes,
> And apples of ten thousand tribes,
>   And quick peculiar quince.
>
> "The wealthy crops of whitening rice,
> 'Mongst thyine woods and groves of spice,
>   For adoration grow;
> And, marshall'd in the fencèd land,
> The peaches and pomegranates stand,
>   Where wild carnations blow.

> " For adoration, beyond match,
> The scholar bullfinch aims to catch
> The soft flute's ivory touch ;
> And, careless on the hazel spray,
> The daring redbreast keeps at bay
> The damsel's greedy touch."

How much the *Song to David* perplexed Smart's contemporaries may be gathered from the fact that it, the only real jewel in his crown, was omitted from the posthumous collection of his works. Of late, full justice has tardily been done to the highly-coloured phrases and daring adjectives of the *Song*, and Mr. Browning, in his recent *Parleyings*, has celebrated the magic of Smart's disordered but glowing imagination in fervid iambics. In reference to the mediocrity of Smart's other poems, the greater modern poet compares the *Song to David* to a gorgeous chapel lying *perdue* in some dull old commonplace mansion.

The latest and brightest of Goldsmith's poems would scarcely have been written if the manner of rhyming had not been suggested to him by the popularity of a very whimsical and elegant trifle. *The New Bath Guide*, which appeared in quarto in 1766, was the herald of a new school of society verse, and led the way towards Praed and Oliver Wendell Holmes. The author was a Cambridge scholar of distinction, a fox-hunting country squire, and an inglorious member of Parliament, Christopher Anstey (1724-1805). This gentleman had for many years frequented Bath, then in the heyday of fashion, and he determined to lampoon the society of that city in a rhyming satire. The sub-title of *The New Bath Guide* is " Memoirs of the B—r—d Family," and the poem takes the form of fifteen letters addressed by members of that family, who are drinking the Bath waters for their health. The first correspondent remarks :

> " From water sprung, like flowers from dew,
> What troops of Bards appear !
> The God of Verse—and Physic too—
> Inspires them twice a year."

And accordingly all the Blunderheads, male and female, express their feelings, whether cynical or romantic, in rhyme. The whole poem, though coarse in parts, and in others darkened by lost allusions, remains one of the lightest and most sparkling of purely mundane compositions in the language; the "letters," written in anapæstic verse of four stresses, being decidedly the best. It is in these latter that we see the coming Goldsmith foreshadowed.

From *The New Bath Guide* to *Retaliation* the transition is easy, and we now approach the chief poetic name of the period, Oliver Goldsmith (1728-1774), whose interesting personal career it will be desirable to defer treating till we reach him, in his more important character of a prose-writer, in the next chapter. Goldsmith, if carefully examined, is seen to mark a retrograde step, a momentary phase of reaction. In versification he returned, in company with Churchill, to the heroic couplet, which had received no support of any great weight, save that of Samuel Johnson, in the preceding generation. For the Spenserian stanza and the blank verse of Thomson, for the ode-forms of Gray and Collins, Goldsmith did not conceal his disdain. He looked back beyond these naturalistic poets, and took his place in direct succession to Pope. His disdain, in non-dramatic poetry, of blank verse, the employment of which had become general since 1725, is not more seen in the remarks in the *Polite Learning* and the dedication to *The Traveller*, than in Goldsmith's total repudiation of it in his own work. He studied the couplet with great care, and he contrived to introduce into it an ease, an unstudied simplicity, which raise Goldsmith far above Johnson and Churchill, and sometimes place him, in mere charm, above Pope himself. The keyword of Goldsmith's verse is grace. He is not, as a poet, very strong, or very original, or very frequently inspired; but his simplicity is often touching, his ear is commonly delicate, and his rectitude of feeling always takes a polished and yet a natural form of expression. But here it becomes necessary to distinguish, since Goldsmith claims our attention in two classes of imaginative art, as a dramatist and as a descriptive poet. We touch on the former first.

Goldsmith's earlier comedy, *The Good Natur'd Man*, was produced at Covent Garden in January 1768, having been written in the two preceding years. It enjoyed but a comparative success, although good judges, such as Dr. Johnson, pronounced it the best comedy seen on the English stage since Cibber completed Vanbrugh's *Provoked Husband* in 1728. The period of forty years contained between these two representations had certainly been one of the most sterile in the dramatic history of the country. Cibber had been succeeded by Foote (1721-1777), in whose numerous dramas the development of characteristic dialogue was entirely subordinated to the illustration of such oddities and whimsical singularities as could be emphasised by the talent for mimicry possessed by the author-actor himself; and not one of Foote's plays holds a niche in literature. Near the close of the half-century a change came over dramatic taste; the mere farce or burlesque grew to be less in favour, and the audiences welcomed attempts at a purer and more legitimate comedy of intrigue. There is still a savour of the salt of wit to be tasted in *The Suspicious Husband* of Dr. Benjamin Hoadly (1706-1757) and in the *Miss in Her Teens* of Garrick, both produced in 1747; while if *High Life Below Stairs* (1759) of the Rev. James Townley (1714-1778) be a trifle, it is one which keeps any audience alive with laughter to the present day. When Goldsmith's attention was first called to the drama the popular taste had once more changed, and the favourite of the moment was Hugh Kelly (1739-1777), the Irish staymaker, who made himself, for a short time, pre-eminent with a series of five comedies, all of the *larmoyante* sentimental class recently introduced from France, in which everything that was vulgar or vigorous was carefully omitted. It was one of Kelly's pieces, *False Delicacy*, which was produced at Covent Garden six days before *The Good Natur'd Man*, and so sorely interfered with the success of that play. Goldsmith defined the compositions of Kelly and Cumberland as "sentimental comedies, in which the virtues of private life are exhibited, rather than the vices exposed; and the distresses rather than the faults of mankind make our interest in the piece." His own *Good Natur'd Man*, although strong comic writing is introduced, shows to a considerable extent this sentimental quality. It is a play that has scarcely preserved its vitality; when it is revived, it is before an audience that accepts it from an antiquarian point of view, and consents to be only occasionally amused. Yet Croaker is a good creation, and Jack Lofty a better one.

The hero-worship of Goldsmith's biographers has obscured the memory of a play which is really a far better and livelier comedy than *The Good Natur'd Man*, and much more worthy to precede *She Stoops to Conquer*. It occurred to Garrick and to George Colman that an entertaining drama might be drawn up on the lines of Hogarth's " Mariage à la mode," and the result of their joint labours was *The Clandestine Marriage* (1766), a play now wholly neglected, but worthy of revival as much on the stage as in the study. Two years earlier, in 1764, Macklin had, in his *True Born Scotchman* (afterwards known as *The Man of the World*), sketched, rather inartistically, the outline of a most laughable play. The Lord Ogleby of the former comedy, and the Sir Pertinax Mac-Sychophant of the latter, are characters which display very brilliant qualities of comic invention, and it is to do their authors a gross injustice to pretend, as the worshippers of Goldsmith are accustomed to do, that the latter arises, like a phœnix, out of the absolute ashes of the drama. In all other branches of literature Goldsmith's originality shows itself in the art with which he excels those who had been doing well on the same lines; and it is this praise, and no other, which is due to him as a comic dramatist.

The famous "low" scene in *The Good Natur'd Man*, between young Honeywood, Miss Richland, and the bailiffs, which is so funny to read and so distressing to see that Goldsmith was forced to cut it out, is really that which most characteristically prepares us for the playwright's second and far more genuine dramatic success. If one swallow could make a summer, *She Stoops to Conquer* would make the eighteenth century a period of genuine dramatic vitality, for it is one of the great comedies of the world. It lives mainly by the vigour of its broad humour. "The genteel thing is the genteel thing any time, if so be that a gentleman bees in a concatenation accordingly," but the public is not always in a mood to dance the Minuet in *Ariadne*. Sometimes it likes to be reminded of its Tony Lumpkins and the frolics at the Three Pigeons, and then *She Stoops to Conquer* is once more in all its glory. This inimitable comedy, with all its innocent wit and frank good-nature, was put on the stage, after extraordinary objections on Colman's part, in March 1773, just a year before the author's death, and brought Goldsmith considerable pecuniary profit and endless personal distresses. At the present day it is probably the best known of the author's works, and, outside Shakespeare and Sheridan, the English play with which the greatest number of persons are familiar. Of post-Elizabethan comedies which preceded it in this country, those of Congreve alone can be named by its side; and if it is less artistically constructed, somewhat less carefully written, and much less witty, its moral purity and wholesomeness, its fund of good spirits, and its wonderful flow of natural dialogue, are qualities that raise it almost to a level with *Love for Love* or *The Way of the World*. Of succeeding comedies, but one has approached it in lasting popularity—the *School for Scandal*, produced four years later, by Sheridan.

No earlier poem of Goldsmith than *The Traveller* is known to exist, for this piece belongs, at least in part, to the year 1757, when the poet was wandering over the face of Europe on foot. But it was not published until the last days of 1764, in a quarto form dated 1765. In plan *The Traveller* is a perfect example of an eighteenth-century didactic or descriptive poem in heroics. The person who speaks the verses—Goldsmith himself in his Swiss exile—sits pensively on an Alpine rock, and moralises on the condition and the limitations of European society. The poem pleased Goldsmith's contemporaries; Johnson, who deigned to complete it with couplets of his own, declared it to be the best poem since the death of Pope, but this was a mistake. *The*

Traveller is far from being so good a poem as the *Churchyard Elegy* or even the *Vanity of Human Wishes*, but it is a delicate and pathetic piece of idealism in highly-finished verses. It is far inferior, however, to *The Deserted Village*, a poem in the same manner and measure,—and of about the same length, each containing less than five hundred lines,—which Goldsmith published, also in quarto, in 1770. The descriptions in the later piece are not merely superior in freshness and reality to those in *The Traveller*, but they have a truth of detail, an exquisite simplicity and penetrative sweetness, which are hardly rivalled elsewhere in the language :

> " Sweet was the sound, when oft, at evening's close,
> Up yonder hill the village murmur rose ;
> There, as I passed with careless steps and slow,
> The mingling notes came soften'd from below ;
> The swain responsive as the milk-maid sung,
> The sober herd that low'd to meet their young ;
> The noisy geese that gabbled o'er the pool,
> The playful children just let loose from school ;
> The watch-dog's voice that bay'd the whispering wind,
> And the loud laugh that spoke the vacant mind,—
> These all in sweet confusion sought the glade,
> And fill'd each pause the nightingale had made.
> But now the sounds of population fail,
> No cheerful murmurs fluctuate in the gale,
> No busy steps the grass-grown footway tread,
> But all the bloomy flush of life is fled !"

The last ninety lines may be charged with a certain heaviness, due to the requirements of the age, which, like Horace Walpole, called for "edification" in its art; but if these are omitted, the rest of the contrast between the smiling Auburn of old and its hag-haunted ruins is in the highest and truest sense felicitious and poetical. The heroic couplet was never employed, even by Pope himself, with more melody, and there is an easy lightness about the best descriptive passages which is hardly to be discovered elsewhere in English heroic verse.

With the single exception of the anapæsts of his latest years, the remainder of Goldsmith's poetry is inconsiderable. *Edwin and Angelina* is absurd; even Shenstone could do this sort of thing better, and Johnson's burlesque sums up all criticism. The songs and lyrics are poor, always excepting the comic ballads of "Mary Blaize" and the "Mad Dog," to which a fresh vitality has been given by the sympathetic genius of Randolph Caldecott. The best of Goldsmith's minor pieces is the very carefully polished "Description of an Author's Bedroom":

> "Where the Red Lion, staring o'er the way,
>   Invites each passing stranger that can pay;
>   Where Calvert's butt, and Parsons' black champagne,
>   Regale the drabs and bloods of Drury Lane;
>   There, in a lonely room, from bailiffs snug,
>   The Muse found Scroggen stretched beneath a rug.
>   A window, patched with paper, lent a ray
>   That dimly showed the state in which he lay;
>   The sanded floor, that grits beneath the tread;
>   The humid wall, with paltry pictures spread.
>   The Royal Game of Goose was there in view,
>   And the Twelve Rules the Royal Martyr drew;
>   The Seasons, fram'd with listing, found a place,
>   And brave Prince William show'd his lamp-black face.
>   The morn was cold; he views with keen desire
>   The rusty grate unconscious of a fire;
>   With beer and milk arrears the frieze was scor'd
>   And five crack'd tea-cups dress'd the chimney-board;
>   A night-cap deck'd his brows instead of bay,
>   A cap by night—a stocking all the day!"

But after the publication of *The New Bath Guide*, Goldsmith adopted the ambling measures in which he wrote three posthumously-printed masterpieces, *Retaliation* (1774), *The Haunch of Venison* (1776), and the *Letter to Mrs. Bunbury* (1837), and it is in these of all his works in verse that he attains his easiest movement and most racy vocabulary. In *The Traveller* and *The Deserted Village*, with all his brilliancy and charm, he was really returning consciously to a form of writing which the world had already decided to condemn. In *Retaliation*, although clinging to the modes of his generation, his style was prophesying of a freer and a more courageous period:

> " Here lies David Garrick, describe me, who can,
> An abridgment of all that was pleasant in man;
> As an actor, confess'd without rival to shine,
> As a wit, if not first, in the very first line;
> Yet with talents like these, and an excellent heart,
> The man had his failings, a dupe to his art;
> Like an ill-judging beauty his colours he spread,
> And beplastered with rouge his own natural red.
> On the stage he was natural, simple, affecting;
> 'Twas only that when he was off he was acting.
>
> . . . .
>
> But let us be candid, and speak out our mind,
> If dunces applauded, he paid them in kind;
> Ye Kenricks, and Kellys, and Woodfalls so grave,
> What commerce was yours, while you got and you gave!
> How did Grub Street re-echo the shouts that you raised,
> While he was be-Rosciused and you were bepraised!
> But peace to his spirit wherever it flies,
> To act as an angel and mix with the skies;
> Those poets who owe their best fame to his skill,
> Shall still be his flatterers, go where he will.
> Old Shakespeare receive him with praise and with love,
> And Beaumonts and Bens be his Kellys above."

On the whole, however, we must deny to the verse of Goldsmith any great importance in the procession of English literature. It presents us with certain very graceful and delicate numbers, but it marks no progress in the art of poetry.

Still less can be claimed for the satirist who towered for a moment so high above his contemporaries, and who leaves upon us the same impression of greatness as a knock-kneed giant at a country fair may leave. The Rev. Charles Churchill (1731-1764) has faded to the merest shadow of himself, and the writer who of all others aimed at being virile, robust, and weighty, has come to be regarded as the ideal of a pasteboard hero. Churchill was at Westminster and would have been at Trinity; but he disqualified himself at seventeen by marrying, and was forced by poverty to

prepare for the uncongenial profession of a clergyman. He held
curacies in Wales and Somerset, and in 1758 he came back to
London as a curate and, regardless of his cloth, plunged into a
succession of debaucheries which carried him off within six years,
at the age of thirty-three. His literary career was brief and full of
activity. In 1761 he began by publishing *The Rosciad*, a satire in
the manner of Dryden, on the actors of the day. This piece was
short (it does not contain more than one thousand lines); it
lampooned the masters of the stage openly, by name; and it was
written in rough but very vigorous verse. To this rapidly succeeded *Night* (1762), addressed to Lloyd, *The Prophecy of Famine*,
an abominable assault upon the Scotch nation, and *An Epistle to
William Hogarth*, which drove its illustrious but thin-skinned
subject into a passion of distress:

> "Virtue, with due contempt, saw Hogarth stand,
> The murderous pencil in his palsied hand;
> What was the cause of Liberty to him,
> Or what was Honour? Let them sink or swim,
> So he may gratify, without control,
> The mean resentments of his selfish soul.
> Let Freedom perish, if, to Freedom true,
> In the same ruin Wilkes may perish too.
> With all the symptoms of assured decay,
> With age and sickness pinch'd and worn away,
> Pale, quiv'ring lips, lank cheeks, and faltering tongue,
> The spirits out of tune, the nerves unstrung,
> Thy body shrivell'd up, thy dim eyes sunk
> Within their sockets deep, thy weak hands shrunk
> The body's weight unable to sustain.
> The stream of life scarce trembling thro' the vein,
> More than half-kill'd by honest truths, which fell,
> Thro' thy own fault, from men who wish'd thee well,
> Can'st thou, e'en thus, thy thoughts to vengeance give,
> And, dead to all things else, to malice live?
> Hence, Dotard, to thy closet! Shut thee in,
> By deep repentance wash away thy sin;
> From haunts of men to shame and sorrow fly,
> And, on the verge of death, learn how to die."

This was written to revenge Hogarth's plate of "The Times," into which Wilkes and Churchill, till lately friends of the painter's, had been introduced with ridicule. The cruelty of the satire consisted in its truth, for Hogarth was actually dying, though he lingered for another year.

Churchill was so ill-advised as to turn from the composition of these pamphlets in heroic verse, which were at least readable and brief, to a poem in no less than five thousand lines—*The Ghost*, written in dull octosyllabic couplets. He acknowledges in one of his reckless passages of self-appreciation that he has "nothing of books and little known of men," and his writings are tiresome in their wholesale denunciation of persons and things which the author is utterly unable to appreciate. He returned to the heroic couplet, which suited his hasty talent best, in *The Conference* and *The Author*, each 1763; *The Duellist* (1763) is in the Swiftean eight-syllable verse. Churchill contrived to publish no less than five separate poems during the last year of his life, one of these, *Gotham*, being issued in three distinct instalments. He became at last so truculent and foul that he dared not print his name on his title-page, and copies of *The Times* and *Independence* are often found to be franked with the poet's signature in ink. The friendship of Wilkes was very unfortunate for Churchill, whose character was much more liable to be injured by excess; but it must be admitted that the patriot was faithful to his coarse associate and laureate. Churchill was visiting Wilkes in Boulogne, when he died of fever, prematurely exhausted, in November 1764.

Feared and admired for his force, with his tempest of uncouth and vituperative verse, his rattling facility, and his reckless swaggering courage to support him, Churchill exercised a genuine power so long as he lasted, and to some of his contemporaries he appeared another Dryden. But he was really scarcely even an Oldham. His work is crude and unfinished to excess, he has no ear and no heart, and he fails to please us the moment that our surprise at his violence is over. His latest works are positively execrable, whether in morals or in style, and he alternates in them between the universal attribution of hypocrisy to others, and the cynical confession of vice in himself. He is a very Caligula among men of letters; when he stings his Muse to the murder of a reputation, he seems to cry "Ita feri, ut se mori sentiat." The happiness of others is a calamity to him; and his work would excite in us the extremity of aversion, if it were not that its very violence betrays the exasperation and wretchedness of its unfortunate author. Even more than Goldsmith, Churchill exemplifies the resolute return to the forms of poetic art in vogue before the age of Thomson and Gray. A satellite and boon-companion of Churchill was Robert Lloyd (1733-1764), who survived him but a few weeks. Cowper, who was his schoolfellow, says that Lloyd was "born sole heir and single of dear Matt Prior's easy jingle." Lloyd collected his fables, epistles, and translations in quarto in 1762.

Two minor versifiers, who could ill pretend to compete with Goldsmith in sweetness or with Churchill in strength, nevertheless arrest the attention of the critic as having done more than either of those more eminent writers to secure the progress of poetry. Thomas Percy (1728-1811), Dean of Carlisle and then Bishop of Dromore, wrote some songs and tinkered up some ballads, but his real contribution to literature was his epoch-making *Reliques of English Poetry*, published in 1765. Thomas Warton of Basingstoke (1728-1790), the most inspired of a respectable family of songsters, has, in like manner, immortalised his name, not by his easy verses, but by his resuscitations of the forgotten masterpieces of the elder poets, in particular his *Observations on Spenser* (1754), and his *History of English Poetry* (1777-78-81),—books which Johnson, who disliked such excursions, was shrewd enough to acknowledge would "show to all, who should afterwards attempt the study of our ancient authors, the way to success." Neither Percy nor Warton escaped the strictures of Ritson, that "blackletter dog," a tame and affected pedant of no critical importance, but far more careful as an editor than either of them. Warton, a very gentle and enlightened scholar, was Professor of Poetry at

Oxford for ten years, and lectured, of course in Latin, on the Greek pastoral poets. He eventually succeeded Whitehead for a little while as poet-laureate. As an original versifier he was copious and careful, in the school of Gray, but not strong or vivid. Johnson, with unerring skill, packed the whole of Warton's lyrical work into the compass of one cruel copy of verses:

> "Wheresoe'er I turn my view,
> All is strange, yet nothing new;
> Endless labour all along,
> Endless labour to be wrong;
> Phrase that time has flung away,
> Uncouth words in disarray,
> Trick'd in antique ruff and bonnet,
> Ode and elegy and sonnet."

But he was prompt to add, "Remember that I love the fellow dearly—for all I laugh at him."

The result of studies less complete and authoritative than those of Percy and Warton, but undertaken in the same direction, is seen in the work of a group of small poets, whose names once occupied a prominent position in the history of English literature, but are now slipping out of notice altogether. For auld lang syne, their existence may here be briefly recognised, although not one of them is really significant. William Falconer (1732-1769), a common sailor in the merchant-service, published, in 1762, *The Shipwreck*, a long heroic piece in couplets, in three cantos, describing the disaster which attended a vessel in which he himself had been wrecked, in Greek waters, in a style which is partly pompous, partly crude with realism. The technical part of Falconer's poem, expressed in such verses as these—

> "The swelling stud-sails now their wings extend,
> Then stay-sails sidelong to the breeze ascend;
> While all to court the wandering breeze was placed,
> With yards now thwarting, now obliquely braced";

or—

> "To each yard-arm the head-rope they extend,
> And soon their earings and their robans bend;

> This task performed, they first the braces slack,
> Then to the chesstree drag the unwilling tack;
> And, while the lee clue-garnet's lowered away,
> Taut aft the sheet they tally, and belay,"—

is said to be extremely accurate. Falconer was congratulated on having rivalled Virgil in his own line, and was appointed purser on board a royal frigate to encourage the others. But his triumph was brief; his ship, "The Aurora," sailed away and was never heard of again, and Falconer is supposed to have been drowned off the coast of Mozambique, sinking, like his own hero Albert, "amid the vast profound." Of James Beattie (1735-1803) it is enough to record that he published incoherent fragments of a mock-antique *Minstrel*, in the Spenserian stanza, in 1771 and 1774. William Julius Meikle (or Mickle) (1734-1788) essayed many things, and succeeded once with a tender ballad of *Cumnor Hall*, which had the honour of inspiring Sir Walter Scott with the story of *Kenilworth*. It was either Michael Bruce (1746-1767), or his friend John Logan (1748-1788) who wrote a lyric "To the Cuckoo," which is one of the freshest strains of unpremeditated song that meet us in the arid flats of late eighteenth-century poetry:

> " Hail, beauteous stranger of the grove!
>   Thou messenger of Spring!
> Now Heaven regains thy rural seat,
>   And woods thy welcome sing.
>
> " What time the daisy decks the green,
>   Thy certain voice we hear;
> Hast thou a star to guide thy path,
>   Or mark the rolling year?
>
> " Delightful visitant, with thee
>   I hail the time of flowers,
> And hear the sound of music sweet
>   From birds among the bowers.
>
> " The schoolboy, wandering through the wood,
>   To pull the primrose gay,
> Starts, the new voice of Spring to hear,
>   And imitates thy lay.

> " What time the pea puts on the bloom,
>   Thou fliest thy vocal vale,
> An annual guest in other lands,
>   Another Spring to hail.
>
> " Sweet bird! thy bower is ever green,
>   Thy sky is ever clear;
> Thou hast no sorrow in thy song,
>   No winter in thy year!
>
> " O could I fly, I'd fly with thee!
>   We'd make on joyful wing,
> Our annual visit o'er the globe,
>   Companions of the Spring."

The influence of this little ode "about a gowk" on the genius of Wordsworth was direct and unquestionable.

It would be inexcusable to linger over names even less than these—names of versifiers who stood out for a moment above the general level of mediocrity, but did nothing to stem or even to hasten the final deluge. At the close of the third quarter of the century the ruin of the classical school almost abruptly became complete. But we must pass on to consider the clever artificer of verse, in whom the manner of Pope at once culminated and became hopelessly ridiculous. The antithesis to Edmund Waller is Erasmus Darwin (1731-1802). The greater part of the life of this remarkable man was spent at Lichfield, where he practised as a physician, and reigned as a local king of letters. From 1756 for nearly fifty years a clique of scientific and literary people, male and female, surrounded the doctor, and gave emphasis to the natural bent of his character; in the "Darwinian sphere," as Lichfield was called, the author of *The Botanic Garden* was confidently pointed to as "equal in science, superior in genius" to the "arrogant" Dr. Samuel Johnson. It was in this provincial hotbed that in 1771 was begun, slowly polished through nearly a quarter of a century, and in 1794, published, the *Zoonomia*, Darwin's valuable treatise on the laws of organic life, a work which is understood to foreshadow in a singular degree the discoveries of his illustrious descendant.

While engaged in these scientific studies, Darwin, who had cultivated with the success of an amateur an easy gift of verse, was persuaded in 1779 to embody the botanical system which bears the name of Linnæus in an elaborate poem, *The Botanic Garden*, on which for many years he expended all his leisure moments. The first instalment, containing the second part of the poem, *The Loves of the Plants*, appeared in 1789; the first part, *The Economy of Vegetation*, followed in 1792; each contains four cantos. *The Botanic Garden* is written in heroic couplets, studiously imitated from Pope, and, in a certain sense, polished to a degree that surpasses even the skill of that consummate artist. It is the extraordinary nature of Darwin's theme, however, that first attracts attention. At the opening of *The Economy of Vegetation* we find the Goddess of Botany descending to earth; she is met by Spring, attended by gnomes, nymphs, sylphs, and fire-spirits, to whom she addresses, in pompous soliloquy, the four cantos that follow. Electricity, water-nymphs in general, Captain Savery's steam-engine, the circulation of the blood, terrestrial volcanoes, the statuary of Mrs. Damer, azotic gas (represented as the Lover of the Virgin Atmosphere), Mr. Wedgwood's porcelain, the Slave Trade, the architectural taste of the Duke of Devonshire, the mechanism of the common pump, the Tornado, the Plague in Holland, and a great many other subjects, among which not the least singular is an account of the Nuptials of Pure Air and Inflammable Gas, make up the broidery of this extraordinary work. *The Loves of the Plants* is yet more luxurious and unparalleled. Here we have described "The Ovidian metamorphosis of the flowers, with their floral harems," and witness in succession the transformations of a great variety of plants, all described by their Latin names, and introduced as living personages:

> " Sofa'd on silk, amid her charm-built towers,
> Her meads of asphodel, and amaranth bowers,
> Where Sleep and Silence guard the soft abodes,
> In sullen apathy, Papaver nods.
> Faint o'er her couch, in scintillating streams,
> Pass the light forms of Fairy and of Dreams."

The machinery of the poem becomes bewildering and incongruous to the last degree; "The gnomes suspend the again silent lyre on the shrine of Hygeia; the sylphs slacken the strings, and catch the rain-drops on their shadowy pinions, whilst a Naiad prepares the Tea-Urn"; at last, while the brain whirls with preposterous images and learned array of fancy, the Goddess of Botany dismisses her gnomes and sylphs, and retires, leaving the nightingale to carry on her descant.

Darwin's object was to instruct in physical science, and to introduce to the abstruser forms of knowledge those who shrank from the routine of an educational course. He thought that by drowning it in gorgeous imagery, and by gilding it with what he conceived to be poetry, he could make idlers swallow the pill of vegetable physiology. He was, indeed, an extraordinary being, and if verve, knowledge, a brilliant vocabulary, and boundless intellectual assurance could make any man a poet, Darwin might have been one. But he has no imagination, and almost every fault of style. When he desires to seem glowing, his verses have the effect of ice; his very versification, for which he was once greatly admired, is so monotonous and so exasperatingly antithetical, that it reads like a parody of the verse of the earlier classicists. His landscapes, his sketches of character, his genre-pieces, his bursts of enthusiasm, are all of them ruined by his excessive insincerity of style, his lack of genuine vivacity, and his unceasing toil and tumidity of phrase. In his abuse of personation, as in many other qualities, he is the typical helot of eighteenth-century poetry, and the great temporary success of his amazing poem led to the final downfall of the school. To rival the *hortus siccus* of Darwin was more than the most ambitious of grandiose poetasters could hope to do. It would take us beyond the scope of the present volume to show how Darwin was ridiculed by Canning and Frere in *The Loves of the Triangles*.

In the darkness of the final decline there appeared two cometary lights which criticism finds it very difficult to assign to any definite place in the poetical heavens. Of these Ossian is one, and Rowley the other. To mention first that which seems of essentially the greater value, and that of which we certainly know the most, we find ourselves confronted with the problem of the talent of the "marvellous boy," Thomas Chatterton (1752-1770), whose fate appealed so directly to the sympathies of Wordsworth and of Keats. He was the posthumous son of a Bristol schoolmaster, and was born, on the 20th of November, in the very shadow of the noble minster of St. Mary Redcliffe. Before he was seven years of age he began to show signs of an extraordinary antiquarian precocity. His uncle was sexton of the great church, "that wonder of mansions," and the child spent his leisure hours in a chamber called the Muniment Room, where there existed certain mediæval parchments of little value. It seems certain that at a very early age Chatterton began to imitate these documents. When he was ten, he contributed poems to the local magazines; the satire called "Apostate Will" belongs to his twelfth year, and about this time (1764) he began to create the series of poetic forgeries entitled the *Rowley Poems*.

In the summer of that year the child was heard to speak mysteriously of marvellous vellum MSS. which he had discovered in Redcliffe Church, and already he found dupes among his adult acquaintance. A surgeon named Barrett, and a conceited local bibliophile, George Catcott, were the chief of those on whose credulity the adroit boy played his tunes. To these patrons he began to dribble out a series of astonishing transcripts from unknown poets of the fifteenth century—ballads, eclogues, interludes, tragedies, and the like, the whole surrounding the figure of a mythical T. Rowley, secular priest, historiographer, and laureate of Bristol. In December 1768 he sent some of the Rowley poems to the publisher Dodsley, who took no notice, and in March 1769, at the age of sixteen years and four months, Chatterton wrote the famous letter which gulled Horace Walpole, who presently formed a suspicion of the truth, and was finally enlightened by the superior critical taste of Gray. In May of the same year *Elinoure and Juga*, one of the best of the Rowley poems, appeared in a magazine, and Chatterton began to be known to the editors of journals. In April 1770 he determined to leave Bristol, and to try his fortune in London. He was tolerably successful at first, and a clever burletta, *The Revenge* (not published until 1795), was brought out at Marylebone Gardens in July. The *Balade of Charitie*, the latest of the Rowley poems, was written at the same time, but was rejected by the editors. Chatterton found himself starving. He had long contemplated suicide, and on the 24th of August 1770 he poisoned himself with arsenic in his Brook Street lodgings. His dead body was found surrounded by torn fragments of his latest poetry and prose. He had lived only seventeen years and nine months.

Chatterton's work was not allowed to disappear. Public curiosity in it grew, and when in 1777 Tyrwhitt collected it for the first time it excited a storm of controversy. Of the Rowley poems the most important were found to be the *Bristowe Tragedie*, a ballad on the death of Sir Charles Baldwin; *Ælla*, a tragical interlude in various lyrical forms, containing " As Elinor by the green arbour was sitting," and "Oh sing to me my roundelay," but mainly in a sort of Spenserian stanza; *Goddwyn*, a tragedy of the same semi-lyrical kind; *A Ballad of Charitie*, in a seven-line stanza; *The Tournament*, another "tragedy"; *The Battle of Hastings*, a heroic poem, re-written in the pseudo-Spenserian form; and a dramatic interlude called *The Parliament of Sprites*. These stanzas form part of the dialogue in *Ælla*:

" The budding floweret blushes at the light,
 The meads are sprinkled with the yellow hue;
In daisied mantles is the mountain dight,
 The nesh young cowslip bendeth with the dew;
 The trees enleafèd, unto heaven straught,
When gentle winds do blow, to whistling din are brought.

" The evening comes, and brings the dew along;
 The ruddy welkin shineth to the eyne;
Around the ale-stake minstrels sing the song;
 Young ivy round the door-post doth entwine,
 I lay me on the grass, yet, to my will,
Albeit all is fair, there lacketh something still."

So small was the critical experience of even lettered persons in that age, when what professed to be mediæval work came under their attention, that it was by no means generally admitted at first that these productions were wholly composed and deliberately presented as forgeries by the unaided hand of Chatterton. But the controversy has now ceased, and as knowledge of genuine fifteenth-century documents has become extended, the absurdity or anachronism of the Rowley alphabet, rhymes, phraseology, and metre has become evident to the most superficial student. Professor Skeat, in 1875, closed the whole dispute, and placed Chatterton's work for the first time on a firm basis, by modernising, or rather correcting, his preposterous spelling, under which his true character as a poet lay hidden as the body of the cuttle-fish lies concealed in the profusion of its ink. Chatterton's ignorance of real fifteenth-century literature was profound; his knowledge was confined to a slight acquaintance with Speght's *Chaucer*. Almost all his strange words have been traced to Kersey's *Dictionary*, and from this very incorrect authority he compiled his odd Rowley dialect. It is therefore desirable, if we wish to consider Chatterton as an original poet,—and this is the only claim he has upon our consideration,—to remove the useless curtain of his bad spelling, and to minimise his use of mechanical synonyms. This is what his wonderful mock-antique spelling looks like:

> " Whanne Sprynge came dauncynge onne a flowrette bedde,
> Dighte ynne greene Raimente of a chaungynge kynde;
> The leaves of Hawthorne boddeynge on hys hedde,
> Ande whyte Prymrosen coureynge to the Wynde;
> Thanne dydd the Shepster hys longe Albanne spredde
> Uponne the greenie Bancke and daunced arounde
> Whilest the soft Flowretts nodded onne hys hedde,
> And hys faire Lambes besprenged on the Grounde,
> Anethe hys Fote the brookelette ranne alonge,
> Whyche strolled rounde the Vale to here hys joyous Songe."

It is possible that the reaction from supposing Chatterton to have been the ignorant transcriber of ancient works of high merit has led critics to an exaggerated opinion of the value of verses now certainly written between 1760 and 1770 by a child. A very acute and learned authority has styled the *Ballad of Charitie* "the most purely artistic work perhaps of the time"; the saving "perhaps" suggesting that a doubt occurred to the writer at the moment of his enthusiasm. It is not to be denied that, in relation of his years and equipments to the vigour and bulk of his work produced, Chatterton is—let us say it boldly—the most extraordinary phenomenon of infancy in the literature of the world. To an intellect so untrammelled, to a taste so mature, to an art so varied and so finished at the age of seventeen, twenty years more of life might have sufficed to put the possessor by the side of Milton and perhaps of Shakespeare. But when we come to think not of what was promised, but of what was actually achieved, and to compare it with the finished poems of Thomson and Goldsmith, of Collins and Gray, some moderation of our rapture seems demanded. Our estimate of the complete originality of the Rowley poems must be tempered by a recollection of the existence of *The Castle of Indolence* and *The School-mistress*, of the popularity of Percy's *Reliques* and the *Odes* of Gray, and of the revival of a taste for Gothic literature and art which dates from Chatterton's infancy. Hence the claim which has been made for Chatterton as the father of the Romantic School, and as having influenced the actual style of Coleridge and Keats, though supported with great ability, appears to be overcharged. So also the positive praise given to the *Rowley Poems*, as artistic productions full of rich colour and romantic melody, may be deprecated without any refusal to recognise those qualities in measure. There are frequent flashes of brilliancy in Chatterton, and one or two very perfectly sustained pieces, but the main part of his work, if rigorously isolated from the melodramatic romance of his career, is surely found to be rather poor reading, the work of a child of exalted genius, no doubt, yet manifestly the work of a child all through. His acknowledged poems are more mature, but still less pleasing. His satires show

how very little mental training or knowledge of the world were needed to equip a Churchill. *Kew Gardens* is quite as good, or as bad, as *Gotham* or *The Times;* while *The Prophecy*, of which we give a couple of stanzas, is perhaps the most terse and vivid political lyric of the age :

> " When vile Corruption's brazen face
> At council-board shall take her place ;
> And lords and commoners resort
> To welcome her at Britain's court ;
> Look up, ye Britons ! cease to sigh,
> For your redemption draweth nigh.
>
> " See Pension's harbour, large and clear,
> Defended by St. Stephen's pier !
> The entrance safe, by current led,
> Tiding round Grafton's jetty-head !
> Look up, ye Britons ! cease to sigh,
> For your redemption draweth nigh."

The Ossian problem has not proved so easy of solution as the Rowley problem. The wild Gaelic rhapsodies which formed the taste of so many would-be lovers of romance, from David Hume to the great Napoleon, were first given to the world under very suspicious circumstances by James Macpherson (1738-1796), an ambitious Highland schoolmaster, in 1760, in the form of a tiny volume of fragments from the Erse language. The reading public was very much interested in these supposed translations, and certain friends of literature, including Boswell, "Douglas" Home, Hugh Blair, and Lord Lynedoch, subscribed to enable Macpherson to travel through the Highlands and the Hebrides in search of oral poetry. The result was the most important of all the Ossian literature—the ancient epic of *Fingal*, in six books, published in quarto in 1762. To this volume Macpherson prefixed an essay on the antiquity of these verses, which he confidently attributed to Ossian, a Gaelic bard of the third century. Sixteen other pieces were appended to *Fingal*, to fill up the volume. Of these the most striking were *Temora, Oithoma*, and *Croma;* but so far as style and subject were concerned there was really very little to choose between them all. This was the sort of thing, a rhapsody in modulated prose :

"Pleasant is thy voice in Ossian's ear, daughter of car-borne Scroglan ! But retire to the hall of shells : to the beam of the burning oak. Attend to the murmur of the sea : it rolls at Dunscaich's walls : let sleep descend on thy blue eyes, and the hero come to thy dreams.

"Cuchullin sits at Lego's lake, at the dark rolling of waters. Night is around the hero ; and his thousands spread on the heath : a hundred oaks burn in the midst ; the feast of shells is smoking wide. Carril strikes the harp, beneath a tree ; his gray locks glitter in the beam ; the rustling blast of night is near, and lights his aged hair. This song is of the blue Togorma, and of its chief, Cuchullin's friend."

Temora proving attractive, Macpherson enlarged it to eight books, and published it separately in 1763. A controversy instantly sprang up between those who believed and those who disbelieved in the authenticity of these works. For ten years, till the very name of Ossian became a weariness, people argued up and down. Macpherson found a sturdy sceptic in Dr. Johnson, and, becoming insolent, dared to provoke the sage with personal threats, so that Johnson provided himself with a strong oaken plant, headed with a knob as large as an orange. As an original writer Macpherson became more and more discredited, but as an individual more and more wealthy ; and, to prove that no honour lies beyond the grasp of unprincipled mediocrity, he was buried in Poet's Corner.

The vagueness and unreality of the natural phenomena described in Ossian have long been felt to be one of the great objections to its genuineness. No particulars are vouchsafed which enable us to form a distinct idea of the dress or food of the warriors, of their customs or religion, or even of the animal world in which they moved, for the eagle and the whale positively exhaust the list of Ossian's finned and feathered fauna. Again, the uncultured and inartistic measures in which Macpherson's originals are composed are understood to be wholly foreign to the genius of ancient Gaelic poetry, which is ruled by a complex and elaborate metrical system. Moreover, such certainly genuine examples of Gaelic verse as have been preserved, going back, not indeed to the third, but possibly to the eleventh century, are archaically pure and simple in style, with no trace of the turgid pomp of Ossian. But most important of all, perhaps, is the statement of the best Gaelic scholars, that the language of Ossian is a modern and mutilated form of Erse which did not exist five hundred years ago. Macpherson was extremely disingenuous with regard to his documents, and what he did at last produce was so much rubbish. Even Dr. Johnson could gauge the antiquity of "the dusky manuscript of Egg." Curiously enough, although Macpherson died suddenly, his papers were searched in vain for a scrap of evidence for or against his culpability. In these days few will be credulous enough to pin their faith to the misty songs of Ullin; but there are probably some persons of intelligence, especially north of the Tay, who still "indulge the pleasing supposition that Fingal fought and Ossian sang."

Although the plan of this work excludes partial reference to writers the main part of whose production belongs to the period dealt with in the succeeding volume, an exception must be made by a brief allusion to the plays of Richard Brinsley Sheridan (1751-1816), whose career as a dramatist practically closed when he was twenty-seven years of age. His first appearance was with *The Rivals* (1775), an amazing feat in comedy for a young man of twenty-four, not much resembling life indeed, but full of whim and wit and theatrical activity. In the same year Sheridan not merely brought out a farce, but took the town by storm with the laughable opera of *The Duenna*. In this he owed something to Wycherley, and he borrowed more from Vanbrugh in his comedy of *A Trip to Scarborough* (1777); but in May of the same year he suddenly achieved a very great and entirely original success with what is perhaps the best existing English comedy of intrigue, *The School for Scandal*. This play was produced by Sheridan in his capacity of proprietor of Drury Lane Theatre. For years the popularity of *The School for Scandal* "damped the new pieces," and it is still one of the safest favourites of the public. Two years later the brilliant extravaganza of *The Critic* closed the list of Sheridan's dramatic successes. These dramas are among the most familiar of all products of English genius. A period of only one month separated the first appearance of *The Rivals* from that of *Le Barbier de Séville*, and it is not unworthy of notice that Sheridan is in a certain sense the Beaumarchais of the English stage. Each of these playwrights marked the return of theatrical taste to the Molière ideal of conventional comedy, after a brief interval of *drame larmoyante*. In Sheridan's case the direct inspiration came, not so much from Molière, as from the masters of English Restoration comedy, whose merits he imitated with a happy exclusion of their worst faults. The decade from 1770 to 1780 was a blossoming-time for English comedy, since it saw the performance not only of *She Stoops to Conquer*, and of Sheridan's pieces, but of *The West Indian* of Richard Cumberland (1732-1811), *Three Weeks after Marriage* of Arthur Murphy (1727-1805), and *The Belle's Stratagem* of Hannah Parkhouse (Mrs. Cowley—1743-1809). These pieces are of various literary value, but they are all in possession of a considerable share of the *vis comica*, and all agree in making laughter and the amusement which arises from brisk movement and incisive wit, rather than didactic moralising or an appeal to sentiment, their principal aim. In other words, so far as they went, they marked a distinct return to the pure tradition of comedy.

While all the forms of serious poetry were declining in England, and the higher species of lyric for a time absolutely disappeared, verse of the native order and a strain of spontaneous song began to flourish north of the Tweed. The scholars of Allan Ramsay, with Hamilton of Bangour at their head, take hands with the precursors of Burns through Alexander Ross of Lochlee (1699-1784), who, at the age of eighty, collected his pastoral Doric ditties in a volume called *Helenore*, in 1778. The poem which gives its name to this volume, "Helenore, or the Fortunate Shepherdess," seems to have been written before 1740, in direct rivalry with Allan Ramsay. It is in some respects unique, particularly as being the most ambitious narrative work in Scots written, perhaps, down to the present time; it is composed in the heroic measure, and extends to more than four thousand verses. An elaborate story of homely Scottish life is told with some skill, an almost Chaucerian simplicity, and much occasional picturesqueness, disguised by the rough dialect. This is a portrait of the heroine:

> " Now Nory was the bonniest lassie grown
> Was to be seen a-landward or in town;
> Three halyears younger she than Lindy was,
> But for her growth was meikle about a pass;
> Her hair was like the very threads of goud,
> First hang well down, then back in ringlets row'd;
> Pure red and white, her mother o'er again,
> And bonnier,—gin bonnier could ha' been.
> Ye could na look your sairin' at her face,
> So meek it was, so sweet, so fu' o' grace.
> Her cherry-cheeks ye might bleed wi' a strae;
> Syne was she swift and souple like a rae,
> Swack like an eel, and calour like a trout."

Alexander Ross eked *Helenore* out with some good songs—in particular, "Woo'd and married and a'," and "What ails the lasses at me?" But he wrote nothing so spirited as the *Tullochgorum* of the Rev. John Skinner (1721-1807), which Burns called "the best Scotch song Scotland ever saw":

> " There needs na' be sae great a phrase,
>   Wi' dringing dull Italian lays;
> I wadna gie our ain strathspeys
>   For half a hundred score o' 'em.
>
> " They're douff and dowie at the best,
>   Douff and dowie, douff and dowie,
> They're douff and dowie at the best
>   Wi' a' their variorum.
>
> " They're douff and dowie at the best,
>   Their allegros and a' the rest,
> They canna please a Scottish taste
>   Compar'd wi' Tullochgorum."

About 1765 there began to spring up all over the Lowlands a tendency to put the homely events of life and its tender emotions to untrammelled and tuneful ballad-measures. Tibbie Pagan (1740-1821), the hunchbacked hostess of an Ayrshire alehouse, was the first to prophesy of the full music of Burns in her sincere and thrilling "Ca' the Yowes":

> "Ca' the yowes to the knowes,
> Ca' them where the heather grows,
> Ca' them where the burnie rows,
> My bonnie dearie."

In 1771 Lady Anne Barnard (1750-1825) wrote her immortal "Auld Robin Gray." Jean Adams, to whom is now commonly attributed the honour of having enriched the language with "And are ye sure the news is true," belongs to a slightly earlier period:

> "Sae true his words, sae smooth his speech,
> His breath's like caller air!
> His very foot has music in't,
> As he comes up the stair.
> And will I see his face again?
> And will I hear him speak?
> I'm downright dizzie wi' the thought,—
> In troth, I'm like to greet."

It is indeed remarkable how prominent a place was taken by women of every rank in this revival of North British song. At first the stream was often clouded by the conventional phraseology of the age, as in "Lewie Gordon" we read, side by side with

> "O to see his tartan trews,
> Bonnet blue and laigh-heel'd shoes,
> Philabeg aboon his knee;
> He's the lad that I'll gang wi'."—

such a Whitehead or Langhorne stanza as,

> "This lovely lad of whom I sing
> Is fitted to become a king;
> And on his breast he wears a star,
> You'd tak' him for the god of war."

The only cure for such errors of convention was a complete plunge into the pure local dialect. This was not fully understood until it was exemplified in the practice of Fergusson.

Thirteen years before Burns arrived in Edinburgh there had passed away in a Scotch lunatic asylum, under circumstances acutely distressing, a youth whose temperament and genius had been the foreshadowing of Burns's own. The memory of Robert Fergusson (1750-1774), indeed, awakened in the breast of Burns an almost excessive passion of sympathy, admiration, and regret. It was the reading of Fergusson's little volume of 1773 which had induced Burns to take up the art of native poetry seriously, and it has been happily said that the works of the earlier and lesser minstrel were the *juvenilia* of this great poet. After Burns's ecstatic praise, the reader turns to Fergusson with some disappointment. A great part of his little book is filled with odes in the manner of Collins, with eclogues, with Shenstonian ballads. His burlesque heroics are better, and celebrate phases of Edinburgh society in smart English couplets. But his genius is revealed by the narrow section of his *Scots Poems*, and particularly by those lyrics in what we think of as the Burns stanza, "Caller Oysters," "Daft Days," "Caller Water," and "To the Tron Kirk Bell." In his "Hallow-Fair," his "Ode to the Gowdspink," and "Auld Reikie," he comes nearer to Burns than any other Scottish poet of earlier or later times:

> " At Hallowmas, whan nichts grow lang,
> And starries shine fu' clear,
> Whan fouk the nippin' cauld to bang,
> Their winter hap-warms wear,
> Near Edinburgh a fair there hauds,
> I wat there's nane whase name is,
> For strappin' dames and sturdy lads,
> And cap and stoup, mair famous
>   Than it that day.

> " Upo' the tap o' ilka lum
> The sun began to keek,
> And bade the trig-made maidens come
> A sightly joe to seek

> At Hallow-Fair, where browsters rare
> Keep gude ale on the gantries,
> And dinna scrimp ye o' a skair
> O' kebbucks frae their pantries
> Fu' saut that day.
>
> "Here chapman billies tak' their stand,
> And shaw their bonny wallies;
> Wow! but they lie fu' gleg off hand
> To trick the silly fallows;
> Hech, sirs! what cairds and tinklers come,
> And ne'er-do-weel horse-coupers,
> And spae-wives fenzying to be dumb,
> Wi' a' sic-like landloupers,
> To thrive that day!"

Fergusson is familiar, however, as Burns never was, with the town life of the poor in Edinburgh, and he is perhaps most himself when he paints the world as he saw it from his desk in the office of the Commissary Clerk. Not very great in himself, a knowledge of Fergusson is yet a necessary introduction to the complete study of Burns.

In closing a description of the poetry of an age, there is a great temptation to draw the threads neatly together in an effective conclusion. But in the case of the eighteenth century this can be done only at the expense of truth. That system of poetics which sprang into existence with Waller, became dominant under Dryden, reached its pinnacle in Pope, and was continued by Goldsmith and Johnson, after being partially transformed by Thomson and Gray, did not finish in any glow of Alexandrianism, nor reach, except in Darwin, any final Gongorian extravagance. It simply divided its current into shallow streams and sank in the desert, leaving a dry district between itself and the approaching flood of romanticism. By 1780 every poem which we have mentioned was either produced or planned, and nothing in a similar style, of even fifth-rate promise, was being given to the world. The names of the candidates for fame were such as John Wolcot, Anna Seward "the Swan of Lichfield," the guileless Anna Letitia

Barbauld, and the amorous votaries of Della Crusca. Even these nonentities belong to a slightly later date. Of the great, or even of the considerable poets of the new era, only two had hitherto given any specimens of their art, and those most unimportant ones, to the public; since of what was in store for English poetry little could be guessed from *The Olney Hymns* or *The Candidate*. If Cowper and Crabbe were still unknown, the rest of the chorus was immature indeed. Blake, the visionary engraver's apprentice, had still his *Poetical Sketches* snug in the table-drawer. Burns, yet unambitious, was roving "where busy ploughs are whistling thrang," a fresh-coloured farmboy and no more. Wordsworth was a child of ten, Scott and Coleridge eight years old, Landor five, Campbell three, Byron and the rest not born. So, partly by the accidental shortening of the lives of the most eminent poets of the passing age, since neither Gray nor Thomson nor Collins nor Goldsmith nor Chatterton lived to be an elderly man, a calm and fallow period was left between the extinction of the old and the creation of the new school. The artificial poetry died of sheer exhaustion, as last year's leaves fall off without waiting for the new buds to push them from their places. When Cowper and Crabbe, Wordsworth and Coleridge, were ready to try their new effects, there was no resistance to their music. They piped upon an empty stage to an audience whose appetite for song had been whetted by a long interval of perfect hush, in a theatre where even the nibblings of such a mouse as Hayley could be heard through the portentous silence.

CHAPTER XI

THE PROSE OF THE DECADENCE

THE presence of two writers of incomparable splendour makes the prose field of the close of our period seem more attractive than the poetic. But in reality we trace the same elements in the former as in the latter. The anxieties of the American War, the hollow calm which preceded the French Revolution, the general interest in and apprehension regarding purely political questions, seem to have deadened the intellectual life of the country, or to have diverted it into the channels of action. Between 1770 and 1780 the pamphlet once more became the vehicle of what was most strenuous and impassioned in contemporary writing, and books, though still numerous enough, did not, with a few exceptions, possess much vitality. Johnson was dictator through all this generation, and beyond it; and what was best in prose was supported, directly or indirectly, by his influence—directly in the cases of Burke, Goldsmith, and Boswell; indirectly in that of Gibbon. Magnificence of phrase, something of the tumid pomp of Johnson, became requisite in all serious prose writing; and both Gibbon and Burke added the glory of colour to the splendour of form of the Lexicographer. In the hands of these two masters the prose of the eighteenth century did not sink into insignificance, as poetry did in the hands of the versifiers, but became so heavy with gold and jewels, so radiant with massy ornaments of bullion, that the first duty of the next generation was to simplify it, and to reduce the volume of the sonorous sentences. In this regard, Gibbon, who died unaffected in style by a coming post-revolutionary age, is more typical of the school than Burke, who carried his impassioned rhetoric over into a new atmosphere, and became almost a modern nineteenth-century writer.

Entirely untouched by this magnificence, which we have suggested as characteristic of the period, is Oliver Goldsmith (1728-1774), whose graceful poetry and cheerful comedies have already occupied our attention, and who must now be considered as one of the most delicate of English prose-writers. Goldsmith was born in Pallas, in County Longford, on the 10th November 1728, but spent his childhood at Lissoy, in Westmeath, the putative "Auburn" of *The Deserted Village*. In 1744 he went to Trinity College, Dublin, as a sizar, and enjoyed a wretchedly undistinguished university career. He was rejected for holy orders, he proposed to run away to America, he tried the law, and at last, in 1753, he managed to be admitted into the Medical School in Edinburgh. Goldsmith was idle, unattractive, and unpromising as a youth, and at six-and-twenty seemed to be as fine an example of the hopeless ne'er-do-weel as any one might wish to see. At that age he went over to Leyden, took a very obscure and dubious degree at Louvain, and then, in imitation of Baron Holberg, set out as a pedestrian flute-player, or, as he observed to Johnson, "disputed his passage through Europe" for a year.

His first introduction to the purlieus of literature was made by his appointment as proof-reader to the press of Samuel Richardson, while in 1757 he engaged himself to work for the *Monthly Review* of the bookseller Griffiths. Goldsmith's life was still for a long while full of troubles; no man was ever slower in finding work to which he could successfully set his hand. One appointment after another came to nothing; he tried at last to earn his bread as an hospital mate, but was rejected in Surgeon's Hall as not qualified. It was in his thirty-second year that his first original book saw the light, a little *Enquiry into the Present State of Polite Learning in Europe* (1759), a presumptuous, but very bright and daring little treatise in criticism. Goldsmith now got plenty of journalistic work to do, and in 1762 he achieved a place in literature with the two volumes of his delightful *Citizen of the World*, at first anonymous. In these letters he frankly imitated Montesquieu, but in a manner so fresh and brisk, with so gay a vein of satire, that this little book remains one of the classics of the century.

The biographers of Goldsmith, however, have rightly observed that his success had become assured before this, and that the "birthday of his life" was the 31st of May 1761, when Percy brought the great Johnson, in a new wig, to sup at Goldsmith's lodgings in Wine Office Court. From this moment to the close of Goldsmith's life the great good tyrant of literature watched over him like an elder brother, and took care that Goldsmith's delicate and easily disheartened temperament should never be so strained by dejection as to lack elasticity for the rebound. One of the mysteries of eighteenth-century biography is the tangled web of anecdote which attributes to Johnson the sale of a novel which Goldsmith had in 1762 already planned, if not completely written, *The Vicar of Wakefield*. Exceedingly confused is the whole history of this famous book, which seems to have been sold in sections, at various times, to various publishers. Meanwhile, Goldsmith was engaged in hack-work of all kinds, and never again, until the close of his weary career, was he free from the toil of book-building, the compilation of readable, but above all, of saleable summaries of second-hand knowledge. The names of these works, which do not belong to literature, although Goldsmith signed their title-pages, cannot be expected here. The miracle is that, doomed as he was to trail a pen in the service of these freebooters of Grub Street, he ever found time or inclination for the production of his private masterpieces. In 1765 he arrests our attention, not merely by his appearance as a poet, but by the facts that he collected his agreeable *Essays* into a volume, and that he moved from Islington into lodgings, first in Wine Office Court, and then in the Temple, where he received his friends in purple silk breeches and a scarlet roquelaure buttoned to the chin.

Goldsmith was now fairly well known to the literary public, and in March 1766 he became more so by the publication of his belated novel, *The Vicar of Wakefield*. Mr. Austin Dobson has lately proved that this famous book did not please so quickly and so completely as has been taken for granted. Goldsmith received £60 for it, but it hardly paid its expenses during his lifetime. It has been pointed out that Goethe was one of the first critics to give *The Vicar* its full and unstinted measure of praise, and to insist on its recognition as not merely a pleasing or a well-written but as an immortal story. Its place in literature is now fixed beyond all possibility of dislodgment. In the sudden and unexplained decline of the English novel it is the only book of the second generation which holds its rank with the masterpieces of the first, with the novels of Richardson, Fielding, and Smollett. It is deeply to be deplored that this fresh and bright, though immature, *Joseph Andrews* of Goldsmith's was succeeded by no *Tom Jones* of its author's finished prime. But the entire body of Goldsmith's works is a collection of specimens and fragments. In 1768 the success of *The Good Natur'd Man* emboldened the improvident Goldsmith to fit out another and a too splendid apartment in Brick Court, and with this he was shackled until he died. Many a child of twelve has a juster sense of the value of money, and what it will or will not fetch, than this adult creature of genius.

Writing copiously and continuously, Goldsmith from this time forth added nothing to prose literature which has lived. Biographies and histories, "brevities" and "abridgments," make up the tale of his hurried and painful struggle to win enough to keep his payments abreast of his engagements. He was an honest soul, if ever there lived one, but he had none of the convenient Philistine virtues, and all the good advice and sound sense of Johnson could not keep him from dying £2000 in debt. It has been thought that he was describing himself when, in the *Enquiry into Polite Learning*, he speaks of an author as one whose "simplicity exposes him to all the insidious approaches of cunning, his sensibility to the slightest invasions of contempt, though possessed of fortitude to stand unmoved the expected bursts of an earthquake, yet of feelings so exquisitely poignant as to agonise under the slightest disappointment." In 1769 Goldsmith was appointed Professor of History to the new Royal Academy; but as this honour brought no emolument, he said it was like a pair of ruffles to a man without a shirt. Almost the last event in his troubled life was the production of *She Stoops to Conquer* in 1773; before the bustle which attended this play in its first success had subsided, the author succumbed, in his forty-sixth year, to a complaint which fed with ease on his exhausted constitution. This was on the 4th of April 1774.

In prose style, as in poetic, it is noticeable that Goldsmith has little in common with his great contemporaries, with their splendid bursts of rhetoric, and Latin pomp of speech, but that he goes back to the perfect plainness and simple grace of the Queen Anne men. He aims at a straightforward effect of pathos or of humour, accompanied, as a rule, with a colloquial ease of expression, an apparent absence of all effort or calculation. It is remarkable that it is only in his *Enquiry into Polite Learning*, which was written before he personally knew Johnson, that he makes any pretension to the sesquipedalian bow-wow. Perhaps, when he came to know Johnson privately, he was influenced less by that great man's writings than by his simple, humorous, and powerful conversation. Few English writers, always excepting Johnson, hold so prominent a place as Goldsmith in literary anecdote. We know him as though we had lived with him, and see the rough ugly face, with its bright smile, the awkward limbs tricked out beyond the fashion with the Tyrian bloom of velvets and of satins, the guttural Irish voice that tripped itself up upon the hesitating lips,—in short, the living portrait of the wonderful man who wore his heart upon his sleeve and found plenty of daws to peck at it. No figure, for all its shortcomings, is more endeared to us than his; and above all criticism of the poems, the prose, the dramas, some of which, to say the truth, a less interesting person than he might have composed, there rises the extraordinary sympathy and curiosity with which we follow the individual Oliver Goldsmith, and to this day our hearts are stirred in thinking of him by the "sodalium amor" and the "amicorum fides" quite as much as by the "lectorum veneratio."

His most sustained prose-work, *The Vicar of Wakefield*, is founded in form upon the tradition of the novel as Fielding had laid it down. It is, however, less carefully constructed than the most shambling of that writer's stories, and shows a retrograde step towards the incredible and conventional romances of an earlier generation. With these faults of construction, however, *The Vicar* mingles such a modern sweetness and tenderness, such grace of portraiture, and, above all, such inimitable humour, that we never think of comparing it to its disadvantage with its stronger and coarser forerunners. But if we set aside our familiarity with it as a tale, and try to think of it afresh as a literary work, we shall probably be inclined to admit that it is more like an extended episode, in the *Spectator* manner, than a story, and that Fielding would have discoursed in vain if the British novel, after its superb start, had gracefully trotted back again into its stable in this way. As Goldsmith wrote but one novel, we cannot tell how far he might have succeeded in developing his powers of narrative construction; but the happiest passages in *The Citizen of the World* and the *Essays* give us the impression that a long and realistic study of the development of emotion was beyond his powers, or, which is perhaps the same thing, contrary to his inclination. He loved to draw the portrait of a single creation, half-grotesque, half-pathetic,—a Beau Tibbs or a Man in Black, a Dr. Primrose or a Moses,—and to finish it so highly that we can see it to this day like a figure by some great Dutch master; but he was not very successful in making these people move in concerted action, and it is when he tries to set them about the work of human life that we smile indulgently because we see that they are puppets. To select a fragment from one of Goldsmith's highly-finished episodes is difficult, and cannot be satisfactory. From the trilogy of Beau Tibbs, from the three superb chapters dedicated to that famous gentleman's gentleman in *The Citizen of the World*, we may borrow a page:

"We waited some time for Mrs. Tibbs's arrival, during which interval I had a full opportunity of surveying the chamber and all its furniture, which consisted of four chairs with old wrought bottoms, that he assured me was his wife's embroidery; a square table that had been once japanned; a cradle in one corner, a lumbering cabinet in the other; a broken shepherdess, and a mandarin without a head, were stuck over the chimney; and round the walls several paltry unframed pictures, which, he observed, were all his own drawing. 'What do you think, sir, of that head i' the corner, done in the manner of Grisoni? There's the true keeping in it; it is my own face, and though there happens to be no likeness, a Countess offered me a hundred guineas for its fellow; I refused her, for, hang it, that would be mechanical, you know.'

"The wife at last made her appearance, at once a slattern and a coquette, much emaciated, but still carrying the remains of beauty. She made twenty apologies for being seen in such odious dishabille, but hoped to be excused, as she had stayed out all night at Vauxhall Gardens with the Countess, who was excessively fond of the horns. 'And, indeed, my dear,' added she, turning to her husband, 'his lordship drank your health in a bumper.' 'Poor Jack!' cries he, 'a dear good-natured creature, I know he loves me. But I hope, my dear, you have given orders for dinner; you need make no great preparations neither, there are but three of us; something elegant, and little will do,—a turbot, an ortolan, a ——' 'Or what do you think, my dear,' interrupts the wife, 'of a nice pretty bit of ox-cheek, piping hot, and dressed with a little of my own sauce?' 'The very thing!' replies he; 'it will eat best with some smart bottled beer; but be sure to let us have the sauce his Grace was so fond of. I hate your immense loads of meat; that is country all over;. extremely disgusting to those who are in the least acquainted with high life.'"

The historian of literature will scarcely reach the name of Edward Gibbon (1737-1794) without emotion. It is not merely that with this name is associated one of the most splendid works which Europe produced in the eighteenth century, but that the character of the author, with all its limitations and even with all its faults, presents us with a typical specimen of the courage and single-heartedness of a great man of letters. Wholly devoted to scholarship without pedantry, and to his art without any of the petty vanity of the literary artist, the life of Gibbon was one long sacrifice to the purest intellectual enthusiasm. He lived to know, and to rebuild his knowledge in a shape as durable and as magnificent as a Greek temple. He was content for years and years to lie unseen, unheard of, while younger men rose past him into rapid reputation. No unworthy impatience to be famous, no sense of the uncertainty of life, no weariness or terror at the length or the breadth of his self-imposed task, could induce him at any moment of weakness to give way to haste or discouragement in the persistent regular collection and digestion of his material or in the harmonious execution of every part of his design. His life was not long, but it sufficed to bring him his reward, and he survived to finish what is, no doubt, the most majestic solitary work which comes before us for mention in the present volume. On this work he was engaged without intermission for fifteen years, and it must not be forgotten that to this period should properly be added one at least as long during which the future historian was charging his mind with the learning that afterwards sat so lightly on his memory. No man who honours the profession of letters, or regards with respect the higher and more enlightened forms of scholarship, will ever think without admiration of the noble genius of Gibbon.

Like Gray, Gibbon was the sole survivor of a numerous family of children, and retained through life a certain physical sluggishness and the proofs of an inelastic constitution. He was born on the 27th of April 1737, at Putney. He was of gentle birth, and would have been very wealthy, but that his father squandered the family resources. Notwithstanding this last fact, however, Gibbon was relieved all his life from the necessity of working for his bread. Had it not been so, with his temperament, we may confidently say that he would never have become famous. His health as a child was miserable; but at fifteen his complaints left him, and his father immediately sent him, backward and ignorant as he was, to Magdalen College, Oxford. His experience of the university was most unfavourable. He says: "I spent fourteen months at Magdalen College; they proved the most idle and unprofitable of my whole life." The fact is that the universities were, at that time, what Junius called them, "peaceful scenes of slumber and thoughtless meditation." At the age of sixteen Gibbon became a Catholic, a step of which he has given us a curious and minute description in his *Memoirs*. As the religious disposition was never developed in him, we must suppose that it was as a logician that he was converted. He says that he "fell by a noble hand," that of Bossuet. The result of taking a step so unusual in English society of that day was, that his father instantly exiled him to Lausanne, to the house of a distinguished pastor, whose instructions were to reconvert Gibbon to Protestantism. At the close of 1754 this task was successfully achieved, but Gibbon continued to remain at Lausanne, where he was very happy, for five years. It was during his Swiss sojourn that the intense thirst for literary knowledge sprang up in him and began to be satisfied. He read incessantly, and with fine judgment, not only the whole range of classical, and particularly Latin authors, but all that was worth reading in the recent literature of France. He had been transplanted from England so early, and in so crude a condition, that he threw off, to a degree not equalled by any of his contemporaries, the insular prejudices of his age.

In 1758 Gibbon hastily returned to England, and in the breach which this step made in the regular course of his studies was induced to enter the militia, which proved a most absorbing distraction. It has been thought wholly incongruous that the author of the *Decline and Fall* should spend several years marching from a guard-room to a country inn, and then back again to barracks; and he himself declares that the militia was unfit for and unworthy of him. But he took a great interest in military tactics, and carried Quintus Icilius with him when he camped under canvas. The result is seen in the lucidity and vigour of his battle-pieces. As he says in the *Memoirs*, "the Captain of the Hampshire Grenadiers (the reader may smile) has not been useless to the historian of the Roman Empire." While he was in the militia, in 1761, Gibbon published, in French, his first work, an

Essai sur l'Etude de la Littérature, which, to say the truth, shows but little promise. In January 1763, being freed from the bondage of his marchings and countermarchings, Gibbon escaped once more to the Continent.

Passing leisurely through France and Switzerland, Gibbon reached Italy at last, and it was here that the central object of his life suddenly flashed upon his consciousness. In a famous sentence he tells us "it was at Rome, on the 15th of October 1764, as I sat musing amid the ruins of the Capitol, while the barefooted friars were singing vespers in the temple of Jupiter, that the idea of writing the Decline and Fall of the City first started to my mind." He returned home, and from a phrase in the *Memoirs*, we may believe that he very soon began to accumulate materials. His life now became sequestered and disturbed. His father had wasted the family property, and the son was threatened with poverty. We know little more of Gibbon's career until 1770, except that he started one or two unsuccessful historical projects, which have survived in fragmentary form. In the latter year his father died, and Gibbon withdrew from the country, to keep house as a bachelor in what was then the West End of London. Before making this change he plunged into polemics by publishing a pamphlet of *Observations on the Sixth Book of the Æneid*, designed, if possible, to ruffle the complacency of Warburton. When settled in London he began, for the first time, to move in society, and to form literary friendships; but his gifts do not seem to have awakened as yet any general notice.

From 1770 to 1773 Gibbon worked away quietly and secretly on the three opening volumes of his *Decline and Fall*. No one, not even John Baker Holroyd, afterwards Lord Sheffield, and Gibbon's most intimate friend through life (1741-1821), suspected what was the magnitude or importance of this undertaking. On a subject so interesting as the inception of his masterpiece, no words can equal in value those of the historian himself. He says: "At the outset all was dark and doubtful; even the title of the work, the true era of the decline and fall of the empire, the limits of the introduction, the division of the chapters, and the order of the narrative." After seven years, he was sometimes inclined to destroy all that he had written. "Many experiments," he continues, "were made before I could hit the middle tone between a dull tone and a rhetorical declamation. Three times did I compose the first chapter, and twice the second and third, before I was tolerably satisfied with their effect. In the remainder of the way I advanced with a more equal and easy pace." Yet the difficulty in starting is still felt by the reader in a certain restlessness of style and comparative lack of charm throughout the first volume.

From 1774 to 1783 Gibbon was in Parliament. His life as a member and as a civilian is, happily, of no interest to us here, and we need not be concerned to know that he undertook a public career without ambition and pursued it without patriotism. He was desirous of being no worse than his neighbours as a citizen of England, but in truth he cut a sorry figure as the representative of Liskeard, and as a *fainéant* Lord of Trade. This was not his world, and his laxity as a politician contrasts strangely with his modesty, ardour, and unshaken sincerity as a scholar and man of letters. Early in 1776 the first volume of the *Decline and Fall of the Roman Empire*, a large quarto, containing exactly as much as two of the ordinary octavo volumes of the reprint, appeared in London. It enjoyed an immense and instant success. It "was on every table and almost on every toilet." In 1781 volumes ii. and iii. appeared. Superior as they were in charm and finish, weightier in judgment and purer in style, they did not please so completely. The town was accustomed to the manner that had seemed so unique, and the clergy, disgusted with the tone of the last two chapters of volume i., had raised no inconsiderable cabal against the book. Gibbon thought it needful to pause, and to reply, but he was not born to be a disputant. It was more to the point that, though he revoked nothing, he altered his tone towards Christianity, and the remainder of the history contains nothing which can be compared for offence with the too-famous fifteenth and sixteenth chapters.

Finding it needful to retrench his expenses, in 1783 Gibbon broke up his London house, and transported all his household gods to Lausanne, where an old and intimate friend, M. Deyverdun, resided. Here he was very calm and happy for several years of strenuous, patient labour. Volume iv. was almost finished before he left London; v. and vi. were entirely written in Lausanne. It was on the night of the 27th of June 1787 that, a little before midnight, rising from the last lines of the last page, which he had just completed, he walked to and fro on the moonlit terrace over the Lake of Geneva, and formulated those reflections, at once so simple and so pathetic, which are familiar to us all. The *Decline and Fall of the Roman Empire*, the most magnificent trophy of historic art in the eighteenth century, was now complete, to the most delicate carvings on its elaborate architrave. In the summer of 1788 the three last volumes were published in London.

The rest of Gibbon's record is the story of physical collapse and decline, the withering of the aloe which had put forth one such momentous blossom. Friend after friend was taken from him; the French Revolution passed over Lausanne, and in the summer of 1793 the exhausted and invalided Gibbon made a painful flight back to England. Old long before his years, and weighted with a cluster of complaints, he passed away in London very stoically early on the morning of the 15th of January 1794. In person Gibbon was stout and grotesquely hideous; "his mouth, mellifluous as Plato's, was a round hole nearly in the centre of his visage." Shy and hesitating among strangers and those who were indifferent to him, he shone as a talker in the best society, and Colman, who often heard him, has an ingenious passage comparing him with Johnson as a social figure. "Johnson's style [in conversation] was grand, and Gibbon's elegant; the stateliness of the former was sometimes pedantic, and the latter was occasionally finical. Johnson marched to kettledrums and trumpets, Gibbon moved to flutes and hautboys." Gibbon never married, but he preserved through life a Platonic sentiment for the charming Suzanne Necker, the mother of Madame de Staël; he was eminent for the warmth and duration of his friendships, and for his loyalty to those who were connected with him by family ties. In religion, after his early escapade to Catholicism, he was a pronounced free-thinker, yet this fact is rather divined from than revealed in his writings, where he is usually careful to preserve all possible religious decorum. The absence, however, of any apparent conception of what was mystical and enthusiastic in the creed of the early Church is a serious blot on a work, the historic temper of which might else seem nearly perfect.

It is proper to compare Gibbon with Hume and Robertson, but he is as different from them both as they are like one another. With those his predecessors, when charm of language, variety of reflection, and vigour of narrative are put aside, comparatively little that is serious remains, except a certain freshness of vision and clearness of tact that often enables each of them, but particularly Hume, to be right when he had taken no trouble to be so. Gibbon has all these qualities, but he has one which is far greater. As Freeman has put it, " He remains the one historian of the eighteenth century whom modern research has neither set aside nor threatened to set aside." His design, as the same authority remarks, is encyclopædic, and his execution so accurate, so broad, so free of the distortions of prejudice, founded upon so vast a knowledge of documents, that it can never become antiquated. " Whatever else is read, Gibbon must be read too."

Gibbon's great work falls into three divisions, at the end of each of which it might, if needful, have closed with propriety, namely, from the Antonines to Constantine, thence on to the Fall of Rome, and thence to the Capture of Constantinople by the Turks. In covering this vast area without sign of fatigue, Gibbon showed the scope of his genius; but to enter in the smallest degree into any analysis of the work as history would here be out of place. As to the style of Gibbon, opinion has been strangely at variance,—strangely, we say, because it seems a style about which a sharply-defined judgment might appear inevitable. It might be expected that friends and foes would unite to admit that it is singularly correct, full, and harmonious, too pompous upon trivial occasions, too ornate in matters of common narrative, somewhat lacking in variety and sprightliness, yet for general historic purposes superb in its richness of colour and unflagging energy of movement. This passage is one out of many which dilate on the splendours of the Eastern Empire in the tenth century :

> " The economy of the Emperor Theophilus allowed a more free and ample scope for his domestic luxury and splendour. A favourite ambassador, who had astonished the Abbassides themselves by his pride and liberality, presented on his return the model of a palace, which the Caliph of Bagdad had recently constructed on the banks of the Tigris. The model was instantly copied and surpassed : the new buildings of Theophilus were accompanied by gardens, and by five churches, one of which was conspicuous for size and beauty ; it was crowned with three domes, the roof of gilt brass reposed on columns of Italian marble, and the walls were incrusted with marbles of various colours. In the face of the church, a semicircular portico, of the figure and name of the Greek *sigma*, was supported by fifteen columns of Phrygian marble, and the subterraneous vaults were of a similar construction. The square before the sigma was decorated with a fountain, and the margin of the bason was lined and encompassed with plates of silver. In the beginning of each season, the bason, instead of water, was replenished with the most exquisite fruits, which were abandoned to the populace for the entertainment of the prince. He enjoyed this tumultuous spectacle from a throne resplendent with gold and gems, which was raised by a marble staircase to the height of a lofty terrace. . . . The long series of the apartments was adapted to the seasons, and decorated with marble and porphyry, with painting, sculpture, and mosaics, with a profusion of gold, silver, and precious stones. His fanciful magnificence employed the skill and patience of such artists as the times could afford : but the taste of Athens would have despised their frivolous and costly labours ; a golden tree, with its leaves and branches, which sheltered a multitude of birds, warbling their artificial notes, and two lions of massy gold, and of the natural size, who looked and roared like their brethren of the forest."

As the work advances, the style improves ; the faults which are commonly attributed to Gibbon are confined in large measure to his first volume, and when he was fairly sailing on the deep waters of his theme he proved himself a master in all the craft of language.

It is peevish to refuse credit to those who do things admirably well, because there is something incomprehensible in their capacity. Those who think that James Boswell (1740-1795) was a vain and shallow coxcomb of mediocre abilities, without intellectual gifts of any eminence, are confronted with the fact that this supposed fool was the unaided author of two of the most graphic and most readable works which the eighteenth century has left us. It is right that Boswell's claim to a high independent place in literature should be vindicated, and the fact is that, after Burke and Goldsmith, he is by far the most considerable of the literary companions of Johnson. That he has risen into fame on the shoulders of that great man is true, but the fact has been insisted upon until his own genuine and peculiar merits have been most unduly overlooked. He was of good family, a Scotchman from Auchinleck in Ayrshire. He had long been an admirer of the Sage, when, in his twenty-third year (May 16, 1763), he had at last the happiness of meeting him in Davies's back-parlour. On that very day he began to take notes of Johnson's conversation. He pleased Johnson at once, and was promptly taken into his awful familiarity, with the result that we all know, and should all be thankful for. In 1768, Boswell, having visited Pascal Paoli, the patriot-bandit, in his home, published *An Account of Corsica*, the personal part of which is far better written than the hasty critic is wont to acknowledge. In 1773 Johnson took unusual pains to insist that Boswell (as "the most unscottified of Scotchmen") should be elected into the club, and later in the same year the friends set out on their extraordinary visit to Scotland. Boswell kept a minute diary of this excursion, and published it in 1785 as the *Journal of a Tour to the Hebrides*. Six years later, in 1791, he produced, in two volumes quarto, his famous masterpiece, the *Life of Samuel Johnson, LL.D.*, dedicated to Sir Joshua Reynolds. The universal verdict of mankind has placed this work among the five or six most interesting and stimulating of the world's books.

Biography was one of the latest branches of literature to

blossom in this country. There were interesting and affecting lives of eminent men produced, no doubt, such as Walton's *Donne* and *Herbert*, Sprat's *Cowley*, and Oldys's *Raleigh;* but no biography, in anything like the full modern sense, had been published in this country till William Mason (1725-1797) published his *Life and Letters of Gray* in 1775. This timid and imperfect work, the system of which embraced the correspondence of the subject of the memoir, was the model on which Boswell constructed his infinitely bolder and more powerful work. The theory of this new kind of biography was, that the subject should as far as possible tell his own story and throw light upon his own character, instead of forming a central nodus round which the eloquence and piety of the biographer should crystallise in fine language. Bold as the experiment was, Boswell rose at once to the summit of success. The faculty of forming and retaining impressions of social phenomena was developed in him to an extraordinary degree, and if Boswell had chosen to describe the rest of his world as searchingly as he has observed Dr. Johnson we should have a matchless collection of eighteenth-century portraits. Meanwhile this is how the lexicographer lives in Boswell's photography :

"That the most minute singularities which belonged to him, and made very observable parts of his appearance and manner, may not be omitted, it is requisite to mention, that, while talking, or even musing as he sat in his chair, he commonly held his head to one side towards his right shoulder, and shook it in a tremulous manner, moving his body backwards and forwards, and rubbing his left knee in the same direction with the palm of his hand. In the intervals of articulating he made various sounds with his mouth, sometimes as if ruminating, or what is called chewing the cud, sometimes giving a half-whistle, sometimes making his tongue play backwards from the roof of his mouth, as if clucking like a hen, and sometimes protruding it against his upper gums in front, as if pronouncing quickly under his breath, *too, too, too:* all this accompanied sometimes with a thoughtful look, but more frequently with a smile. Generally, when he had concluded a period, in the course of a dispute, by which time he was a good deal exhausted by violence and vociferation, he used to blow out his breath like a whale. This, I suppose, was a relief to his lungs ; and seemed in him to be a contemptuous mode of expression, as if he had made the arguments of his opponent fly like chaff before the wind.

"I am fully aware how very obvious an occasion I have given for the sneering jocularity of such as have no relish of an exact likeness, which, to render complete, he who draws it must not disdain the slightest strokes. But if witlings should be inclined to attack this account, let them have the candour to quote what I have offered in my defence."

There has never been since, and there probably never will be, seen, a literary portrait so rich, so well-proportioned, and so detailed. Johnson lives in Boswell's pages, and lives at full length.

Among Boswell's qualities as a narrator, his dramatic power ranks very high. In rendering long dialogues, the minutiæ of which cannot have lingered in his memory, he seldom fails to preserve the utmost propriety of speech, the utmost regard for what would be characteristic in the mouth of each speaker. Johnson praised his "justness of discernment and fecundity of images"; Boswell observed very exactly, and with a happy regard for the picturesque touches of daily action. We feel that he did not live among savages in Scotland and rakes in England to no purpose; no man of that age saw the ground about his own feet more clearly, with less prejudice, less obscured by reverie, or vanity, or indifference. His style, from a man who idolised Johnson, and could reproduce "the bow-wow" so faithfully, is remarkably simple and unstudied; he is as free as Goldsmith is from imitation of their common idol. Boswell was petulant and foppish, excessively jealous of the attentions other men received from Johnson, but at bottom as simple and honest as he was vivacious. The adjective "clubbable" was invented to describe him; his "good humour and perpetual cheerfulness" were proverbial. His great originality as a literary artist is best proved by the fact that although every biographer since his day has imitated him, not one has successfully competed with him. It is really not fair to Johnson to suggest a comparison between the two existing accounts of their Tour to the Hebrides, but it is a parallel which those provoke us to make who insist on giving all the praise to Johnson and all the contempt to Boswell.

The decline of fiction during this period was complete, and

was the more emphasised from the fact that so brilliant a school of novelists had adorned the preceding generation. The portraiture of real life, of the tragi-comedy of contemporary existence, gave way to an affected pathos and a morbid excess of sentiment. The success of Sterne, imperfectly understood by a host of feeble imitators, naturally led to this result, and at the head of the parodists of Sterne stood Henry Mackenzie (1745-1831), whose life was prolonged so as to touch those of Mr. George Meredith and Mr. Blackmore. Although wedded to the following of Sterne, Mackenzie affected the moral earnestness of Richardson also, and the characters in his three principal fictions move, meekly robed in gentle virtue, through a succession of heartrending misfortunes. There is no observation of life, no knowledge of the world, in Mackenzie's long-drawn lachrymose novels of feeling. The personal affection of Sir Walter Scott for this amiable man has done much to preserve Mackenzie's memory.

Dr. Johnson greatly admired the *Memoirs of Miss Sydney Biddulph*, a tragic novel of manners written by Frances Chamberlaine (1724-1766), the wife of Thomas Sheridan, and mother of the dramatist. Johnson wrote to her, "Madam, I know not that you have a right to make your readers suffer so much." For the lively wife of "Sherry the dull" is as tearful in her novels as Mackenzie is in his. Just after the close of this generation, a whole group of lively novelists, all tinged with the new spirit of romance, suddenly sprang into prominence, but none of these writers, "Zeluco" Moore, Beckford, Bage, Holcroft, Sophia Lee, or Ann Radcliffe, belongs to the present volume. We may, however, claim to deal here with Frances Burney (1752-1840), whose *Evelina*, the one great comic novel between Smollett and Jane Austen, appeared in 1778. Miss Burney was the daughter of Dr. Burney, the historian of music. She had observed the droll and farcical side of life with great acumen, and the frank laughter which her pages provoked was indescribably welcome after the tear-inspiring episodes of the Sensibility school. It is to be desired that Miss Burney had remained the author of one book.

Her *Cecilia* is only read because it is by the creator of *Evelina*, and her *Camilla* is never read at all. Her life became cramped and tiresome, and the natural vivacity of her mind was subdued by the intolerable boredom of court servitude. In 1793 she became Madame d'Arblay, and at the close of her long life she left behind her five volumes of *Diary and Letters*, which are paradoxically lively and tiresome at the same time.

The sprightliness of Fanny Burney is well exemplified by her account to Windham of the effect produced upon her own nerves by Burke's oration, in February 1788, at the trial of Warren Hastings:

"Mr. Burke's opening had struck me with the highest admiration of his powers, from the eloquence, the imagination, the fire, the diversity of expression, and the ready flow of language with which he seemed gifted, in a most superior manner, for any and every purpose to which rhetoric could lead. And when he came to his two narratives, I continued; when he related the particulars of those dreadful murders, he interested, he engaged, he at last overpowered me; I felt my cause lost. I could hardly keep on my seat. My eyes dreaded a single glance towards a man so accused as Mr. Hastings; I wanted to sink on the floor, that they might be saved so painful a sight. I had no hope he could clear himself; not another wish in his favour remained. But when from his narration Mr. Burke proceeded to his own comments and declamation,—when the charges of rapacity, cruelty, tyranny, were general, and made with all the violence of personal detestation, and continued and aggravated without any further fact or illustration,—then they appeared more of study than of truth, more of invective than of justice; and, in short, so little of proof to so much of passion, that in a very short time I began to lift up my head, my seat was no longer uneasy, my eyes were indifferent which way they looked, or what object caught them, and before I was myself aware of the declension of Mr. Burke's powers over my feelings, I found myself a mere spectator in a public place, and looking all around it, with my opera-glass in my hand!"

History was magnificently represented in this generation by Gibbon, and no other name even approaches his in magnitude. But few miscellaneous writers of the time have retained anything of their fame. John Jortin (1698-1770), besides being a writer of elegant sermons in an age when pulpit literature had greatly decayed, may be remembered as the author of various contributions to ecclesiastical history, in which he showed liberality of thought.

Jortin was persistent and fairly successful in controversy with Warburton. Jean Louis Delolme (1745-1807), a Genevese lawyer, wrote a superficial but very enthusiastic work on *The English Constitution*, which he brought to this country, and published in a remarkably good English version of his own in 1775. A Scottish "moderate," Dr. George Campbell (1719-1796) was long famous as apparently the most successful of the many opponents of Hume; his *Dissertation on Miracles* in 1763 was the only attack which the philosopher deigned to answer in correspondence. Campbell was a man of great intellectual liberality, and he rose to be the leading spirit among the Scotch clergy of his time; he was Principal of Marischal College, Aberdeen. The labours of Joseph Priestley (1733-1804), the unitarian natural philosopher of Birmingham, of Richard Price (1723-1791), and of Tom Paine (1736-1809) had begun before 1780; but the real significance of these revolutionary forces, so far as they concern literature at all, belongs to a subsequent period.

As was natural in an age of extreme political uneasiness, the publicist became more and more a power in the state as the century wore on. Between January 1769 and 1772 the attention of the entire public was riveted by the appearance of a rapid series of letters in the "Public Advertiser," signed Junius, which surpassed anything which had been previously known in ferocity of criticism. They were issued in support of Wilkes, as a constitutional hero, and in vehement opposition to the Government, especially to Grafton, North, and Mansfield. All attempts to discover the perpetrator of these outrages was in vain; as Lord North said, "the great boar of the wood, this mighty Junius, broke through the toils and foiled the hunters." Thirty-seven persons have at different times been suggested as candidates for the mask of Junius, and the pseudonymity of these *Letters* was preserved with such astonishing adroitness and success that to this day it is not every careful student of the subject who is persuaded that they were written by Sir Philip Francis (1740-1818), a clerk in the War Office. The literary value of Junius seems to have been absurdly overrated. The letters are vigorous, of course, but their malignity is atoned for or relieved by no philosophical enthusiasm, while the indignation itself appears to be personal first and patriotic afterwards. It is an instance of the difficulty which attends contemporary criticism that Johnson, so eminent a judge of language, thought that Junius was Burke. To us it seems amazing that brass should thus be mistaken for gold. At the same time the *Letters* have "polish," a quality for which Francis preserved an exaggerated affection; the balance and modulation of their merciless sentences may still please the ear. The principal objects of the hatred of Junius were the king and the Duke of Grafton, but perhaps the loftiest flights of his sarcastic genius are those in which he wheels and swoops around the figure of the Duke of Bedford, the Verres of Woburn, in attacking whom Junius attains for a moment a veritable splendour of invective:

"Let us consider you, then," he says to the tormented Duke, on the 19th of September 1769, "as arrived at the summit of worldly greatness; let us suppose that all your plans of avarice and ambition are accomplished, and your most sanguine wishes gratified in the fear as well as the hatred of the people. Can age itself forget that you are now in the last act of life? Can gray hairs make folly venerable? and is there no period to be reserved for meditation and retirement? For shame! my Lord: let it not be recorded of you, that the latest moments of your life were dedicated to the same unworthy pursuits, the same busy agitations, in which your youth and manhood were exhausted. Consider that, although you cannot disgrace your former life, you are violating the character of age, and exposing the impotent imbecility, after you have lost the vigour, of the passions.

"Your friends will ask, perhaps, Whither shall this unhappy old man retire? Can he remain in the metropolis, where his life has been so often threatened, and his palace so often attacked? If he returns to Woburn, scorn and mockery await him. He must create a solitude round his estate, if he would avoid the face of reproach and derision. At Plymouth, his destruction would be more than probable; at Exeter, inevitable. No honest Englishman will ever forget his attachment, nor any honest Scotchman forgive his treachery, to Lord Bute. At every town he enters he must change his liveries and his name. Whichever way he flies, the hue and cry of the country pursues him."

While Junius and John Wilkes, with many others, were the active sharpshooters of Whig journalism, the Tories upon their side sought in vain for a stirring mouthpiece in the press, and found nothing better adapted to their purpose than an occasional sonorous pamphlet from the pen of Dr. Johnson, in which the advantages of blind subordination to the will of the sovereign were expanded in a strain that was not strictly popular. But whether Whig or Tory, there was only one really great political writer then in England, and with some brief summary of his career and work we may close this chapter of our history.

As the minor political literature of the close of the eighteenth century passes more and more into the background, the remnants of the eloquence of the master-politician become more and more the objects of critical panegyric. It now surprises no one to hear it maintained that Edmund Burke (1729-1797) was the greatest prose-writer of the century. Some critics have not hesitated to place him at the absolute summit of English prose. With all due enthusiasm for the majestic merit of his style, that extremity of praise will not be reached here. Notwithstanding all its magnificence, it appears to me that the prose of Burke lacks the variety, the delicacy, the modulated music of the very finest writers. When Sir Leslie Stephen applauds the "flexibility" of Burke's style, he attributes to him the very quality which to my ear he seems most to lack. A robe of brocaded damask is splendid, sumptuous, and appropriate to noble public occasions, but it is scarcely flexible. To be a perfect prose-writer, a man must play sometimes upon thrilling and soul-subduing instruments, but Burke never takes the trumpet from his lips. To those few who may think him humorous, I resign him in despair; and surely still fewer will be found to think him pathetic. The greatest of English prose-writers, we may be sure, would be found to have some command over laughter and tears, but Burke has none. The ferocity and ungoverned passion of his attacks, on the other hand, are not critically distasteful to me. They seem to correspond with a conception of the man as a filleted as well as togated senator, a certain priestly passion being fitly mingled with this parliamentary zeal. Without such outbursts his rich rhetoric might seem too polished to be quite sincere. In short, the prose of Burke may be felt to be the finest expression of a particular phase of the eighteenth-century mind—a phase from which all the coarse fibre of the Renaissance, to its very last filament, had been extracted, where all is civilised, earnest, competent, and refined, but where the imagination is almost too completely under control. So much may, in the face of the modern idolatry of Burke, be suggested, without weakening in any degree the effect which his unexampled majesty of rhetoric must ever, and probably to an increasing degree, exercise upon those who are moved by the loftier parts of language.

It is with some hesitation that I allow myself the pleasure of closing my survey with this noble figure, since in 1780 Burke was still comparatively undistinguished as a writer. His greatest triumphs of style succeed the French Revolution, and he may therefore be considered as a resident in the domain of my successor. But Burke, though his genius developed late, belonged to an earlier generation, and can properly be no more divided from the immediate circle of Johnson than Boswell, Goldsmith, or Reynolds. He learned to write between 1750 and 1760, and he belongs to the group of men whom circumstances encouraged to blossom into literature at that time. It should perhaps here be insisted upon that Burke's figure must of necessity appear dwarfed and distorted in a mere history of literature. He belongs to the history of politics, and to the history of thought, and in each of these he holds a more commanding place than in pure literature. For a great part of his career he is absolutely submerged by the practice of political life, and during these years it would be a licence to follow him minutely in such pages as these. There is no greater instance of the difficulty of treating in purely literary criticism a writer whose first object was not literary expression. To pass over into a consideration of the general work of such a man would be to go beyond the limits of our inquiry, yet to keep it out of sight seems to be doing less than justice to his genius. In these days, however, the reader may be presumed able and willing to fill up the blanks in Burke's intellectual portrait.

It is not quite certain that it was on the 12th of January 1729 that Burke was born, but the event undoubtedly took place in Dublin, of which city or its neighbourhood he was a resident until he became of age. At Trinity College he read much, but on lines of his own, and had little ambition for academic honours. In 1750 he came to London, to study law in the Middle Temple; and here for some years he almost entirely disappears from view. All we know is what he tells us himself, that during this part of his life he was "sometimes in London, sometimes in remote parts of the country, sometimes in France." He gave hostages to society in 1756 by marrying a wife, and by making his first essays in literary publication. These two volumes bear little weight in relation to Burke's subsequent and far more authoritative writings, but their positive cleverness was interesting enough. The *Vindication of Natural Society* professed to be a letter to a lord, by a late noble writer—that is to say, by Bolingbroke, whose sentiments it held up to ridicule in an exceedingly close and temperate parody of his style. It has excited surprise that so original a writer as Burke should make his first appearance in the very dress of so second-rate a rhetorician as Bolingbroke. But it must be recollected that in 1756 Bolingbroke was considered absolutely first-rate, and that it was no slight exercise in self-education for a young man to force himself to forge the admired style of a great favourite with so much success as to take in the St. Johnians themselves. Even thus early Burke looked upon any relaxation of the curb of government on the popular mouth as being not less infamous than perilous; and it really is astonishing that there should have been readers of the *Vindication* who did not perceive that the arguments in that work were absurd, and the whole thing a piece of polemic by parody. It is very interesting to those who have mastered the needful elements of irony to trace in this his first publication the same burning zeal for constitutional forms of accepted rule which inspired the great speeches of his later manhood. One unfortunate result of this early *pastiche* has been noted by Mr. John Morley, namely, that Burke never got entirely clear from the influence of the style of Bolingbroke.

To the same year belongs the once-famous but now little consulted æsthetic *Inquiry into the Sublime and Beautiful*. This essay, in a somewhat dark and tentative manner, opened up a new field of speculation, and has been regarded as containing the germ of all later art-criticism. The *Polymetis* of Joseph Spence (1698-1768), which had appeared nine years before, had enjoyed a success which its artless ignorance of the principles of art had not deserved. The field was open to Burke, but public ignorance on the subject was excessive, and his own artistic experience ludicrously limited. Thirteen years were to elapse before Reynolds was to deliver his first *Discourse* before the students of the infant Royal Academy. Meanwhile Burke's *Inquiry* had the honour of attracting the attention of Lessing, who is said to have just read it through at Breslau when he began his *Laokoon* in 1760. It is claimed also that this essay had a powerful influence on the mind of Kant; and in Germany the *Sublime and Beautiful* has always been held in greater respect than in England, where subsequent art-criticism has tended to become more empirical and less philosophical than on the Continent. In 1759 Dodsley started *The Annual Register* under Burke's editorship; and in 1761 we find Horace Walpole considering that Mr. Burke is too much exercised with "authorism." The reproof is strange, for Burke's first period of authorism had by that time closed; and, immersed in active affairs, he did not resume his pen for many years.

Certain pamphlets, of an occasional nature, and inconsiderable size, are the next publications of Burke's which we meet with. In these we find that his style has ripened to a more independent eloquence, and that he has become a master of the arts of rhetoric. His *Observations on the Present State of the Nation*, in 1769, and his *Thoughts on the Cause of the Present Discontents*, in 1770, revealed the young Whig statesman as by far the most effective publicist of the age. These tracts had nothing of the rancour of Junius or of Wilkes, but they hit harder, because the tone of them was infinitely more elevated and philosophical. Yet even in these admirable pamphlets, and especially in the *Present Discontents*, the modern student may discover faults which were seldom entirely absent even from the most rapid of Burke's polemical writings. The author is too long getting under weigh; in his anxiety to be superior to all petty considerations, he is too particular and too verbose; and, to pass from style to subject, he is already too obviously alarmed at the dangers which threatened the prestige of rank and office. It has been noted that Burke by this time had come very directly under the influence of the ideas of Montesquieu, an influence which henceforth became paramount over his intellect. Finally, it may be confessed that the contents of these pamphlets, and of the speeches and letters which combine to form with them the product of Burke's second literary period, are often rendered so obscure by the cessation of the transitory interests which called them forth, that the works appeal more to the historical student than to the general reader. The *Speech on American Taxation*, of 1774, should perhaps be excepted from this judgment.

It would be impossible for us to follow in detail Burke's career as an orator, noble as are those fragments of his eloquence which have come down to us. Enough to say that his speeches are more stimulating and more convincing after one hundred years have elapsed than any others which exist under the pretence of being literature. But in 1790 Burke once more reappeared in the open field of letters, and it was between this date and that of his death, 1797, that his main contributions to our literature were published. This magnificent series of books opened with the *Reflections on the Revolution in France*, in the form of a letter to a French gentleman. In this extraordinary volume, inspired by his constant intellectual mentor, the author of the *Esprit des lois*, Burke contrasts the ancient monarchy of France, and the possibility of reforming its institutions, with the calamity of utter revolution which had just burst over that unfortunate country. In

1789 Price, in addressing a harmless body called the Revolutionary Society, had given, as Burke considered, "the solemn publick seal of sanction" to what was going on in France. The publication of Price's *Discourse on the Love of our Country*, which had been widely read, upset Burke's equanimity still further, and he blazed forth, like an angry prophet, with the vial of his *Reflections*. The weak point of the book now is that it contains too much about Price and the Revolutionary Society—entities which have ceased to move our timidity or our curiosity. But such as it is, it is a masterpiece. It spoke with the thrilling accents of vehement sincerity, and with an enthusiasm which rose above all private and vulgar considerations of decorum :

"Why do I feel so differently from the Reverend Dr. Price, and those of his lay flock, who will choose to adopt the sentiments of his discourse ? For this plain reason,—because it is *natural* that I should ; because we are so made as to be affected at such spectacles with melancholy sentiments upon the unstable condition of mortal prosperity, and the tremendous uncertainty of human greatness ; because in those natural feelings we learn great lessons ; because in events like these our passions instruct our reason ; because when kings are hurled from their thrones by the Supreme Director of this great drama, and become the objects of insult to the base, and of pity to the good, we behold such disasters in the moral, as we should behold a miracle in the physical order of things. We are alarmed into reflexion ; our minds (as it has long since been observed) are purified by terror and pity ; our weak unthinking pride is humbled under the dispensations of a mysterious wisdom. Some tears might be drawn from me, if such a spectacle were exhibited on the stage. I should be truly ashamed of finding in myself that superficial, theatric sense of painted distress, whilst I could exult over it in real life. With such a perverted mind, I could never venture to show my face at a tragedy. People would think the tears that Garrick formerly, or that Siddons not long since, have extorted from me, were the tears of hypocrisy ; I should know them to be the tears of folly."

The author was exactly twelve months sharpening the burning arrows of his sarcasm with infinite pains and zest, and he was rewarded by a success the like of which no political book had ever enjoyed before. Its appeal to the passions, its cruel force and wit, its magnificent direct incentive to reaction, all these gave the *Reflections* an amazing interest to those who had just witnessed, with bewilderment, the incomprehensible and unexampled progress of events in France. Upon all the trembling kings of Europe, upon the exiles on the Rhine especially, the book fell like rain after long drought; and a French version of it was attributed to no less a pen than that of the most exalted of the Emigrants.

Burke's disapproval of the French Revolution did not grow calmer as events began to show that in many of his predictions he had been a wise prophet. In the *Letter to a Member of the National Assembly*, published early in 1791, he goes to still more violent extremes of invective. There was distinctly a less angry unreasonableness in the beautifully modulated *Appeal from the New to the Old Whigs*, of August in that year, but he returns to his fiercest diatribes in the *Thoughts on French Affairs* of the subsequent winter. There was again a silence, amid the claims of public life, and then, in February 1796, appeared the famous *Letter to a Noble Lord*, which remains, perhaps, the most typical of Burke's writings, the most accomplished and surprising in matter, the most splendid, melodious, and refined in manner. The Duke of Bedford and the Earl of Lauderdale had attacked the pensions which Burke was by this time enjoying, and the old debater was far too acute not to perceive in a moment the incongruity of such attacks from the head of the vastly-pensioned house of Russell. He therefore soon leaves Lord Lauderdale alone, and concentrates his anger, irony, and scorn on the head of the Duke of Bedford, that "leviathan among all the creatures of the crown," whom he alternately tortures with ridicule and with threats of coming ruin from French ideas. Nothing could be happier than the main portion of this letter, nothing more dignified than Burke's references to his loss in the deaths of his son and of Lord Keppel. But, as in other cases, the rhetoric is a little overdone; the golden rolling sentences occasionally leave a blank upon the mind; and the matter under discussion is certainly approached too slowly.

The great patriot was now very near the close of his wonderful career, and the latest months of it were spent in composition.

To 1796 and 1797 belong the letters *On a Regicide Peace*. They were three in number, the third a fragment; but a fourth, which was really the first, was found among Burke's papers, and published in 1812. There can be no doubt that in these celebrated compositions, the imaginative fervour of which has dazzled many critics, there are signs enough of the decay of the author's physical powers. To many it is merely distressing to see this Chrysostom of the English language descending to scurrilities unworthy of a fishwife, and relinquishing all remnants of judgment, decorum, reason, and good sense in ravings about "sanguinary cannibals" and the tyrannies of a regicide jacobinism. Yet, to those who can stifle their sentiments of indignation and pity,—indignation at an injustice so extreme, and pity at the decay of such noble qualities of the heart,—to read the *Regicide Peace* is one of the most fascinating of literary exercises. And there are more dignified phases, even in his anger :

"This business was not ended, because our dignity was wounded, or because our patience was worn out with contumely and scorn. We had not disgorged one particle of the nauseous dose with which we were so liberally crammed by the mountebanks of Paris, in order to drug and diet us into perfect tameness. No; we waited, till the morbid strength of our *boulimia* for their physic had exhausted the well-stored dispensary of their empiricism. It is impossible to guess at the term to which our forbearance would have extended. The Regicides were more fatigued with giving blows than the callous cheek of British Diplomacy was hurt in receiving them. They had no way left for getting rid of this mendicant perseverance but by sending for the Beadle, and forcibly driving our Embassy 'of shreds and patches,' with all its mumping cant, from the inhospitable door of Cannibal Castle. I think we might have found, before the rude hand of insolent office was on our shoulder, and the staff of usurped authority brandished over our heads, that contempt of the suppliant is not the best forwarder of a suit ; that national disgrace is not the high road to security, much less to power and greatness. Patience, indeed, strongly indicates the love of peace. But mere love does not always lead to enjoyment. It is the power of winning that palm that insures our wearing it. Virtues have their place, and out of their place they hardly deserve the name. They pass into the neighbouring vice. The patience of fortitude and the endurance of pusillanimity are things very different, as in their principle, so in their effects."

The decline in Burke's case was moral—it was not intellectual, and to the very last he grew in power as an artificer of sonorous prose. The second of the letters on a *Regicide Peace* is much shorter than the others, and more decent in its effusion, and all its author's old acuteness will be marked in the study of the character of Louis XVI. Inveighing to the last against "that mother of all evil, the French Revolution," Burke passed away at Beaconsfield, not old, but worn out, on the 9th of July 1797. The total number of his separate publications is nearly sixty.

It is a matter of regret to the purely literary student that, as a writer, Burke is displayed at his best only in those works in which the sanity and probity which so eminently distinguished his character are clouded by his rabid prejudice against France. Hence it is that those who read only his masterpieces must carry away so vague and so distorted an idea of what it was in which the greatness of Burke consisted. In his youth Johnson, with his fine and generous discrimination, had said, "We who know Mr. Burke know that he will be one of the first men in the country." As his career developed, there is no doubt that he became *the* first man in the country, and it was when his powers as a statesman and an orator were at their zenith, and when his partial retirement gave him leisure for literary composition, that this strange madness of anger seized and convulsed him. We must, however, beware of exaggerating its mark on his work. It is true that it pervades his more important later writings, yet much came from his lips, even when that agonising robe of Nessus was wrapt around his spirit, that was calm and clear and noble.

We learn that Burke was devoted to the study of Dryden's prose, and resolutely endeavoured to imitate it. The resemblance cannot be said to be very striking, except in the elaborate art of balancing and adjusting the parts of the sentence, so as to produce upon the ear the exact effect required. But in doing this, though Burke carried to a greater perfection than any one else except Gibbon what Dryden had been the first to invent, yet it cannot be said that Burke's rhetoric, which is always golden, and sometimes jewelled and enamelled as well, has much superficial likeness to the strong uncoloured prose of Dryden. In the class of declamatory writers Burke stands easily first; his tracts and orations do not speak reflectively, with the still small voice which the cloistered student loves, but in resonant accents, so that even in the study their effect is completed to the imagination by cries of defiance or rounds of applause from an unseen audience. It may be questioned whether books conceived and executed in this spirit can ever be held among the most precious possessions of the true lover of pure literature. But as illustrations of a wonderful public career, and as specimens of oratory at its loftiest pinnacle of success, they outshine all rivalry; and although it is probable that Burke, as a writer, has enjoyed his fullest panegyrics in the immediate past, the future can never be entirely disloyal to a publicist so chivalrous, so fervid, and so logical.

CHAPTER XII

CONCLUSION

WHEN we approach the close of the seventeenth century in English literature, we begin to be confronted by a practical difficulty. A door must be open or shut, and the chamber of our studies will hold but a limited number of forms or ideas at a single time. What is to be excluded, and what retained, becomes a burning question. In the early stages of civilisation, everything written takes its place as literature, but with the widening of the habit of penmanship there springs up an ever-increasing mass of script which is by no means to be treated as literary art. Even in the Elizabethan age there were two branches of written and published work which mainly passed outside the conception of literature, namely, theology and law. But still, throughout the seventeenth century, poetry remained the normal class of expression, while prose retained its conscious character as something which had to compete with poetry and share its graces. It is at the point where these graces of language are entirely subordinated (in the discussion of practical subjects) to exact statement of fact, that there arises a class of books which cannot be treated as literature, in spite of their importance as contributions to thought and knowledge. During the last quarter of the seventeenth century a spirited effort was made to chronicle the new observations of science in the best literary form of the age, but it could not be sustained. The reader has but to compare the *Acetaria* of Evelyn and the *Anti-Elixir* of Boyle with any authoritative modern treatise on the cookery of cucumbers or the composition of alloys, to see how very much the absence of all literary elegance is of advantage in obtaining exact information upon practical subjects. Accordingly, the graces were tacitly and gradually excluded from all treatment of purely utilitarian problems and exact observations, and this exclusion divided the vast body of what was written into literature and non-literary matter.

We must, therefore, prepare ourselves, on approaching the year 1700, to find the history of English literature no longer identical with the history of English thought. There has recently been developed a tendency to go in the opposite direction, and instead of narrowing the field of study to enlarge it. It has been proposed to combine with an examination of English literature a survey of contemporary history and politics, science and learning, theology and speculation. Such a curriculum is fit only for an archangel, dowered with eyes "that run thro' all the heavens," and with a memory and a comprehension beyond a mortal span. No doubt a direct benefit in the exact study of any one province of knowledge is gained by a correct superficial acquaintance with all that is contiguous to it; but common sense and experience unite to show that with the increase of facts, and the minute subdivision of science, the field of any one particular study, to remain exact, must be rigidly narrowed. It is, therefore, I think, useful for the student of English literature, on reaching the eighteenth century, to make up his mind to the acceptance of a formula less extended than he has hitherto brought with him down from the Renaissance. He will so contract his field of study as to embrace only what may be contained within the denomination of *belles-lettres* in its widest sense, to the exclusion of whatever is purely technical or occasional.

It is difficult, no doubt, in practice, to draw any hard and fast line between what is and is not literature in this sense. In a rough kind of way we may see that while *The Public Spirit of the Whigs* and the *Letter to a Noble Lord* are inside, the *Behaviour of the Queen's Ministry* and the *Duration of Parliaments* are outside the frontier of literature; yet, on the whole, it will be convenient to give everything of such masters as Swift and Burke the benefit of the doubt. It is when we descend to less accomplished forces than these that it becomes obvious that the epoch-making work of the Methodist and the Deist, the politician and the savant, the jurist and the economist, although so important in the history of society, of thought, and of the state, must, from the point of view of the mere student of literature, be, for the future, left unexamined, or very briefly and inadequately touched. We must restrict ourselves severely to what remains in some degree linked with the art of poetry, to what aims at giving delight by its form, to what appeals to the sentiments and the pleasure-receiving instincts, and is not merely a vehicle for instruction or edification.

If, however, it becomes necessary in approaching the Augustan age to confine our study of English literature within closer limits, we are encouraged in so doing by the tendency of that age itself. The seventeenth century had been a period of extraordinary literary adventure. Every species of intellectual stimulus had stirred the educated classes throughout the reign of the last of the Tudors, and one amazing achievement had followed on the heels of another. Greece, Italy, Rome, and Spain had been laid under contribution for the enrichment and enlargement of the genius of this country, and a magnificent literature was borne, like a triumphal procession, heavy with the spoils of Europe, in front of the throne of Elizabeth. But this glowing triumph had tailed off, by the time the Commonwealth was reached, into a grotesque and anarchical body of camp-followers, with here and there a majestic Milton or Taylor to recall the greatness of the past. When the Restoration was complete, and the babel of voices had died away, the new generation had no desire to recall the deafening chorus of Jacobean decadence, but rather proposed to reduce its own manifestations to the most decent and prosaic forms. The tradition of eighteenth-century reserve was formed in the intellectual fatigue that succeeded the decline of Elizabethan greatness, and the last thing which the contemporaries of Dryden proposed to themselves was a new crusade of literary adventure.

Where there is life, however, there must be experiment, and in spite of its studied quiescence, eighteenth-century literature is full of new departures. To detect these, and to analyse them correctly, is one of the first tasks which the student must set himself to undertake, when once he has mastered the chart of the period. At first sight there seems to be an absence of general tendency; the forces appear to be wielded by certain master-spirits at their individual pleasure, without much relation to contemporary feeling. We have no longer, certainly, those well-defined schools, or, to change the image, those prominent ranges, culminating in peaks, which diversify the map of seventeenth-century literature, and make its general aspect so rich and full. We find movements less absorbing and men more prominent. In the development of literary society, the personage of letters emerges from the obscurity of professional life, and poses as an important single figure. Literary history in the eighteenth century, however, is far from being the chronicle of a series of brilliant units. Perhaps because of that very meagreness of outside influence which has been alluded to, the transmission of forces from generation to generation was never more marked than between 1660 and 1780. The continuity of metaphysical speculation from Locke onward, the long-resisted and slowly-adopted new literary profession of journalism, the evolution of the modern novel from the expiring schools of comedy, the gradual resumption of an observant interest in the phenomena of society and of landscape, the dawning of a taste for Gothic romance,—these are but the most salient of a number of experimental movements, rising from the dead surface of the century, and pursued across wide sections of its extent.

These experiments, these feats of literary adventure, are not hurried forward during the eighteenth century as they were at the close of the sixteenth or the beginning of the seventeenth. Then it took but a year or two to create, introduce, and make fashionable a whole new form of literature. Any match, whatever wind was blowing, would set the prairie then on fire. But after the Restoration, whatever was done had to be done in the green tree. The judgment had grown sedate, enthusiasm was waxing cold, and the changes were slow and not obviously apparent. The close observer detects, for instance, a change of style between the *Astræa Redux* of 1660 and the *Dispensary* of 1699; but the alteration is by no means obvious. An equal period would take us from the *Steel Glass* of Gascoigne, across Spenser and Shakespeare, to *Britannia's Pastorals* and the songs of Carew—an excursion which bewilders the brain with its variety. But no more suggestive instance of the slowness of post-Restoration changes can be given than is offered by the history of a return to the observation of nature. In 1660 it seemed as though all use of the physical eyes had been abandoned in prose and verse; those who wrote appeared to see everything blurred and faint, as through clouded spectacles. Dryden is perhaps the only great writer—he is certainly the only English poet of high rank—who appears to be wholly destitute of the gift of observation. In Congreve, in such touches as Lady Wishfort's "Thou bosom-traitress that I took from washing of old gauze and weaving of dead hair, with a black-blue nose over a chafing-dish of starved embers, and dining behind a traverse rag in a shop no bigger than a bird-cage," we see the art returning. But still no one looks beyond the street; till years roll on, and Lady Winchelsea and Gay and Green, venturing into country places, successively open the field of vision each a little wider than the other; they pass away, and Thomson arrives with a mannered but genuine vision of something more grandiose, of mountain and lake and long, billowy champaign; he gives place to Gray, with his intuition of beauty among the genuine Alps and under the forehead of Helvellyn; and by the time we reach the Gilpins and the Gilbert Whites, we perceive that a slow and slender, but ever-broadening stream of natural observation has been meandering down the whole length of that very century which is supposed to be so characteristically devoid of it.

To facilitate the study of eighteenth-century literature, it is convenient to divide the one hundred and twenty years which succeeded the Restoration into three equal parts. Each of these is dominated by one figure of far greater intellectual prestige than any other of the same period. No one will question that the first of these is the generation of Dryden and the last that of Johnson. It may not perhaps be quite so readily conceded that the age of Anne lay under the tyranny of Swift. It will, however, be found, I think, upon close examination that neither Pope nor Addison has an equal claim to be considered the centre of the action or the hero of the story. They wrote with consummate skill, but Swift it was who laid the torch to the standing-corn of thought; his was the irradiating, the Promethean mind from 1700 to 1740 and his force of character, the thrill of personal genius, that rivets to itself the main attention of students throughout that brilliant period.

The age of Dryden was the most prosaic in our literary history. In its course theology, philosophy, even poetry itself, were chained either to common sense, or to a ranting rapture which dispensed with literary sincerity, and was, in fact, more prosaic than all prose. What mainly flourished under the strong leaden sceptre of Dryden was satire, in new and stringent forms; artificial comedy, brutal at first, and harsh, but polished at length to the last extremity of cynical elegance; burlesque verses, very smart and modern, which passed for poetry; the political pamphlet; the clear, limpid art of the letter-writer, modelled, through Roger L'Estrange, on the directness of the *Lettres Portugaises;* the sincere, naked thought of Locke, with its dislike of ornament and carelessness of authority; the first grotesque babble of modern criticism; the dryness of the polemical divines; and over it all, covering its defects as with a garment, the new graces of the competent current prose of the day. This is the vestibule of the eighteenth century, and across its very threshold the rich brocaded wit of Congreve takes hands with the urbanity and grace of Addison.

The age of Swift is fuller of intellectual activity, more genial, more varied, more enthusiastic. The coldest period is over, and already a faint flush of the summer of romanticism is discoverable. This fuller life takes many forms. In philosophy the age is no longer content with the bald presentment of Locke's ideas, but, with something less of positive originality, calls to its aid the fancy and ingenuity of Shaftesbury, the brilliant imagination of Berkeley. In poetry, though the general type is artificial still, there is no longer the protracted cultivation of one form; satire takes urbaner and less brutal shapes, and half way through the period the landscape poets push in with their blank verse, and the lyrists with their octosyllabics. The drama somewhat abruptly expires, and while the nation is waiting for the development of the novel, Addison holds its ear with the humour and dainty sentiment of his essays. A delicate amenity, a sweetness of expression, marks the age of Anne; and even the ferocities of Swift and Mandeville do not belie this general impression of increasing civilisation of the mind, since the very wounds inflicted by these writers show the tenderness of the contemporary epidermis. Such satire would not have penetrated a generation grown pachydermatous under the flail of Oldham or Lord Dorset. There was a rapid development of the power of ridicule by prose and verse, a general sharpening and pointing of every literary weapon, and it was in this age of Swift that English prose reached its maximum of strength, elegance, and elasticity combined.

Something was again relinquished in the third period, that of Johnson. Here, to secure more strength, needless weight was superadded to language; elasticity was lost in a harmony too mechanically studied. What was really best in this third age was directly recovered from the early Anne writers, as Goldsmith, its best author, is seen returning to the traditions of Addison and Congreve. The main contribution of this period to literature is the novel, which opens with *Pamela* in its first year, 1740. Before the generation closed, the earliest development of fiction was over and the novel in decline. In verse, what was not imitative of the old schools was suggestive of what did not come till the next century began. On one hand we have Goldsmith, Johnson, and Churchill reviving the manner of Pope; on the other we have Gray and Collins in their odes, and Chatterton in his verse-romances, prophesying of Coleridge and Shelley. Everywhere during this third period the buried and forgotten seeds of romantic fancy were becoming stimulated, and were pushing their shoots above ground in a Percy's *Reliques*, in a *Castle of Otranto*, in a *Descent of Odin*. Meanwhile, what was mainly visible to the public was the figure of Dr. Samuel Johnson, a sesquipedalian dictator, not writing very much or in a superlatively excellent manner, but talking publicly, or semi-publicly, in a style hitherto unprecedented, and laying down the law on all subjects whatever. Around this great man collects whatever there is of normal genius in the generation—Goldsmith and Burke, Gibbon and Reynolds, Boswell and Garrick,—and a group is formed, to the student of personal manners the most interesting that literary history can supply. So rich is the age in anecdote, so great in critical prestige, that the student must look closely and carefully to perceive that it is rapidly declining in intellectual force of every kind, and by 1780 is only waiting for the decease of two or three old men to sink completely into a condition of general mediocrity. When Doctor Johnson dies, the literature of the eighteenth century is practically closed, and the work of removing the débris to prepare for the nineteenth begins.

A rough criterion of the vitality of English literature in the eighteenth century may be gained by seeing at what points it was able to influence foreign literatures, and at what points it was influenced by the latter. The old theory that the whole business of the hardening and de-romanticising of English poetry came from France is now exploded. It has been shown beyond dispute that Waller was, at least, as early in the field as Malherbe. But the artificial verse-product was never thoroughly at home in England, and at one moment only, in the hands of Pope, was able to lay down a tradition for Europe. It is a proof of the force of Pope's art that, while Dryden remained, and still remains, a mere name on the continent of Europe, Pope had direct followers and imitators among the leading poets of Germany, Italy, Sweden, and even Holland.

Thomson had the good fortune to be imitated also, and to found a sort of French school, of which Saint-Lambert is the most prominent member. Pope might be said to owe much to Boileau, and his influence to be therefore continental in a second degree; but whatever the author of *The Seasons* might give to Europe was wholly our own.

Yet far more important than any foreign influence from English verse was the stimulus given abroad by the English novel. Here again it was a Frenchman, Lesage, who first started the modernisation of the Spanish story of adventure, and so prepared the way for Fielding and Smollett; while another, Marivaux, may possibly have had some slight effect on the manner of Richardson. But the French critics immediately received the first great English novels with enthusiasm, and acknowledged them to be, in almost every respect, far superior to their own. This admiration for *Tom Jones* and *Clarissa* being admitted, it is strange that Crébillon, rather than Richardson or Fielding, continued to be imitated in France almost to the end of the century; but the influence of the English novel abroad, although suffused, was manifested in many ways before the age of Rousseau, and is to be considered as perhaps the most vivid which our purely eighteenth-century literature exercised on the continent of Europe. In history, also, the pre-eminence of the English writers made itself felt during the last years of our period. The French and Italians excelled already in memoir-writing and in the compilation of historical essays; but it was not until they had comprehended what Hume and Gibbon had done that they realised the true function of history. It may perhaps be maintained that the *Decline and Fall* was the most epoch-making work of the English eighteenth century as regards the entire literature of Europe.

In speaking of the direct influence of English literature in the eighteenth century upon foreign nations, there are three names which naturally recur to the memory, those of Montesquieu, Lessing, and Rousseau. The famous *Esprit des Lois*, published in 1748, contains a glowing panegyric of the principles of the English

Constitution, and one which could only have been written by a man permeated by the ideas of Locke. Montesquieu knew this country well, and he paid it the compliment of saying, "*L'Angleterre est faite pour y penser.*" When he returned to La Brède in 1731 his leisure was divided between his English garden and his English books. Nevertheless, the traces of the study of English literature on his style are insignificant, and Montesquieu is rather the master of Hume and Burke than the pupil of Locke. Lessing was deeply read in English drama and essay of the Orange and Anne periods, and was the first continental critic to admit the full greatness of our literature. Voltaire, to a less degree, exercised a similar critical spirit, but it was Rousseau in whom the Anglicising influence abroad culminated. Rousseau borrowed from England on all sides, from Hobbes and the Deists, from Locke and the political philosophers, from Clarke and from Richardson, taking whatever he needed, in substance or in form, and throwing it indiscriminately into the fiery crucible of his genius. This fascinating and perilous theme might easily be pursued too far, especially where the expression of literary work rather than its substance is under review; but while we speak of Rousseau as owning, as a novelist, the sway of Richardson, we must not fail to remember that the same is true of Marmontel and of Bernardin de Saint-Pierre, while Goethe no less has acknowledged the debt of all the early German novelists to Goldsmith and Fielding.

As far as the novel is concerned, we cannot be surprised at the attention excited on the continent by this branch of English literature in the eighteenth century. When the period we are considering begins, the ablest exercise of English fiction current was the *Parthenissa* of Roger Boyle (1621-1679), a weak imitation of the Scudéry romances; when it closes, *Evelina* is the novel of the hour, and a great school of original prose narration has adorned the intervening years. Between Boyle and Miss Burney there lies the monument of a vast literary reform, in some respects the most important which the eighteenth century achieved. This reform, which swept away the pinchbeck heroism that was so ridiculous in that singularly unheroic age, which dethroned from fiction the vague worship of rank and substituted a spirit of minute and realistic observation of life and character, had its first exponent in Defoe, who returned, nevertheless, to the *picaresque* tradition, and moved in a world of brigands and bandits which was not entirely genuine. It was much to have got rid of Almahide and Almanzor, but it was necessary to dismiss the cynical pirates of Defoe's lesser romances also, in order to clear the field for perfectly sincere and genuine fiction. The *Gil Blas* of Lesage was an inspiration and a snare to English novelists, who were more healthily, but much less keenly, stimulated by the *Roman Bourgeois* of Furetière. The transition between the harsh, direct narrative of Defoe, without sympathy or insight, and the tender, penetrating fiction of Richardson, is to be found in the urbane essays of Addison and Steele.

So untended was the field of prose narrative in England that a ploughshare was needed to break up the fertile but unready soil, and this instrument was provided by the genius of Defoe, with its clearness of vision, justice of observation, and facility of superficial analysis. But Defoe, that interesting and most difficult of intellectual problems, was too much a creation of his age, was too completely the outcome of a blunt and unsympathetic generation, to comprehend that touch of enthusiasm without which the English novel could not flourish. We see, accordingly, that, twenty years after *Robinson Crusoe* had shown Englishmen what to demand, in a story which, in certain qualities of narrative, would never be excelled, the English novel seemed, nevertheless, as far as ever from coming to the birth. It is the absence of a recognition of this fact which impairs one of the most valuable contributions of recent criticism to the history of the development of the European novel, the *Réforme Littéraire de Defoe*, by M. Jusserand. It is not enough to show what marvels Defoe performed; the picture gives a false impression, unless what Defoe could not perform be also insisted upon.

It was in the fulness of time, when the drama had totally deceased, when the essay of the age of Anne was also in complete decline, when new airs were beginning to blow from the land of romance, when Thomson's landscape and Young's funereal mystery, the starry speculation of Berkeley and the daring imagination of Swift, had prepared men's minds for what was less mundane, less superficial than the observation of material facts, that the novel of feeling began to take its place. It was welcomed from the very first. So weak and faulty a book as *Pamela* must be confessed to be awakened instant and universal enthusiasm, and all mistakes of execution were forgotten in the European acclamation which hailed Richardson as a great creative talent. It was fortunate for our literature that he was immediately succeeded and accompanied by a man of genius still greater than his own; and these two, Fielding and Richardson, remain after a century and a half, in spite of the immense cultivation of the novel, acknowledged masters as well as founders of this vast branch of literature, not superseded and scarcely surpassed by the Scotts and Dumas, the Thackerays and Tolstoïs, the race of giant novelists that have sprung from their loins.

Scarcely less rich or less influential was the chain of metaphysical, or at least philosophical, literature which flourished in England throughout the eighteenth century. But here it seems necessary, in dealing with literature alone, to guard against the obvious manner of observing this group of writers, namely, as a sequence. Berkeley succeeds to Locke, Mandeville to Hobbes, Butler to Shaftesbury, and the student is almost certain to be led away from a consideration of the contributions of these writers to style, into an inquiry into their intellectual relation one to another. We must return to our opening reservation, and remind ourselves that what is written, what is contributed to thought, is not valuable in literature in proportion to its intellectual quality. From the point of view of the philosopher, Berkeley owes his existence to Locke, and is a planet of considerably lesser magnitude, if not absolutely a satellite. From the point of view of style, Berkeley is totally distinct, is divided by a chasm, from Locke, and is a very great, as distinguished from a perfectly ordinary and mediocre, writer.

Taking this standpoint, the most influential philosopher of the first half of the century is Shaftesbury. No one will ever again contend that this unequal writer owed this influence wholly to his merits, or will quarrel with Brown for saying that, in the *Characteristics*, Shaftesbury "hath mingled beauties and blots, faults and excellencies, with a liberal and unsparing hand." But with all its faults, with all its absurdities, the manner of Shaftesbury was stimulating and inflaming to a remarkable degree, and for one eighteenth-century writer who was affected by the noble simplicity of Berkeley, there were a dozen who imitated the ingenuities, the subtle fancies, the curious æsthetic warmth of Shaftesbury. It was not in this country only that the *Characteristics* affected thought and expression. Diderot and Voltaire, in France, Herder, Lessing, and Wieland, in Germany, are only the most illustrious of the direct disciples of "the Virtuoso of Humanity." Much of the admiration of these foreign writers was directed, of course, to Shaftesbury's ethical system; but his style also affected them vividly, and no English metaphysical writer of the eighteenth century has left so strong a mark on European expression.

It is not to deny merit to Shaftesbury to assert that, on the whole, this effect of his upon style was wholly deleterious. He wrote with great care, but with an eagerness to attain grace which was only partially successful, and which, when not successful, gives an impression of strange affectation. Under this quaint air of the fine gentleman, he moves briskly and clearly, and those who felt his charm hastened to imitate his insipidities and oddities. It is Shaftesbury above all other men to whom the guilt must be brought home of having fostered and legitimatised those vague and trite generalities, those empty and ornate forms of expression, those rotund commonplaces, which are so distressing to a modern reader of eighteenth-century literature, and constitute its worst blot. Nor does the propriety of this charge exclude the other, but less material, fact that the writings of Shaftesbury abound, to a degree now but very rarely acknowledged, in passages of genuine and rare beauty. The main circumstance is that Shaftesbury, for some reason which it would be difficult to define, although a second-rate thinker and not a first-rate writer, stamped a caricature of his individuality on the style of the succeeding half century.

It would take us too far, and would, on the whole, lie outside the limits of the particular questions now under consideration, to discuss the relations of the great English and French economists of the centre of the eighteenth century. Although what Adam Smith owed to Quesnay and to Gournay, what Turgot owed to Hutcheson and to Adam Smith, was very considerable, and although such facts as the appearance of the tract, *Sur la Formation et la Distribution des Richesses*, ten years before the publication of *The Wealth of Nations*, are most interesting in themselves, they have no distinct relation to the history of style.

We are on safer ground when we turn from the influence exercised on foreign literature by English writing to the reverse action. The English language was, as a rule, so imperfectly understood on the continent of Europe, and French was so completely the tongue of travelling Englishmen, that what was borrowed from English thought was apt to be taken through the medium of translation. When the century was already half through, such men as Gibbon and Hume were glad to make French the vehicle for their ideas; there is perhaps no other instance than Delolme of the opposite practice, and Delolme was a Swiss. Hence, in the politer and more precise departments of literature, where matter counted for less, and manner more, there was much more apt to be French influence at work in England than English influence at work in France. We see this French spirit active mainly in three principal fields, which may now be examined in some detail. They are non-dramatic poetry, drama, and literary criticism.

In a general survey of English poetry from 1660 to 1780, the first thing that strikes us is that, without ceasing to be either popular or abundant, poetic work has become, and remains to the close of the eighteenth century, subordinated to prose, and of a second order of interest. This was a new thing. Until the end of the sixteenth century, literature in England, broadly speaking, was in verse, and we chronicle its fluctuations without special regard to anything but the quality of this kind of writing. With the Elizabethan period, prose begins to take a very great prominence, and to claim a large place in the history of English style; this place, however, until the Commonwealth, is decidedly subordinated to that occupied by verse. Shakespeare is, on the whole, a more luminous figure than Bacon, and Spenser than Hooker, while, if we go further down in the ranks, the superiority of the poets becomes more and more obvious. We may take an image from the lighthouse service. The Elizabethan poets carry white lights, the prose-men carry red ones, and, as we recede from them all, the red rays do not seem to penetrate so far as the white ones. But with the Restoration this state of things ceases; the art of verse becomes monotonous and mechanical, the prose-writers assert themselves more, are brighter, more various, and more entertaining; and though the poets are slow to lose their personal prestige, the poetic art is no longer paramount. If Dryden dominates the first age, he was a great prosaist as well as a great poet; Swift, though a hardy rhymester, does not live among the poets at all, and Johnson is only admitted by personal favour, on the credit of two paraphrases of Juvenal, among the ranks of those who put on singing raiment. Verse is very active and prominent throughout the eighteenth century, but it plays the part of Mascarille in the comedy of literature. It is no longer the master, but the entertaining and irrepressible domestic, of the imagination.

The eccentricity and lawlessness of seventeenth-century poetry are now recognised even by those who exaggerate its qualities of simplicity, naïveté, and nobility. The necessary reaction which followed the lyrics of Quarles, the epics of the Fletchers, the tragedies of Goff and Cartwright, stranded English poetry high and dry upon the shore of common sense. Where invention had been strained into monstrosity, a decent sterility of imagination began to reign, and a generation of readers whose taste had been positively tortured enjoyed a complete respite from enthusiasm, familiarity, and surprise. In Dryden the English nation found the best possible leader of the chorus for a condition of things so peculiar. The poetic genius of this man was eminently robust and unromantic; sustained at a considerable, but never at a transcendent, height, his shoulders were broad enough and his patience was great enough to support the poetry of his country through a period of forty years, when all that was most essential was that after so many violent oscillations the tradition of verse should for one whole generation be unruffled, and that nothing should be done to destroy the hold which poetry still contrived to maintain, wounded and shaken as it had been, on the respect of men of average intelligence. In order to do this it was necessary to secure a strong popular poet of little invention, indisposed to formal experiment of any kind, more desirous to accompany public taste than to lead it, and such a poet the Restoration revealed in the panegyrist of the *Coronation*. When the entire generation had passed away, the same voice was heard, merely mellowed to a deeper cadence, in the nervous couplets of *Cymon and Iphigenia*. The long dictatorship of Dryden, uninspiring as it seems in various superficial degrees, ought to be regarded with gratitude by every lover of English. Had Dryden been other than he was, or had his life been cut off in early manhood, it is difficult to see what could have prevented our brilliant national poetry from sinking into fantastic ruin, and expiring in a sort of frenzied Gongarism.

Until near the close of the seventeenth century, the direct influence of France upon our poetry is rather surmised than discovered. So far as we can prove its existence, it seems to have been the result of the reading of the French critics rather than of the French poets. Malherbe, it might be supposed, would affect English style, but there seems no evidence that the very name of the Norman reformer had crossed the Channel. Voiture was read, and to some extent imitated; the *vers de société* of this elegant master were distinctly beneficial to the humorous versifiers of the

Revolution and of the Orange period, and through Oldham and Vanbrugh the lighter poetry of our own age claims direct descent from the band who fought around the *Uranie* sonnet. The narrative style of Dryden, perhaps, and of the English poets of the age of Anne, certainly, was strengthened by a study of the *Contes* and *Fables* of Lafontaine. In Prior we at last reach an English poet who can manage the mechanism of a *conte* as well as the most skilful Frenchman. The workmanship of the heroic couplet was probably affected—but on this subject it is most dangerous to dogmatise—not so much by French narrative poetry as by the alexandrines of Corneille and Molière. Probably what had more effect on the Royalist poets than all the practice of the versemen and the dogmas of the critics, was the regular fall of the distich on their ears when they went to see a tragedy or a comedy in Paris before the Restoration.

After 1700 the relation between English and French poetry, though still far from intimate, becomes closer and more definite. St. Evremond in London and Maynwaring in Paris brought the two literary worlds nearer in contact. The story of Maynwaring's visits to the aged Boileau, who, when Dryden died, was glad to be assured that England had possessed a poet, gives us the earliest distinct evidence of the looking to Paris for poetical encouragement. Boileau, thenceforward, though often disrespectfully used in this country, becomes a kind of dictator of taste to English poets, until in 1711 the sceptre seems to descend again to an Englishman, to Pope. In the succeeding generation there is no talk over here of the clever artificial work of the school of Boileau, and Voltaire presently proceeds to London in the same spirit which took Maynwaring to Paris. The result of all this relation, when closely studied, is to persuade us that what is so similar in the English and French poetry of the eighteenth century is mainly an accidental parallelism or a likeness due to simultaneous action of similar intellectual forces, and is not to be accounted for by any very definite discipleship on one hand or on the other. What is very odd is the similarity in phrase, in colour, in the adoption of tricks and fripperies almost exactly identical, the apparent deliberation with which a basis of style is prepared, upon which, at the appointed hour, either an André Chenier or a Wordsworth, a Keats or a Victor Hugo, may build his romantic structure.

From the age of Anne onward the sole object of interest, to the student of broad effects, is the gradual development, as from a grain of mustard-seed, of the mighty tree of naturalism. The prosaic poetry of English rhetoric, which stands, like the Cathedral of Chartres, with its two great towers, the one solid and majestic, the other a miracle of grace and lightness, is an object of definite critical interest. But when we pass Dryden and Pope, we reach a long stretch of country where no poetical structure of complex significance meets us until we arrive at the temple of Wordsworth and Coleridge. During the sixty years which intervene, much was done of a beautiful and accomplished character, but the interest of it is either confined to its relation with the past or to its intuition of the future. The verse of Goldsmith and Churchill has to be considered in the light of Pope, that of Gray and Cowper in the light of Coleridge; all the tract between 1740 and 1800 is covered with accidental, diffused, and tentative work in verse, the work of a period virtually preserved from anarchy only by its lack of animation.

The conditions of drama during the period we are considering were, in some degree, analogous to but much more extraordinary than those of non-dramatic poetry. Between 1660 and 1700 the English stage cannot be called sterile or inanimate, nor was it supported only by the prestige of a single man. Both in its tragic and its comic department it was crowded with figures, enjoyed a lively professional existence which was also literary, and produced a body of work which is very large in quantity and not despicable in quality. The drama of the Restoration is an important fragment of the literature of this country, and if it contains but two names, those of Congreve and Otway, which are in the first rank, it boasts a whole galaxy of the second and third. Tragedy had the marks of decrepitude upon it, but it was alive until the days of Southerne ; sentiment, character, passion, though all clouded by a prevailing insincerity of style, were present. A gulf divides such a drama as Crown's *Thyestes* from *Douglas* or *The Revenge*, a gulf on the earlier side of which are all the traditions of poetry and literature. Of comedy there is still more to be said. To Etheredge belongs a merit above that of any other poet of the age, that of introducing into England a new and vigorous form of imaginative art. Needless to say that this was the Comedy of Manners, sweeping away the old decayed Comedy of Humours, and giving us in its place something of Molière's love of truth and penetration of character. Through Wycherley, Congreve, and Vanbrugh, this school rose to proportions genuinely considerable ; but from the first the English stage, unable to perceive the charm of the purity of French comedy, had defiled our scenes with a cynicism that grew to be intolerable, and English comedy of manners fell before an incursion of indignant puritanism. This fall of comedy is an extraordinary phenomenon. In 1699 England possessed the most vigorous and vivacious school of comic dramatists in Europe; ten years later the chorus was absolutely silenced, or vocal only in the feeble pipe of Colley Cibber. Through the remaining years of the eighteenth century, dramatic vitality was accidental and sporadic ; a good play appeared from time to time, but there was no school of dramatic literature, no school of capable literary writers for the stage.

Some hints of the modern drama, pure and simple, are to be met with in writers who scarcely demand a word from the historian for their personal merits. A Moorgate jeweller, George Lillo (1693-1739), amused the town with some perfectly unreadable plays, principally *George Barnwell* and *The Fatal Curiosity*, which are interesting as the first specimens of " *tragedie bourgeoise* " or modern melodrama. These artless dramas were composed in the interests of morality and virtue, and are the parents of a long line of didactic plays of crime and its punishment. Of somewhat the same character were the sentimental comedies, influenced by the " *comédies larmoyantes* " of La Chaussée. There were various other innovations, mostly of a non-literary or anti-literary kind, such as the introduction of popular opera early in the reign of Anne, and the fashion for pantomimic drama which came in some forty years later. All tended to sever more and more completely the marriage between literature and the theatre, and to destroy that art of drama which had existed until the close of the seventeenth century. The four or five best plays of the eighteenth century are comedies in which Goldsmith, Colman, and Sheridan have deliberately gone back to the Congreve and Wycherley tradition, and have resumed, with the reprehensible elements omitted, the style and method of the great comedians of manners. But these are exceptions, and only enough to prove the rule of dramatic insignificance in England from 1700 onward.

Too little attention has been given to the growth of literary criticism in England. It begins, so far as a modern conception of the critical faculty is concerned, with the Restoration and in the famous prefaces of Dryden. Before this what passed for criticism had been the pseudo-philosophical reflections of rhetoricians. The first professional criticism in England, if we ignore the dissertations of Dryden, was that introduced about 1675 from France, where the Jesuit critics, Le Bossu and Rapin, began to formularise and adapt to modern poetry the rules of Aristotle. These rules were soon adopted in this country, particularly by a writer, Thomas Rymer (1638-1713), who made himself highly ridiculous by using them as a standard by which to measure and condemn Shakespeare and Fletcher. These Jesuit critics, by no means wanting in wit, knowledge, or even, in the case of Rapin, taste, were more fitted to deal with French literature than English. They were ready cheerfully to undertake to shut up all individual inspiration within limits which they rigorously defined, and they were only serviceable so long as men were passing through that curious condition of craving for order and regularity.

In John Dennis, a writer to whom great injustice has been and still is done, a critic appeared who, with great faults of temper, had a far higher idea than Rapin or Rymer, or even Dryden, of certain classes of poetic work. The praise is due to Dennis of having been the first to dwell judicially on the sublime merits of Milton, and to give him his right place among the poets of the world. Literary criticism, by which was principally meant the analysis of poetry and the poetic art, received further contributions from Shaftesbury and Addison. As the century proceeded, more and more was attempted in this direction, until it may be said that critical analysis began to take a part in general literature which was unwholesomely prominent. Some parts of the work of men like Lord Kames and Hurd are good and readable as literature, though not very useful as criticism; most of it is deliberately to be condemned as empirical, dull, and preposterous, and as leaving out of discussion the only elements worthy to be included. The criticism of Matthew Arnold or Sainte-Beuve is not a development of such criticism as that of Hurd; it is something wholly different in kind, starting from another basis and aiming at another goal. To the comparative student a few words which Gray has scattered here and there in his prose, and some sturdy positive pages in Doctor Johnson, comprise all of literary criticism which is really noteworthy after the age of Anne is over. In Dennis and Addison criticism possessed something of the personal accent, and faintly suggested a *causerie*. But this was soon lost in the pretentiousness of a false philosophy, and criticism ceases to be the expression of genuine individuality.

The place of theology in eighteenth-century literature, properly so called, has been greatly exaggerated. The importance of theology in the vicissitudes of thought during the same period could hardly be overrated. The progress of independent speculation, whether tending toward scepticism as in the Deists, or toward a closer puritanism as in the Methodists, or toward the more conservative reaction of the Evangelicals, is of great historical interest. But a florid page of Jeremy Taylor gives a critic of style more to talk about than all Toland's tracts or Whitefield's sermons. Berridge's *Christian World Unmasked*, which just comes within our period, is a typical instance of divinity produced solely to rouse the conscience and excite the belief in a supernatural creed, without a single appeal, in the turn of a sentence or the choice of a word, to any other purpose. With such a writer all the charms of intellectual expression were so many narcotics provided to dull the soul's sense of its awful condition. With the Deists, with those curious Chubbs and Annets and Collinses who wandered about in sheepskins and goatskins under George I., and whose scattered leaves have been so tenderly examined by Sir Leslie Stephen, —with these, also, the substance was everything and the form nothing, except when, like Shaftesbury and Conyers Middleton, they rose upon a politer sphere, and only hinted their deism incidentally. Needless to add that the same spirit, so inimical to literature, actuated those orthodox divines who denounced these dry and uninspired opponents.

It became no better when the rage for speculation died away, and calm fell upon the theologians. The rationalism of the English Church after 1750 gave no encouragement to enthusiasm or imagination; it even kept in check what had inspired a good deal of seventeenth-century Church literature, personal oddity. The principal representative of this late class of theologian is William Paley (1743-1805), who summed up the dry and almost mathematical manner of his age when it had nearly closed. The *Horæ Paulinæ*, it is true, did not appear until 1790; but Paley may very well be taken as characteristic of the theological style of the forty years preceding, and between Paley's literary form and the sapless legal style of Clarke, in the age of Anne, there is so little difference that we are tempted to regard these two as typical of their respective groups. If, then, we can say that in the generation of Swift leading theologians wrote like Clarke, and in the age of Burke like Paley, we are almost justified by that very circumstance in conjecturing that the contributions of eighteenth-century divinity to literature are so small that they are hardly worth considering. Among all the divines, the one who wrote most vigorously is perhaps that very ingenious and powerful Tertullian of the nonjurors, William Law.

The student will not omit to note, as one of the interesting features of the eighteenth century, the school of history which arose in England toward the end of the reign of George II. History at its best had been what Lamb, with an intention wholly laudatory, calls the chronicles of Burnet, "good old prattle," garrulous and pleasant. Early in the century, the laborious compilations of Strype, Carte, and Echard, which were innocent of any general horizon, of any clear or correct view of the relation of one part of history to another, were accepted as contributions to the science. Rapin's *History of England* and Rollin's *Ancient History*, which were well known in England, aimed somewhat higher, but no other French historian, before Voltaire, had any influence in this country; and when the new school made its appearance, it was of purely English growth. The year 1754, in which Hume printed the first volume of his *History of England*, is the date of the burgeoning of English history; it came to its full greatness in 1776, with the publication of the first volume of Gibbon's *Decline and Fall*. The sudden efflorescence of this school of historians, with Hume, Gibbon, and Robertson at its head, may be not too fantastically compared with that of the first great generation of novelists, who began to appear twelve years prior to Hume, and who sustained their glory about as long as the historians did. After Gibbon's death there occurred a period of relapse analogous to that which succeeded the death of Smollett.

The condition of England had, since late in the Renaissance, afforded no general opportunities for the cultivation of purely provincial literature until the eighteenth century began. The existence of work in dialects or inspired by provincial feeling became from that time forth too evident to be overlooked. But it is the revival of letters in Scotland which is likely first of all to attract the notice of a student, and it is the more necessary to dwell on this because that revival, although more important than any other of its class, was at first so imitative, and remained so feeble until near the end of the century, that it may easily be lost sight of in the glare of English literature. There went on a curious struggle between pure Scots and classic English—men who, as Ramsay of Ochtertyre puts it, "spoke their mother-tongue without disguise," finding it exceedingly difficult to suppress that native idiom when they came to emulate the *Spectator* or the *Tatler*. The worst of it was that the Scots tongue was looked upon as rude and contemptible, and for a long time even the preachings and the practice of Allan Ramsay did not contrive to make the dialect fashionable. The revival of popular poetry came at last, and culminated splendidly in Burns. The use of Scotch prose, except by the novelists in dialogue, has never been seriously accepted, and probably never will be. Toward the close of the eighteenth century America began to supply herself with a species of literature, which, however, gave at first but little promise of all she has done within the last hundred years. By far the most eminent of the early American writers was Benjamin Franklin (1706-1790), whose works, first collected in 1779, only just come within our chronological limits. Franklin's style is notoriously graceful and charming, but he is almost the only American writer before the Independence who can be named with the recognised masters of eighteenth-century English. It is curious to reflect that in 1780, a date which to the historian of English literature seems late indeed, neither Washington Irving nor Bryant, neither the father of American prose nor the father of American poetry, was yet born.

This so-called classic age of ours has long ceased to be regarded with that complacency which led the most flourishing part of it to adopt the epithet "Augustan." It will scarcely be denied by its greatest admirer, if he be a man of wide reading, that it cannot be ranked with the poorest of the five great ages of literature. Deficient in the highest intellectual beauty, in the qualities which awaken the fullest critical enthusiasm, the eighteenth century will be enjoyed more thoroughly by those who make it their special study than by those who skim the entire surface of literature. It has, although on the grand scale condemned as second-rate, a remarkable fulness and sustained richness which endear it to specialists. If it be compared, for instance, with the real Augustan age in Rome, or with the Spanish period of literary supremacy, it may claim to hold its own against these rivals in spite of their superior rank, because of its more copious interest. If it has neither a Horace nor a Calderon, it has a great extent and variety of writers just below these in merit, and far more numerous than what Rome or Spain can show during those blossoming periods. It is, moreover, fertile at far more points than either of these schools. This sustained and variegated success, at a comparatively low level of effort, strikes one as characteristic of an age more remarkable for persistent vitality than for rapid and brilliant growth. The Elizabethan *vivida vis* is absent, the Georgian glow has not yet dawned; but there is a suffused prosaic light of intelligence, of cultivated form, over the whole picture; and during the first half of the period, at least, this is bright enough to be very attractive.

Perhaps, in closing, the distinguishing mark of eighteenth-century literature may be indicated as its mastery of prose as a vehicle for general thought. It is customary to note the Restoration as marking the point where English prose took a modern form. This is true, but there was nevertheless much left to reform in the practice of authors. At the close of the reign of Charles II., we find the most accomplished prose-writer of the age still encumbering himself in the toils of such sentences as this:

"That which is not pleasant to me, may be to others who judge better, and to prevent an accusation from my enemies, I am sometimes ready to imagine that my disgust of low comedy proceeds not so much from my judgment as from my temper, which is the reason why I so seldom write it, and that when I succeed in it, I mean so far as to please the audience, yet I am nothing satisfied with what I have done, but am often vexed to hear the people laugh and clap, as they perpetually do, where I intended them no jest, while they let pass the better things, without taking notice of them."

A hundred years later, such a sentence had become an impossibility. It is not merely that we should search Burke or

Robertson in vain, at their weariest moments, for such a flaccid chain of clauses, but that the ordinary newspaper-man, the reporter or inventor of last night's speeches, would no longer endure this clumsy form, this separation of the noun from its verb, and the pronoun from its noun. It was the work of the period which we roughly describe as the eighteenth century to reform and regulate ordinary writing. It found English prose antiquated, amorphous, without a standard of form; it left it a finished thing, the completed body for which subsequent ages could do no more than weave successive robes of ornament and fashion.

BIBLIOGRAPHY

ADDISON, JOSEPH, vols. i.-iv., Oxford, 1830.
Akenside, Mark. Ed. Dyce. In the Aldine Poets.
Amory. Life of John Buncle, 4 vols. New edition, 1770.
Anstey, C., Poetical Works. Ed. Anstey, 1808.
Arbuthnot, John. [Not yet edited.]
Armstrong, John. In Chalmers's English Poets, vol. xvi.

BARROW, ISAAC, vols. i.-viii. Theological Works, Oxford, 1830.
Baxter, Richard, Works. Ed. Orme, vols. i.-xxiii., 1830.
Beattie, James. In Chalmers's English Poets, vol. xviii.
Behn, Mrs. Aphra, Dramatic Works. Ed. Pearson, 1874.
Bentley, Richard, Works. Ed. Dyce, vols. i.-iii., 1836-38.
Berkeley, George, Works. Ed. Fraser, 3 vols., Oxford, 1871.
Blackstone, Sir William, Commentaries. Ed. Kerr, 4 vols., 1876.
Blair, Hugh. Ed. Finlayson, 4 vols., 1815, and 3 vols., 1817.
Blair, Robert. In Chalmers's English Poets, vol. xv.
Bolingbroke, Viscount, Philosophical Works. Ed. Mallet, 5 vols., 1754.
Boswell, James, Life of Samuel Johnson. Ed. Birkbeck Hill, 6 vols., 1887.
Boyle, Hon. Robert, Works. Ed. Birch, 5 vols., 1744.
Brooke, Henry, The Fool of Quality. Ed. Kingsley, 2 vols., 1859.
Broome, William. In Chalmers's English Poets, vol. xii.
Bruce, Michael, Poetical Works. Ed. Grosart, Edinburgh, 1865.
Buckingham, G. Villiers, 2d Duke of, The Rehearsal. Ed. Arber, 1868.
Buckinghamshire, John Sheffield, Duke of. In Chalmers's English Poets, vol. x.
Budgell, Eustace. [Not yet edited.]
Bunyan, John, Works. Ed. Offor, 3 vols., Glasgow, 1855.
Burke, Edmund, Works. 16 vols., 1826-27.
Burnet, Gilbert, History of His Own Time. 6 vols., Oxford, 1833.
Burnet, Thomas. [Not yet edited.]
Butler, Joseph, Works. Ed. Halifax, 2 vols., Oxford, 1835-36.
Butler, Samuel. 2 vols., Aldine Poets.
Byrom, John. In Chalmers's English Poets, vol. xv.

CARTE, THOMAS, History of England. 4 vols., 1747-55.
Chalmers, A., English Poets. 21 vols. 1810.
Chatterton, Thomas, Works. Ed. Skeat, 2 vols., Aldine Poets, 1875.

BIBLIOGRAPHY

Chesterfield, Earl of, Letters. Ed. Mahon, 5 vols., 1845-53.
Churchill, Charles, Poetical Works. 2 vols., Aldine Poets.
Cibber, Colley, Dramatic Works. 5 vols., 1736.
Clarke, Samuel, Works. Ed. Hoadly, 4 vols., 1738.
Collins, William, Poetical Works. Ed. Mon. Thomas, Aldine Poets.
Colman, George, the Elder, Dramatic Works. 4 vols., 1777.
Congreve, William, Dramatic Works. Ed. Ewald, 1887.
Cowley, Abraham, Works. Ed. Grosart, 2 vols., 1881.
Creech, Thomas. [Not yet edited.]
Crown, John, Works. 4 vols., Edinburgh, 1873-74.
Croxall, Samuel. [Not yet edited.]
Cudworth, Intellectual System. Ed. Birch, Andover, U.S.A., 1837-38.
Cumberland, Richard, Dramatic Works. British Theatre, vol. xx.

DARWIN, ERASMUS. [Not yet edited.]
Davenant, Sir William, Works. 5 vols., Edinburgh, 1882-84.
Defoe, Daniel, Miscellaneous Works. 20 vols., Oxford, 1840-41.
Delolme, Jean Louis, Constitution of England, 1807.
Denham, Sir John, Poetical Works. Chalmers's English Poets, vol. vii.
Dennis, John. [Not yet edited.]
Doddridge, Philip, Works. 10 vols., Leeds, 1802-5.
Dorset, Charles, Earl of, Poetical Works. Chalmers's English Poets, vol. viii.
Dryden, John, Works. Ed. Scott and Saintsbury, 19 vols. (vols. i.-xiii. issued), 1882-88, etc.
Dyer, John, Poems. Chalmers's English Poets, vol. xvii.

ETHEREDGE, SIR GEORGE. Ed. Verity, 1888.
Evelyn, John, Diary. Ed. Wheatley, 4 vols., 1879.

FALCONER, WILLIAM, Poems. Aldine Poets.
Farquhar, George, Dramatic Works. Ed. Leigh Hunt.
Fergusson, Robert, Works. Ed. Peterkin, 1807.
Fielding, Henry, Works. Ed. Leslie Stephen, 10 vols., 1882-83.
Fielding, Sarah. [Not yet edited.]
Foote, Samuel, Dramatic Works. Ed. Bee [Badcock], 3 vols., 1830.
Franklin, Benjamin, Works. Ed. Sparks, 10 vols., Boston, U.S.A., 1840.

GARTH, SIR SAMUEL, Poetical Works. Chalmers's English Poets, vol. ix.
Gay, John, Works. 6 vols., 1772-78.
Gibbon, Edward, Miscellaneous Works. Ed. Sheffield, 5 vols., 1814.
    Decline and Fall. Ed. Milman, 12 vols., 1838-39.
Glover, Richard, Poetical Works. Chalmers's English Poets, vol. xvii.
Goldsmith, Oliver, Works. Ed. Gibbs, 5 vols., 1884-86.
Grainger, James, Poetical Works. Chalmers's English Poets, vol. xiv.
Gray, Thomas, Works. Ed. Edmund Gosse, 4 vols., 1884.
Green, Matthew, Poems. Chalmers's English Poets, vol. xv.

HALIFAX, GEORGE SAVILE, Marquis of. Ed. Foxcroft, 2 vols., 1898.
Hartley, David, Observations on Man. Ed. Pistorius, 3 vols., 1801.
Head, Richard, The English Rogue. 4 vols. [n.d. 1875?]
Hoadly, Benjamin, Works. Ed. Hoadly, 3 vols., 1773.

BIBLIOGRAPHY 403

Home, John, Works.   Ed. Mackenzie, 3 vols., 1822.
Howard, Sir Robert, Dramatic Works, 1722.
Hughes, John.   [Not yet edited.]
Hume, David, Philosophical and Miscellaneous Works.   Ed. Green and Grose, 4 vols., 1874-75.
Hurd, Richard, Works.   8 vols., 1811.
Hutcheson, Francis.   [Not yet edited.]

JOHNSON, SAMUEL, Works.   Ed. Murphy, 12 vols., 1824.
Junius.   Ed. Wade, 2 vols., 1850.

LAW, WILLIAM, Works.   9 vols., 1762.
Lee, Nathaniel.   [Not yet edited.]
Lillo, George, Dramatic Works.   2 vols., 1775.
Lloyd, Robert, Poetical Works.   Chalmers's English Poets, vol. xv.
Locke, John, Works.   10 vols., 1812.
Logan, John, Poems.   Chalmers's English Poets, vol. xviii.
Lyttelton, George, 1st Lord, Works.   Ed. Ayscough, 3 vols., 1776.

MACKENZIE, HENRY, Works.   8 vols., Edinburgh, 1808.
Mandeville, Bernard de.   [Not yet edited.]
Marvell, Andrew, Works.   Ed. Grosart, 4 vols., 1872-75.
Mason, William, Works.   4 vols., 1811.
Middleton, Conyers, Miscellaneous Works.   5 vols., 1755.
Montagu, Lady Mary Wortley, Letters and Works.   Ed. Thomas, 2 vols., 1887.

OLDHAM, JOHN, Political Works.   Ed. Bell, 1854.
Oldys, William, Life of Raleigh.   Oxford, 1829.
Otway, Thomas, Works.   Ed. Thornton, 3 vols., 1813.

PALEY, WILLIAM, Works.   Ed. Paley, 4 vols., 1838.
Paltock, Robert, Peter Wilkins.   Ed. Bullen, 2 vols., 1884.
Parnell, Thomas, Poetical Works.   In the Aldine Poets.
Pearson, John, Exposition of the Creed.   Ed. Chevallier, Cambridge, 1849.
Pepys' Diary.   Ed. Braybrooke and Mynors Bright, 6 vols., 1875-79.
Philips, Ambrose, Poems.   Chalmers's English Poets, vol. xiii.
Philips, John, Poems.   Chalmers's English Poets, vol. viii.
Pix, Mary.   [Not yet edited.]
Pope, Alexander, Works.   Ed. Elwin and Courthope, 11 vols., 1870-1889.
Prior, Matthew, Poetical Works.   2 vols.   In the Aldine Poets.

RAMSAY, ALLAN, Works.   Ed. Tennant, 2 vols., Paisley, 1877.
Reid, Thomas, Works.   Ed. Hamilton, 2 vols., Edinburgh, 1872.
Richardson, Samuel, Works.   Ed. Leslie Stephen, 12 vols., 1883.
Robertson, William, Works.   Ed. Stewart, 9 vols., 1824.
Rochester, John Wilmot, Earl of, Poems.   Chalmers's English Poets, vol. viii.
Roscommon, Wentworth Dillon, Earl of, Poems.   Chalmers's English Poets, vol. viii.

SAVAGE, RICHARD, Works.   Ed. Johnson, 2 vols., 1777.
Secker, Thomas, Sermons.   Ed. Porteus, 7 vols., 1771.
Sedley, Sir Charles, Works.   2 vols., 1778.

Settle, Elkanah. [Not yet edited.]
Shadwell, Thomas, Dramatic Works. 4 vols., 1720.
Shaftesbury, A. A., Earl of, Characteristics. Ed. Hotch, vol. i. only, 1870. Baskerville Edition, 1773.
Shenstone, William, Works. 3 vols., 1791.
Sheridan, R. B., Dramatic Works. Ed. Leigh Hunt, 1841.
Sherlock, Thomas, Works. Ed. Hughes, 5 vols., 1830.
Smart, Christopher, Poems. Chalmers's English Poets, vol. xvi.
Smith, Adam, Wealth of Nations. Ed. Thorold Rogers, 2 vols., Oxford, 1869.
Smollett, Tobias George, Works. Ed. Browne, 8 vols., 1872.
Somerville, William, Poetical Works. Chalmers's English Poets, vol. xi.
South, Robert, Sermons. 7 vols., Oxford, 1823.
Southerne, Thomas, Dramatic Works. 2 vols., 1713.
Steele, Sir Richard, Selected Works. Ed. Dobson, 1885.
Sterne, Laurence, Works. Ed. Browne, 2 vols., 1885.
Swift, Jonathan, Works. Ed. Sir Walter Scott, 19 vols., 1883-84.
Sydney, Algernon, Works. Ed. Robertson, 1772.

TEMPLE, SIR WILLIAM, Works. 4 vols., 1770.
Thomson, James, Poetical Works. Ed. Nicholas. In the Aldine Poets.
Tillotson, Archbishop, Works. 12 vols., 1742-43.

VANBRUGH, SIR JOHN, Dramatic Works. Ed. Leigh Hunt.

WALLER, EDMUND, Poetical Works. Ed. Fenton, 1740.
Walpole, Horace, Works. 5 vols., 1798.
    Letters. Ed. Cunningham, 9 vols., 1857-59.
Warburton, William, Works. Ed. Hurd, 7 vols., 1788.
Warton, Thomas, Poetical Works. Ed. Mant, 2 vols., Oxford, 1802.
    History of English Poetry. Ed. Hazlitt, 4 vols., 1871.
Welsted, Leonard, Works. Ed. Nichols, 1787.
Wesley, John, Works. 14 vols., 1829-31.
West, Richard, Poems. Anderson's British Poets, vol. x.
White, Gilbert, Works. Ed. Bell, 2 vols., 1877.
Whitehead, William, Poetical Works. Chalmers's English Poets, vol. xvii.
Wilkins, John, Works. 2 vols., 1802.
Williams, Sir Charles Hanbury, Works. Ed. Horace Walpole, 3 vols., 1882.
Wilson, John, Works. Edinburgh, 1884.
Winchelsea, Anne, Countess of. [Not yet edited.]
Wycherley, William, Dramatic Works. Ed. Ward, 1887.

YALDEN, THOMAS, Poems. Chalmers's English Poets, vol. xi.
Young, Edward, Poetical Works. 2 vols. In the Aldine Poets.

[This Bibliography is intended to serve as an indication to the student of the most conveniently accessible text of the principal writers mentioned in this volume. Where the author is described as "not yet edited," the reader is referred to the original forms of publication.]

INDEX

Absalom and Achitophel, Dryden, 14, 15, 16, 18, 59.
Acetaria, Evelyn, 79, 375.
Adams, Jean, 340.
Addison, Joseph, 99, 101, 105-7, 112, 114, 117, 123, 137, 138, 147, 150, 177, 186, 187-191, 192, 193-5, 243, 271, 311, 380, 381.
Admiral Hosier's Ghost, Glover, 228.
Advancement of Learning, Cowley, 77.
Adventurer, Hawkesworth's, 289.
Adventures of an Atom, Smollett, 262.
Akenside, Mark, 196, 311, 312.
Alcander, Pope, 109.
Alcibiades, Otway, 54.
Alciphron, or the Minute Philosopher, Berkeley, 201.
Alexander's Feast, Dryden, 22.
Alfred, Thomson and Mallet, 225.
All for Love, Dryden, 13, 45, 92.
Allies, Conduct of the, Swift, 155, 167.
Alma, Prior, 134.
Almanzor and Almahide, Dryden, 42-4, 91.
Amelia, Fielding, 244, 256, 257.
American Taxation, Burke's *Speech on*, 369.
Amory, Thomas, 278, 279.
Amphitryon, Dryden, 45.
Analogy of Religion, Butler, 275.
Anecdotes of Painting, Walpole, 300.
Annual Register, 368.
Annus Mirabilis, Dryden, 10, 11, 91.
Anstey, Christopher, 315, 316.
Anti-Elixir, Boyle, 376.
Antony and Cleopatra, Dryden, 13.
Appius and Virginia, Dennis, 111.
Arbuthnot, John, 156, 159, 160, 167-9.
Arbuthnot, Pope's *Epistle to Dr.*, 129.
Architectura, Evelyn, 78.

Armstrong, John, 227, 228.
Arnold, Matthew, 24, 90, 395.
Articles, Exposition of the Thirty-nine, G. Burnet, 102.
Assignation, Dryden, 44, 92.
Astræa Redux, Dryden, 10, 379.
Atterbury, Francis [Bishop of Rochester], 103, 104, 127, 199.
Atterbury, Lewis, 103.
Auld Langsyne, Sempill, 33.
Auld Robin Gray, Barnard, 340.
Aureng-Zebe, Dryden, 13, 44, 92.
Austen, Jane, 272.

Badman, Life and Death of Mr., Bunyan, 84, 85.
Barbauld, Anna Letitia, 246, 343.
Barnard, Lady Anne, 340.
Barrington, Hon. Daines, 303.
Barrow, Isaac, 88, 89.
Barry, Mrs., 54.
Bastard, The, Savage, 217.
Battle of the Books, Swift, 140, 143.
Battle of the Frogs and Mice, Parnell, 119.
Baucis and Philemon, Swift, 153.
Baxter, Richard, 76.
Beattie, James, 327.
Beauty, Inquiry concerning, Hutcheson, 277.
Beaux' Stratagem, The, Farquhar, 71.
Beggar's Opera, Gay, 135.
Behn, Mrs. Aphra, 32, 51, 242, 244; her *Songs*, 32, 54.
Bellamira, Sedley, 50.
Belle's Stratagem, The, Parkhouse (Mrs. Cowley), 338.
Benevolence, Armstrong, 227.
Bentley, Richard, 103, 104, 147.
Bergerac, Cyrano de, 160.

Berkeley, George [Bishop], 95, 156, 197-203, 277, 381, 386.
Berridge's *Christian World Unmasked*, 395.
"Bickerstaff, Isaac," 151, 152, 188.
Blackstone, Sir William, 307, 308.
Blair, Hugh, 302, 335.
Blair, Robert, 220, 221.
Blenheim, Philips, 108.
Boileau, 132, 133, 383, 391.
Bolingbroke, Viscount, 126, 128 173, 174, 367.
Boswell, James, 291, 292, 358.
Botanic Garden, Darwin, 328, 329.
Boyle, Hon. Robert, 81, 149, 376.
Boyle, Roger, 384.
Brooke, Fulke Greville, Lord, 9.
Brooke, Henry, 218, 271.
Broome, William, 119.
Browne, Dr. Peter, 197.
Browne, Isaac Hawkins, 229.
Browne, Sir Thomas, 194.
Browning, Robert, 315.
Bruce, Michael, 327.
Brutus, Lucius Junius, Lee, 58.
Buckingham, George Villiers, 2d Duke of, 43, 60, 61.
Buckingham [Mulgrave, *which see*], Duke of, 31.
Budgell, Eustace, 190.
Bunyan, John, 82-6, 242.
Burke, Edmund, 362, 365-74, 377.
Burnet, Gilbert [Bishop], 102, 103, 149, 204, 305.
Burnet, Thomas, 99, 100.
Burney, Miss Frances, 361, 362.
Burns, Robert, 33, 339, 341, 342.
Busiris, Young, 211.
Butler, Joseph [Bishop], 273, 274-7, 280.
Butler, Samuel, 26-8, 61, 134.
Byrom, John, 214, 215.

Cadenus and Vanessa, Swift, 162.
Caldecott, Randolph, 321.
Caleb Williams, Godwin, 244.
Caligula, Crown, 58.
Call to the Unconverted, Baxter, 76.
Cambyses, Settle, 59.
Campaign, The, Addison, 106, 107.
Campbell, Dr. George, 363.
Canterbury Tales, Chaucer, 3.
Captain Singleton, Life of, Defoe, 179, 181.

Careless Husband, The, Cibber, 70.
Carte, Thomas, 397.
Carter, Elizabeth, 288.
Caryll, John, 112, 131.
Castle of Indolence, Thomson, 225, 226, 227.
Castle of Otranto, Walpole, 244, 271, 301, 302.
Catalogue of Royal and Noble Authors, Walpole, 300.
Cato, Tragedy of, Addison, 106, 116, 190, 199.
Cave, Edward, 284.
Caylus, Comte de, 302.
Chamberlaine, Frances, 361.
Chapone, Mrs. *See* Mulso.
Character of a Trimmer, Savile, 89.
Characteristics of Men, etc., Anthony, 3d Earl of Shaftesbury, 171, 311, 387.
Charles V., History of Reign of, Robertson, 304.
Charleton, Walter, 74.
Chase, The, Somerville, 138.
Chatterton, Thomas, 331-4.
Chaucer, Geoffrey, 3, 22.
Cheats, The, Wilson, 39.
Chesterfield, Philip Dormer, Earl of, 228, 280, 289.
Choice, Pomfret, 107.
Christian Hero, The, Steele, 187.
Christianity, Argument against Abolishing, Swift, 150.
Christianity not Mysterious, Toland, 175.
Christie, W. D., 18.
Chrysal, Johnstone, 244, 271.
Chubb, Thomas, 273.
Churchill, Charles, 231, 322-5.
Cibber, Colley, 69, 70, 122, 124, 317, 393.
Cicero, Life of, Middleton, 278.
Cider, Philips, 108.
Circassian, The Fair, Croxall, 138.
Citizen of the World, Goldsmith, 346, 349.
Clandestine Marriage, Colman and Garrick, 318.
Claremont, Garth, 34.
Clarendon, Earl of, 74.
Clarissa, Richardson, 244, 247-9, 383.
Clarke, Samuel, 195, 196, 198, 273, 274, 384, 396.
Cleomenes, Dryden, 45.

INDEX

Cleveland, John, 28.
Coleridge, Samuel Taylor, 334.
Collier, Jeremy, 67, 69.
Collins, Anthony, 175.
Collins, William, 208, 231-5.
Colman, George, the Elder, 318, 319, 355.
Colonel Jack, Defoe, 179, 181.
Comical Revenge, Etheredge, 46.
Commentaries on the Laws, Blackstone, 307.
Conduct of the Allies, Swift, 155, 167.
Confederacy, The, Vanbrugh, 68, 69.
Congreve, William, 53, 64-7, 141, 150, 319, 379, 380.
Conscious Lovers, Steele, 187, 192.
Constant Couple, The, Farquhar, 70.
Contentment, Hymn to, Parnell, 137.
Contests and Dissensions in Athens and Rome, Swift, 149.
Conversation, Polite, Swift, 164.
Cooper's Hill, Denham, 5, 34.
Coriolanus, Thomson, 228.
Corneille, 93.
Coronation Panegyric, Dryden, 10.
Corsica, Boswell, 358.
Count Fathom, Smollett, 261.
Country Wife, Wycherley, 52.
Courthope, Mr. W. J., 106, 131.
Cowley, Mrs. *See* Parkhouse, Hannah.
Cowley, Abraham, 5-8, 77, 78, 101.
Cowley, Life of, Sprat, 359.
Cowper, William, 325.
Crabbe, George, 220.
Craggs, Robert. *See* Nugent, Lord.
Crébillon, 383.
Creech, Thomas, 21.
Creed, Exposition of the, Pearson, 76.
Critic, The, Sheridan, 61, 337.
Critical Review, Smollett, 261.
Criticism, Essay on, Pope, 111.
Cromwell, Discourse concerning Oliver, Cowley, 77.
Crown, John, 58, 59.
Croxall, Samuel, 138, 139.
Cuckoo, To the, Bruce, 327.
Cudworth, Ralph, 77, 81.
Cumberland, Richard, 338.
Cumnor Hall, Meikle, 327.
Curll, Edmund, 122.
Cythereia, 118.

Damascus, Siege of, Hughes, 188.
Darwin, Erasmus, 4, 219, 310, 328.

Davenant, Sir William, 8, 9, 38, 39, 60.
David Simple, S. Fielding, 243, 254, 264, 265.
Davideis, Cowley, 6.
De Quincey, Thomas, 241.
Death, Practical Treatise on, Sherlock, 101.
Decline and Fall of the Roman Empire, Gibbon, 352, 353, 354-7, 383.
Defoe, Daniel, 176-185, 242, 385.
Deists, Short and easy Method with the, Leslie, 174.
Delolme, Jean Louis, 363, 388.
Denham, Sir John, 4, 5, 34.
Dennis, John, 111, 114, 122, 185, 394.
Description of an Author's Bedroom, Goldsmith, 321.
Deserted Village, The, Goldsmith, 320, 321.
Diary of Evelyn, 79.
Diary of Pepys, 97.
Dictionary, Johnson's, 280, 289, 290.
Discourses, Sir J. Reynolds, 308.
Dispensary, Garth, 34, 379.
Dissenters, The Shortest Way with the, Defoe, 177.
Divine Legation, Warburton, 281.
Dobson, Mr. Austin, 195, 206, 254, 347.
Doddridge, Philip, 228.
Don Carlos, Otway, 54.
Don Quixote, Smollett's trans., 261.
Don Sebastian, Dryden, 45.
Donne, Satires of Dr., Pope, 130.
Dorset, Charles Sackville, Lord, 20, 32.
Double Dealer, Congreve, 65.
Douglas, Rev. J. Home, 232.
Dramatic Poetry, Essay on, Dryden, 91.
Drapier's Letters, Swift, 156-9.
Drummer, The, Addison, 191.
Dryden, John, 4, 5, 9-26, 30, 31, 37, 41-6, 48, 49, 60, 62, 65, 89, 90-4, 105, 131, 133, 142, 373, 379, 380, 389, 390.
Dryden's *Songs*, 12, 25.
Duncan Campbell, Mr., Defoe, 179.
Dunciad, The, Pope, 119, 123, 132, 159.
Dunciad, The New, Pope, 124, 130.
Dyer, John, 219.

Earth, The Sacred Theory of the, Burnet, 98.
Earth may be a Planet, That the, Wilkins, 75.

INDEX

Echard, Laurence, 397.
Economy of Love, Armstrong, 227.
Education, Thoughts concerning, Locke, 95.
Elegy on Anne Killigrew, Dryden, 19.
Elegy to the Memory of an Unfortunate Lady, Pope, 120.
Elegy written in a Country Churchyard, Gray, 207, 236, 239, 240.
Eloisa to Abelard, Pope, 120, 121, 207.
Elysium Britannicum, Evelyn, 79.
English Commerce, The Plan of, Defoe, 179.
English Language, Proposal for correcting the, Swift, 155.
English Poets, Account of the Greatest, Addison, 106.
English Poets, Lives of the, Johnson, 293.
Englishman, True-born, Defoe, 177.
Enquiry into Polite Learning, Goldsmith, 345, 347, 348.
Enthusiasm, Letter concerning, Shaftesbury, 171.
Epistle to Dr. Arbuthnot, Pope, 129.
Epistle to the Earl of Dorset, Philips, 137.
Epsom Wells, Shadwell, 49.
Esprit des Lois, 383.
Essay on Man, Pope, 126, 127, 132, 171.
Essays, Cowley, 77, 78.
Essays, Goldsmith, 346, 349.
Essays, Hume, 296.
Etheredge, Sir George, 32, 41, 46-8, 51, 64, 393.
Evelina, Miss Burney, 244, 361, 384.
Evening, Ode to, W. Collins, 233.
Evergreen, The, Ramsay, 139.
Evelyn, John, 53, 78-80, 376.
Examiner, 155, 206.
Executions at Tyburn, Causes of the Frequent, Mandeville, 170.

Fable of the Bees; or, Private Vices, Public Benefits, Mandeville, 169.
Fables, Gay, 135.
Fables, Ancient and Modern, Dryden, 22, 93.
Falconer, William, 326, 327.
Familiar Letters, Richardson, 245.
Farquhar, George, 53, 70-2.
Fatal Marriage, The, Southerne, 62.
Fawkes, Francis, 312, 313.
Fenton, Elijah, 119.

Ferdinand, Count Fathom, Smollett, 261.
Fergusson, Robert, 341, 342.
Fielding, Henry, 247, 251-8, 386.
Fielding's *Miscellanies*, 253.
Fielding, Sarah, 247, 254, 264, 265.
Fingal, 335.
Flavel, John, 88.
Flecknoe, Richard, 48.
Fleece, The, Dyer, 219.
Fontenelle, 160.
Fool of Quality, The, H. Brooke, 218, 271.
Foote, Samuel, 317.
Forc'd Marriage, The, Behn, 51.
Forced Marriage, The, Armstrong, 227.
Forster, John, 154.
Fourth Moral Essay, Pope, 126.
Fox, George, 88.
Francion, Sorel, 242.
Francis, Sir Philip, 363.
Franklin, Benjamin, 398.
Freeholder, The, 191, 192.
Freeman, E. A., 356.
Freethinking, Discourse on, Collins, 175.
Funeral, The, Steele, 187.
Furetière, 242, 385.

Gallant, The Wild, Dryden, 41.
Gardening, Evelyn, 78.
Gardiner, S. R., 298.
Garrick, David, 229, 284, 287, 317, 318, 322.
Garth, Sir Samuel, 33-5.
Gay, John, 135, 136, 379.
"Gazette in rhyme," Waller, 107.
Gentle Shepherd, Ramsay, 139.
Gentleman's Magazine, 284, 285.
Ghost, The, Churchill, 324.
Gibbon, Edward, 203, 228, 278, 345, 350-7, 397.
Gil Blas, Le Sage, 385.
Gloriana, Lee, 57.
Glover, Richard, 228.
Godolphin, Sidney, 5.
Goethe, 384.
Goldsmith, Oliver, 217, 272, 316-22, 345-50, 381.
Goldsmith's *Essays*, 346, 349.
Gondibert, Davenant, 9, 10.
Good Natur'd Man, Goldsmith, 317, 347.
Government, Locke, 95.
Government, Discourses concerning, Sydney, 81.

Grace Abounding, Bunyan, 84.
Grainger, James, 312.
Granada, The Conquest of. SEE *Almanzor.*
Granville, George, Lord Lansdowne, 110, 116.
Grave, The, R. Blair, 220.
Gray, Thomas, 25, 63, 208, 231, 235-41, 302, 331, 379.
Gray's *Elegy,* 207, 236, 239, 240.
Gray's Life and Letters, Mason, 359.
Gray's *Odes,* 237, 239.
Great Britain, Hume's *History of,* 298.
Green, Matthew, 215-7, 379.
Gresset, J. B. L., 216.
Grongar Hill, Dyer, 219.
Grub Street Journal, 126.
Grumbling Hive, The, Mandeville, 169.
Guardian, The, 190, 199, 210.
Guise, Vindication of the Duke of, Dryden, 91.
Gulliver's Travels, Swift, 147, 159, 160-2, 242.

HALIFAX, Earl of. *See* Montague.
Halifax, Marquis of. *See* Savile.
Hamilton of Bangour, 209, 338.
Hanmer, Epistle to Sir Thomas, Collins, 232.
Harleian Miscellany, Oldys, 280.
Harmony in an Uproar, Arbuthnot, 168.
Hartley, David, 295, 305.
Haunch of Venison, The, Goldsmith, 321.
Hawkesworth, Dr. John, 285, 289.
Hazlitt, William, 279.
Head, Richard, 180, 242.
Health, Art of Preserving, Armstrong, 227.
Hebrides, Tour to the, Boswell, 358.
Helenore, Ross, 338.
Herbert, George, 230.
Hermit, The, Parnell, 136.
Hervey, William, stanzas by Cowley on, 6.
High Life Below Stairs, Townley, 317.
Hill, Aaron, 222, 225.
Hind and the Panther, The, Dryden, 19.
Historic Doubts, Walpole, 301.
History of England, Smollett, 261.
History of Great Britain, Hume, 298.
History of My Own Times, G. Burnet, 102.

History of Reign of Charles V., Robertson, 304.
History of Scotland, Hume, 304.
History of the Devil, The Political, Defoe, 179, 182.
Hive, The Grumbling, Mandeville, 169.
Hoadly, Dr. Benjamin, the elder, 196.
Hoadly, Dr. Benjamin, the younger, 317.
Hogarth, William, 318, 324.
Hogarth, An Epistle to William, Churchill, 323.
Holland, The Character of, Marvell, 29.
Holroyd, J. B. [Lord Sheffield], 353.
Holy War, Bunyan, 84, 85.
Home, Henry. *See* Kames, Lord.
Home, Rev. John, *Douglas,* 232, 335.
Homer, Pope's translation, 117, 118.
Horæ Paulinæ, 396.
House of Fame, Pope's Paraphrase, 117.
Howard, Sir Robert, 42, 60.
Hudibras, Butler, 27, 134.
Hughes, John, 188, 189, 190.
Human Knowledge, Principles of, Berkeley, 198.
Human Nature, Hume, 296, 297.
Human Understanding, Locke, 73, 95.
Hume, David, 203, 295-300, 304, 306, 397.
Hume's *History,* 298.
Humphrey Clinker, Smollett, 244, 262, 263.
Hunt, Leigh, 107, 195.
Hurd, Richard, [Bishop], 281, 395.
Hutcheson, Francis, 277, 305.
Hylas and Philonous, Berkeley, 198.
Hymn to Contentment, Parnell, 137.
Hymn to the Naiads, Akenside, 311.

Idea of a Patriot King, Bolingbroke, 174.
Idler, Johnson, 289, 290.
Iliad, Pope's translation of the, 117, 119.
Imitations of Horace, Pope, 128-130.
Indian Emperor, The, Dryden, 41, 42, 91.
Indian Queen, The, Dryden, 41.
Inn at Henley, Written in an, Shenstone, 231.
Innocence, The State of, Dryden, 92.
Inquiry into the Sublime and Beautiful, Burke, 368.
Intellectual System of the Universe, Cudworth, 77.
Irene, Johnson, 287.

INDEX

Italy, Letter from, Addison, 106.

JEBB, Prof. R. C., 104.
Jesuits, Satire upon the, Oldham, 30.
John Bull, The History of, Arbuthnot, 168.
John Buncle, T. Amory, 278, 279.
Johnson, Dr. Samuel, 26, 77, 217, 271, 280, 281, 282-95, 302, 314, 321, 325, 326, 336, 337, 346, 355, 358, 365, 373, 380, 382, 389.
Johnson, Boswell's *Life of*, 358.
Johnson, Esther. See "Stella."
Johnstone, Charles, 271.
Jonathan Wild, Fielding, 253.
Jonson, Ben, 39, 40, 48, 92.
Jortin, John, 362.
Joseph Andrews, Fielding, 243, 252, 254.
Journal to Stella, Swift, 154, 155.
Journey to the Western Islands, Johnson, 292.
Juliana, Crown, 58.
"Junius," *Letters of*, 363-5.
Jusserand, Mons. J. J., 385.

KAMES, HOME, Lord, 280, 302, 395.
Keats, John, 331, 334.
Kelly, Hugh, 317.
Kersey's *Dictionary*, 333.
Killigrew, Anne, *Elegy* on, Dryden, 19.

LA BRUYÈRE, 194, 204.
Lamb, Charles, 182.
"Lancelot Temple" [J. Armstrong], 227.
Lansdowne, Lord. See Granville.
Last Day, The, Young, 210.
Law, William, 203, 273, 396.
Law, In Memory of William, Blair, 220.
Law is a Bottomless Pit, Arbuthnot, 168.
League, History of the, Dryden's translation, 93.
Lee, Nathaniel, 57, 58.
Lee, Mr. William, 179.
L'Estrange, Sir Roger, 89, 380.
Leonidas, Glover, 228.
Le Sage, 181, 383, 385.
Leslie, Charles, 174.
Lessing, 368, 383, 384.
Letters of Junius, 363-5.
Letters of Lord Chesterfield, 280.

Letters of Phalaris, 104.
Letter to a Noble Lord, Burke, 371, 376.
Lettres Portugaises, 380.
Liberty, Thomson, 225.
Lillo, George, 393.
Lives of the English Poets, Johnson, 293.
Lloyd, Robert, 323, 325.
Lobo's *Voyage to Abyssinia*, 283.
Locke, John, 94-7, 171, 197, 277, 378, 380, 381, 386.
Logan, John, 327.
London, Johnson, 284.
Love, Sydney, 81.
Love, All for, Dryden, 92.
Love and a Bottle, Farquhar, 70.
Love and Business, Farquhar, 72.
Love, An Evening's, Dryden, 42, 91.
Love of Fame, The Universal Passion, Young, 211.
Love for Love, Congreve, 66.
Love in a Wood, Wycherley, 51.
Love makes a Man, Cibber, 70.
Love Triumphant, Dryden, 45.
Love Tyrannic, Dryden, 42.
Love's Last Shift, Cibber, 70.
Loves of the Plants, The, E. Darwin, 329.
Loves of the Triangles, The, Canning and Frere, 330.
Loyal Brother, The, Southerne, 62.
Lucretius, Creech, 21.
Lying Lover, The, Steele, 187.
Lyttelton, George, 1st Lord, 225, 227, 228, 254.

MacFlecknoe, Dryden, 15, 17, 48.
Mackenzie, Henry, 272, 361.
Macklin, Charles, 318.
Macpherson, James, 292, 335-7.
Madagascar, Davenant, 9.
Maiden Queen, The, Dryden, 42.
Malebranche, 199.
Malherbe, 390.
Man, Essay on, Pope, 126.
Man of Feeling, Mackenzie, 272.
Man of Mode, Etheredge, 46, 47.
Man of the World, Macklin, 318.
Man's the Master, The, Davenant, 39.
Mandeville, Bernard de, 169-70, 201, 381.
Manley, Delarivière, 205, 206.
Marianne, Marivaux, 247.
Marivaux, Pierre de, 243, 247, 383.

Marriage à la Mode, Dryden, 44.
Martinus Scriblerus Club, 159, *Memoirs of*, 168.
Marvell, Andrew, 14, 28-30.
Mason, William, 359.
Massacre of Paris, Lee, 58.
Maynwaring, Arthur, 187, 391.
MDCCXXXVIII. Pope, 130.
Medal, The, Dryden, 14, 16, 93.
Meditation on a Broomstick, Swift, 81, 148.
Meikle *or* Mickle, William Julius, 327.
Memoirs, Gibbon, 352.
Memoirs of a Cavalier, Defoe, 179, 181, 182.
Mercury, Wilkins, 75.
Messiah, The, Pope, 115, 189.
Mickle *or* Meikle, W. J., 327.
Middleton, Conyers, 278, 396.
Mill, Letter to Dr., Bentley, 103.
Mill, James, 295.
Milton, John, 3, 11, 58.
Miracles, Essay on, Hume, 299.
Miraculous Powers, Free Inquiry into, Middleton, 278.
Miscellanies, Fielding, 28.
Miscellanies, Swift, 152, 154, 165.
Miscellanies, J. Armstrong, 227.
Miss in Her Teens, Garrick, 317.
Miss Sydney Biddulph, Chamberlaine, 316.
Mistress, The, Cowley, 5.
Mistress, The Fortunate, Defoe, 179. See *Roxana*.
Mithridates, Lee, 57.
Moll Flanders, Defoe, 179, 180, 181.
Montagu, Lady Mary Wortley, 122, 129, 192, 204, 205.
Montague, Charles, Earl of Halifax, 106.
Montesquieu, 346, 369, 383, 384.
Moon may be a World, That the, Wilkins, 75.
Moral Essays, Pope, 127, 128.
Moralists, The, Shaftesbury, 171, 173.
Morley, Mr. John, 368.
Morocco, The Empress of, Settle, 59.
Mourning Bride, Congreve, 67.
Mrs. Veal, The Apparition of, Defoe, 178.
Mulberry Garden, The, Sedley, 50.
Mulgrave, John Sheffield, Earl of, 31.
Mulso, Hester, 288, 303.
Murphy, Arthur, 338.

Musset, Alfred de, 249.
Mysterious Mother, Walpole, 301.

Naboth's Vineyard, 14.
Naiads, Hymn to the, Akenside, 311.
Natural History of Selborne, White, 303.
Navigation and Commerce, Evelyn, 78.
Nero, Lee, 57.
New Atalantis, Mrs. Manley, 206.
New Bath Guide, Anstey, 315, 316, 321.
Night Piece, The, Parnell, 137.
Night Thoughts, Young, 212.
Nocturnal Reverie, Lady Winchelsea, 35.
Nugent, Lord, 229.

Odes, Collins, 232.
Odyssey, Pope, 119.
Old Bachelor, Congreve, 65.
Old English Baron, C. Reeve, 302.
Oldham, John, 14, 30, 31, 391.
Oldmixon, John, 124.
Oldys, William, 279, 280.
Oldys' *Life of Raleigh*, 280, 359.
Ormond, Duchess of, *Dedication* by Dryden to, 23, 113.
Oroonoko, Southerne, 62.
Oroonoko, Aphra Behn, 244.
Orphan, Otway, 55, 62.
Ossian, 240, 335-7.
Otway, Thomas, 54-7, 62, 220.

Pagan, Tibbie, 340.
Paine, Tom, 363.
Painter, Last Instruction to a, Marvell, 28.
Paley, William, 396.
Paltock, Robert, 244, 245.
Pamela, Richardson, 243, 246, 247, 251, 252, 253, 381, 386.
Parkhouse, Hannah, 338.
Parnell, Thomas, 119, 136.
Parthenissa, Roger Boyle, 384.
Partridge, John, 151, 152.
Partridge's Death, An Account of, Swift, 151.
Passions, The, Collins, 233.
Pastorals, A. Philips, 110.
Pastorals, Pope, 110.
Pastoral Ballad, Shenstone, 230.
Patriot King, Idea of a, Bolingbroke, 174.

Peacock, T. L., 312.
Pearson, John, Bishop of Chester, 76.
Pennant, Thomas, 303.
Pepys' *Diary*, 97.
Pepys, Samuel, 97, 98.
Percy, Thomas, 325, 346.
Peregrine Pickle, Smollett, 244, 260, 263.
Persian Eclogues, Collins, 232.
Peter Wilkins, Paltock, 245.
Petition of Francis Harris, Swift, 148.
Phalaris, Letters of, 104.
Philips, Ambrose, 110, 111, 117, 135, 137.
Philips, John, 108.
Pilgrim, Beaumont and Fletcher, 45.
Pilgrim's Progress, 73, 84-6.
Pindaric Odes, Swift, 142.
Pindarique Odes, Cowley, 7.
Pix, Mary, 51.
Plague Year, The, Defoe, 179.
Plain Dealer, Wycherley, 52, 54.
Plays, Essay on Heroic, Dryden, 91.
Pleasures of Imagination, Akenside, 311.
Poems, Prior, 134.
Poems, Swift, 153.
Poetry, Essay on, Mulgrave, 31.
Poetry, History of English, Warton, 325.
Poetry, Roscommon's *Paraphrase of Horace's Art of*, 32.
Polite Conversation, Swift, 164.
Political Lying, The Art of, Arbuthnot, 168.
Polly, Gay, 135.
Polymetis, Spence, 368.
Pope, Alexander, 24, 36, 53, 105-34, 135, 137, 156, 159, 171, 185, 189, 204, 207, 224, 281, 284, 380, 382, 391.
Pope, his Safe Return from Troy, Gay's *Alexander*, 135.
Predictions for the year 1708, Swift, 151.
Price, Richard, 363, 370.
Priestley, Joseph, 363.
Princess of Cleve, The, Lee, 58.
Prior, Matthew, 101, 134, 391.
Procession, The, Steele, 187.
Projectors, The, Wilson, 40.
Prophecy, The, Chatterton, 335.
Proposal for correcting the English Language, Swift, 155.
Provoked Husband, Cibber and Vanbrugh, 317.
Provoked Wife, Vanbrugh, 68.

QUESNAY, 306, 388.

RACINE, 7.
Raleigh, Oldys's *Life of*, 280, 359.
Rambler, The, 192, 288.
Ramsay, Allan, 139, 208, 209, 338, 398.
Rape of the Lock, Pope, 112-4, 119, 132.
Rasselas, Johnson, 244, 271, 290, 291.
Ray, John, 81.
Recruiting Officer, The, Farquhar, 71.
Reeve, Clara, 302.
Reflections on the French Revolution, Burke, 369.
Reformation, History of the, G. Burnet, 102.
Regicide Peace, Burke *On a*, 372.
Regicide, The, Smollett, 258.
Rehearsal, The, Villiers, 44, 60, 101.
Reid, Thomas, 295.
Relapse, The, Vanbrugh, 68.
Religio Laici, Dryden, 18.
Religion of Nature delineated, Wollaston, 175.
Religion, Project for the Advancement of, Swift, 151.
Religion, The Force of, Young, 211.
Reliques of English Poetry, Percy, 325.
Retaliation, Goldsmith, 321.
Revenge, The, Young, 211.
Reynolds, Sir Joshua, 308, 309, 368.
Rhodes, Siege of, Davenant, 39.
Richardson, Samuel, 243, 245-51, 258, 265, 345, 383, 386.
Ritson, Joseph, 325.
Rival Ladies, The, Dryden, 41, 91.
Rival Queens, Lee, 57.
Rivals, The, Sheridan, 337.
Rivarol, 145.
Robertson, William, 304, 305.
Robinson Crusoe, Defoe, 160, 179, 180, 181, 184, 185, 242, 245, 385.
Rochester's *Songs*, 32, 33.
Rochester, John Wilmot, Earl of, 11, 31, 32, 55, 102.
Roderick Random, Smollett, 244, 258, 259, 260.
Rogue, The English, Head, 180.
"*Rolls*" *Sermons*, J. Butler, 274, 275.
Roman Bourgeois, Furetière, 242, 385.
Rome, Ruins of, Dyer, 219.
Rosamund, Addison, 106.
Rosciad, The, Churchill, 323.
Roscommon, Wentworth Dillon, Earl of, 31, 32.

INDEX 413

Ross, Alexander, 338, 339.
Rousseau, 383, 384.
Rover, The, Behn, 51.
Rowe, Nicholas, 112, 288.
Rowley Poems, Chatterton, 331-5.
Roxana, Defoe, 179, 180, 181, 182, 184.
Royal and Noble Authors, Catalogue of, Walpole, 300.
Royal Society, History of the, Sprat, 101.
Rule Britannia, 225.
Rymer, Thomas, 394.

Sacramental Test, Letter on the, Swift, 152.
Saint Lambert, 383.
Saintsbury, Mr. G., 13, 44.
Saints' Everlasting Rest, Baxter, 76.
Salamander, The, Swift, 152.
Satire, Essay on, Mulgrave, 31.
Satire 1740, Pope, 130.
Satires, Pope, 130.
Savage, Richard, 217-8, 285, 293.
Savage, Johnson's *Life of*, 285.
Savile, George, Marquis of Halifax, 89, 90, 93.
Scarron, 39.
Schoolmistress, The, Shenstone, 230.
Scotland, Robertson's *History of*, 304.
Scots Poems, Fergusson, 341.
Scots Songs, Ramsay, 208.
Scott, Sir Walter, 94, 272, 327, 361.
Scriblerus Club, 159, 168.
Scriblerus, Memoirs of, Pope, 159, 168.
Sculptura, Evelyn, 78.
Seasons, Thomson, 222.
Secker, Thomas, 210, 274, 275, 276.
Sedley, Sir Charles, 32, 50.
Sempill, Francis, 33.
Sense and Sensibility, Jane Austen, 244.
Sentimental Journey, Sterne, 268, 269.
Sentiments of a Church of England Man, Swift, 150.
Serious call to a Devout and Holy Life, Law, 204.
Sermons of Mr. Yorick, Sterne, 267.
Servants, Rules for, Swift, 165.
Settle, Elkanah, 18, 48, 59.
Seward, Anna, 342.
Shadwell, Thomas, 8, 15, 17, 18, 48-50.
Shaftesbury, Anthony Ashley, 3d Earl of, 147, 170, 171-3, 201, 218, 276, 277, 280, 295, 302, 311, 381, 387, 396.
Shaftesbury, 1st Earl of, 14, 15, 16, 95.
She Stoops to Conquer, Goldsmith, 318, 319, 338, 348.
Sheffield, John, Earl of. *See* Mulgrave.
Shelley, Percy, Bysshe, 226.
Shenstone, William, 230, 321.
Shepherd's Week, Gay, 135.
Sheridan, Richard Brinsley, 337-8.
Sheridan, Thomas, 361.
Sherlock, Thomas, 197.
Sherlock, William, 101.
She Would if She Could, Etheredge, 46.
Shilling, The Splendid, Philips, 108.
Shipwreck, The, Falconer, 326.
Shirley, James, 38.
Siege of Rhodes, Davenant, 39.
Singleton, Life of Captain, Defoe, 179, 181.
Sir Charles Grandison, Richardson, 244, 249.
Sir Courtly Nice, Crown, 59.
Sir Lancelot Greaves, Smollett, 261.
Siris, Berkeley, 202, 203.
Skeat, Professor W. W., 333.
Skinner, Rev. John, 339
Smart, Christopher, 313, 314.
Smith, Adam, 277, 296, 305-7, 388.
Smith, Edmund, 293.
Smollett's *History of England*, 261.
Smollett, Tobias George, 258-64.
Snake in the Grass, Leslie, 174.
Soliloquy, or Advice to an Author, Shaftesbury, 171.
Solomon, Prior, 134.
Somerville, William, 138, 219.
Song to David, Smart, 314.
Songs, Aphra Behn, 32.
Songs, Dryden, 12.
Songs, Rochester, 32.
South, Robert, 100, 101.
Southerne, Thomas, 62, 63.
Sophonisba, Lee, 57.
Spanish Friar, The, Dryden, 45.
Spectator, The, 189-91, 192, 194, 214, 243.
Spleen, The, M. Green, 216.
Sprat, Thomas, 10, 101.
Sprat's *Cowley*, 359.
Spring, Thomson, 207, 222, 223.
St. Cecilia's Day, Song for, Dryden, 20, 22.

INDEX

St. John, Henry, Viscount. *See* Bolingbroke.
Stanhope, Philip Dormer. *See* Chesterfield.
Stanhope, Philip, 280.
Steele, Sir Richard, 105, 114, 186-92, 194, 195, 199, 206, 243.
"Stella," 148, 154, 161, 162, 206.
Stella, Journal to, Swift, 154.
Stephen, Sir Leslie, 113, 119, 152, 170, 196, 281, 306, 365, 396.
Sterne, Laurence, 265-71, 361.
Stillingfleet, Edward, 101, 104.
Strype, John, 397.
Sublime and Beautiful, Inquiry into the, Burke, 368.
Sullen Lovers, The, Shadwell, 48.
Summer, Thomson, 222, 223.
Superstitions of the Highlands, On the popular, Collins, 232.
Suspicious Husband, The, Hoadly 317.
Swift, Jonathan, 81, 117, 122, 130, 136, 140-69, 188, 189, 199, 206, 377.
Swift, On the death of Dr., 163, 164.
Swinburne, Mr., 233, 240.
Sydney, Colonel Algernon, 80, 81.
Sylva, Evelyn, 78.

TALBOT, Catherine, 288.
Tale of a Tub, Swift, 140, 143-7, 167, 193.
Tate, Nahum, 15.
Tatler, 152, 153, 186, 188, 189, 192, 271.
Tea Table Miscellany, Ramsay, 139, 208.
Temple, Sir William, 86-8, 142, 143.
Temple of Fame, Pope, 117.
Tender Husband, The, Steele, 187.
Terra, Evelyn, 79.
Thackeray, William, 64, 257.
Thebais of Statius, Pope's trans., 109.
Theobald, Lewis, 123.
Thirty-nine Articles, Exposition of the, G. Burnet, 102.
Thomson, James, 208, 209, 217, 219, 221-7, 232, 383.
Thomson's *Spring* 207.
Three Weeks after Marriage, Murphy, 338.
Tickell, Thomas, 117, 138, 188, 191.
Tillotson, John, 76, 88, 89.
Tindal, Dr. Matthew, 174.
Tobacco Pipe of, J. H. Browne, 229.
Toland, Janus Junius, 175, 197.

Toleration, First and Second Letters concerning, Locke, 95.
Third letter, Locke, 96.
Tom Jones, Fielding, 244, 254-6, 383.
Tongue, Government of the, J. Butler, 274.
Tonson, Jacob, 187.
Tour to the Hebrides, Boswell, 358.
Town Eclogues, Lady M. W. Montagu, 205.
Townley, Rev. J., 317.
Tragedy of Tragedies, Fielding, 251.
Translated Verse, Essay on, Roscommon, 32.
Traveller, The, Goldsmith, 217, 319, 321.
Tristram Shandy, Sterne, 244, 266-8, 269.
Trivia, Gay, 135.
True Born Scotchman, Macklin, 318.
Tullochgorum, Skinner, 339.

Universal Beauty, H. Brooke, 218.
Universe, True Intellectual System of the, Cudworth, 77.

Vanbrugh, Sir John 45, 67-9, 152, 217, 337, 391.
"Vanessa," 154, 162, 200.
Vanhomerigh, Hester. *See* "Vanessa."
Vanity of Human Wishes, Johnson, 286.
Vegetation, The Economy of, E. Darwin, 329.
Venice Preserved, Otway, 55.
Vicar of Wakefield, Goldsmith, 244, 272, 346, 347, 349.
Villiers. *See* Buckingham, 2d Duke.
Vindication of Natural Society, Burke, 367.
Vindication of the Duke of Guise, Dryden, 93.
Virgil, Dryden's, 22.
Virtue, Inquiry concerning, Shaftesbury, 171, 172.
Virtuoso, The, Shadwell, 49.
Vision, Essay towards a New Theory of, Berkeley, 198.
Voiture, 12, 390.
Voltaire, 146, 200, 384, 391.
Voltaire's *Candide*, 290.
Volunteers, Shadwell, 48.

WALLER, EDMUND, 2-5, 9, 10, 106, 107, 382.

INDEX

Walpole, Horace, Earl of Orford, 236, 271, 300-2, 331, 368.
Walsh, William, 109, 110.
Wanderer, The, Savage, 217.
Warburton, William [Bishop], 127, 131, 281, 353.
Ward, Edward, 124.
Warton, Thomas, 303, 325, 326.
Way of the World, Congreve, 67.
Wealth of Nations, Adam Smith, 305, 306, 388.
Webster, Dr. Alexander, 229.
Welsted, Leonard, 124.
Wesley, Charles, 230.
Wesley, John, 204.
West Indian, The, Cumberland, 338.
West, Richard, 236.
White, Gilbert, 303, 304, 379.
Whitehead, William, 131, 327.
Wild, Jonathan, 243.
Wild, Robert, 28.
Wilkins, John [Bishop], 75, 76.
William and Margaret, Mallet, 209, 222.

Williams, Sir Charles Hanbury, 229.
Wilson, John, 39, 40.
Willughby, Francis, 81.
Winchelsea, Anna Finch, Countess of, 35, 36, 379.
Windsor Forest, Pope, 116.
Wit and Humour, Essay on the Freedom of, Shaftesbury, 171.
Wolcot, John, 342.
Wollaston, William, 175.
Woman's Wit, Cibber, 70.
Wordsworth, William, 35, 219, 328, 331.
Wotton, William, 147.
Wrestling Jacob, C. Wesley, 230.
Wycherley, William, 51, 109, 110, 337.

YALDEN, THOMAS, 152.
Yarrow, Braes of, Hamilton, 209.
Young, Edward, 209-14, 220.

Zola, M. 182.
Zoonomia, E. Darwin, 328.

THE END